AMERICAN TAPESTRY

A rigorous, absorbing family account that offers a microcosm and a macrocosm...Sherman is a competent writer and is passionate about the downtrodden...Readers get a very thoughtful panorama of 250 years of history, change, and how this 'middling' family dealt with all of it. She is a formidable and patient researcher.

—KIRKUS REVIEWS

Sherman's historic account weaves detailed chronicles of her Colonial-era ancestors, based on her extensive original research, with a clear-eyed view of American history, demonstrating the vital role of small-town civil activities, labor, and commerce in the nation's development and never shying away from the past's brutal realities...Sherman emphasizes the treatment of Native Americans during the Revolutionary War era, pointing out that the destruction of the Iroquois nation—and the "centuries-long genocide of Native Americans, in all of its malignant forms"—is too rarely the focus in accounts of the American story...The original research and the book's confrontation with the American past are invaluable.

—BOOKLIFE REVIEWS

The fascinating family biography *American Tapestry* collects an in-depth series of historical accounts together to trace the early history of the Eastern and Central United States....Their lives are shared to reflect the progress and setbacks that the nation weathered thanks to the dedicated labor of ordinary individuals. The fact that each person in [Sherman's] story is more or less average...results in an intriguing demonstration of how the consequences of major events...manifested in places far removed from their scenes of action.

—FOREWARD CLARION REVIEW

Pat Speth Sherman proves herself a skilled chronicler of America's past in this account of her family's role in various epochal events... her writing never becomes dryly recitative, but remains vividly pictorial and even poetic throughout...Genealogy buffs will especially admire the detective work Sherman performed in excavating her family's past, but anyone interested in a fresh perspective on American history can profit from her rich work.

—BLUE INK REVIEW

American Tapestry

Portrait of a
'Middling' Family
1746-1934

PAT SPETH SHERMAN

LUMINARE PRESS
WWW.LUMINAREPRESS.COM

Luminare Press
442 Charnelton St.
Eugene, OR 97401
www.luminarepress.com

LCCN: 2021910422
ISBN: 978-1-64388-672-5

To Eric
Colleen, Tim and Erin
Tom, Sharon, Patti and Mike
Blair and Kelly

Contents

Note on Terminology

Teaching generations of Americans that the United States' westward expansion was the nation's "manifest destiny" was dreadfully wrong. The concept ignored the fact that Euro-Americans waged a more than four-centuries-long campaign to steal Native Americans' lands, exterminate their families and erase their multitudinous cultures.

The early chapters of *American Tapestry* describe fierce encounters between Euro-Americans and Native Americans during the French and Indian War, the Revolutionary War and beyond. Most of the contemporaneous accounts written about these events, all of which were written by white men, use the undifferentiated word *Indian* to describe all Native Americans. Other pejoratives were also used. Current practice favors words that reflect tribal sovereignty. I have chosen instead to use words that were used at the time. To do otherwise, I believe, would nourish the whitewashing that has distorted our history lessons for far too long.

Note on Methodology

I am not a professional historian, sociologist, attorney, genealogist or statistician. I am a storyteller. My methods may not consistently conform to the various professions' standards. All errors of commission, omission and method are my own.

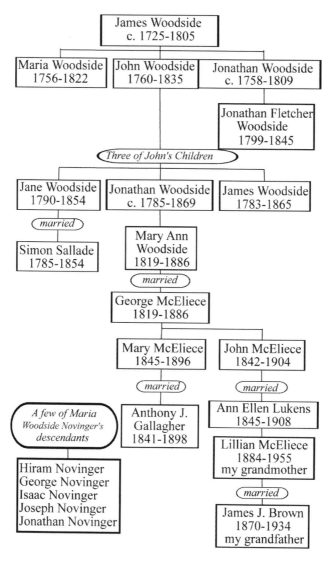

Family Tree

Introduction

Our Founding Fathers created the blueprint. Business titans, political leaders, and military heroes oversaw the construction. But it was the ordinary people—the middling people—who cemented the foundation, put up the walls, and roofed our enduring republic. Unfolding in Pennsylvania, New York, Ohio, Virginia, Missouri, and Mexico, and spanning the years between 1746 and 1934, *American Tapestry* is a ride through American history in the company of a family of local community leaders. Today, the family, my family, would belong to the middle class—financially stable men and women who often volunteer on school boards or city councils or for other service organizations. In their day, the family members were farmers, wheelwrights, millwrights, teachers, engineers, managers, physicians, and of course, husbands, wives, and parents. In public affairs they served as overseers of the roads, overseers of the poor,[1] school board members, city councilors, county officials, state legislators, and in one case, a United States ambassador. In wars they marched as foot soldiers, and in times of peace they were officers in local militias. Thus, the family members were part of a group who stood somewhere between the struggling masses and the political, industrial, and military leaders of their time. That one family consistently fulfilled this societal role over a long period presented an opportunity for me to partially fill an underrepresented piece of the American story.

INITIALLY I INTENDED TO WRITE A SHORT NARRATIVE ABOUT my great-grandfather John McEliece. He was among the dozens of obscure men who were profiled in *Biographical Sketches of Leading*

Citizens of the Seventeenth Congressional District, Pennsylvania.
The volume was one of the many books of biographies—derisively
referred to as "mug books" because they typically required a fee for
inclusion—that were published toward the end of the nineteenth
century. As a Civil War veteran, a justice of the peace, a captain of
the local militia, a community leader, and a colliery superintendent,
he was lionized as a man "of steady purpose and constant industry."[2]
But when I came across a Lewis Wickes Hine photograph of little
boys working in a colliery, I realized that there may be another side
to John's story (see figure 1).

*Figure 1. A view of Ewen Breaker of the Pennsylvania Coal Company.
The dust was so dense at times as to obscure the view. This dust
penetrates the utmost recesses of the boy's lungs. A kind of slave driver
sometimes stands over the boys, prodding or kicking them into
obedience. Location: South Pittston, Pennsylvania. Courtesy of the
National Child Labor Committee collection, Lewis Hine photographs,
Library of Congress, Prints and Photographs Division,
https://www.loc.gov/resource/nclc.01127/.*

As I gazed at the photo, I considered the predicament of the little
boy, probably nine years old, in the bottom row in front of the man

with the club. I saw the little boy's eyes—afraid to look left or right, fearful lest he be clubbed again by the man with the stick. I saw his thin and raggedy jacket, the hard wooden bench, his ungloved hands, the coal dust on his cheek. Then I took notice of the fixed glower of the man behind him—probably no more than twenty years old—ready to enforce discipline on the youngster. I observed the dust-laden air and the rows of boys. Then I tried to imagine what it was like for these young boys to sit at their task of separating rock and slate from the coal for ten or twelve hours, six days a week.

The worst of Charles Dickens was better than this. And my great-grandfather was in charge of it all. Compelled to come to terms with the disparity between the flattering biographical sketch and the reality of John's life as a colliery superintendent, I hoped to find the answer to a simple question—how could this be?—by exploring my family's past.

ON MY JOURNEY THROUGH THE ARCHIVES OF HISTORY, I dis-covered a family whose lives were interwoven with the often glorious and sometimes dark chapters of the American struggle. Being that they were neither war generals nor captains of industry, the memory of most of the family members was preserved only in commonplace documents—baptism, marriage, and death records; land transactions; the census—and an occasional weatherworn gravestone. Yet, in the stories of those whose lives went beyond the ordinary—and there were many of those—a picture emerged of a family who was remarkably engaged from the very beginning. The story of their sometimes heroic, occasionally unlawful, but always unsung lives—woven into the soft greens and rich browns of the soil, the steely grays and bloody reds of war, the vibrant and inventive colors of commerce, and the glorious hues of honor found in frequent public service—is the fabric of the American tapestry.

American Tapestry tells the stories about selected family mem-bers—the Woodsides and Novingers, the Sallades, and the McE-lieces and Browns—by contextualizing their activities with concurrent events that faced the growing nation. They were real-life people who contended with real-life situations, and their stories bring history to life in a way that standard history texts do not. *American Tapestry* is not an account of the entire American experience. But with its long chronological focus on one family in localized settings, the narrative offers a fresh perspective on a wide range of less-well-documented developments such as the Whiskey Rebellion, the canal- and railroad-building period, xenophobia and religious bigotry in the nineteenth century, the relative importance (or not) of the Molly Maguires in Pennsylvania's anthracite coal-mining region, the nineteenth-century child labor situation, and the progress of the medical profession in the progressive era.

My quest to unravel the family's story caused me to acknowledge surprising facts about some of my forebears. Can you imagine my reaction when I discovered that Jonathan Woodside Sr. (see family tree) was arrested during the Whiskey Rebellion? Better yet, I remember when I clicked on a web page of Berner's Auction Gallery of Springfield, Ohio, and learned from their offering that Jonathan Fletcher Woodside, the son of the Whiskey Rebellion arrestee, had been appointed by president Andrew Jackson as chargé d'affaires of the United States of America at the Court of His Danish Majesty. Surely, there was a story behind that! When I saw the names of three of my relatives on the witness list in the 1877 murder trial of some Molly Maguires, I could hardly believe my eyes. Was my family somehow connected to a secret society of murderous Irish thugs? And there was worse.

But it was not the discovery of startling facts that brought me joy; it was sniffing out the backstory. Sometimes the problem lay in putting a puzzle together when the pieces were scattered or missing, as with James Woodside's experiences during the French and Indian War and in the 1776 Battle of Long Island. Other times I felt like a special prosecutor, trying to make sense of several seemingly isolated but ultimately interconnected events. Simon Sallade was a politician in Dauphin County, Pennsylvania, who is remembered for the construction of the Wiconisco Canal. But who would guess that, in order to build the canal—it was only twelve miles long—he tangled with Nicholas Biddle and his little Bank War, and Thaddeus Stevens and the corrupt Canal Commission. At the same time, the project was impeded by Pennsylvania's infamous Buckshot War; the aftermath of the Panic of 1837, including Pennsylvania's default on its debt; numerous construction delays; and corporate infighting. There was George McEliece, the poor Irish immigrant whose life was portrayed in the nineteenth-century biographies as a classic rags-to-somewhat-fancier-rags story. His highest public achievement lay in being elected as Northumberland County's treasurer. But in the aftermath of a vicious yearlong nativist attack on him and others, a previously hidden part of George's story came to light. Next, I learned about John McEliece's experience as a private and corporal in the Forty-Sixth Pennsylvania Volunteer Regiment during the Civil War: his unit was involved in two major battles, several skirmishes, and a lot of marching. But on his second tour of duty, serving as a sergeant in the Thirty-Sixth Pennsylvania Emergency Volunteer Regiment, John's unit was assigned the dreadful task of cleaning up the Gettysburg battlefield, an aspect of the war that is seldom studied by historians. And then there was the story about the little breaker boys whose predicament inspired me to undertake this project. Was their miserable situation entirely a consequence of poverty and greed? Or was something else going on? Finally, there was the story of gentlehearted James J. Brown, the loyal and devoted physician, the "revered and honored friend" of the suffering poor of South Buffalo, New York.[3]

My research experience also induced me to reevaluate my basic understanding of American history. I grew up in the 1950s and early 1960s, and my concept of history was shaped by the paternalistic lessons of that period: classes focused on white men's achievements and trivialized, or avoided altogether, discussion of our country's imperfections. I came of age in the late 1960s and early 1970s amid the upheaval of the civil rights movement and Vietnam War protests. And then I got caught in the flurry of life—as a nurse, an accountant, a businesswoman, a politician, a wife, and a mother—never paying attention to what had been instilled in me as a youngster.

The image of the little breaker boy shook me out of my coma. And my studies, especially of the colonial and early republic periods, led to the discovery that America's first original sin—the centuries-long genocide of Native Americans, in all of its malignant forms—had been completely ignored in the classrooms of my youth. Thus, in addition to my family's story, *American Tapestry* explores aspects of the Native American experience from the perspective of a white woman who learned late in life of their travails.

Woven together, *American Tapestry* became more than a chronicle of family memory. Rather, the manuscript unfolded as a series of historical essays bound together by one family's experience. Indeed, it was only after I completed my story that the similarities between James Woodside (c. 1725–1805), Jonathan Woodside (c. 1758–1809), Jonathan Fletcher Woodside (c. 1799–1845), Simon Sallade (1785–1854), George McEliece (1819–1886), John McEliece (1842–1904), and Dr. James J. Brown (1870–1934) came into focus. Imperfect though they were, each of them responded to the challenges of the time, challenges that exemplify the universal experience of the human condition. Importantly, the traditions the family members established and the values they embraced live on today in the millions of Americans who continue to volunteer in a multitude of organizations. Thus, a unifying theme of this long story—that middle-class values have endured through two centuries and countless historical transformations—offers assurance that we can overcome our present-day and future challenges as long as we remain true to those values. Borrowing the words of David Brooks, *American Tapestry* embodies a story that embraces the "democratic culture that captures, celebrates and ennobles the way average Americans live day to day."[4]

Part I

WOODSIDE AND NOVINGER

"Let us welcome, then, the strangers,
Hail them as our friends and brothers,
And the heart's right hand of friendship
Give them when they come to see us.
Gitche Manito, the Mighty,
Said this to me in my vision.
"I beheld, too, in that vision
All the secrets of the future,
Of the distant days that shall be.
I beheld the westward marches
Of the unknown, crowded nations.
All the land was full of people,
Restless, struggling, toiling, striving,
Speaking many tongues, yet feeling

But one heart-beat in their bosoms.
In the woodlands rang their axes,
Smoked their towns in all the valleys,
Over all the lakes and rivers
Rushed their great canoes of thunder.
"Then a darker, drearier vision
Passed before me, vague and cloud-like;
I beheld our nation scattered,
All forgetful of my counsels,
Weakened, warring with each other:
Saw the remnants of our people
Sweeping westward, wild and woful,
Like the cloud-rack of a tempest,
Like the withered leaves of Autumn!"

—HENRY WADSWORTH LONGFELLOW,
"The Song of Hiawatha"

CHAPTER 1

CLASHING CULTURES

———◆———

W hen I was little, one of my favorite TV shows was *Davy Crockett*. It was broadcast on Sunday nights at seven o'clock. Our entire family watched it. Us kids were given our weekly ration of Dad's Old Fashioned Root Beer, and we made popcorn, which was served to us in small brightly colored plastic bowls: green, red, blue, and yellow. My mother—college graduate, Latin scholar, classical pianist, brilliant and organized—invented color coding.[1] Each of us was assigned a color: Rick was green, Sue was red, I was blue, and Ginny was yellow. The system was applied mostly to personal items—toothbrushes bought from the Fuller Brush salesman, towels, and washcloths—but my mother extended the color-coding system to the popcorn bowls.

Every Sunday evening the family gathered around the TV, rabbit ears atop, root beer in our hands, and color-coded popcorn bowls in our laps while we watched Davy Crockett, "King of the Wild Frontier." Davy, dressed in buckskins and a coonskin cap, dashed across the twelve-inch black-and-white screen, chopping down trees, living in a log cabin, plowing fields, growing crops, killing critters, gathering wild nuts and berries, helping his neighbors, and instructing his young 'uns. Little did we know at the time that Davy Crockett had been a real-life folk hero of the American frontier.

THE NEAT AND TIDY STORIES ABOUT THE FRONTIER AS REPRE-
sented in Disney's adaptation crossed my mind when I considered
the lives of James and Margaretha Woodside. Disney's stories
meshed nicely with my initial impression of pioneer life after a visit
to the Woodside homestead one October: life in the wilderness
was hard, but as beautiful as Dauphin County's Lykens Valley is,
it must have had its rewards.

When the Woodsides finally settled in this lush valley bordering
the Susquehanna in about 1765, they had been in America for nearly
twenty years. But prior to 1765, the document trail for the family is
thin. James Woodside's name appears on a ship's passenger manifest, in a journal recording his indenture, on a list recording his
marriage, and on an early tax record for Paxtang. These everyday
documents suggest that James and his family spent their early years
in America quietly making their way. But that scenario is unlikely,
for the Woodsides lived on the fringe of the Pennsylvania frontier
when two brutal conflicts—the French and Indian War (1754–1763)
and Pontiac's War (1763–1764)—made a quiet life impossible.

JAMES'S AMERICAN STORY BEGAN IN SEPTEMBER 1746 WHEN,
after a twelve-week voyage from Belfast and Larne, he sailed into
Delaware Bay aboard the privateer *William and Mary* and dis-
embarked at New Castle, Delaware.[2] He was one of hundreds of
thousands of Irish, Anglo-Irish, and Scots-Irish who emigrated
between 1719 and 1775 from Ireland to America. As detailed by
historian David Hackett Fischer, this group of emigrants shared a
common culture.[3] In religion they were almost entirely Protestant,
mostly Presbyterian. (The emigration of Irish Catholics during
this interval was negligible.) The Scots-Irish fled Ireland for many
reasons: economic hardships due to repeated crop failures (not to
be confused with the nineteenth-century potato blight famines);
burdensome British trade restrictions; rack-renting (a practice of

doubling or tripling the land rent when a lease expired); and religious intolerance.[4]

In particular, in 1740–1741 a devastating famine occurred in Ireland after which an estimated four hundred thousand people perished from starvation. Near famine conditions returned in 1744. These famines prompted a wave of increased emigration from Ireland that persisted for ten years.[5] Even so, while there were many reasons for people to leave Ireland for America in search of a better life, most remained in their homes. Considering that James Woodside was among those who had the courage to leave his family and country behind, and risk a perilous sea voyage to start a new life in the unknown New World, he was exceptional. What relief he must have felt as his ship sailed into Delaware Bay, when his eyes beheld Cape Henlopen on the "starboard in the west, with its low, white sandy beaches and fine woods of oak, hickory and firs."[6]

Many of the immigrants of the early and mid-eighteenth century, German as well as Scots-Irish, arrived as indentured servants. Historian James Leyburn estimates that as many as 90 percent of the new arrivals from northern Ireland were thus obligated.[7] James was among them. Upon his arrival in 1746, he was assigned on September 25 by William and David McIlvaine, shipping merchants, to Adam Farquhar of Philadelphia as a laborer for four years for the price of £16 plus customary dues.[8] Four years later he went forth with his dues—"two Compleat Suits of Apparel, whereof one was new, one Axe, one Grubbing hoe, and one Weeding hoe, at the charge of his master"—as a freeman, prepared to make his way on his own.[9] Having learned the customs of his new country, James Woodside decided where to live.

The townships of Derry and Paxtang, located in the portion of Lancaster County that would eventually lie within Dauphin County, were erected in 1729. Both townships were near present-day Harrisburg. Derry was south of Swatara Creek. Paxtang extended from the mouth of Swatara Creek north to the Blue Mountain, also known as Kittatinny Ridge, a distance of about twenty miles. It was in Derry that James Woodside and Margaretha Trotter were married by Reverend Johann Casper Stoever, a Lutheran minister, on September 12, 1754.[10] It was in Paxtang that the Woodsides settled sometime prior to 1758, and it was there that they lived the life of the early pioneers.[11]

Pioneer life in the colonial era was tied to taking care of basic needs. On the frontier this meant building a log home, clearing land and farming, hunting and gathering, and engaging in home industries. A typical Lancaster County farm included about 135 acres, of which about 40 acres was cleared and only about 9 acres were planted in grain.[12] In the garden the family grew squash, corn, beans, pumpkins, and other vegetables. Peter Kalm, a Swedish botanist who visited North America in 1749–1751, described the Pennsylvania farms as "very pretty, with a walk of trees frequently leading from the farm to the high road....Every countryman, even though he was the poorest peasant, had an orchard with apples, peaches, chestnuts, walnuts, cherries, quinces and such fruits and sometimes...vines climbing among them."[13]

The planting and harvest seasons were the most demanding. The farmers worked with their neighbors from dawn to dusk, using only hand tools. Harvesting the hay was a particularly laborious process, with the best workmen able to cut about one and a half to two acres a day.[14] When not working in the fields, the pioneers threshed their grain, preserved their food, and manufactured tools, candles, soap, and other essential items. Much time was spent making the family's clothing. What today we accomplish with a quick trip to a department store or an online purchase, in those days consumed countless hours and required many steps—fascinating processes that are replicated at living history museums such as Plimoth Plantation and Colonial Williamsburg. The men generally wore hunting shirts and leggings, Davy Crockett style, fashioned from deerskins. Women preferred to make their dresses with linsey-woolsey, a fabric with a linen warp and a woolen weft.[15] Before the dress could be made, however, the cloth had to be woven. Before the cloth could be woven, the fiber had to be spun. Before the fiber could be spun, it had to be cleaned and processed. And before the fiber could be processed, it had to be either sheared from the sheep (wool) or grown in the field (linen was made from the stems of flax). Clothing, hats, caps, bonnets, stockings, and moccasins—everything was made in the home.[16] What a family had was limited by the skills of its members. If an item could not be made, the family usually went without it.[17] In 1755 this endless cycle of chores was all in a day's work, and as newlyweds, James and Margaretha would have faced these challenges with the vigor and enthusiasm of youth.

—————◆—————

BUT YOUTHFUL OPTIMISM IS NO MATCH FOR WAR, AND JUST AS the Woodsides were beginning their life together south of the Blue Mountain, trouble was brewing on the far side of the hill. Simply put, the French and Indian War (the American theater of the Seven Years' War) was a contest between the French and English for control of North America, with the focus in Pennsylvania being the lands west of the Allegheny Mountains. But war is rarely simple, and just below the surface a continent was seething. Among the Indian nations were the Six Nations of the Iroquois (the Mohawk, Oneida, Onondaga, Cayuga, Seneca, and Tuscarora), the Delaware and Shawnee, the Catawba, the Cherokee, and the Indian allies of the French. Some had long-standing rivalries, some were resentful of past injustices, and others were divided within.[18] Among the separate colonies, Virginia, Maryland, Pennsylvania, and Connecticut quarreled about conflicting land grants. Among Pennsylvanians, the Scots-Irish and German settlers of the frontier regions had trouble getting along, and the Quaker-dominated assembly, constrained by the Society of Friends' peace testimony, failed to perform a government's most basic obligation of protecting its citizens. Global conflict. Clashing cultures. Shifting alliances. Internal bickering. The stage was set for the New World to explode in bloody fight.

The explosion came after the defeat of British General Edward Braddock near Fort Duquesne (located near present-day Pittsburgh) in July 1755. Focusing on the Pennsylvania frontier, the Delaware and Shawnee caused the most trouble. Those nations were distressed by Braddock's mismanagement of his campaign and especially by his contempt for the Indians' sage advice regarding frontier warfare, and they were embittered by fraudulent land purchases by Pennsylvania and Connecticut in the Delaware and Wyoming valleys. Fearing an attack by the French-allied Indians and disgruntled by insults of their "uncles"—the British-allied Iroquois—the Delaware and Shawnee nations defiantly sided with the French and launched guerilla attacks on the frontier settlements.[19] Massacres, scalping, and other heinous atrocities including kidnapping and the destruction of homes and crops or even entire villages were frequent events. Still, almost three centuries later, reading the brutal accounts of these wars in the colonial records, old newspapers, and old history books, as well as in modern accounts, sends a chill through the soul.[20]

It was as dark and dismal a time as the Civil War but absent any pretense of chivalry. No truces were called to bury those slain in battle; women, children, and infants were sometimes butchered, often carried away. I cannot imagine the macabre scene of the little nine-year-old Mackey boy—reportedly forced to stretch his dead father's scalp after the father was murdered and the boy was captured in the summer of 1757 just south of the Blue Mountain in Hanover—stroking the relic with his hand while softly murmuring the lament, "my father's pretty hair."[21] Such incidents were not isolated events and were often reported in the newspapers of the day.[22]

With a provincial military response stymied by political wrangling between the colonial assembly and the proprietary governor, the settlers did what they must in self-defense. With but limited arms and ammunition, they aided their neighbors as best as they could. They built blockhouses. They formed groups called rangers who patrolled the frontier. And they fled. The inhabitants of the remote regions abandoned their plantations en masse, often fleeing in terror with only the clothes on their back. The exodus involved Paxtang as well, as attested by the change in its tax lists between 1756 and 1758. Indeed, the tax collector in 1756 noted the names of those who had already "fled from ye Indians."[23] More would follow. By 1758, seventy-five of the 192 names listed in the 1756 assessment were no longer there.[24]

Against this backdrop, how strange it seems that James Woodside's name appears on the Paxtang tax list in 1758 for the first time! Why would he move his family to Paxtang while others were fleeing? Although it may be tempting to claim his family possessed uncommon courage, to do so based on a single entry in a tax list would be unwarranted. No surviving records show that the family members were participants in or direct victims of the war or that they were community leaders at that time. Still, extant colonial records are notably incomplete. And Paxtang and the neighboring townships were not immune from attack. Throughout the troubled period there were incursions in the adjacent townships of Lebanon and Hanover, and late in 1757 murders were reported in Paxtang and south of Derry, in the Swatara region, and near Fort Hunter.[25] Hence, being an able-bodied young man with a family to protect, it is possible that James was at least involved with the informal groups called rangers who patrolled the nearby frontier.

That James and Margaretha would be deeply disturbed by the war's events is undeniable. That they would be anxious for their own safety, fearful for the well-being of their children, and aggrieved by the horrific events experienced by their neighbors and countrymen year after year is beyond question. While the particulars of their situation will never be known, it is safe to conclude that this was a distressing period in their lives.

Nevertheless, people are resilient and somehow go on, doing what they do in spite of adversity. Farm life continued in its seasonal rhythm. People got married and babies were born. And so it was with James and Margaretha Woodside. Daughter Maria was born on February 19, 1756, just as the hostilities got underway. Jonathan was probably born in 1758, the year before the French and Indian War came to a close in Pennsylvania after a treaty was signed between the Indians and the English at Easton.[26] Although the war continued in other venues in North America, Pennsylvania would enjoy five years of peace.

The war was not forgotten, although sad memories soon lost their sting. Life returned to normal, and people went about their business of plowing their fields, doing their chores, socializing with neighbors, and watching children play. They talked about everyday matters, just as we do today: late frosts in the spring, early ones in the fall, the local political drama, how the children grow too fast. James and Margaretha's third child, John Woodside, was born March 9, 1760.[27] So by the spring of 1763, Maria was seven, Jonathan was six, and John had just turned three years old. Margaretha was busy tending to the family's needs while James was occupied with providing for them. Their life was not easy, but they were making their way.

Then, in 1763 war broke out again. The cause and objectives of Pontiac's War were clear. The English had broken their treaties with the Indians by which they had promised to withdraw their people to the east side of the Allegheny Mountains after the French were driven from the Ohio Valley. Instead, the English built forts and allowed white settlers to build plantations on the land that the Indians rightfully claimed. Moreover, the policies implemented by the commander of the British army in North America, General Jeffery Amherst, aggravated the already touchy situation. As historian Richard White observed, Amherst "blustered into Indian affairs with the moral vision of a shopkeeper and the arrogance of a victorious soldier."[28] He disrupted the long-standing practice of bestowing presents on the Indians as an essential part of the European-Indian negotiation process. He drastically reduced the supply of gunpowder, which the Indians needed for the hunt. And he treated the Indians with disdain.[29] Because of this, the Indians waged war and intended to kill all the Englishmen or drive them into the sea.

This was a war without mercy. If the atrocities of the French and Indian War make one shudder, then the crimes of 1763 and 1764 make one wonder what it means to be human. Accounts tell of massacres and an orgy of scalping—by Indians and white men on victims both alive (some of whom survived) and dead.[30] Indeed, on July 7, 1764, Pennsylvania's governor John Penn issued a proclamation that offered a bounty of 134 pieces of eight for the scalp of "every male Indian enemy above the age of ten years," and for "every female Indian enemy above the age of ten years," the going rate was fifty pieces of eight.[31]

In Paxtang the reaction was vicious. Provoked by continuing depredations by hostile Indians upon their neighbors, a group of frontiersmen took the law into their own hands. Believing that peaceable Conestoga Indians living near the borough of Lancaster under the protection of provincial authorities were aiding enemy Indians, the Paxton Boys, a group of rangers associated with Reverend John Elder's Presbyterian Church, butchered and mutilated the Indians, young and old alike.

The massacre ignited a political frenzy in the colony, which brought into sharp focus the ideological chasm existing between the backcountry inhabitants and Philadelphia's influential Quakers. Reverend Elder described the murderers as "hot-headed, ill advised persons, & especially by such, I imagine, as suffer'd much in their relations by the Ravages committed in the late Indian War."[32] He further expostulated that "the deed, magnified into the blackest of crimes, shall be considered one of those youthful ebullitions of wrath, caused by momentary excitement."[33] Benjamin Franklin, meanwhile, offered that the Indians "would have been safe in any Part of the known World—except in the Neighborhood of the Christian White Savages of Peckstang [Paxtang] and Donegal!"[34] Amid this turmoil, two of the ringleaders, Lazarus Stewart and Matthew Smith, were identified. But owing to intense public sentiment, they were never brought to justice. While the identities of the remaining participants may have been known at the time, their names have been lost to history.[35] As I ponder whether James

Woodside could have been among the perpetrators, I assuage my concern by reminding myself that there is no evidence that James was a Presbyterian and, at the time, he was in his late thirties—past the age of "youthful ebullition."

In the aftermath of the slaughter, some of the frontier residents marched to Philadelphia, where they presented a formal list of their grievances. They demanded a share in the privilege of legislation for the frontier counties equal to that of the three eastern counties; they condemned a provincial law that deprived "such persons as shall be charged with killing any Indians in Lancaster County" of a long-established British right to a trial by a jury of their peers in the jurisdiction where the crime was committed; and they remonstrated passionately against a government that sheltered their Indian enemies at the public expense while, at the same time, the frontier inhabitants were left defenseless and destitute.[36]

The Paxton Boys' massacre of the Conestoga Indians went down as one of the darkest crimes in the history of Pennsylvania, and it continues to be the subject of historical interpretation today.[37] The events that unfolded in Pennsylvania between 1755 and 1765 engendered an abiding hatred between the white men and Indians. It was in these cruel years that a malignant style of Indian-hating was born. Moreover, among Pennsylvanians, the bitter political divide laid open by the crisis would fester in the decades to come and play an important part in the storm of events to follow.

Ultimately, the Indians lost Pontiac's War. In a masterful battle at Bushy Run (near present-day Harrison City in Westmoreland County, Pennsylvania) in August 1763, Colonel Henry Bouquet defeated a combined force of Delaware, Shawnee, Wyandot, and Mingo Indians. In the fall of the following year, Bouquet marched deep into Ohio's Indian territory where he met with the tribal chiefs at Muskingum and Tuscarawas and dictated the terms of peace.[38]

After hostilities ceased, James and Margaretha Woodside decided to leave their home in Paxtang around 1765 and move to their final destination, the Lykens Valley. It was time to move to a quieter neighborhood.

CHAPTER 2

A FINE VALE

---·◆·---

Peace settled over the valley. In fair weather the pleasant twenty-mile journey along the well-worn Indian path between Paxtang and Wiconisco Creek took a day or two. Above the Narrows, as the Susquehanna Water Gap was called in the 1760s, the Woodsides would have walked past the Blue Mountain, Second Mountain, Peters Mountain, and Berry Mountain as each ridge yielded an opening for the long, crooked river. In the valleys between the ridges, they would have forded each of several creeks— the Fishing, Stony, Clark, Powell, and Armstrong—at last arriving at the Wiconisco. As they cast their eyes on the lush valley that would soon be their home, the Woodside family knew they were not the first to walk among its forest and streams.

Long since, the valley had been a hunting ground for the native Delaware Indians, or the Lenni Lenape people, who gave the creek its name.[1] Later, as an unnamed place between hither and yon, the valley impressed sojourners as they trekked along another old Indian path that wound its way from Tulpehocken through the head of the valley to the Indian village of Shamokin (now Sunbury, Pennsylvania). Accounts written by these early travelers telling would-be settlers of the wonders of the valley drifted south of the Blue Mountain.

In 1742 the Moravian missionary Count Zinzendorf passed through on his quest to save the souls of Indians at Shamokin and beyond. He described the valley as "a very wild region of country."[2] Zinzendorf named the valley "Anna's Valley" after one of his traveling companions, a fellow missionary and his future wife, Anna Nitschmann. Although the valley's name didn't stick, the story of this small and indomitable woman leading her male companions down a treacherous incline along the trail is enough to make anyone smile. We came to "a precipitous hill, scarce as I ever saw," the Count reported. "Anna, who is the most courageous of our number, and a heroine, led the descent. I took the train of her riding habit in my hand to steady me in the saddle, Conrad held to the skirt of my overcoat, and Bohler to Conrad's. In this way we mutually supported each other, and the Savior assisted us in descending the hill in safety."[3]

In 1743 John Bartram, a famous early American horticulturist, recorded his botanic observations of the "fine vale" and surrounding ridges as he traveled to Onondaga (near present-day Syracuse, New York), Oswego, and Lake Ontario.[4] Bartram was accompanied on his trek by the noted cartographer Lewis Evans, who subsequently mapped the region they visited.[5] Two years later, Bishop A. G. Spangenberg, the successor to Count Zinzendorf, followed the trail on his way to the Six Nations capital at Onondaga and noted the valley was "beautiful and pleasing to the eyes."[6]

In a letter to Count Zinzendorf, Bishop J. C. F. Cammerhoff, an assistant to Spangenberg, described the perils of wintertime travel along the same river trail probably traveled by the Woodsides decades later:

"We suddenly saw the [Susquehanna] river before us," he wrote. "In a narrow part of its channel [probably Berry's Falls] the ice was dammed up to the height of ten or twelve feet, and the Narrows, through which the path along the river wound, was overflowed and caked with ice. It was in vain that we endeavored to effect a passage or keep to the trail. Foiled in this, we were compelled to climb the spurs of the mountain which here abut against the river, until we again struck a wide expanse of lowland. It was a laborious task;

but we kept brave hearts, and our poor horses did their part nobly. After toiling on in this way for seven miles we reached the Wiconisco, which ran very far above its banks, with an impetuous current, and was full of floating ice. We were told that any attempt to ford it, would be at the peril of our lives. But Powell rode in, and as I followed, I encouraged him by the word of the text. It was a special Providence that we reached the farther bank in safety. A short distance beyond we came to a house [probably James Berry's house] where we halted."[7]

Surely, what we might consider an extreme sport today was a matter of fact for eighteenth-century travelers.

At the mouth of Wiconisco Creek, James Berry's house had been a stopping point on June 15, 1744, for Six Nations' chiefs and their party of 245 men, women, and children as they traveled from Onondaga to Lancaster to meet with Marylanders and Virginians. At the treaty a dispute between the Six Nations and the southern colonies about land ownership was resolved.[8] In his response to the Marylanders, who (supported by the Virginians) contended that the Six Nations had no right to any lands within its borders, Canasatego, an Onondaga chief, delivered the Iroquois' opening statement.[9] The address includes the allegory of the chain of friendship—the precept underlying the evolving relationship between the Six Nations of the Iroquois and the English and the Americans. The importance of the allegory becomes clear in chapters about the Revolutionary War and the later fate of the Indians. That said, the speech is remarkable for its imagery and eloquence.

Canasatego spoke:

When you mentioned the affair of the Land Yesterday, you went back to the old Times, and told us you had been in Possession of the Province of Maryland above One hundred years, but what is One hundred Years in comparison to the length of Time since our Claim began? Since we came out of this Ground? For we must tell you, that long before One hundred years Our Ancestors came out of this very Ground, and their Children have remained here ever since; you came out of the Ground in a Country that lyes beyond Seas, there you have just Claim, but here you must allow Us to be your elder Brethren and the Lands belong to Us long before you knew anything of them. It is true that above One hundred Years ago the Dutch came here in a Ship and brought with them several Goods such as Awls, Knives, Hatchets, Guns and many other particulars which they gave Us, and when they had taught Us how to Use their things, and we saw what sort of People they were, we were so well pleased with them that we tyed their Ship to the Bushes on the Shoar, and afterwards likeing them still better the longer they stayd with Us, and thinking the Bushes to Slender, we removed the Rope and tyed it to the Trees, and as the Trees were liable to be blown down by high Winds, or to decay of themselves, We, from the affection We bore them, again removed the Rope, and tyed it to a Strong and big Rock [Here the Interpreter said they mean the Oneido Country] and not content with this, for its further Security We removed the Rope to the Big-Mountain [Here the Interpreter says they mean the Onondago Country] and there we tyed it very fast and rowled Wampum about it, and to make it still more Secure We stood upon the Wampum and sat down upon it, to defend it, to prevent any hurt coming to it, and did our Best endeavors that it might remain uninjured forever. During all this Time the Newcomers the Dutch acknowledged Our Rights to the Lands, and Sollicited us from time to time to grant them Parts of Our Country, and to enter into League and Covenant with Us, and to become one People with Us.

After this the English came into the Country, and, as we were told, became one People with the Dutch. About two years after the Arrival of the English, an English Governor came to Albany, and finding what great friendship subsisted between Us and the Dutch he approved it mightily, and desired to make as Strong a League and to be upon as good Terms with us as the Dutch were, with whom he was United, and to become One People with Us, and by his further care in looking at what had passed between Us he found that the Rope which tyed the Ship to the Great Mountain was only fastened with Wampum which was liable to break and rot and to perish in a Course of Years. He therefore told us that he would give us a Silver Chain, which would be much stronger and last for Ever. This we Accepted, and fastned the Ship with it and it has lasted ever since.[10]

At the same treaty, Gachradodow, a Cayuga chief, spoke for the Indians on the occasion of bestowing an honorific name on Lord Baltimore, the governor of Maryland. Gachradodow was graceful and bold in his speaking style, "without the buffoonery of the French or over-solemn deportment of the haughty Spaniards," such that the governor observed of him that he "would have made a good figure in the forum of Old Rome."[11]

The interpreter at the Treaty of Lancaster was Conrad Weiser, the son of a German immigrant and a friend of colonist and Indian alike. Having learned the Mohawk language in his youth, Weiser was the interpreter who had also accompanied the missionaries, the botanist, and the cartographer. When the Indians rested at James Berry's home on their way to Lancaster, he was the person who provided them with food. His frequent visits to his good friend in Shamokin, Shikellamy, the great Oneida chief entrusted with the care of the Six Nations and their dependents in Pennsylvania, kept the path well worn. Moreover, Weiser's name regularly appears in the provincial records as the official interpreter at Indian treaties and as an emissary to the Six Nations. One of the most interesting characters of Pennsylvania's colonial period, Weiser was a "hot-headed, true-hearted, whimsical Jack-of-all-trades."[12] Today, Weiser State Forest, located near the trails he so often tread, memorializes this colonial leader.

The land that includes the Lykens Valley was reluctantly sold to the provincial authorities by the Six Nations of the Iroquois, the Delaware, and the Shawnee for £500 in a deed executed on August 22, 1749 (approximately £58,000 in today's currency).[13] A condition of the sale was that the provincial authorities would forcibly remove white trespassers living on hunting grounds bordering the Juniata River, west of the Susquehanna.[14] Soon after the purchase of 1749, pioneers began to settle along the Wiconisco. Among them was Ludwig Schott, whose land was adjacent to the future Woodside homestead. Another settler was John Rewalt. But the most notable of the early arrivals was Andrew Lycans, who came after he had been evicted from land on the Juniata, twenty-five miles from its mouth.[15] The three men lived in the valley at the outset of the French and Indian War and came under attack on the morning of March 7, 1756. Lycans later died from wounds suffered in the attack, but his name would live on; for it is after Andrew Lycans that the Lykens Valley was named.[16]

IN THOSE EARLY DAYS SETTLEMENT OF THE VALLEY WAXED AND waned. Trailblazing farmers cleared scattered patches of land only to later withdraw amid the threat of renewed hostilities. When peace was finally restored in 1765, permanent settlers began to arrive. The Woodsides were among the first. The scene that greeted them was that of a virgin oak-chestnut forest.[17] And what a splendid forest it must have been! As revealed by old township survey maps, it included all kinds of oak trees.[18] The eastern white oak, with its broad and spreading branches, provided the family with a "sort of second home, an outdoor mansion of shade and greenery and leafy music."[19] There was the soldierly chestnut oak, the black oak, and the Spanish oak—"handsome and gallant."[20] Lowliest among the oaks was the scrub oak, which "trudged with scrub pine in places where otherwise you might have no trees at all."[21] Sharing the namesake forest, the magnificent American chestnut, prized for its appearance, its food, and its valuable timber, grew on the hillsides. On the valley floor, along Wiconisco Creek, there were hickory and black walnut groves and an occasional white walnut. And scattered here and there were black birch, wild cherry, maple, ash, and the sassafras tree. Rounding out this wonderful forest were the pines, the scrubby jack pine and the enormous eastern white pine. The white pine towered above all other trees, growing to 150 feet, clear of limbs and knots for the first eighty feet or so. They mingled among the oaks on the valley floor and stood in pure stands on the hillsides above.[22]

Amid this grand forest, on May 25, 1767, James Woodside submitted applications for two adjacent pieces of land to Pennsylvania surveyor general John Lukens. One tract, named Deer's Watering Place, included 48¼ acres on both sides of Wiconisco Creek. The other, named Indian Encampment, included 124½ acres of rich bottomland (see figure 2).[23]

Figure 2. A view of Wiconisco Creek adjacent to the Woodside property that was known as Indian Encampment. Photo by author.

The stream and forest provided the Woodsides with basic necessities in their new home. Wiconisco Creek was crystal clear back then and, like other Susquehanna tributaries, teamed with fish: trout, bass, catfish, mullet, eels, and anadromous species—shad and salmon.[24] The forest abounded with bear and deer to provide meat for food and hides for clothing. Turkey and grouse were plentiful, and in the spring, "cities" of nesting passenger pigeons—now extinct—provided easy meals for the settlers.[25] But in the eyes of James Woodside, farmer that he was, the woodlands were menacing. Predacious animals, the panther and the timber wolf, prowled unseen.[26] Fear of Indian attacks lingered, and imagined hostile Indians seemingly lurked behind every fallen tree. Giant trees blocked sunlight where grain would grow and orchards could flourish.

These enormous trees, growing to heights of one hundred feet or more, were felled by James and other early settlers with the ax. I can imagine James as a lean, muscular man, standing amid a cathedral of trees, choosing one tree, raising his ax high overhead, bringing it down with all the might that the muscles of the shoulders and back could give, thrusting it deep into the trunk of the monstrous tree, and repeating the stroke hundreds, thousands of times. At the end of each day, with calloused hands and an aching back, he would look with pride at what he had done and reckon what he had yet to do. Then with a gritty inward smile, James would whisper to the trees: "I shall beat ye back." Day after day would be the same. Weeks would pass, then months. One by one the massive trees would fall. Fallen logs would lie helter-skelter on the forest floor. Finally, what few neighbors there were would bring their tools and teams of draft animals, wrestle the logs into tremendous heaps, and set them all aflame.[27] In this way James and the other early settlers cleared their scattered patches of land. They tilled the soil around the remaining stumps, and ever-so-slowly transformed the virgin forests of the valley into productive farmland. Such a mental image of James clearing land, surely with his sons, Jonathan and John, working beside him, removing brush and smaller trees, is within my grasp. After all, these manly occupations remain prevalent today.

But what of Margaretha's life in the wilderness? What a treasure it would be if one day I were to find a bundle of dusty letters from Margaretha, perhaps addressed to a sister or her mother, describing her life on the frontier! Such bundles of old letters have been discovered from other settlers. Those letters often told of an unrelenting longing to be reunited with distant kin. They spoke of the labors of frontier life. Encounters with Indians were a frequent theme, captivity stories being fairly common. But women's letters from the frontier also revealed a sense of pride in accomplishment. They described little bits of joy—social events such as house-raisings and corn-husking parties, and comforting visits from neighbors. In the end, however, Margaretha's life remains a mystery. Knowledge of her family, when and where she was born, and the time and circumstance of her death are elusive. Margaretha, a woman whose name exists only on a list of marriages, remained the nameless "beloved wife" in her husband's last will and testament.[28] Like countless other pioneer women, she lived in obscurity, struggling from day to day, bearing her share of the load.

WHILE JAMES AND HIS WIFE WERE OCCUPIED WITH DEVELOPING their homestead, other settlers trickled into the valley. In 1764 there was one land application; in 1765, eleven; in 1766, nine; and in 1767, eighteen.[29] German-speaking immigrants were the largest group of arrivals, and, unusual for the period, they intermingled and intermarried with their Scots-Irish and French Huguenot neighbors. The names and lives of the early settlers—Schott, Wert, Hoffman, Deibler, Jora, Sheesley, Novinger, Messner—became intertwined. By working together for a common purpose, these families established an enduring community. They helped one another in times of need. They stayed constantly alert for threats to themselves and their families. They shared the joy of a bountiful harvest and suffered together through the lean years, and when all else failed, they accepted setbacks as the hand of God.

In this young community, James and Margaretha's thrift and endurance was at last rewarded. Unimaginable in Ireland, by 1771 James was taxed three shillings and six pence for one hundred acres of land, two horses, and two cattle that he claimed as his own. In

1773 he was taxed five shillings and six pence for one hundred acres, two horses, and five cattle.[30] Although they were not wealthy, the Woodsides were slightly above average by the living standards of the day.[31] Undoubtedly they participated in the burst of consumerism that followed the French and Indian War.[32] Imported items such as glass windows, colorful fabric, kitchen utensils, tools, tea, and spices graced their little cabin in the woods.

The family felt more secure in their home. At the 1768 Treaty of Fort Stanwix (present-day Rome, New York), Pennsylvania had extended its proprietary lands. Legal settlements in the Juniata valley and the north and west branches of the Susquehanna provided a buffer against the wilderness. Sunbury was laid out in 1772 by surveyor general John Lukens. Located twenty miles north of Lykens Valley near the site of the Indian village (Shamokin), the town was the county seat of the newly erected Northumberland County.

I think these years were probably the best of their lives. In their prime, James and Margaretha watched their children mature into strong, capable adults accustomed to the rigors of pioneer life. In 1773 young Jonathan filed a warrant for 165 acres of land adjacent to his father's, and in 1775 he added 150 acres to that.[33] Maria got married. She was just eighteen when she married Dewalt Novinger, a man almost twice her age. Dewalt fell in love with Maria, so the story goes, when he was out with a group chasing Indians, and instead of capturing Indians, he got captured…by Maria.[34] The first in a long line of Novingers, the Woodsides' first grandson was born in 1774.[35] Also in 1774 James was elected as overseer of roads, one of five township officials, and thus he began what would become a pattern of family leadership in community affairs.[36]

On the eve of the American Revolution, the farmers of the valley still lived in an intensely localized world. Their vision seldom extended beyond their neighborhood or county to their province and even more rarely to other provinces.[37] The men of the "Upper End" sometimes gathered at the local polling place—Garber's Mill near the mouth of Fishing Creek—where they talked about their families, their crops, and local news. Through the years onerous British tax laws had caused some grumbling. But generally, there was little ado in rural Lancaster County. Compared to the zealous residents of the Massachusetts colony, the reaction of Pennsylvanians to the Stamp Act, the Townshend Acts, and other restrictive laws was restrained, and any potential for rousing patriotic fervor seems to have dissipated as soon as the British modified offensive laws.

But the mood in the quiet Appalachian valley changed with the arrival of alarming news from Boston in the spring of 1774. The closing of the port of Boston as punishment for the Boston Tea Party, and the New Englanders' plea to their sister colonies for help were the catalysts that would drive the colonists to unite in a common cause. As the cloud bank of a tempest gathered on the horizon, the silence of the valley once again surrendered to the thunder of a gathering storm.

CHAPTER 3

FLYING CAMPS

In some ways the early summer of 1776 was like any other. I can imagine the warm July sun beating down as the men of Lykens Valley tend to their fields. The pungent smell of sweat mingles with a sweet aroma of new-mown hay as the farmers, scythes in hand, stoop at their labor, methodically advancing through fields of tall grass. Young women, warm under their dark woolen dresses, follow close behind, humming as they rake, pausing at times to nurse newborn babes. Boys, being boys, are wrestling, challenging, and jostling as they gather the hay into sheaves and then stack them into shocks. Sounds of young girls fill the air—once laughing, now scolding as they watch their young charges play. And at last, the older women arrive with whiskey, water, and a bite to eat. What a peaceful, romantic scene!

And yet, in most ways, the summer of '76 was unlike any other. Hot conversation warmed the cool breeze when the farmers paused for their refreshments. Passionate discussion of adverse events of recent years replaced familiar talk of weather and families. Soon after the British had closed the port of Boston on June 1, 1774, resolutions in support of the farmers' New England countrymen were unanimously approved at a meeting organized by Timothy Green on June 4, in nearby Hanover Township. The resolutions expressed the men's feelings in plain and unmistakable language: "That in the event of Great Britain attempting to force unjust laws upon us by strength of arms, our cause we leave to heaven and our rifles."[1] As the only colony without an organized militia, however, Pennsylvanians were unprepared to match their bold language with courageous action.

Stuck with a Provincial Assembly controlled by a coalition of pacifist Quakers, lawyers, and wealthy merchants, Pennsylvanians needed the help of the First Continental Congress to effect change. The critical moment arrived on October 20, 1774, when Congress adopted the Articles of Association.[2] Intended to pressure the British to repeal a series of punitive laws, later collectively called the Intolerable Acts, the Articles of Association established a nonimportation and nonconsumption pact among the colonies and, most importantly for Pennsylvanians, authorized committees of observation and inspection in every town, city, and county to enforce the boycott.

The members of the Lancaster County Committee of Observation and Inspection were elected on December 15, 1774. James Burd, Timothy Green, and William Brown were among those elected from the county's northern district, which included the Lykens Valley.[3] The fact that the people elected three men who had fought on the frontier during the French and Indian War served both as a reflection of the electorate's militaristic values and a portent of the committee's priorities. The committee, soon after news of the Battles at Lexington and Concord arrived in Lancaster on April 25, 1775, acted independently of the Provincial Assembly and on May 1 resolved to organize a voluntary militia throughout the county. Among the Lancaster County volunteers, known as Associators, were the Fourth Battalion commanded by Colonel James Burd and the Hanover Rifle Battalion commanded by Colonel Timothy Green.[4]

By the spring of 1776, the dynamics in Pennsylvania had changed. General George Washington was collaborating with the Continental Congress to devise a comprehensive plan for defense of the southern colonies, the middle colonies, and New England. The plan for the middle colonies involved the formation of a Flying Camp, which was authorized by Congress on June 3, 1776.[5] But on June 14, Pennsylvania's discredited Provincial Assembly was no longer able to procure a quorum and announced that it was unable to carry out Congress's directive to muster Pennsylvania's quota of troops. Therefore, it was left to a provincial conference, convened at the statehouse on June 18, to usurp the authority of the assembly. The conference delegates paved the way for the Continental Congress to adopt the Declaration of Independence, and they recommended to the committees of inspection and observation for each city and county to order the militia for the Flying Camp to be raised.[6]

SHELTERED FROM THE MIDDAY SUN BY THE SHADE OF AN OLD oak tree, the farmers of Lykens Valley considered these bewildering developments. Their joy about the Declaration of Independence and their satisfaction about the demise of the Provincial Assembly were tempered by apprehension. News had arrived that the British were landing in New York with foreign mercenaries in tow. And the Lancaster County Committee of Observation and Inspection was hastily securing the county's quota for the Flying Camp. A sense of urgency prevailed as the farmers decided who among them would respond to General Washington's call to arms and who would stay behind to put in the fall crops. In the Woodside family, it appears that sixteen-year-old John, perhaps guided by his neighbor and brother-in-law, Dewalt Novinger, assumed responsibility for the homestead. James and possibly Jonathan, father and son, joined together with their poorly trained, ill-equipped neighbors as they marched off to fight the British army and navy, the most formidable military force in the world.

The record of Jonathan's service in 1776 is unclear. It includes a letter dated 1896 from the State Library of Pennsylvania to a descendant of Jonathan Woodside, which states that Jonathan was with Captain William Brown's company of Colonel Timothy Green's battalion. Captain Brown's company, or at least a part of it, was among those of the militia that went to the Jerseys. Nothing more is known of Jonathan's service in 1776.[7]

Tracing James's footsteps through the battles of 1776 presents a challenge. One problem arises from the fact that, although Pennsylvania furnished altogether about 4,500 men for the Flying Camp, the names of only about five hundred officers and men have been preserved. A few muster rolls of the period have survived, but there is no guarantee that a person named on a muster roll of a certain date, say, March 13, 1776, fought in a battle with the same company on, say, August 27, 1776. Nor can one conclude that a person unnamed on a muster roll of a particular date was not a member of the company present at a different date.[8]

Adding to the confusion, it appears that some of the extant documents are inaccurate, contradictory, or both. For example, an undated report signed by Lancaster County's Colonel James Burd claims that James Woodside was reimbursed for a gun that he lost when he served as a Flying Camp soldier at the surrender of Fort Washington on November 16, 1776. The same document lists Albright Deibler's widow and Adam Wert, both Woodside's Lykens Valley neighbors, with loss of a gun in the same battle.[9] But two additional reports undermine the accuracy of that report. According to one of the reports, a portion of Captain Deibler's company, including Deibler, was captured at the Battle of Long Island and not released until 1778 and further states that Deibler was wounded at Long Island and died from his wounds.[10] Second, casting more doubt on Burd's Fort Washington claim, Lancaster County's Flying Camp companies were not among the Pennsylvania units listed in the order of battle at Fort Washington.[11]

The aforementioned James Burd report places James Woodside, Wert, and the deceased Deibler in Captain James Murray's company, even though Deibler was captain of the company of Associators organized in the Lykens Valley. Was Burd also wrong about this? Perhaps not. The discrepancy might be explained if one understands how the soldiers of the Flying Camp were recruited, later organized, and served.

THE FLYING CAMP WAS A HYBRID UNIT, CONTAINING ELEMENTS of the Continental army and the state militias. General Hugh Mercer was appointed by General Washington as the division's commander. Intended to serve as a mobile reserve, the Flying Camp was to be composed of men selected from the militia: 6,000 from Pennsylvania, 3,400 from Maryland, and 600 from Delaware. It appears that Lancaster County met its initial quota of 746 men—which was increased to 1,069 on August 12, 1776—by drafting three or more soldiers from each of the county's companies and paying each draftee a bounty of three pounds.[12] Further, although the soldiers marched to Flying Camp headquarters under the command of their local officers—Murray's and Deibler's draftees probably marching together—upon arriving at their encampment in Perth Amboy in the Jerseys, the troops were reorganized into Lancaster County's Flying Camp battalion commanded by James Cunningham, newly appointed as colonel. I assume that the draftees from Murray's and Deibler's companies, including their captains, were assigned to Timothy Green's Flying Camp company because all three men—Green, Murray, and Deibler—lived in the same vicinity. In fact, Green and Murray were neighbors—they owned adjacent properties in Clark's Valley. Although Timothy Green had been a colonel in the Lancaster County state militia, he accepted the lower rank of captain of the Eighth Company in Cunningham's Flying Camp battalion. Finally, because Deibler was killed at Long Island, it seems logical that Burd's later report of guns lost would be credited to Murray's company because he was the surviving captain. Taken together, it appears that James Woodside was initially in Captain Deibler's company, that he fought in the Battle of Long Island alongside Deibler in Captain Timothy Green's Flying Camp company, that he was not captured in the battle, and that he eventually returned home with Murray's company.

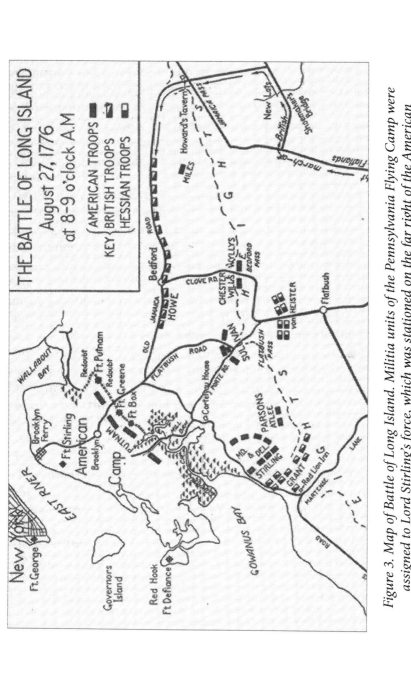

Figure 3. Map of Battle of Long Island. Militia units of the Pennsylvania Flying Camp were assigned to Lord Stirling's force, which was stationed on the far right of the American line on the Gowanus Heights. Courtesy Delaware Historical Society.

IN ANY EVENT, BY AUGUST 20, 1776, CUNNINGHAM'S BATTALION WAS stationed at Fort Lee, located in New Jersey on the Hudson River opposite Fort Washington in Manhattan. They weren't there long before detachments from the battalion were sent to Long Island under the command of Colonel William Hays, Cunningham's second-in-command. Colonel Hays, Captain Green, and about two hundred men, possibly including James Woodside, were assigned with Flying Camp battalions of Berks and Northampton Counties to General John Sullivan's division, which was part of Lord Stirling's brigade, which would put them on the Narrows Road, the American right flank (see figure 3).[13]

Meanwhile, on August 22, British General William Howe began massing his army on southern Long Island, and on the eve of battle, his force numbered about 20,000 encamped on the Long Island plains. They faced an American army including more than 5,000 men located behind entrenchments in Brooklyn and about 3,800 men stretched out along a six-mile-long defensive line on a wooded ridge overlooking the plains.

At about two o'clock in the morning of August 27, Colonel Edward Hand's rifle battalion, which had been on picket duty guarding the right flank for several days, was relieved by a detachment from the Berks County Flying Camp.[14] At three o'clock in the morning, the recently arrived picket was surprised by a British patrol. There was a brief exchange of fire, several Americans were captured, and the remaining men retreated. Thinking this was the beginning of the main attack, Washington sent reinforcements. But Washington had been outmaneuvered, for the British attack on the American right flank was a feint. Only when the Americans heard the British guns in their rear did they realize they were in a trap. In a quiet nighttime march, General Howe had led the main force of the British army far to the east over the lightly guarded Jamaica road, and thereby he had surrounded the American line of defense located on the ridge.

With their path for retreat almost completely cut off, Stirling ordered Colonel William Smallwood's First Maryland Regiment to cover the retreat of the 1,600 or so men under Stirling's command. "Without flinching an inch," these brave soldiers held their ground for nearly three hours, allowing the main body of troops, including the Pennsylvanians, to make a pell-mell retreat across the marshy Gowanus Cove.[15] Although losses were heavy, most made it back to the fortified American line in Brooklyn Heights. Smallwood's regiment sustained the heaviest losses: 256 of a total 684 men were killed or captured.[16] Several officers under Colonel Hays's command (and presumably rank-and-file troops, including Albright Deibler) were captured, killed, or wounded.[17] It was a decisive defeat for the Americans.[18] Where James Woodside was among the melee—whether he panicked and ran at the sight of the Hessian mercenaries' bayonets or stood firm to fight—we will never know.

Two days later, under the cover of a dark and foggy night, Washington and his army made a daring nighttime escape from Brooklyn to Manhattan across the East River. A demoralizing American defeat at Kip's Bay in east Manhattan on September 15 was followed by a heartening display of bravery at Harlem Heights on September 16. Reorganizing his army after an orderly retreat to King's Bridge, on the northern end of Manhattan, Washington assigned Cunningham's battalion, still commanded by Colonel Hays, to Colonel Edward Hand's Pennsylvania rifle battalion. On September 21 Hays's battalion was located at King's Bridge, with 335 men fit for duty and 92 sick. By October 5 the battalion, with Cunningham resuming command, was scattered between Fort Lee, Westchester, and DeLancey's Mills (present-day Bronx). James Woodside was probably with Green's company, which was stationed at DeLancey's Mills together with Colonel Edward Hand's First Continental Regiment and Colonel Henry Haller's battalion from the Berks County Flying Camp. By November 3, Cunningham's battalion, with 429 men, once again in Lord Stirling's brigade somewhere near White Plains, was preparing to withdraw to New Jersey. The brigade crossed the Hudson about twenty miles north of White Plains at Peekskill, New York, on November 11 and began their long slog home.[19]

WHILE WASHINGTON AND HIS MEN WERE FIGHTING FOR THE country's glorious cause in New Jersey and New York, the people in Lykens Valley were having problems of their own. Reports that Indians might attack stirred up horrifying memories of the brutalities of the last wars. On August 27 John Harris Jr., a member of the Lancaster County committee, wrote that he had been informed that the Indians to the northward, southward, and westward were for war against them. "About twenty Indians (enemies) men, women and children," he wrote, "have been many days past at Sunbury and made the report."[20] Harris made application to the Lancaster County committee for gunpowder for use in the township "as we do not know the day or hour we may be attacked by a frontier enemy."[21] Fear of Indians wasn't the only problem. Not long after the valley's farmer soldiers marched off, John Hoffman, the lieutenant in Deibler's company who remained behind, and Ludwick Gratz, a neighbor, requested gunpowder and lead in order to suppress "Tory riots that might happen in the neighborhood…from some evil-disposed persons lately appearing among them, who rob spring-houses and other houses, frightening women and children."[22] And at a time when a successful harvest was needed to survive, the Paxton committee ordered four men from Deibler's militia company to assist with putting in the fall crops.[23] Obviously, the local militia was intimately involved in meeting the community's needs. As a matter of fact, the Associators and the adult male population of the valley were essentially one and the same.

BY NOVEMBER 30, WASHINGTON'S ARMY WAS IN DISARRAY. CONfidence in Washington was at an all-time low. Even his most trusted adjutant general, Colonel Joseph Reed, had written to second-in-command General Charles Lee expressing his displeasure with the commander in chief.[24] Defeat had followed defeat. The fall of Fort Washington on November 16 cost the Americans dearly:

ninety-six men were wounded in the battle and fifty-nine were killed, but most devastating of all, the capture and imprisonment of 2,837 soldiers cut the size of Washington's army in half. Four days after taking Fort Washington, the British crossed the Hudson River with 5,000 men, forcing the evacuation of Fort Lee. With Lord Cornwallis snapping at his heels, the remnants of Washington's army, barely 2,500 men fit for duty, plodded through New Jersey and crossed to the Pennsylvania side of the Delaware River. Hunkered down with the army, James Cunningham's Flying Camp battalion, surprisingly strong at 432 men, reappeared in the record for the last time in General Edward Hand's brigade on December 1.[25] The British, encamped on the Jersey side of the Delaware River across from Washington's bedraggled army, stood at Philadelphia's doorstep. Washington himself conceded that "the game is pretty near up."[26]

Enlistments were about to expire. In Philadelphia, Congress sent the eloquent General Thomas Mifflin, accompanied by Lancaster County's George Ross, on a tour of the counties to "devise…the best mode of calling forth the strength of the country."[27] In a desperate appeal both to honor and fear, Ross sent an emotional circular to his countrymen, invoking them "to step forth in the field…which will insure victory over enemies glorying in every act of outrage and impiety, and debauching your wives and daughters in the face of the sun…The ravished maiden, the insulted parent, the buffeted hoary head…call on you to drive from this once happy land those bold and impious invaders of the peace."[28] In northern Lancaster County, the appeal had a negligible effect. Writing to General Mifflin from his home in Highspire (near present-day Harrisburg), Colonel James Burd reported that eighteen men in his battalion, plus thirty-one volunteers commanded by Captain Joshua Elder, turned out.[29]

IF EVER THERE IS A MARK OF THE TRUE GREATNESS OF GEORGE Washington, it was in his talent to grapple with this impossible situation, in his ability to rally his troops in this darkest hour and turn on the enemy in order to win two improbable battles. Reinforcements finally arrived, including about 600 men from General Gates's northern division and 2,000 men from General Lee's army, commanded by General John Sullivan, Lee having been ignominiously captured by the British. With reenlistments who responded to Washington and Mifflin's desperate plea, the total number of officers present, together with rank-and-file soldiers fit for duty, was 6,113 men on December 22, 1776.[30]

Observing that the British had left their force dispersed throughout New Jersey, Washington saw an opportunity and seized it. On anything but a silent and holy night, Christmas 1776, Washington made his daring crossing of the icy Delaware River and attacked the Hessian garrison guarding the small town of Trenton. The successful battle was brief, lasting only two hours, but it was enough of a win to bolster the confidence of the populace. Soon after the surprise victory at Trenton, Washington outfoxed Lord Cornwallis and defeated him at Princeton on January 3, 1777. Washington's little army would live to see another day.

While it's possible that James Woodside answered Washington's plea to extend his service, there is no evidence that he did. Neither Cunningham's battalion from Lancaster nor Haller's battalion from Berks, who had fought, camped, and marched together since the warm days of August, appears in the reports after December 1. Presumably the men's term of service expired, the units disbanded, and the men went home.

Much has been written, both at the time and since, of the privations suffered by the winter soldiers of 1776. Descriptive though the accounts may be, I still cannot imagine what James Woodside, fiftysomething years old, endured. Leaving his family behind for almost six months, he marched from his home to New York and back, about 450 miles. Clothed in a stinking, tattered hunting shirt, wearing the same pair of thin-soled shoes, or barefoot when they fell apart, he marched with his comrades along muddy backcountry roads. With only a thin blanket to protect him, he slept on the ground through drenching downpours and frosty nights. Fresh food and pure water were always in short supply. Conditions in camp were deplorable. There were rarely adequate latrines. Body lice, fleas, diarrhea, and fevers were rampant. He endured all this while facing the most powerful army the world had ever known. I stand in awe of the stamina, commitment, courage, and passion that these rebellious, fearless, cantankerous, heroic, stout-hearted, intrepid brothers-in-arms possessed. James returned home—cold, exhausted, and hungry—to a hero's welcome probably with the survivors of Albright Deibler's company. But the revolution had only just begun.

CHAPTER 4

BIG RUNAWAY

⸺◆⸺

Perplexed by British movements during the summer of 1777, General Washington was forced to split his army. Whether the British, led by General William Howe and his brother Admiral Richard Howe, intended to head north to support an attack from Canada led by British General John Burgoyne, head south to Charleston, or attack Philadelphia was unknown. The British objective became clear only when the British army and Hessian mercenaries landed at Head of Elk on the Chesapeake Bay on August 25 and began their slow march toward Philadelphia.

Prior to the British landing, the Pennsylvania militia had already been in motion. Full of youthful bravado, seventeen-year-old John Woodside was mustered into Captain John Rutherford's company at Middleton, Lancaster County, on August 12 on its march to Philadelphia.[1] At Philadelphia, Washington decided to make his stand against his foe south of the city at Brandywine Creek. The creek had several fords, and anticipating an assault at Chadds Ford, Washington formed his main line of battle there under the command of General Nathanael Greene. Two miles below Chadds Ford, General John Armstrong commanded the Pennsylvania militia in the rough ground at Pyle's Ford. Since all of the Pennsylvania militia were under Armstrong's command, we presumably find John Woodside at this location. Opposite Generals Greene and Armstrong, General Howe formed some of his brigades under the command of the Hessian General Wilhelm von Knyphausen (see figure 4).

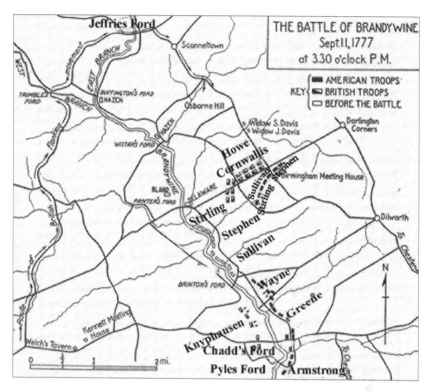

Figure 4. Map of Battle of Brandywine. The Pennsylvania militia was located at Pyles Ford, shown at the bottom of the map. Image courtesy of Delaware Historical Society, and modified by author.

On September 11 the fighting began when Knyphausen engaged in a distracting fire at Chadds Ford. Howe's main army, however, was stealthily advancing through the woods to cross the creek twelve miles upstream at Jeffries Ford; the British intent was to surprise the American right flank under the command of General John Sullivan. As soon as Howe's maneuver was discovered, the Americans adjusted their ranks as best as they could, but they were driven back by a superior force. Then, once the main attack was underway against Sullivan, Knyphausen commenced an all-out attack against the American main line of battle at Chadds and Pyle's. The Americans were driven back there as well, with the poorly trained militia making a disorderly retreat toward Chester.

Young Private John Woodside had seen his first battle and apparently escaped unharmed.

Maneuvers around Philadelphia continued over the following months. On September 20–21, the Americans were defeated at the Battle of Paoli (not far from today's Valley Forge National Historical Park). Howe marched into Philadelphia on September 26. The Americans were defeated again at Germantown on October 4, where we can guess that John Woodside continued to fight in Armstrong's brigade, but with a typical service in the militia lasting two months, he probably returned to Lykens Valley after that.

Beaten back though they were at Philadelphia, the Americans were in good spirits on October 18 when Washington announced that General John Burgoyne had been defeated up north at Saratoga, New York, a victory that would lead France to formally recognize the United States. Next, as if the Woodside family was taking turns, James Woodside was mustered in Captain Martin Weaver's company under the command of Colonel John Rogers.[2] On November 7 the unit was stationed at Whitemarsh, north of Philadelphia, where Washington temporarily staged his army before going into winter camp at Valley Forge. More maneuvers followed, but with winter fast approaching, both armies retired for the season. On a cold January morning in 1778, James Woodside headed for home, where he would spend the remaining years of the war while his two sons fought on.

THE WINTER OF 1777–1778 WAS A CRUCIAL ONE. WASHINGTON utilized the temporary lull in hostilities to harden his army under the disciplined direction of the incomparable Baron von Steuben, who molded the army at Valley Forge into a creditable combat force.[3]

At the same time, two hundred miles to the north at Fort Niagara, Joseph Brant (also called Thayendanegea), the well-educated Mohawk firebrand, consulted with the aged and sagacious Seneca war chief Sayenqueraghta to plan a spring campaign against the Americans.[4] Although the Six Nations of the Iroquois had pledged their neutrality in a treaty with the Americans in 1775, their commitment to peace was repeatedly challenged by Brant and British officials. Arguing that it was the British who had restrained American colonists from establishing settlements across the Allegheny Mountains since the 1763 Treaty of Fort Stanwix, Brant persuaded the Mohawks early in 1777 that their best chance for protecting their homeland against land speculators was to ally with the British. The Seneca, however, hesitated. It was not until July 1777, at a council held at Irondequoit (near present-day Rochester, New York), that the Seneca agreed to take up the hatchet against the Americans. Most of the Cayuga affirmed the silver chain of friendship with their British father. The Onondaga, regrouping after a devastating smallpox epidemic in 1777, mostly remained neutral until 1779 when they allied with the British. The Oneida and most of the Tuscarora, influenced by the compromised Presbyterian missionary Reverend Samuel Kirkland, abandoned the Iroquois Confederacy and sided with the Americans. The split among the Iroquois Confederacy widened on August 6, 1777, at the Battle of Oriskany (near present-day Rome, New York) during which the tribes of the Iroquois fought on opposite sides. The Indians, especially the Seneca, suffered heavy losses in the battle. Back at Fort Niagara after the battle, Sayenqueraghta wavered in his commitment to further engagement until he was won over by Brant's influential older sister, Molly Brant (also called Degonwadonti), the widow of Sir William Johnson, the former British Indian agent for the northern states. Sir Johnson had died suddenly in 1774. With renewed resolve, Sayenqueraghta agreed to attack the Pennsylvania frontier in the spring of 1778 while Joseph Brant and his warriors vowed to raid American rebels located in the Hudson and Mohawk Valleys.[5]

COME SPRINGTIME 1778, THE PEOPLE OF LYKENS VALLEY cringed at grim reports coming in from the west as the British and their Indian allies opened a new battlefront on the frontier. On the West Branch Susquehanna River at Bald Eagle Creek, Pine Creek,

Loyalsock Creek, and Lycoming Creek, Indian raids occurred with increasing frequency.[6] (See figure 5.)

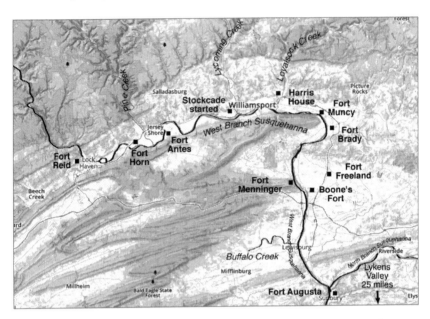

Figure 5. Map of fortifications and streams in north-central Pennsylvania during the Big Runaway. Modern cities are shown for orientation. Lykens Valley is off the map and south of Fort Augusta. United States Geological Survey, https://ngmdb.usgs.gov/topoview/viewer/#4/40.01/-99.93, and modified by author; fort information from Ruhrfisch - taken from US Census website [1] and modified by User: Ruhrfisch., CC BY-SA 3.0, https://commons.wikimedia.org/w/index.php?curid=2009498, and modified by author.

Most frightening of all to the people of Lykens Valley was the news that Indians had penetrated to the Susquehanna and murdered settlers on the Isle of Que, barely twenty miles north of their homes.[7] All of these attacks were a prelude to a major battle.

The cutting blow hit, not on the West Branch Susquehanna, but on the North Branch, sixty miles above Sunbury. On July 3, 1778, with John Butler in command of a group of British Rangers, and Sayenqueraghta and Cornplanter in command of almost five hundred Indians including an untested young warrior named Red

Jacket, the Tories and Indians swept down on the Wyoming Valley (near present-day Wilkes-Barre) and attacked a weak American garrison in what became known as the Wyoming Massacre.[8] The battle was a resounding defeat for the Americans, and although outrageous accounts of the battle have since been debunked, at the time the false or exaggerated stories of atrocities seemed all too real to the settlers.

When news of the battle at Wyoming on the North Branch of the Susquehanna reached Colonel Samuel Hunter at Fort Augusta near Sunbury, he issued an order for the people living on the West Branch to evacuate. Panic ensued. What followed, since called the Big Runaway, involved thousands of backcountry inhabitants who precipitously left their homes, their crops, and their possessions. In makeshift rafts, canoes, or hog troughs—anything they could get their hands on—they made their way downriver to a place they thought safe. The entire country above Fort Augusta was "broken up," and with less than one hundred men left to defend it, Fort Augusta, barely twenty-five miles north of Lykens Valley, was the new frontier.[9]

What must the residents of Lykens Valley have thought as they watched a flotilla of desperate people drifting by? Writing from Lancaster, Bartram Galbraith observed the scene. "On Sunday morning last," he wrote, "the banks of the Susquehanna, from Middletown up to the Blue Mountain, were entirely clad with the inhabitants of Northumberland County who had moved off....Indeed, the inhabitants of Wiconisco valley...were moving on Sunday last, and the people lower down were thinking to follow!"[10] Maria Woodside Novinger and her husband had built their cabin on land adjacent to her father's property. Maria had been raised on the frontier and undoubtedly took her hard life in stride. But she was old enough to have memories of the last war and its aftermath—vivid childhood memories magnified by gory accounts of Indian atrocities. Now Maria, with a child of her own; her mother, Margaretha Woodside; and the other women probably withdrew, taking temporary shelter with neighbors in the next valley downriver.

After the disaster unfolded, the men of Lykens Valley were called into service. John Woodside and his brother, Jonathan, elected sergeant, were mustered in Captain Martin Weaver's company of Upper Paxton.[11] They may have been among the men of the Lancaster County militia ordered to Northumberland County to serve under Colonel Thomas Hartley. Combined with other groups of militia and regulars, a total of seven hundred men were stationed at various points on the Susquehanna. Reportedly this was hazardous duty. The few inhabitants who had returned to their farms with hopes of salvaging their crops, as well as the militia who guarded them, were shot from ambush by "swift-footed bands of Indians."[12]

Later in the summer of 1778, deeming it advisable to take the war into enemy territory, Hartley led a successful expedition of two hundred men beginning at Muncy Hills, following the Indian path up Lycoming Creek into Indian country and returning via Wyoming. He ambushed some Indians at Canton and torched Queen Esther's Town (present-day Athens) and surrounding villages.[13] The Hartley expedition checked the Indians' raids in Pennsylvania for the remainder of the year; but it, along with Indians' outrage about atrocities committed on Indian children by American soldiers under the command of Colonel William Butler during the destruction of the town of Onaquaga (located near present-day Windsor, New York), spawned brutal late-season retaliatory attacks by Indians and Tories in the Mohawk region at Cherry Valley.[14] Thus, by year's end, the frontier regions in New York and Pennsylvania had collapsed into a hellhole of chaos and mutual destruction.

In the spring of 1779, the Iroquois and the western Indians prowled in marauding bands along the frontier. Among the Pennsylvanians who responded, Jonathan Woodside was ordered to Bedford County in April. As part of a detachment under the command of Captain John Rutherford, he protected the inhabitants from Indian and Tory attacks while they sowed their crops.[15]

BACK HOME IN THE LYKENS VALLEY, PEOPLE WATCHED FROM the banks of the Susquehanna as fleets of bateaux worked their way upstream transporting troops and military supplies to Sunbury, and from there to Wyoming in preparation for a massive offensive campaign against the Indians. Although military operations on the main and north branches of the Susquehanna deterred enemy action in those sections, the west branch was left exposed. Consequently, on July 28, a band of two hundred Indians and Tories attacked Fort Freeland. The garrison at the fort surrendered and was taken to Fort Niagara as prisoners. The women with their children escaped unharmed.[16] Following the Fort Freeland raid, Jonathan was among the militia who marched to defend the inhabitants in that region against further attacks. He served from August 11 to October 11, 1779, in Captain John Caldwell's company, somewhere in the vast Northumberland County.[17] By then, however, there was little for the militia to do because the Indians had withdrawn to defend their own country against the ravages of the Americans' scorched-earth counteroffensive.

AMONG THREE ASSAULTS IN THE AMERICAN CAMPAIGN—COLonel Goose Van Schaick's against the Onondaga in the Mohawk Valley, Colonel Daniel Brodhead's in northwestern Pennsylvania, and General John Sullivan's in New York—the latter wreaked the most havoc among the Iroquois. In their journals, the officers of Sullivan's invading army gushed about what they saw as they advanced through the Indian country in the Finger Lakes region and continued their march to the Genesee River Valley (near present-day Geneseo, New York). Extending for hundreds of acres, the officers saw lush cornfields with cornstalks growing sixteen feet high. There were gardens with beans, squash, pumpkins, potatoes, turnips, cucumbers, and watermelons. Peach, apple, and plum orchards swelled with ripening fruit. Well-built homes made with hewn logs and glass windows clustered in scattered towns. A virtual Garden of Eden, this was the home of a sophisticated native people, famously described by Thomas Jefferson in the Declaration of Independence, our revered founding document, as "merciless Indian Savages."

General Washington's orders to Sullivan were clear: to push the "Indians to the greatest practicable distance from their own settlements and our frontiers...throwing them wholly on the British enemy" and to make "the destruction of their settlements so final and complete as to put it out of their power to derive the smallest succor from them in case they should attempt to return this season."[18] The Battle of Newtown, in which Red Jacket again appeared briefly before he reportedly ran away, was the only major engagement of the campaign. As historian Barbara Graymont aptly observed, the campaign was largely "warfare against vegetables."[19] In his official report to Congress, Sullivan boasted that his army had destroyed 160,000 bushels of corn (about enough to fill a six-story, 3,600-square-foot grain elevator), a vast quantity of vegetables of every kind, and a number of orchards, including one with 1,500 fruit trees. His army destroyed forty towns and numerous scattered houses. "Every creek and river has been traced," he recorded, "and the whole country explored of Indian settlements, and I am well persuaded, that except one town situated near the Allegany..., there is not a single town left in the country of the Five [Six] nations."[20] Thus, in 1779 our young nation delivered a devastating blow against the Iroquois, a blow that offered a striking contrast to the gracious welcome so elegantly memorialized by Onondaga Chief Canasatego in his oration at Lancaster in 1744!

Curiously, learning that Red Jacket had been a participant in the frontier war piqued my interest in this side of the revolution story, for Red Jacket Parkway was one of several intriguing place names of my childhood neighborhood. Other place names as well—Seneca Street, Indian Church Road—suggested that the frontier war had a peculiar nexus with my childhood home abutting the Triangle neighborhood of South Buffalo. I wondered, What was this part of our revolution all about? Indeed, it seemed incredible that this aspect of the war was never mentioned in the classrooms of my childhood, especially since it touched the very ground where I grew up and went to school. Fortunately, in examining the American Revolution from different perspectives, eminent historians have recently presented a more comprehensive view of our revolution. Their research has brought to light many tragic stories about what happened to Native Americans. For my part, the haunting thought that something profound must have happened to the Indians on the ground where I played my childhood games compelled me to find out what took place near the banks of Buffalo Creek so very long ago.

CHAPTER 5

CHILLING OMENS

By the time Jonathan Woodside returned from his tour of duty in Northumberland County in October 1779, the people of the valley were celebrating news that General John Sullivan's army had vanquished the Indians. Crisp autumn evenings found the family gathered around their hearthstone, taking stock of the recent past and planning for the future. They gave thanks that the threat of Indian raids had never materialized in the valley and that their farm had been spared the ravages of trampling armies and military foraging parties. Above all, the family was grateful that James, Jonathan, and John had survived their repeated calls to duty unharmed.

Pragmatic people, they developed strategies for adjusting to a wartime economy and an economic collapse. The size of their homestead, now exceeding five hundred acres, with one hundred acres in cultivation, enabled them to reap profits from demand by the army for wheat and other commodities. In response to the worthlessness of continental dollars, they likely increased their production of flaxseed, which was universally acknowledged as an intrinsically valuable nonperishable commodity and was useful, at the time, in a barter economy. Being self-sufficient, they were largely immune from a shortage of basic provisions that precipitated bloody riots by mobs in Philadelphia. As an example, on October 4, 1779, a band of desperate militiamen, aggravated by wealthy merchants' profiteering and hoarding of wheat, seized four "detested merchants" and "paraded them around the city with a drum beating 'The Rogue's March'" until they arrived at the house of James Wilson, a leading conservative lawyer and future co-author of the United States Constitution.[1] Barricaded inside his house with other conservatives including Robert Morris, Wilson confronted the angry mob. At the end of the ensuing battle, six men were dead and seventeen injured.[2]

In spite of the fact that the prospect for success of the rebellion looked increasingly gloomy, the Woodsides hoped that the end of their ordeal was near and that victory over the British and their Indian allies was close at hand. But a chilling omen blew in from the north. Although images of soldiers trudging bloody-footed through a winter storm toward Trenton in 1776 and suffering in miserable hovels at Valley Forge in 1777–1778 endure in the public memory, it was actually the winter of 1779–1780 that caused the most distress to the soldiers and ordinary families. The most severe winter of the century, the mercury in the thermometer at Philadelphia on only one day rose to the freezing point. Long Island Sound was frozen over. In the mountains, such deep snow had never been seen by the oldest natives. Deer and turkeys died by the hundreds for want of food. Smaller animals such as partridges and squirrels also perished.[3] This harsh winter took its toll on the Woodside family. A measure of their suffering is that they lost three cattle and six sheep, three-fourths of their livestock.[4] I shiver at the thought of the family (and thousands of others just like them) hunkered around a crude fireplace during that long, cold winter as icy winds swirled about their drafty cabin.

BUT IF THE WOODSIDES SUFFERED IN THEIR LITTLE HOME, THEN the fate of the Iroquois was far worse. After Sullivan's whirlwind tour of central New York, the Indians had fled to Fort Niagara, where they joined refugees of earlier assaults. The refugees were a remnant of the Iroquois Confederacy whose numbers prior to European invasion are estimated to have been 21,740. Indeed, the total number of pre-Columbian northern Iroquois-speaking Indians—the Iroquois Confederacy, Huron Confederacy, Neutral Confederacy, Erie Confederacy, and independent nations of the Petun, Wenro, Susquehannock—is estimated to have been 95,840 in 1630. Through the century and a half of European presence, the number of Iroquois had been reduced by migration, warfare—both with other Indians and with Europeans—and disease. For example, a smallpox epidemic in 1634–1635 reduced the Mohawk population from 7,740 to about 3,000 in a matter of weeks. Prior to the American Revolution, the number of Iroquois living in New York had been reduced to an estimated 7,680 people.

In any case, as the winter of 1779 approached, 5,036 Indians were encamped in a makeshift village that stretched for eight miles along the portage road near the Niagara River. The British, unexpectedly faced with this crisis, ordered additional provisions from Montreal and Detroit in order to feed and clothe the Indians. They encouraged the Indians to go to Montreal or to return to their villages in Genesee Valley to garner any remaining crops. Some did, but about three thousand remained—"a disorganized mob...who during that terrible winter dotted the plain about the Fort with their flimsy, nondescript cabins, and roamed the snow-covered wastes in search of anything that might appease their hunger."[5] In spite of British efforts, many of the Indians, a number that was never recorded, perished of cold, starvation, and disease.[6]

In the spring of 1780, the Indians searched for locations likely to produce sustenance. Some fled to Canada. Some settled along Cattaraugus Creek in southwestern New York, "a beautiful river, surrounded by a most beautiful country and excellent land."[7] Others, including Sayenqueraghta, led their families to settle among the sweet-smelling basswoods of the fertile bottoms of the Buffalo Creek valley. By summer's end the banks of Buffalo Creek, a place known to the Seneca since their defeat of the Wenro in 1639, became the new home of over 1,200 Indians, and their number was increasing fast.[8] As soon as the men cleared the land, the women planted their corn, beans, and squash—the traditional "three sisters" of Iroquois' sustenance. Their warrior husbands, meanwhile, had other work to do.

⸺⸻✦⸻⸺

WHEN SPRINGTIME ARRIVED IN THE LYKENS VALLEY, THE WOOD-side family was somewhat relieved to learn that major fields of battle in the fight for independence had shifted to the southern states. But their hope for a peaceful Appalachian spring was dashed on April 25, 1780, when news arrived that Indians had carried off members of the Gilbert family, who lived in nearby Berks County.[9] Soon afterward, they learned that four settlers had been killed on May 16 in Buffalo Valley (near present-day Lewisburg), and on June 12 there was an attack seven miles east of Sunbury. Trouble persisted throughout the summer, including in Penn's Valley and at Fort Rice, thirteen miles north of Sunbury.[10] Folks discovered that, rather than subduing the Indians, Sullivan's invasion had stirred up a hornet's nest. For the next two years, 1780 and 1781, the Iroquois and the western Indians waged a furious war against the inhabitants of the New York, Pennsylvania, and Virginia frontiers. Sir Guy Johnson, the British commander at Fort Niagara, boasted in 1780 that in July, 836 Indians were in service. Moreover, he proudly claimed that the raids were important in keeping the rebels in a continual state of alarm and apprehension, and destroying their resources.[11] Indeed in 1780 alone, damage on the frontier amounted to 330 killed or taken prisoner, six forts and several mills and over seven hundred houses and barns destroyed, and nearly seven hundred head of cattle driven off. In 1781 sixty-four war parties comprising 2,945 warriors completed the devastation.[12] Again, the militia of the valley responded to the call. Jonathan Woodside, who had been elected ensign in Captain Martin Weaver's company in 1780, and his younger brother, John, offered their final duty of the war, serving somewhere in Northumberland County in the spring of 1781.[13]

At home during this critical period, the Lykens Valley men stayed on alert. A second evacuation of homesteads on the north and west branches of the Susquehanna had once again put the valley on the fringe of the frontier. Separated from the Indian menace by one low mountain ridge and a shallow Susquehanna, terror penetrated every cabin. Gruesome reports and graphic drawings of scalpings and body mutilations committed upon white settlers amplified dread of the Indian enemy. In fear of attack, farmers carried their guns while they tilled their soil. Even the itinerant preacher, Reverend William Hendel, was at risk: several men were obliged to accompany him whenever he made his holy rounds to the valley. As the reverend preached within David's Church, located a short distance from the Woodside land, the guards stood around the door with their rifles "so they could both keep a look out for their enemies, and also listen to the servant of God delivering unto them the glad tidings of salvation."[14]

WELCOME NEWS OF LORD CORNWALLIS'S DEFEAT AT YORKTOWN, Virginia, by a joint Franco-American operation arrived in October 1781. In spite of the surrender, however, war raged on in the backcountry. Significantly, at Gnadenhutten, Ohio, on March 8, 1782, a gang of miscreant Pennsylvania militiamen under the command of Colonel David Williamson brutally bludgeoned to death ninety-six members of a peaceful faction of Christian Delaware Indians while they were praying. Like the Paxton Boys of an earlier generation, the militiamen justified the slaughter by accusing the particular Indians of being involved in hostilities against white settlers. In revenge for the murders, Mingo, Shawnee, Wyandot, and Delaware warriors launched attacks on nearby settlers.[15] In retaliation, in June 1782, Colonel William Crawford led an expedition to destroy enemy Indian villages along the Sandusky River in Ohio. Crawford was captured and gruesomely tortured and executed. Probably referring to the incidents, the great Seneca war chief Sayenqueraghta, in a council at Fort Niagara, asserted that the Americans "gave us great Reason to be revenged on them for their Cruelties to us and our Friends, and if we had the means of publishing to the World the many Acts of Treachery committed by them on our Women and Children, it would appear that the title of Savages wou'd with much greater justice be applied to them than to us."[16] In truth, the Gnadenhutten massacre and its aftermath demonstrated what the frontier war had become: a dehumanized, bare-knuckle brawl between white Americans and Indians in which both sides committed atrocious acts. Sad as it could be, the silver chain of friendship would never shine again.

Soon after Crawford's demise, General Washington received intelligence that the British had "called in all the savages" and that no more war parties would be sent out against the frontier.[17] He therefore issued an order to abort a planned military expedition into the Indian country from Fort Muncy, located ten miles north of Sunbury.[18] With Washington's September 23, 1782, order, the military maneuvers on the Susquehanna came to an end, and the people in the Lykens Valley, at long last, could return to peaceful pursuits.

The Woodsides had been involved in two sides of the war for independence. In the east, they engaged in a fight for freedom. On the frontier, they played their part in a brutal struggle to survive. Almost eight years after James Woodside had marched off to war, the Treaty of Paris was ratified on January 14, 1784. No longer subjects of the king, when the Woodsides and other Americans put their plow to the ground in the following spring, they were beginning to sense what it meant to be citizens in a free nation. This was the revolution within each person that would soon empower a nation of people to challenge the existing social order and turn the political world on its head.

CHAPTER 6

OUT OF THE CHAOS

W ith the threat of Indian attacks forever gone, bright prospects for a peaceful future were welcomed by the people of
the Lykens Valley. For the Indians, however, the outlook
was grim. Thunderstruck that their British allies had forsaken
them in the Paris peace negotiations, the Iroquois and the western
Indians had to work out a separate deal with the victorious Americans. And Americans were not in a kindhearted mood. Disguised
by expressions of generosity in the treaties with the Indians, the
motives of Americans were clearly stated in a committee report to
the Confederation Congress on September 19, 1783:

> That although motives of policy, as well as clemency, ought
> to incline Congress to listen to the prayers of the hostile
> Indians for peace, yet…it is just and necessary that lines of
> property should be ascertained and established between
> the United States and them, which will be convenient to
> the respective tribes, and commensurate to the public
> wants: because the faith of the United States stands pledged
> to grant portions of the waste and uncultivated lands as a
> bounty to their army, and in reward of their courage and
> fidelity: and the public finances do not admit of any con-
> siderable expenditure to extinguish the Indian claims upon
> such lands: because it is become necessary, by the encrease
> [sic] of domestic population, and emigrations from abroad,

to make speedy provision for extending the settlement of the territories of the United States; and because the public creditors have been led to believe, and have a right to expect, that those territories will be speedily improved into a fund towards the security and payment of the national debt.[1]

In short, by rook or by crook, the Americans intended to take all the Indian lands north of the Ohio River and east of the Great Miami and Maumee Rivers, near the present-day border of Indiana and Ohio.

In the first of three post-revolution treaties between the United States and the Indians, signed at Fort Stanwix on October 22, 1784, the Iroquois were forced to accept humiliating terms of peace in which they surrendered claims to land in western New York adjacent to the Niagara River and Lake Erie, and they relinquished all claims in Ohio. However, there was a problem with the treaty: it was the long-standing custom of the Iroquois to sell land only when approved in their council. Since the signers of the 1784 Treaty of Fort Stanwix had not been authorized to cede land, the treaty was subsequently rejected when the Iroquois met in council. The United States, as perhaps could be expected, ignored the rejection.

On the next day, October 23, the state of Pennsylvania agreed to pay £3,402 in goods, plus an additional $1,000 in goods to be delivered later, to the Six Nations for a vast tract of land, the so-called Last Purchase. In the land deal of the century, the Pennsylvanians paid about 6.9 cents per acre (in today's US dollars) for about 10 million acres of land.[2] Thus, in spite of later protests by the Indians that they had been tricked, the last of their Pennsylvania lands were surrendered in a fire sale.[3] (See figure 6.)

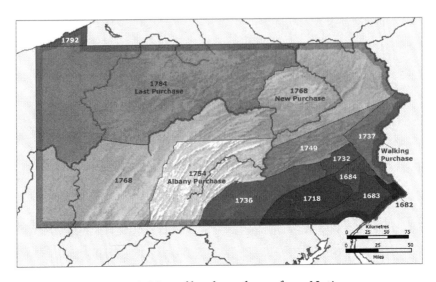

Figure 6. Map of land purchases from Native
Americans in Pennsylvania (1682–1792). Courtesy of
https://en.wikipedia.org/wiki/Treaty_of_Fort_Stanwix_(1784).

In the Lykens Valley, the Woodside homestead was now filled
with the happy echoes of youngsters playing childhood games.
And there were plenty of children. John Woodside was nineteen
years old when he married Margaret McMullen in 1779.[4] Their
first child, James, was born in 1783. Nathan, John's second child,
was born on February 8, 1784. It is unknown why the name of
Nathan's mother was not recorded on the baptism record. Nathan
may have been illegitimate, an idea that is consistent with the fact
that he was omitted in his father's will. Soon after Nathan's birth,
Jonathan (whom I will refer to as Jonathan Jr.) was born about 1785.
Meanwhile, Maria Woodside Novinger's family was growing. She
was now the mother of four boys and a baby girl, well on her way
to bearing ten children: Jonathan C., James, Walter, John, Mary,
Margaret, Catherine, Jane, Isaac, and Jesse.

John's brother, Jonathan (whom I will refer to as Jonathan Sr.),
was still unmarried. He had become a wheelwright, a trade that
suggests what abilities he had: physical strength, skill at working with his hands, an aptitude for mechanics and artistry, and

an understanding of materials including the characteristics of a variety of woods. He also would have acquired a shop and a set of good tools.[5]

On the surface the Woodsides' postwar story portrays a happy picture of continuing success. But all was not well in the state of Pennsylvania. Indeed, the years between 1776 and 1790 were tumultuous. To be sure, the family endured, along with their neighbors, the postwar economic collapse. In fact, between 1774 and 1800, the economy went through volatile swings. In the 1790s, for example, brisk growth rates masked the full extent of the immediate postwar collapse in which the drop in per capita income of 28 percent might have been America's greatest slump ever, worse than the Great Depression.[6]

The twin scourge of high taxes and lack of circulating cash was the most serious problem affecting farmers. Estimated to be about $160 million, the cost of the revolution amounted to about $200 per household, an amount that was well beyond the means of most farmers.[7] Undoubtedly, the irony of being presented with a tax bill to pay for a war that was ostensibly about onerous taxes must have hit the Woodsides squarely in the face.

The high taxes came about as part of financier Robert Morris's plan for handling the war debt: he considered his plan to "be the primary engine of wealth redistribution to enrich moneyed men."[8] Specifically, speculators who had purchased various war debt certificates at deep discounts were demanding to be repaid for the certificates and interest at full value. As Morris saw it, "Taking money from ordinary taxpayers to fund a huge windfall for war debt speculators was what was needed to make America great."[9]

The farmers' sense of injustice toward the Morris plan was exacerbated by a requirement to pay taxes in hard money—meaning gold and silver—a demand that was indefensible at a time when hard money was scarce. To wit, on the eve of the revolution, there was approximately $5.33 in government currency in circulation per person. By 1786 there was only $1.88 per person in circulation, and by 1790 the amount had plummeted to $0.31 per person.[10]

Without hard money, many farmers could not service their private debts or pay their taxes. By county, unpaid taxes per adult white male ranged from £0.114 in Fayette to £7.39 in Cumberland with a statewide average of £3.237. Even in Dauphin County, unpaid taxes amounted to £1.006 per adult white male.[11] There is little wonder that officials feared that the people would rise up and oppose the tax collectors. At a time when people unable to pay their debts were sent to debtors' prison, foreclosure on farms would be punishment for entire families.[12] As one can see, anti-tax fervor has long been part of Americans' DNA.

How the newly sovereign nation would govern itself remained another unsettled question. After years of wrangling over many perplexing problems including representation, taxation, and the disposition of competing claims to western lands, the newly independent states finally ratified the Articles of Confederation, America's first constitution, on March 1, 1781. Deliberately intended to keep the central government's power in check, the articles kept sovereignty in the states. Furthermore, under the Articles of Confederation, it was the states, and not Congress, that had the power to lay a direct tax on the people. Congress could raise money only by selling western lands, borrowing from foreign governments, or asking the states for funds. And Congress was sometimes ignored when it requisitioned money from the states.

Congress's control over commerce was also limited. After the war concluded, British merchants flooded the American market with low-priced, much-desired commodities, thereby creating a trade deficit. But there was little Congress could do to rectify the situation, especially when the British Parliament refused to repeal laws that prohibited profitable American trade with the West Indies. Compounding the international trade imbalance problem, several states waged persistent trade wars with neighboring states.

Further, rural rebellions threatened stability. The most alarming uprising was in western Massachusetts where farmers had closed the courts in order to prevent foreclosures. Interpreted as an insurrection, the so-called Shays' Rebellion not only provoked

Governor James Bowdoin to send state troops to the region but also was an important factor that induced twelve states—Rhode Island excepted—to send a total of fifty-five delegates to the Grand Convention at Philadelphia in May 1787. The authorized purpose of the convention, namely, to amend the Articles of Confederation, was merely a pretense. As we know, several delegates planned to scrap the Articles of Confederation and instead frame a new form of government, the United States Constitution. Indeed, one of the primary motives for writing the Constitution was to tame the forces of democracy unleashed by the revolution, forces that had overturned the ages-old doctrine that only the "better sort" were destined to rule.[13]

Completed on September 17, 1787, the Founding Fathers submitted the Constitution to the Confederation Congress, then sitting in New York, for approval. Before Congress had time to approve the new document (Congress's approval was not required; it was a formality only), the rush for ratification was underway in Pennsylvania. The Pennsylvania ratification convention met from November 23 through December 16. James Wilson, a primary author of the Constitution, was its leading proponent. William Findley of Westmoreland County and others led the opposition and pressed hard to promote the need for amendments to guarantee states' sovereignty and individuals' liberties. Given the makeup of the delegates, however, the outcome of the convention was predetermined. Indeed, not only did the Federalists succeed with a vote of 66–23—Dauphin County's delegates John Hanna, Adam Orth, and William Brown among the nays—they also contemptuously refused to include the statement of the dissenting minority in the convention's minutes. Thus, Pennsylvania became the second state, and the first large state, to ratify.

Given that Dauphin County's Anti-Federalist representatives to the state assembly and to the ratifying convention were repeatedly elected to serve in public office after ratification, it is clear that the local electorate had not changed their minds. In spite of losing a desperately fought political battle, however, the people submitted to the will of the majority. Perhaps the promise to amend the Constitution in the first session of Congress was enough to calm anxiety. It could be that the people were simply sick and tired of fighting. Then again, maybe their opposition to the new form of government silently smoldered, waiting to emerge if and when the tide turned once more in their favor. In any event, the people were ready to return their attention to activities close to their hearts: their families, their homes, their farms, and their communities.

NO SOONER HAD THE RATIFICATION CONVENTION ADJOURNED on December 16, 1787, than John Woodside's fourth son was born on December 18. Perhaps honoring the author of the Declaration of Independence, and as a tribute to Jefferson's advocacy for states' rights, John named the boy Thomas. Children Jane, Eleanor, William, Margaret, John, Isaac, and Polly would eventually add more clamor to John and Margaret Woodside's household. With plenty of mouths to feed and much teaching to be done, John and Margaret certainly had their hands full. And as the children grew, there were more hands to help with farm chores. All the while John remained actively involved in the community. He was elected ensign of his militia company in 1793 and served once as overseer of the poor.

Farming in the Lykens Valley again became profitable. Hard work, rich soil, and abundant water boosted production. Proximity to the Susquehanna and the markets downstream kept transportation costs low, thereby increasing profits. But life along the Susquehanna was changing. Not so much earlier the Woodsides had witnessed the downstream flotilla of despairing refugees and, later, the upstream transport of military supplies. Now, once again, the river was bustling with activity. This time, however, flat-bottomed arks loaded with grain, maple sugar, and other products were making their way downstream, destined for markets in Philadelphia or Havre de Grace or the world beyond.

By 1790, less than a decade after the war, the region above Sunbury had about 35,000 residents, and by 1800 the population exceeded 75,000.[14] Attracted by fertile ground, lush forests, and a built-in transportation network, the region appealed to squatters, small landholders, and Continental soldiers alike. It was, however, wealthy people who "plunged into the speculative boom" and dominated the market.[15] Robert Morris, the revolution's primary financier; James Wilson, a representative to the Confederation Congress and a primary author of the Constitution; and John Nicholson, Pennsylvania's comptroller general, were among the speculators.

The Lykens Valley benefitted from the real estate boom as well, but large land purchases by absentee speculators were not part of the landscape. Rather, tracts were comparatively small, one hundred to three hundred acres in size, suitable for large families. Many land warrants were issued to people already living in the valley—Ferree, Hoffman, Elder, and Buffington. As these families intermarried, they strengthened the bonds within the community.[16] John Woodside was among the buyers. He filed warrants for seventy-nine additional acres in 1792 and forty-five acres in 1794, bringing the family's combined holdings in the Lykens Valley to over six hundred acres.[17] Newcomers were welcomed as well, none more than the family of John Sallade and his wife, Margaret Eberhardt; their sons, two of whom would marry into the Woodside family, would later figure prominently in building America's "internal improvements," what we refer to today as infrastructure.

James Woodside Sr. was getting on in his years when he acquired a proud possession, a windmill. Heaven only knows what he used it for—perhaps pumping water, perhaps grinding grain. I am amused, however, and maybe his neighbors were as well, that James would build a windmill in an area not noted for strong winds. In fact, the region where the Woodsides lived is in something of a doldrums.[18] Nevertheless, James's windmill was listed along with his house, his wagon, and his land when he marked his last will with an X in 1796.[19] His will was probated on December 20, 1805, when he would have been about eighty years old. What a life he had lived! From a poor lad in Ireland to an indentured servant to a free British subject to a prosperous American citizen: if he was not proud of his achievements, he should have been.

Sometime in 1788, Jonathan Sr. pulled up stakes.[20] More adventurous than his younger brother, perhaps he sought to escape the tedium of life on the family farm. He may have seen an opportunity to ply his trade as a wheelwright along the westward migration route. Or possibly, feeling that the ideals of the revolution had been betrayed, and recalling his service in Bedford County during the war, he sought a place where the rebellious spirit of 1776 still thrived: he would find it between the Allegheny Front and Laurel Hill in a spectacular place located where Casselman River, Laurel Hill Creek, and the Youghiogheny River come together. There, Jonathan settled in Turkeyfoot Township. It was in the heart of the Appalachians—whiskey country.

CHAPTER 7

THE REBEL

⸻ ◆ ⸻

Whiskey Rebellion. It's a name that conjures up the spirit of a rough-and-tumble frontier conflict in a way that similar agrarian uprisings—Shays' Rebellion in 1786 and Fries' Rebellion in 1799—do not. With a cast of thousands, the insurrection that began in 1791 and lasted until 1794 pitted western yeoman farmers, laborers, and merchants against eastern politicians and land speculators. Emerging populist leaders such as Albert Gallatin and William Findley were set against revolutionary heroes George Washington and Alexander Hamilton. Playing a bit part in the drama, Jonathan Woodside Sr. was one of the ordinary men who participated in the unfolding events.[1]

Jonathan had been a true patriot in the revolution. Among his many tours of duty in the fight for independence, he had marched to Bedford County in 1779 to protect the inhabitants against depredation by a frontier enemy. Retracing his steps in 1788, he joined a stream of settlers searching for opportunity in the Ohio River watershed. He probably traveled on the Old Forbes Road where, upon reaching the town of Bedford on the western aspect of Sideling Hill, he headed southwest through the glades between Allegheny Mountain and Laurel Hill to the small town of Berlin. From there he continued through the rolling hills of southwestern Pennsylvania, eventually making his home among a group of Irishmen in a place pejoratively named Paddytown in Turkeyfoot Township.

Situated near the ford where Nemacolin's Trail (later named Braddock's Road, the Cumberland Road, the National Turnpike, and eventually US Route 40) crossed the Youghiogheny River, Jonathan was well located for a wheelwright. There he probably built his wilderness cabin, cleared some ground for potatoes, and settled in. In 1793 he warranted two tracts of land. Sometime in the 1790s he married Jane Drury, daughter of his neighbor John Drury, and began to raise a family. Surviving records point to a man who continued to be an integral part of the community—a hardworking American living his life as best as he could. How strange it seems, then, that Jonathan would be arrested in 1794. And how ironic that his offense would be for an act that would have earned him praise in the olden days of 1776!

The problem that led to his arrest began quietly enough on March 3, 1791, when Congress approved Treasury secretary Alexander Hamilton's financial plan, which included an excise tax on whiskey and stills. Soon thereafter, at a meeting in Pittsburgh, delegates from Westmoreland, Washington, Allegheny, and Fayette Counties laid out their grievances in a petition to Congress. Among other complaints, the delegates asserted that the tax on domestic spirits and stills infringed on liberty, was expensive to enforce, was liable to abuse, and was uneven in its application.[2]

The westerners had a legitimate gripe. While farmers east of the mountains were profiting by means of selling grain to Europe, access to the world market for the grain that grew abundantly in the trans-Appalachian region was limited: transporting their grain down the Ohio and Mississippi Rivers was blocked by Spain, then in possession of the lower Mississippi; sending it by packtrain over the mountains to Philadelphia was prohibitively expensive. The only way for the western farmers to make a little profit was by distilling their excess grain into more easily transportable whiskey and sending it to Philadelphia or down the Ohio River to Kentucky. Consequently, the western people had more stills and made more whiskey than an equal population in any other part of the country. Thus, they saw and felt that the tax pressed on them more heavily than on any other part of the Union.[3]

In response to the westerners' and other peoples' petitions, Congress modified the law. Regardless, over the next few years, opposition to the tax snowballed, spreading throughout the Appalachian regions of Virginia, Kentucky, Maryland, North Carolina, Georgia, and Pennsylvania, including the part of Bedford County where Jonathan Woodside lived. Mostly the protests involved threats against anyone cooperating with the law. Occasionally, violent attacks—notably including the brutal practice of tarring and feathering—were inflicted on those who refused to yield to the threats.

But the crisis point came in mid-July 1794. Following a confrontation in which United States Marshal David Lenox and local tax collector John Neville attempted to serve a warrant on a delinquent still owner near Pittsburgh, over five hundred well-organized rebels attacked Neville's expansive homestead, Bower Hill, and burned it to the ground. During the attack the rebels' popular militia leader, James McFarlane, was killed, thereby infuriating the local populace. Soon thereafter, David Bradford, a successful attorney, local businessman, and Washington County's deputy attorney general, emerged as the radicals' leader.[4] On July 26 Bradford's group robbed the mail and, finding several letters that condemned the rebels, Bradford called for a military assembly to meet at Braddock's Field, near Pittsburgh. Attendance at the August 1 rally was estimated between five thousand and seven thousand men, an amazing response considering that the voting population in four of Pennsylvania's western counties was about fifteen thousand.[5] At Braddock's Field there was talk of attacking the federal arsenal in Pittsburgh, of declaring independence from the United States, and of joining with Spain or Great Britain. Radicals flew a specially designed flag that proclaimed their independence. The flag had six stripes, one for each county represented at the gathering: five Pennsylvania counties (Allegheny, Bedford, Fayette, Washington, and Westmoreland) and one Virginia county (Ohio County).[6] At the assembly, however, Hugh Henry Brackenridge, a well-regarded local citizen and owner of the *Pittsburgh Gazette*, prevailed upon the raucous crowd to limit the protest to a defiant march through the town.

IN THE MEANTIME BACK IN PHILADELPHIA, WASHINGTON AND his cabinet were trying to figure out how best to respond to what they believed was an existential threat to the young nation's sovereignty. Although the US Constitution had been ratified in 1788, it remained an open question whether a republic encompassing such a vast territory could survive. Exacerbating the federal government's situation, international and domestic threats abounded. On the high seas the British were seizing American ships. Algerian pirates were raiding American vessels in the Mediterranean. In the Old Northwest the British had refused to abandon forts located on American soil and continued to support Indians' raids against settlers.[7] In the west, Spain, then in possession of the lower Mississippi, prevented the transport of American products. In the countryside and on the frontier, agreement with domestic and foreign policies of the federal government was far from universal. One consideration in particular, Americans' support for the French Revolution, which by 1794 had degenerated into what became known as the Reign of Terror, provoked fear among the Washington administration that the United States could descend into mob rule. Bolstering this concern, Democratic-Republican societies—local political organizations that were critical of the Washington administration—had sprung up in rural and urban settings alike. Furthermore, street festivals celebrating the French Revolution reached a peak during 1794. On August 11 one such festival held in Philadelphia—only "a stone's throw away from the homes and work spaces of the members of the Washington administration"—was the "largest and perhaps the most frightening to Federalists."[8] Further, a dispute between Pennsylvania's government officials and Washington's Federalists over sovereignty, worsened by personal enmity between the president and governor Thomas Mifflin, presented a formidable political obstacle for resolving the situation in the west.[9]

The president, concerned about public sentiment and uncertain about constitutional issues, proceeded cautiously. On August 7 he issued a proclamation calling on the rebels to disperse and invoking the Militia Acts of 1792, thereby preparing the way for military intervention.[10] On August 8 he directed three commissioners, US senator James Ross of Pennsylvania, Pennsylvania Supreme Court judge Jasper Yeates, and US attorney general William Bradford, to proceed to the western country to meet with the rebels. The federal commissioners were joined by a delegation sent by Governor Mifflin.

⁂

BACK IN THE PITTSBURGH AREA, RESISTANCE WAS BEGINNING TO fragment. At an August 14 rebel meeting organized at Parkinson's Ferry (present-day Monongahela, Pennsylvania), a variety of resolutions, intended to express the sentiments of the assembled crowd, were referred to a committee of four for editing. The committee included the radical David Bradford and moderates Mr. Brackenridge and Mr. Gallatin, and Herman Husband of Bedford County.

Husband, considered by some a crazy man and by others a prophet, was one of two men (the other was David Bradford) who President Washington and Secretary Hamilton thought were the leaders of the rebellion. Husband had written extensively about his vision for a future democratic society, and he had proposed elaborate plans for a new constitution. Although his polemics were not the immediate cause of the rebellion, it was said that his ideas of an egalitarian society had inspired the lower classes. While that may be true, his proselytizing would have been spread through speech rather than the written word. Unlike Thomas Paine's 1776 blockbuster, *Common Sense*, Husband's pamphlets did not sell. He either gave them away to his unpersuaded neighbors or left copies in a local store where they were removed "years afterword."[11] In any event, at the August 14 Parkinson's Ferry meeting, Husband was one of the four men appointed to write resolutions addressed to the peace commission that had been sent to the region by President Washington.[12]

The three resolutions as adopted included a complaint that taking citizens from their vicinity to be tried for real or supposed offences was a violation of their rights, an authorization to organize a standing committee to conduct business relative to the current problems, and a statement of commitment to obeying the laws of the states and preventing violence.[13] But the rebels' meeting was interrupted by news that Washington's delegation of commissioners had arrived. Consequently, the Parkinson's Ferry rebel group appointed a committee of twelve persons who were to meet with the commissioners and report back to the rebels. At the August 20 meeting between the rebels' committee of twelve and the commissioners, the commissioners demanded that the rebels submit to the law. Yet another rebel meeting was organized. At that meeting, convened at Brownsville, Fayette County, on August 28, the rebels were to make known their decision whether they would submit to the law. The atmosphere at the meeting was tense. Courageously leading the speakers, Albert Gallatin presented a long, thoughtful speech in favor of submission. Brackenridge, referring to upheaval in France, admitted that he was afraid of being treated in the manner of "the French Connection, the knowledge of which was familiar here."[14] Speeches by Brackenridge and a James Edgar in support of Gallatin were followed by David Bradford's fiery rant in which he alluded to the American and French Revolutions and advocated for war. Herman Husband was among those who advocated for peace.[15] With difficulty, a vote was taken of which the results were 34 yeas in favor of submission to 23 nays. Given the divided response, the federal commissioners ordered that a vote be taken among the entire populace of the western counties on September 11. The results of the September 11 vote being unsatisfactory, the commissioners recommended that "it was absolutely necessary that the civil authority should be aided by a military force in order to secure a due execution of the laws."[16] No results were submitted from Bedford County.[17]

ANTICIPATING THE COMMISSIONERS' NEGATIVE REPORT, President Washington had already called up troops in Pennsylvania, Maryland, New Jersey, and Virginia. However, raising an army among Pennsylvanians was difficult. Specifically, Dauphin County's 250 volunteers fell far short of the county's quota of 410.[18] According to secretary of the Commonwealth Alexander Dallas's report to the Senate, the men were "not willing to march to quell the insurrection in the western parts of Pennsylvania, [saying] that they are ready to march according to the former orders against a foreign enemy, but not against the Citizens of their own State."[19] The use of the word *Citizens* (capitalized in the original) is revealing because it may reflect sympathy with the egalitarian ideals of the French Revolution. Despite the resistance, Washington eventually raised an army of thirteen thousand.

In a last-ditch effort to dissuade Washington from sending the army, on October 2 the rebels dispatched congressman William Findley and Washington County prothonotary David Reddick to Carlisle, where the northern flank of the army was mustering.[20] Their effort failing, the army, led by the president, began its westward march. When the army arrived in the town of Bedford on October 19, one of the first actions against the insurgents was to arrest Herman Husband and Robert Philson, Bedford County's leaders in the insurrection. Washington then headed back to Philadelphia on about October 20 while the army proceeded to the Pittsburgh area, arriving on October 24.

After an investigation that lasted several days, hundreds of supposed rebels were rounded up on what became known locally as "the dreadful night," November 13, 1794. While some of the alleged offenders were treated with humanity, others were dragged from their houses in the middle of the night and "obliged to lie, all night upon the wet earth, without covering; under a season of sleet, rain, and snow; driven from the fire with bayonets, when some of them perishing had crawled, endeavoring to be unseen, towards it; next day empounded [*sic*] in a waste house, and detained there five days; then removed to a newly built and damp room, without fire, in the garrison at Pittsburgh."[21] Twenty of the prisoners were marched to Philadelphia where they joined Husband, Philson, and four other men. Most of the men's cases, however, were referred to the state courts and tried at the courts of quarter sessions in their respective counties.[22]

Caught in the dragnet was Jonathan Woodside. While apparently not subjected to the mistreatment and violation of civil rights that were inflicted on his neighbors to the west, he was "held at bail at the November term of Bedford County court to answer charges of riot and other treasonous proceedings, and in assisting and abetting in setting up a seditious pole in opposition to the laws of the United States."[23] But it wasn't only Jonathan who was drawn into the fracas; it was most of his Paddytown neighbors, including William Pinkerton, James Conner, Daniel McCarty, and John Killpatrick, and several prominent residents of Turkeyfoot Township—Peter Augustine, John Peck, and Henry Everly.[24] A pocket of protest, no doubt the men were fired up by one of their neighbors who was none other than the previously arrested Robert Philson. Philson, as it turned out, owned 403 acres touching McCarty's, Kilpatrick's, and Pinkerton's properties; Woodside's and Conner's were next to Kilpatrick's and Pinkerton's (see figure 7).

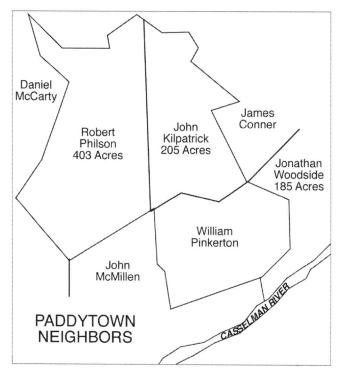

Figure 7. Map of land ownership in Paddytown, Turkeyfoot Township, Bedford County, Pennsylvania, as it was in 1794. Illustration by author.

An Irish immigrant, Robert Philson was the coproprietor, with one John Fletcher, of a mercantile business in the Bedford County town of Berlin. His involvement in the rebellion seems to have begun prior to the August 14 meeting at Parkinson's Ferry, at which he was supposed to be one of Bedford County's delegates. Arriving too late for the meeting, he was probably active behind the scenes in unofficial meetings in the Pittsburgh area. By August 21 he was back in Berlin. Dispersing news of the federal commissioners' demands to submit to the law, Philson encouraged the local citizens to resist the tax and to be prepared "for any steps the government should take."[25] Comments in his September 6 letter, written in Berlin after another visit "over the mountain," presumably to attend the August 27 meeting in Brownsville, reveal that Philson was displeased with moderate leaders of the rebellion and implies that he sided with the more radical faction led by David Bradford.[26] Philson wrote that he was confident the people had not given up. Further, he offered a report from a friend in Franklin County who believed that the militia would not come and, if forced to march, that it would side with the rebels. Finally, Philson called for a public conference to discuss the situation.[27] Documents offering details about the public conference have not survived, but unverified accounts suggest that meetings held sometime in September in Brunerstown—present-day Somerset—and in Berlin, involved speeches and raising of liberty poles with specially designed flags. Jonathan probably committed his "crime" of raising a liberty pole at the event organized by Philson in nearby Berlin. Thus, although some historians have considered Husband to be the leader of the rebellion in Bedford County, it appears to me that Philson was the real rabble-rouser.

TODAY, IT SEEMS STRANGE THAT THE MERE ACT OF RAISING A LIBerty pole would have been considered treason. Indeed, it's not unlikely that the offenders thought they were acting within the bounds of law, especially considering the long-standing tradition that symbolic speech was generally accepted as a legitimate form of protest, and that the First Amendment guaranteed freedom of speech and the rights to peaceably assemble and to petition the government for redress of grievances.[28] But judge Alexander Addison, president of the Courts of Common Pleas of the Fifth Circuit, whose jurisdiction included the western counties of Pennsylvania, had a much different idea. In his charge to the jury in December 1794, he clearly expressed the Federalist opinion about liberty poles, arguing:

> One offence, which I would recommend to your particular consideration, is the raising of liberty poles. What is the liberty, which those pole-raisers wanted? A liberty to be governed by no law, a liberty to destroy every man who

differed from them in opinion, or whom they hated; a liberty to do what mischief they pleased. It is not acts of violence alone, which constitute offences. Offences may be committed by writings, by words, or by other signs of an evil purpose. The mere act of raising a pole is, in itself, a harmless thing; the question is, what is the meaning of it? Those poles were evidently standards of rebellion, and signs of war against the government. They were raised by the seditious, with an avowed intent, to hold under fear all the well-disposed and peaceable part of the community, to keep alive the spirit of riot and confusion in the country, and to prevent the return of law, peace, and safety. And they produced all the ill effects, which were intended. They gave an opportunity to the violent, to know their strength and one another. What was it but those pole-raisings, and their attendant circumstances, that prevented our return to submission and duty, and a general acquiescence with the terms offered by the commissioners, and made it necessary for government to march an army into this country, to subdue that spirit of sedition and riot, which blind madness first excited, and those pole-raisings kept alive? Will any man doubt, therefore, that raising those poles was criminal, that those were especially criminal, who raised them, after the arrival of the commissioners of government in this country? And those, above all, who raised them, after the generous terms offered by government, were made known.[29]

And so, Jonathan and his neighbors were found guilty at the January 1795 term of Bedford County's court. As punishment for their crime, they were fined five shillings to fifteen pounds each, a far cry at least from the usual punishment for treason—death. We'll never know what motivated Jonathan to join the protest. Most likely it was a combination of factors, some arising in the heat of the moment, others from deeply held beliefs. Probably at the top of the list was a reaction to what he believed was an unjust law implemented by an overbearing government. Maybe it was a belief that the principles he'd fought for in the revolution had been betrayed. Such beliefs may have hardened at a time when the ideals of the French Revolution—liberty and equality—were widely celebrated among ordinary people in song, parades, and festivals. Jonathan may have been receptive to the preaching of Herman Husband or, perhaps more likely, to policy statements of the Democratic-Republican societies that had sprung up throughout the nation, including three groups near Pittsburgh.[30] Then again, maybe it was a bond, born of a shared heritage and their experiences on the frontier, with his Scotch-Irish neighbors. Whatever his motives, Jonathan earned his small place in the history of the insurrection.

IN THE END, THE INSURRECTION COLLAPSED WITHOUT A SHOT being fired. But even though the administration had been successful in quashing the rebellion, questions about how legitimate opposition to public policies should be expressed, and about what the limits of freedoms guaranteed in the US Constitution were, had yet to be answered and were the subject of vigorous debate in the young republic. Disputes about these questions would come to a head during president John Adams's administration after the Alien and Sedition Acts were implemented during the American quasi-war with France, a crisis that gave rise to the United States' incipient political party system. The whiskey tax excise law was finally repealed in 1802 after Thomas Jefferson was elected president in 1800. Soon thereafter, judge Alexander Addison, an ardent defender of the Sedition Act, was successfully impeached in 1803 by the Senate of the Commonwealth of Pennsylvania, by a vote of 20–4, for unlawful conduct in the performance of his duty.[31]

With the exception of David Bradford, who fled down the Ohio River, the arrests during the Whiskey Rebellion had no adverse consequences for the accused. More than a few of the rebels went on to lead illustrious careers. Albert Gallatin served at various times as a US senator, US congressman, treasury secretary, minister to

France, and minister to England. Hugh Henry Brackenridge served as associate justice on Pennsylvania's Supreme Court. William Findley continued to serve in Congress, representing the region of Pennsylvania west of the mountains in the Second through Fifth Congresses and again in the Eighth through the Fourteenth. He became known as the "Venerable Findley" and was the first congressman to be awarded with the honorable title of "Father of the House."[32]

Philson and Husband were tried in Philadelphia in 1795. Their indictment, reading as it does like a script for a *Saturday Night Live* sketch, seems ridiculous today; nevertheless, it offers a glimpse into the mind-set that prevailed within the Washington administration toward the insurgents. To wit, according to their indictment, Philson and Husband did not have "the fear of God before his eyes" but were "moved and seduced by the instigation of the devil, wickedly devising and intending the peace and tranquility of the United States to disturb."[33] They were accused of gathering together in Washington County with a great number of persons, "armed and arrayed in a warlike manner…with guns, swords, clubs, staves and other warlike weapons…[and they] most wickedly, maliciously and traitorously did ordain, prepare and levy public war against the United States."[34]

William Findley noted that "the prosecution against [Philson] was conducted with unusual severity. Being first acquitted on a charge of treason, he was tried for a misdemeanor, and in this the verdict also was, not guilty."[35] Husband was also acquitted; sadly the old man died on his way home. Philson, after his return home, served as associate judge of Somerset County for twenty years and as a one-term congressman during the Sixteenth United States Congress. He was commissioned a brigadier general of the Second Brigade, Tenth Division, Pennsylvania militia on May 9, 1800, and he served in that role during the War of 1812.[36]

Peter Augustine, a large landowner, laid out the town of Addison in Somerset County.[37] John Fletcher, Philson's business partner who had posted bail for several of the accused men in Bedford

County and had also been a witness in the Husband and Philson trial in Philadelphia, was elected as one of three county commissioners when Somerset County was first created.[38] Greatly admired by Jonathan Woodside, Mr. Fletcher was the namesake for Jonathan's son, Jonathan Fletcher Woodside, and also one of the administrators for Jonathan's estate.

Jonathan Woodside continued to prosper. He bought two hundred acres of land in January 1795. Ironically, the seller was Hugh Barkley, who had served as an associate judge at the trial in which Jonathan was found guilty; apparently there were no hard feelings.[39] In 1800 Jonathan purchased another ninety-two acres and in 1808 an additional 400 acres.[40] He continued to be involved in the community. He served on both petit and grand juries and was appointed as overseer of the roads for his town. Jonathan's name also appears on an undated court document in which he, along with several others including the popular politician and future congressman Alexander Ogle, was summoned to appear before the Supreme Court of Pennsylvania in Philadelphia. The cause of the summons remains a mystery.[41] Jonathan's last documented contact with his family in the Lykens Valley was in December 1799, at which time he purchased from his father the fifty-acre property, known as the Deer's Watering Place, that James had acquired in 1767. Jonathan died sometime in 1809 at the age of fifty-two and is buried in Younkin Cemetery in Pennsylvania, not far from where he lived. After Jonathan's death, his wife, Jane, and their son, Jonathan Fletcher Woodside, moved to Ohio where Jonathan Fletcher would eventually rise to prominence.

CHAPTER 8

Two Orators

RED JACKET (FROM ALOFT.)
*[Impromptu on Buffalo City's monument to and re-burial
of the old Iroquois orator, October 9, 1884.]*

Upon this scene, this show,
Yielded to-day by fashion, learning, wealth,
(Nor in caprice alone—some grains of deepest meaning,)
Haply, aloft, (who knows?) from distant sky-clouds' blended shapes,
As some old tree, or rock or cliff, thrill'd with its soul,
Product of Nature's sun, stars, earth direct—a towering human form,
In hunting shirt of film, arm'd with the rifle, a half-ironical
smile curving its
        phantom lips,
Like one of Ossian's ghosts looks down.

—WALT WHITMAN, *LEAVES OF GRASS*

As the place where I came to know the world and how to get along in it, South Buffalo has special meaning to me—a fact, I think, that explains my preoccupation with what happened there long before I was born and, less so, after I left. When I grew up there in the 1950s, the neighborhood was a vibrant community. The commercial districts bustled with activity. We claimed two large parks—Cazenovia and South Park—designed by the famous landscape architect Frederick Law Olmsted. Schools were bursting at the seams: in my school, each grade had three classrooms of about forty students each. When school was out, the tree-lined side streets—our playgrounds—were transformed into baseball diamonds in the spring and ice-skating rinks in the winter. Sidewalks were crowded with girls playing jump rope and hopscotch while rambunctious boys created all kinds of mischief. Ethnically, the community was peopled by large numbers of Irish and German Catholics. There were so many Catholics, in fact, that the region supported seven Catholic churches, a godsend for us kids because on Holy Thursday we got to hop on our bicycles and make a "pilgrimage" to all of them. Ostensibly, the objective of this trek was to earn a plenary indulgence, necessary to save us, little sinners that we were, from serving an indeterminate sentence in purgatory after we died. In reality, the outing was probably a contrivance of our mothers, who relished the idea of enjoying a whole day of peace and quiet. Either way, gangs of young pilgrims pedaled through the neighborhoods, visiting the various churches and, when paths crossed, exchanging opinions about which church had the fanciest Easter decorations. And, of course, we never told our mothers about our lunchtime romp in the local haunted house. Fond memories aside, the fact that us kids were allowed to enjoy this all-day adventure without adult supervision bespeaks how safe the neighborhood was.

And yet, this peaceful residential area was surrounded by industrial powerhouses: steel mills, oil refineries, chemical factories, and grain elevators. As a kid, I didn't pay much attention to the layer of orange dust—emissions from the neighboring factories—that settled on everything. But I noticed the smell. Every Saturday my mother drove us through an industrial section bordering Buffalo Creek on our way across town to Dr. Miller's. We went there for eye exercises, a therapy intended to strengthen our eye muscles since we—Sue, Ginny, and I—were cross-eyed and consequently had a visual impairment. It seemed like a long ride. The best part of the trip was listening to a children's story hour on our car radio. The worst part was the drive through the industrial section along

South Park Avenue. First, we passed Republic Steel. Next came one of the most memorable parts, the bridge across Buffalo Creek. I recall how we used to prepare ourselves, holding our noses and chanting in a chorus: "pee-you." What gave off the stink was a big mound of yellow stuff, sulfur, prominently piled right next to the creek; never mind that its runoff flowed unadulterated into the stream after every rainstorm. Sulfur, as it turns out, wasn't the worst pollutant to get dumped into what had become an industrial sewer. Heavy metals of all kinds, municipal waste, and sewage added to the toxic soup. This was white man's idea of progress. Thus, it's hard for me to imagine that this was the place where the Indians were living comfortably and respectably, with the flats surrounding Buffalo Creek planted in one "continued Cornfield."[1] But indeed, for the sixty-six years between 1780 and 1846, the council fire of New York's Haudenosaunee people was kindled at Buffalo Creek.

Such musings bring me to the bothersome question I posed earlier about what took place near the banks of Buffalo Creek so very long ago, and to the complicated answer, introduced in a roundabout way by Jonathan Fletcher Woodside.

"The Jonathan F. Woodside Collection, approx. 100 lots of paintings, books, documents, letters." So read a flyer posted on the web by Berner's Auction Gallery of Springfield, Ohio, announcing its offering for April 11, 2010. Prominently displayed in the auctioneer's announcement was a document dated March 3, 1835, signed by president Andrew Jackson, by which Jonathan F. Woodside had been appointed as chargé d'affaires of the United States of America at the Court of His Danish Majesty. Interesting, I thought. Less conspicuous in the display was a scrap of foxed paper that read, "I Do hereby certify, that Jonathan Woodside hath voluntarily taken and subscribed the Oath of Allegiance and Fidelity, as directed by an Act of General Assembly of Pennsylvania, passed the 13th Day of June, A. D. 1777. Witness my Hand and Seal, the Twenty First Day of August A. D. 1778." The oath was signed by Colonel Timothy

Green of Lancaster County. Aha! The Jonathan F. Woodside whose effects were in the auction was the son of Jonathan Woodside Sr., the revolutionary soldier and whiskey rebel. On a whim, I asked the people at the auction house if they would be willing to help me contact Jonathan F. Woodside's descendants. Soon thereafter, I received an email from a descendant who offered details about Jonathan F.'s life.

After moving to Ohio with his widowed mother, the young Jonathan Fletcher Woodside worked as a clerk in a dry goods store in Chillicothe. Later, he established a store of his own in nearby Portsmouth. When that business failed, he returned to Chillicothe to study law under Edward King, and he was admitted to the bar in 1827. He was joined by a talented duo: William Allen, a fellow student under King, would later serve as a representative in Congress, a US senator, and the thirty-first governor of Ohio; Allen G. Thurman, Allen's nephew, would eventually serve in Congress both as a representative and a senator, as an Ohio Supreme Court justice, and as the Democratic Party's nominee for vice president in 1888.

In 1833 Jonathan F. was elected to the Ohio legislature in which he was appointed to serve as chairman of the House Judiciary Committee. During the session, the legislature adopted a joint resolution endorsing the action of President Jackson in removing the United States' deposits from the Second Bank of the United States.[2] An important issue at the time, the Bank War between President Jackson and Nicholas Biddle, president of the Bank of the United States, over renewal of the bank's charter divided the US Congress. Characterized by President Jackson as an unconstitutional monster that was channeling money into the hands of a wealthy financial oligarchy, the national bank was actually effective in regulating state banks, controlling the money supply, and stabilizing the American credit structure. Regardless, Jackson had made the bank a political issue by which opinions rather than facts controlled the debate.[3] And the opinions were in Jackson's favor. In Ohio's legislature, Jonathan F. made a particularly convincing speech against the bank, and after word of his support reached

Jackson, he was awarded with the post to Denmark in which he served from 1835 to 1841.[4]

As impressive as Jonathan Fletcher Woodside's career in public service may be, another aspect of his career is central to my story. When he was emerging as a public figure, he was invited to deliver a celebratory speech in Chillicothe on July 5, 1830, a speech that conveniently segues to the story about what happened to the Haudenosaunee people in my old stomping ground of South Buffalo. Jonathan F. began the Independence Day speech in a traditional way, heralding the heroic endeavors of our nation's founders and elaborating on the freedoms that Americans, "such a happy people," enjoyed.[5] Then he pivoted. "The Genius of Liberty," he said, "is forced to pause and drop a tear over the fate of the original proprietors of your soil!"[6] He continued:

> The march of your freedom has proved the grave of theirs! The tide of white population has invaded the seats of their former greatness, and swept with a resistless current, over the graves of their fathers! They have retreated from its force—but still the wave has rolled on;—again they have retreated—but still it has pursued. They have seen the forest patrimony of their inheritance, reeling from its mountain basement.—They have seen their vallies disrobed.—They have seen the green borders torn with a sacrilegious hand, from the margin of their mighty lakes, where tradition tells, that the GREAT SPIRIT, stooping from his throne of light, mirrored his form in the prophets of their tribes. They have seen all this, and again plunged into remote wilds; but their retreat has been insecure, their repose has been brief;— scarcely has the smoke of their Wigwams curled above the forest trees, by which they were surrounded, when they are again startled by the roar of the deluge.
>
> Thus driven back from the river to lake, and from valley to mountain top, they have been deprived of profiting by those arts of civilized life that under a permanent establish-

ment of their rights, might have rescued a brave people from a destiny before which many of their tribes have already disappeared, and the brightest Council fires of their nations have gone out; a destiny which appears to yawn around them with an almost exterminating certainty; a destiny embittered by the recollection that the credulity of their fathers pointed the weapon upon which they are expiring.[7]

Turning next in his speech to a discussion of the "fated African," Jonathan F. described America's "peculiar institution" of slavery as "the blackest spot upon the escutcheon of our national fame."[8] He made an unequivocal appeal to the women in his audience to "band together" for the Africans' sake to "dissolve their chains."[9] In contrast to his plea for liberation of slaves, however, Jonathan failed to clarify his opinion about a solution for the Indians' plight, merely asking the women to "plead the justice" of their cause.[10] What did he mean by that? Why did he hedge? A loyal Jacksonian Democrat and an ambitious politician, Jonathan F. was probably caught between the conflicting sentiments of President Jackson and those of Ohioans in the debate over the Indian Removal Act, America's peculiar solution to the "Indian problem." Signed into law by the president on May 28, 1830, Ohio's congressional representatives had voted overwhelmingly (3 yeas to 10 nays) against the act, and later, the citizens of the state had submitted petitions to Congress "praying" to have it repealed.[11]

The Indian Removal Act did not spring out of nowhere. As documented by historian Jeffrey Ostler, the idea of removing Native Americans from their lands is at least as old as the United States.[12] By 1825 president James Monroe had proposed similar legislation that was approved by the Senate but defeated in the House. President Monroe's attitude toward Indian lands was revealed in his First Annual Message to Congress in 1817:

...the rights of nature demand and nothing can prevent, marking a growth rapid and gigantic, it is our duty to make new efforts for the preservation, improvement, and civilization of the native inhabitants. The hunter state can exist only in the vast uncultivated desert. It yields to the more dense and compact form and greater force of civilized population; and of right it ought to yield, for the earth was given to mankind to support the greatest number of which it is capable, and no tribe or people have a right to withhold from the wants of others more than is necessary for their own support and comfort.[13]

In any event, as argued by historian Francis Paul Prucha, the 1830 act was purportedly

the policy adopted to solve the problem of alien groups [the Indians] claiming independence within established states [in particular, Georgia] and territories of the United States; the problem of groups of human beings with communal cultures still only partially dependent upon agriculture owning large areas of land that were coveted for the dynamic white agricultural systems of both the north and the south; and the problem of friction that occurred along the lines of contact between the two societies and the deleterious effect that contact almost universally had upon Indian individuals and Indian society.[14]

The Indian Removal Act authorized the president to negotiate for Indian lands west of the Mississippi. It called for the voluntary removal of Indians living east of the Mississippi River. It compensated the Indians for improvements left behind and offered assistance to the Indians in settling their new lands. On the surface it "seemed harmless and humane enough....But those who knew the policy and practice of Jackson and the Georgians and the adamant stand of the Indians against removal understood that force would be inevitable."[15]

Many champions of removal were motivated by land lust. Nevertheless, some proponents and opponents of the law expressed

sincere, albeit paternalistic, concern about the welfare of American Indians. The compassionate groups believed that the solution
for the problem required assimilation of the Indians into the
Anglo-American culture. Their main difference seemed to rest on
where the assimilation should take place—in the Indians' traditional lands or on lands west of the Mississippi.[16]

Whether Jonathan F. approved of the Indian Removal Act is
difficult to determine. It appears at least that he was opposed to
unconscionable land-grabbers. However, the fact that Jonathan
F.'s rhetoric is strikingly similar to comments made by President
Jackson in his December 1829 annual message to Congress, in
which the president presented his rationale for the Indian Removal
Act, is persuasive evidence that Jonathan F. approved of the law.[17]
I can only hope that he was motivated by benevolence. The law, of
course, set the stage for one of the darkest chapters in our history:
the infamous Trail of Tears by which the southern tribes were relocated to present-day Oklahoma. But the southern Indians weren't
the only ones affected by the law. It also had an impact on tribes
living in the Old Northwest and on the Six Nations Indians who
remained in New York, including those living in the future South
Buffalo. Which brings me to the story about what happened to the
Iroquois who lived at Buffalo Creek. It's a story that unfolded over
a lifetime, a story of death by a thousand cuts.

THE SIX NATIONS' PEOPLE HAD BEEN THROWN ON THEIR BACKS
during General John Sullivan's 1779 scorched-earth campaign
through central New York. After this whirlwind and the frigid
winter that followed, many of the Seneca, Cayuga, Onondagas, and
other refugee tribes settled near Buffalo Creek where they lived in
several villages.[18] In 1784, at the Treaty of Fort Stanwix, the Six
Nations' Indians were forced to cede a vast territory to the United
States, but they had been assured that "they shall be secured in
the peaceful possession of the lands" that they retained.[19] In white
man's parallel world, however, the promise to the Indians was

superseded by conflicting claims of Massachusetts and New York to Six Nations' lands extending westward from Seneca Lake. The claims were based on a legal notion, the right of discovery, by which a king in some far-off land, based only on his say-so, awarded land that was already owned and occupied by Native Americans to those who "discovered" it.[20] The Indians, of course, rejected this idea. In any event, the white man's conflicting claims were resolved to the satisfaction of the contesting states in 1786 when Massachusetts yielded civil jurisdiction to New York while retaining title to the land. The title took the form of a preemptive right to buy the land from the Indians.[21] Massachusetts sold the preemptive right to Oliver Phelps and Nathaniel Gorham in 1788. Later in 1788, Phelps partially exercised the preemptive right when he bought the land located more or less *east* of the Genesee River from the Indians in a council at Buffalo Creek. Phelps's remaining preemptive right on lands *west* of the Genesee reverted to Massachusetts in 1790 when Phelps defaulted on his payment to Massachusetts. In 1791 Massachusetts resold the preemptive right to the lands west of the Genesee to Robert Morris. Soon thereafter, Morris made a deal with the investors of the Holland Land Company in which he sold the preemptive right for most of the lands west of the Genesee. Consummation of the Morris to Holland Land Company deal, however, was contingent on Morris extinguishing Indian title to the land.

All the while that these land speculations were going on, the Indians living in the Old Northwest continued to fight the Americans, winning decisive victories over General Josiah Harmar in 1790 and General Arthur St. Clair in 1792. Fearing that the Six Nations might join the fray on the side of the western Indians, the United States engaged in tense, high-stakes diplomacy with the Six Nations. The negotiations eventually led to the adoption in 1794 of the Treaty of Canandaigua at which Red Jacket emerged as the chief speaker for the Seneca.[22] A high point in the Six Nations' history that is still celebrated today, the treaty pledged a lasting peace, acknowledged Six Nations' sovereignty, and returned to the Six Nations some of the land that had been confiscated in 1784.

Importantly, although the Canandaigua treaty assured the Indians of control of their lands, it also included a provision that the right to purchase the land lay exclusively with the people of the United States. With respect to the Six Nations' land west of the Genesee, the "people of the United States" was, at that time, Robert Morris.

But the Indians were intent on keeping their lands. The land was, after all, a place given to them by the Great Spirit, a place where their forefathers "came out of the ground," a place where they "spread their blankets," a place that gave them sustenance, a place they shared with other creatures and spirits.[23] Moreover, as Red Jacket explained, the Seneca were respected by other tribes because they owned a vast tract of land. To relinquish their lands would be to give up their identity and render them not a free people.[24] Thus, the land and its people were intertwined at their roots in a way that white men could barely comprehend, or if they could, were too greedy to care. Such fierce attachment to the land makes it all the more puzzling that the Seneca would agree to part with it. Indeed, as late as 1796, Red Jacket expressed the Indians' fear of losing their land in a rude but witty description of a dream he had had. In his dream he envisioned that the Indians' land would be "devoured" by the "great Eater with the big belly," Robert Morris.[25] Nevertheless, with the ink on the Treaty of Canandaigua barely dry, Red Jacket's dream became a nightmare when the Seneca sold most of their land to Morris at the Treaty of Big Tree, held between August 20 and September 16, 1797, at present-day Geneseo.

The financially strapped Robert Morris, entangled in a mind-boggling morass of transactions, delegated the delicate task of extinguishing the Seneca's claims to his son Thomas.[26] The trust was well placed: with a thoughtful, well-executed plan, the younger Morris persuaded the Seneca to part with their land for $100,000, to be invested with the Bank of the United States and paid in an annual dividend of about $6,000.[27] But the long tortuous negotiation nearly failed when Red Jacket covered the council fire after Morris refused to accept a Seneca offer of one township near the Pennsylvania state line for a dollar an acre. Morris had done his homework, however. He understood that in "Seneca land polity the ultimate control of lands and household goods rested with the women who were matrons of the clans."[28] In the tradition of the best snake oil salesman, Thomas Morris called together the women and some of the warriors, distributed some baubles, and promised them a life of leisure if they agreed to the sale. The ploy worked. The council fire was rekindled, and the Seneca, including Red Jacket, signed the treaty. Retaining for themselves ten reservations, they sold about four million acres for a mere three cents an acre.[29] Various explanations, none of which are satisfying, have been offered for the Indians' capitulation to Morris. My theory, based on the fact that the women later regretted the sale, is that Thomas Morris not only did a superb job in his sales pitch to the women but also got the women drunk. The idea is supported by Red Jacket's speech delivered on June 22, 1798, at council at Buffalo Creek wherein he commented on behalf of the women: "At the treaty we had reason to think too much use of Liquor was made.... Our request is now free from liquor which ought not to be used to take advantage of Indians. We now speak soberly."[30] Red Jacket, Cornplanter, and Farmer's Brother, speaking on behalf of all the Indians, also expressed seller's remorse. In any event, as a result of the sale, Morris's contractual obligation to extinguish Indian title was fulfilled. The Holland Land Company took possession of the greater part of western New York, and the Indians withdrew to newly defined reservations. (See figure 8.)

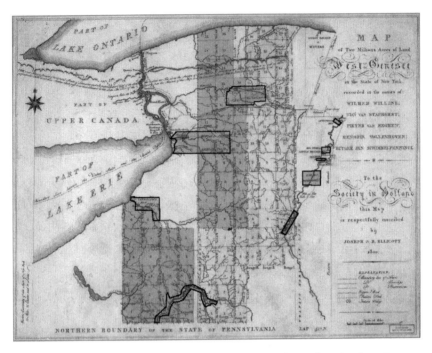

*Figure 8. Map of Holland Land Company purchase showing location
of Indian reservations after the survey was done. Joseph Ellicott,
Benjamin Ellicott, Wilhem Willink, C. Van Baarsel, and Holland Land
Company, Map of Two Millions Acres of land, West Genesee, in the
State of New York: Recorded in the Names of Wilhem Willink, Nic's
van Staphorst, Pieter van Eeghen, Hendrik Vollenhoven, Rutger Jan
Schinnelpenninck (Amsterdam?: Van Baarsel, 1800), Courtesy of Library
of Congress, https://www.loc.gov/item/2012585849, and modified by author.*

Soon after the treaty was signed, Joseph Ellicott was charged with
surveying the lands and setting the boundaries of the reservations, including the 83,557-acre (approximately 130 square miles)
reservation at Buffalo Creek.[31] The Treaty of Big Tree allowed that
the reservations that had not been specifically described in the
treaty, including Tonawanda and Buffalo Creek, "shall be laid off in
such a manner as shall be determined by the Sachems and Chiefs
residing at or near the respective villages where such reservations
are made."[32] Especially interesting to me is how the northwestern
boundary of the Buffalo Creek Reservation was laid out. A map

of the Genesee lands drawn in 1798 shows where the reservation would have been if the Seneca had asserted their prerogative. In having the northern boundary continue in a straight east-west line to Lake Erie, they would have controlled the mouth of Buffalo Creek and most of the future Buffalo harbor and Buffalo downtown, not to mention the site of the Seneca Buffalo Creek Casino. (See figure 9.)

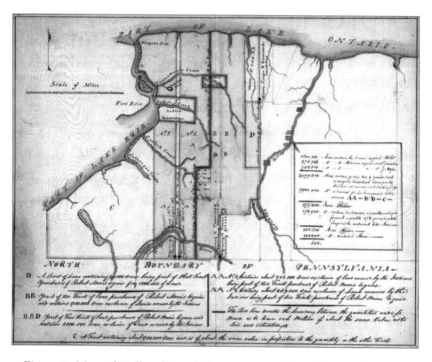

Figure 9. Map of Holland Land Company purchase showing location of Indian Reservations before the survey was done. The reservation map includes the northwest corner of the originally intended reservation (where Buffalo Creek empties into Lake Erie), which was, in the end, excluded from the Buffalo Creek Reservation. "Map of the Genesee Lands, 1798," Courtesy of State University of New York at Fredonia Archives & Special Collections; Municipal Archives of Amsterdam; Nederlandse Document Reproductie B.V., https://cdm16694.contentdm.oclc.org/digital/collection/XFM001/id/95

But it was not to be. A trusted friend, one William Johnston (some-times listed as Johnson) sold the Indians out. Johnston was an early trader who also served on occasion as an interpreter, usually in the British interest. He had a Seneca mother and a Seneca wife. The Seneca had ceded to him about two square miles, including the land where Buffalo Creek emptied into Lake Erie. Asserting that Johnston's deed had no legal validity because he did not hold the preemption right, and intending to exploit Johnston's great influence with the Seneca, Theophile Cazenove, an agent for the Holland Land Company, authorized Ellicott to deed a small portion of the land to Johnston in exchange for Johnston's success in persuading the "Buffaloe tribe" to relinquish that part of their "intended reservation."[33] Acknowledging that the location was one of the "Keys to the Companies lands," Ellicott, after many "desultory conversations" with Johnston, struck a deal with the trader.[34] While the Seneca lost some of their most valuable property, Johnston won his thirty pieces of silver. By 1800 Johnston ranked as the richest settler on the Holland Purchase.[35]

IN THE YEARS THAT FOLLOWED, THE INDIANS DEALT WITH MANY challenges: the War of 1812 for control of the Niagara frontier, disputes with New York regarding law enforcement, divisions over religion, the breakdown of their traditional social structure amid pressure to become "civilized," and encroachment on their lands by white men. But none of these challenges compared with their battle to keep their remaining land. Especially during the construction and after the opening of the Erie Canal, the pressure on the Indians to sell their land was intense. To that end, a "conspiracy of interests" involving local, state, and federal officials in combination with the agents of the rapacious Ogden Land Company, which had purchased the preemptive right to the reservations from the Holland Land Company in 1810, worked with "unparalleled industry, and with perseverance proportioned to the vast amount at stake."[36] What was at stake was the land located at the western terminus of the Erie Canal, the future city of Buffalo.[37]

The first determined attempt by the Ogden Land Company to buy the reservation from the Indians was rebuffed. In a council on July 7–9, 1819, Red Jacket rose to the occasion. In his brilliant rebuttal to two arrogant, condescending harangues—the first by United States' commissioner Morris S. Miller, President Monroe's appointee to the proceedings; the second by David Ogden. Red Jacket, to the amusement of some of the people attending, managed not only to pick his opponents' argument to pieces but also to turn points of their arguments to the Seneca Indians' favor.[38] Defeated and undoubtedly embarrassed, Mr. Ogden and his minions slithered back to wherever they came from.

But the advantage remained with the developer. With the arrival of the Erie Canal, increasing pressure was put on the Seneca to give up their title to Buffalo Creek. To capture this holy grail, the Ogden Land Company changed its strategy. By exploiting religious divisions within the Seneca tribe and by taking advantage of government policies, the company managed to overcome objections raised by Red Jacket and secure more than 33,000 acres of the reservation in a council held at Buffalo Creek in August 1826. (See figure 10.) Soon after the council, however, in an effort to invalidate the sale, Red Jacket began his "last campaign to defend his peoples' lands."[39] He sent memorials to DeWitt Clinton, governor of New York, and president John Quincy Adams in which he described bribery, threats, and intimidation by government officials and prominent local citizens. He visited President Adams in Washington. Although accusations of fraud were later confirmed in an investigation ordered by President Adams, investigator Robert M. Livingston's scathing report was suppressed by newly appointed secretary of war Peter B. Porter, a preeminent Buffalonian.[40] Porter, in a blatant conflict of interest, had sold his share of the Ogden Land Company shortly after the 1826 treaty had been completed and before complaints about the treaty arose.

In retribution for his activity, Red Jacket was deposed as a Seneca chief by a council of leaders of the so-called Christian or emigration party who were "acting on the advice of their Great

Father."⁴¹ The great father, in this case, was apparently a cabal including Oliver Forward, the corrupt federal commissioner who had presided at the treaty; John Grieg, a Canandaigua attorney who had represented the Ogden Land Company at the treaty; Thomas McKenney, superintendent of the Office of Indian Affairs; and their stooge, the Indian agent and translator Jasper Parrish.⁴²

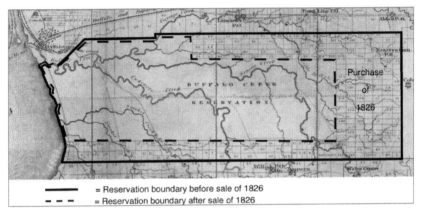

Figure 10. Map of Buffalo Creek Reservation after 1826 sale.
Courtesy of Lionel Pincus and Princess Firyal Map Division, The
New York Public Library, "Map of the County of Erie," http://
digitalcollections.nypl.org/items/510d47da-f276-a3d9-e040-
e00a18064a99, and modified by author.

To his credit, Red Jacket's last campaign had been partly successful. Because of his effort, the 1826 treaty was never ratified by the
United States Senate nor proclaimed by the president as required
by federal law. Nevertheless, because of machinations by the Ogden
Land Company, the sale was allowed to stand.⁴³ Red Jacket was soon
reinstated as a chief. His reputation was restored, and in one of his
final speeches, he bemoaned the fate of his people:

> I am about to leave you, and when I am gone, and my warn-
> ings shall no longer be heard, or regarded, the craft and
> avarice of the white man will prevail. Many winters have I
> breasted the storm, but I am an aged tree, and can stand no

longer. My leaves are fallen, my branches are withered, and I am shaken by every breeze. Soon my aged trunk will be prostrate, and the foot of the exalting foe of the Indian may be placed upon it in safety; for I leave none who will be able to avenge such indignity. Think not I mourn for myself. I go to join the spirit of my fathers, where age cannot come; but my heart fails, when I think of my people, who are soon to be scattered and forgotten.[44]

In spite of his weakness for firewater, Red Jacket had lived a long life. He died at about the age of sixty-eight of cholera on January 20, 1830, at the reservation at Buffalo Creek.

By 1838, the Indian Removal Act had been in force for eight years. "Voluntary" emigrations of the Choctaw, Creek, and Chickasaw had been plagued by varying degrees of hardship and death. The Seminole, some refusing to remove, were engaged in a brutal war with the United States. One of their influential leaders, Osceola, had been captured and had died in prison in January 1838. The Cherokee, in spite of a US Supreme Court ruling in their favor, were faced with a forcible removal, a consequence of a fraudulent treaty effected in 1835.[45] The Seneca were aware of these events.[46] Knowing they were the government's next target, the Seneca agreed among themselves that they faced an existential threat. But they were deeply divided about what to do. The leader of a pro-emigration faction, eighty-year-old sachem Captain Pollard, opined that "we must emigrate or we shall never be happy and prosperous."[47] This faction believed in the beneficence of the US government and in the correctness of the Ogden Land Company's claim to their lands. Publicly, the Ogden Land Company asserted their fee simple ownership of the Indians' land. But in private legal documents, their contract with the Buffalonians, they acknowledged the need to extinguish the Indians' title.[48] An anti-emigration faction believed that remaining in New York was the key to the Indians' happiness and that if they removed to the west, they would be harassed by "warlike tribes" and by "white borderers who infest" the area.[49] This faction believed that the government and the Ogden Land Company were united in an effort to force them to abandon their land.[50] Differences aside, as late as 1835 the disparate factions were willing to accommodate each other by relinquishing part of their land.[51] Further, contracts executed in February 1837 between the Ogden Land Company and four Buffalonians indicate that the Ogden Land Company acknowledged the Indians' division and realized that the company might have to settle for a partial purchase.[52] Maybe, at that point, a compromise was possible.

But something happened on the way to the council house. In the summer of 1837, Reverend John F. Schermerhorn ignored the Six Nations' tribal sovereignty and rules of governance and secretly handpicked a group of pro-emigration Seneca Indians to tour lands in present-day Kansas and issue a favorable report. Schermerhorn had been dubbed "the Devil's Horn" by the Cherokee people for his part as commissioner for the infamous 1835 Treaty of New Echota. In that treaty the majority of Indians had boycotted the proceedings. But that did not stop Schermerhorn from writing into the preamble of that treaty that "those *who did not come...gave their assent...*to whatever should be transacted at this council."[53] Having achieved his objective of removing the Cherokees from Georgia, Schermerhorn turned his sights on the Six Nations, by then the largest group of Indians still living east of the Mississippi.

Also by the summer of 1837, the Ogden Land Company had apparently reconsidered the idea, if it had really ever had it, of settling for less than complete victory. Its four Buffalo subcontractors, led by Heman B. Potter, who had served openly as the Ogden Land Company's attorney for several years, aggressively sought support among the Indians for a sale of their remaining lands.[54] To achieve the company's goal, Potter contracted with at least ten chiefs to the tune of about $21,600 in cash (approximately $537,250 in today's dollars) plus leases for life at nominal rent, and other perquisites.[55]

In exchange, the chiefs were obliged to induce the Indians to comply with the government's and the company's objectives of removing the Indians and selling their land.

It was under these circumstances that the US government and the Ogden Land Company presented the New York Indians with a removal treaty and a deed of sale in December 1837. By the first part of the deal, the New York Indians relinquished land in Wisconsin that had been purchased for them by the government; in exchange, they received a 1,824,000-acre reservation in Kansas to which they were to remove within five years. By the second part of the deal, the Indians sold *all* their remaining New York lands, excepting the one-square-mile Oil Spring Reservation, to the Ogden Land Company for a total of $202,000; $100,000 of this sum was for the land and $102,000 for improvements. The treaty was signed on January 15, 1838.

Then all hell broke loose. Between 1838 and 1840 the treaty was amended by the US Senate, returned to the Indians for reapproval, and tossed back and forth like a hot potato between the Senate and president Martin Van Buren. Evidence of bribery, including both the 1837 "contracts" with the Indians and some new ones amounting to $32,600 (approximately $810,750 in today's dollars), forgery, false impersonation as chiefs, intimidation, misrepresentation of facts, and outright lying emerged.[56] Contrary to Six Nations' rules of governance (and any legislature's rules of governance), most of the Indians' assenting signatures on the reapproval had been obtained out of council, sometimes in a tavern, sometimes in a home, and at times only after a chief had been plied with liquor. Arsonists burned down the council house in protest. Meetings erupted in fisticuffs. Accusations of treachery flew back and forth. Appeals to the president, governors, sympathetic politicians, and the general public in support of and against the sale made the rounds. Amid this acrimony, the amended treaty was approved in the Senate by a majority, rather than a two-thirds vote, on March 25, 1840, and proclaimed into law by President Van Buren on April 4, 1840. It appeared that the

New York lands of the Haudenosaunee people had been sold and that the Seneca would be forced to remove to Kansas.[57]

The Seneca were despondent, but their hopes for an abrogation of the treaty remained. Protests, aided greatly by the Society of Friends (Hicksite branch), continued. The state of Massachusetts, whose consent to the sale was required due to a provision in the 1786 New York–Massachusetts agreement, said that it would not have approved the treaty if it had known about the frauds, but Massachusetts took no action to reverse its approval. In New York, Whig governor William Seward wrote, "The consent of the Senecas was obtained by fraud, corruption, and violence, and that it is therefore false and ought to be held void. The removal of the Indians, under a treaty thus made, would be a great crime against an unoffending and injured people, and I earnestly hope that before any further proceedings are taken to accomplish that object, the whole subject may be reconsidered by the United States."[58] But the governor failed to transform his hope into action.[59] Nevertheless, the delay in enforcing the treaty caused the Ogden Land Company to enter negotiations, not with the Seneca, but with the Hicksite Quakers and the New York Whigs. The resulting compromise, the Treaty of Buffalo Creek of 1842, returned the Allegany and Cattaraugus Reservations to the Seneca. The Indians vacated the Buffalo Creek Reservation, mostly settling at Cattaraugus and Allegany, in 1846.

In the aftermath, Harriet Caswell, a missionary at the Cattaraugus Reservation, observed that "the people who were thus thrust from their homes and driven from the graves of their fathers were not to be comforted or pacified. They were embittered against their chiefs, and the whole race of the Pale Face, including even their own missionaries."[60] Torn apart by strife, in 1848 the Seneca underwent a revolution, replacing their traditional form of government with an elected one. However, the resulting Seneca Nation of Indians did not include the Tonawanda Indians. The Tonawanda Band of Seneca had unanimously refused to sign both the 1838 and the 1842 treaties; they eventually repurchased part of their reservation, and they remain there today.[61]

Such is the long, sickening tale about what happened to the Indians at Buffalo Creek. Now at last I understand why the story was left out of my childhood history lessons. Not only did the story belie the diet of patriotic pabulum that was spoon-fed to us as youngsters, but it also obviated the need to discuss the economic and social disruption, a consequence of centuries of misguided governmental policies, which continue to plague American Indians today. How meaningful those history lessons might have been if they had included observations such as those made by Alexis de Tocqueville when he passed through Buffalo on July 20, 1831. De Tocqueville expressed his complete disappointment upon first seeing a group of Indians at Buffalo. But upon observing a drunken Indian, he made the following comments in his journal:

> Some said to us: "Those men are used to drink to excess and sleep on the ground; they never die from accidents like that." Others recognized that the Indian would proba-bly die, but one could read on their lips this half-expressed thought: "What is the life of an Indian?" The fact is that that was the basis of the general feeling. In the midst of this American society, so well policed, so sententious, so charitable, a cold selfishness and complete insensibility prevails when it is a question of the natives of the country. The Americans of the United States do not let their dogs hunt the Indians as do the Spaniards in Mexico, but at bottom it is the same pitiless feeling which here, as every-where else, animates the European race. This world here belongs to us, they tell themselves every day: the Indian race is destined for final destruction which one cannot prevent and which it is not desirable to delay. Heaven has not made them to become civilized; it is necessary that they die. Besides I do not want to get mixed up in it. I will not do anything against them: I will limit myself to

providing everything that will hasten their ruin. In time I will have their lands and will be innocent of their death. Satisfied with his reasoning, the American goes to church where he hears the minister of the gospel repeat every day that all men are brothers, and that the Eternal Being who has made them all in like image, has given them all the duty to help one another.[62]

Unfortunately, discussion of sentiments like de Tocqueville's were completely absent when I was growing up in the 1950s. And based on my unscientific survey of my nieces and nephews, teaching Native American history in our schools today involves at best a brief glossing over the story. On a brighter note, as a testament to their resilience and adaptability, the Seneca Nation of Indians today includes a population of over eight thousand enrolled members. It is the fifth-largest employer in western New York, creating thousands of new jobs and investing hundreds of millions of dollars to bolster the region's and New York State's economy.[63] Moreover, Red Jacket's memory continues to be reborn. I wonder if he is still looking down, from aloft, with his half-ironical smile, over lands that were once a wilderness, once a cornfield, once an industrial wasteland, and now a restored green space, appropriately named Red Jacket River Front Park.

———————◆———————

JONATHAN F. WOODSIDE'S STORY ALSO HAD A TRAGIC ENDING. He apparently enjoyed himself while serving in Denmark, adequately performing his duties as US ambassador while becoming fluent in Danish, German, and French. He also luxuriated in European culture, adopting a lavish lifestyle as evidenced by his spending on expensive art and jewelry. Following the election of a Whig president in 1840, however, Jonathan F. was recalled from his post in 1841. Upon his return to Ohio, he reentered private law practice. In 1843 he ran for the Democratic nomination for US Congress but was defeated by Allen G. Thurman. The defeat, possibly compounded by difficulty in readjusting to life in a small town, greatly affected Jonathan. He died suddenly at his home on June 25, 1845. He was forty-six years old.

Other than being mentioned on the United States Department of State's website, there are no places or institutions (that I know of) that commemorate Jonathan F. Woodside.[64] But in his shadow lies a far more important legacy. In the brief interval between his return from Denmark and his death, Jonathan F. mentored a law student, Milton Lee Clark, who would marry Jonathan F.'s eldest daughter in 1849. Mr. Clark would eventually become one of the most respected chief judges of Ohio's Supreme Court.[65] Interestingly, he was also a member of the 1860 Ohio delegation at the Republican National Convention in Chicago, the most consequential political convention in US history. William Seward of New York had expected to win the nomination, but his antislavery speeches caused some party members to view him as too radical. At the convention, nominations were offered on the third day, May 18, 1860. After three ballots, none of the candidates had received the 233 votes needed for nomination. Abraham Lincoln came close—231½ votes—and at that point, three of the Ohio delegates changed their votes from Ohio's favorite son Salmon P. Chase to Lincoln, and one switched from John McLean to Lincoln, making Honest Abe the Republican presidential nominee. Judge Clark had cast his vote for Lincoln, the more moderate candidate with respect to the slavery issue, on the first and subsequent ballots. Given his prominence, it is not unlikely that Clark's behind-the-scenes efforts induced other Ohio delegates to change their votes.[66] Of course, Lincoln won the 1860 election, but were it not for the votes of Ohio's delegates, among them Jonathan F. Woodside's son-in-law, how different might the course of our history have been.

Jonathan Woodside Sr. and his son Jonathan Fletcher Woodside both earned their place in the history books—the father because of his "treasonous" act against the United States' government in the Whiskey Rebellion, the son because of his participation in government affairs. More typical of America's emerging middle class were Jonathan Woodside's siblings—Maria Woodside Novinger and my ancestor John Woodside, and their children who scattered far and wide. But before I get to their stories, I have some unfinished business to address about another swindle of the Haudenosaunee people.

CHAPTER 9

CATTARAUGUS

A lthough I grew up in South Buffalo, I spent my summers at our lakeside cottage in a little beach community called Roat Acres, located in the town of Evans in Erie County, New York (see figure 11).

Figure 11. Friends at Roat Acres beach, circa 1950, with Sturgeon Point in the background. Author's collection.

Predictably, I had been unaware that the Roat Acres community was located on land that was initially intended to be part of the Cattaraugus Reservation. But when I was doing research on the history of the Buffalo Creek Reservation, I came across a map of the Cattaraugus Reservation, dated 1798, that had been drawn after the Treaty of Big Tree had been ratified but before the land had been surveyed by Joseph Ellicott on behalf of the Holland Land Company. The boundaries of the Cattaraugus Reservation in the 1798 pre-survey map varied from those shown in the famous post-survey 1800 map, referred to as the Morris map. Specifically, in the 1798 pre-survey map, the reservation was spread out along the lakeshore. Beginning at Eighteen Mile Creek (Catfish Creek on the pre-survey map), the reservation extended to Cattaraugus Creek, then up the north side of the creek. Roat Acres would have been included in this part of the reservation. Another segment of the reservation began on the lakeshore a little south of Cattaraugus Creek and extended to another little creek, Canadaway Creek. The 1800 post-survey Morris map, however, indicated that the reservation was concentrated on both sides of Cattaraugus Creek, and the parts of the reservation that had initially been located along the lakeshore had been eliminated. Why were the two maps different? (See figure 12.)

The 1798 pre-survey map is, as a matter of fact, a sketch of the Cattaraugus Reservation as it was delineated in the 1797 Treaty of Big Tree. The 1800 post-survey Morris map depicts the reservation after a boundary change became official in the treaty of 1802.[1] Why, I wondered, would the Indians agree to exchange a comparatively large region of prime lakeshore—good for hunting and fishing, especially around Sturgeon Point, and potentially excellent agricultural ground—for a smaller region of largely rough terrain? Especially if we take into account the fact that the Seneca prided themselves on owning abundant lands, the exchange is puzzling.

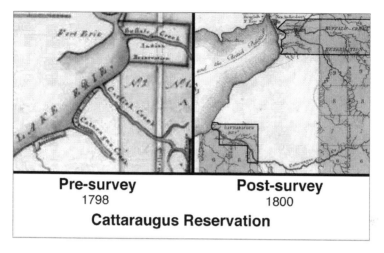

Pre-survey
1798

Post-survey
1800

Cattaraugus Reservation

Figure 12. Map on the left shows Cattaraugus reservation as it was delineated at the Treaty of Big Tree, before survey was done, spread out along the lake shore, and encompassing the north side of Cattaraugus Creek. Map on the right shows Cattaraugus reservation as it was delineated after survey, and before Treaty of 1802, compacted around Cattaraugus Creek. On left, "Map of the Genesee Lands, 1798," Courtesy of State University of New York at Fredonia Archives & Special Collections; Municipal Archives of Amsterdam; Nederlandse Document Reproductie B.V., https://cdm16694.contentdm.oclc.org/ digital/collection/XFM001/id/95, and modified by author; on right, from Map of two millions acres of land, West Genesee, in the State of New York: recorded in the names of Wilhem Willink, Nic's van Staphorst, Pieter van Eeghen, Hendrik Vollenhoven, Rutger Jan Schinnelpenninck, [Amsterdam?: Van Baarsel, 1800], https://www.loc.gov/item/2012585849/, and modified by author.

Searching for an answer, I first came across a reference to the unusual situation in *Pioneer History of the Holland Land Purchase* written by O. Turner in 1850. He wrote:

The Hon. Nathaniel W. Howell of Canandaigua, was, as early as this season [1798], Mr. Ellicott's legal advisor in several matters connected with his primitive duties. Some "embarrassment" occurring connected with the Indian reservation at Cattaraugus, he gave him, by letter, his legal opinion. This circumstance is noted principally to observe, that the author [Turner] has before him the paper above referenced to, and a recent letter from the same hand written plainly and legibly and evincing a memory, and an intellect generally, vigorous and unimpaired. Fifty years intervene between the dates of the two letters.[2]

Although the curators tried their best, inquiries to the Buffalo and Erie County Historical Society and the Monroe County Historical Society (where the Nathaniel Howell papers are located) did not yield an answer to my question about what this "embarrassment" involved or what Howell's legal advice to Ellicott was. Nor did inquiries to the Seneca Nation of Indians, the librarian at State University of New York at Fredonia, or some notable historians. Thus my first blind alley.

Eventually, I found a reference to the 1802 land swap in Granville Ganter's *The Collected Speeches of Sagoyewatha, or Red Jacket*. At a council at Buffalo Creek on June 21–22, 1798, Cornplanter stated that the Cattaraugus Indians made a mistake when they laid out their lands, remarking that the reservation was not compact enough. And Red Jacket stated that Cornplanter's request that the Cattaraugus reservation be laid out in a compact piece was the wish of all those present at the council.[3] Was this the answer? Did either Cornplanter or Red Jacket, neither of whom lived at Cattaraugus, have the right to speak for the Cattaraugus Indians? I remained skeptical.

Running around in circles, I put the problem in the back of my mind until, a few years later, I came across a pertinent article in a small western New York newspaper, the *Westfield Republican*. The article, dated December 5, 2012, included a map of the Cattaraugus Reservation as described in the Treaty of Big Tree. That article led me to Vince Martonis, the historian for the town of Hanover in Chautauqua County. Martonis had spent time doing research on the Holland Land Company while on a sabbatical at Fredonia State University, and, like me, he wondered why the Indians would trade prime lakeshore property for less valuable land. He graciously allowed me to share his findings.

Based on his research, Martonis concluded that "the Holland Land Company had its plans for the Cattaraugus Creek area (also Silver and Canadaway creeks) well before the 1802 treaty was signed."[4] He pointed out that the area's assets included control of three water systems at Canadaway Creek, Silver/Walnut Creeks, and Cattaraugus Creek, as well as potential for harbors at Dunkirk, Cattaraugus Creek, and Silver Creek. The HLC "certainly knew the value of these systems to lumbering, milling, shipbuilding, fishing, and other industry."[5] Martonis noted that non-native settlement had already begun prior to the 1802 treaty. Joseph "Black Joe" Hodge operated a non-Indian trading post in the 1790s. Amos Sottle was located at the mouth of Cattaraugus Creek as far back as 1796, and "by 1800 we can add several other names—Ezekiel Lane, William Sydnor, and others."[6] There was a ferry, a tavern, and a HLC warehouse, all operating prior to 1802. Martonis imagines that an 1803 land deal between David Dickinson and Joseph Ellicott was promoted "well before the treaty was signed": Dickinson's 640-acre parcel includes the entire village of Silver Creek today.[7]

The HLC, Martonis opined, "knew the value of lake shore property to settlement, roads, shipping, etc. The Indians would have valued it much less, so it was probably relatively easy for the HLC to achieve the ratification of the 1802 treaty."[8] And even though there is evidence in their speeches, Martonis doubted "that both Cornplanter and Red Jacket requested the compacting" of the reservation.[9] Rather, Martonis admitted that he would have to "consider what was each personally given in return for their support of the HLC need to acquire that lake shore land."[10] The rapid development of the region once the 1802 treaty was completed offers further evidence of the HLC's designs. A "city" then known as Cattaraugus Village was delineated in early 1800 HLC maps. And "shipbuilding alone at Cattaraugus Creek rivaled Buffalo in the very early 1800s. Piers appeared early, lighthouses later at all three harbors."[11]

Professor Matthew Dennis had this to say about Martonis's observations: "I find Mr. Martonis's analysis compelling—the segments lopped off clearly figured heavily in white development plans, particularly those of the Holland Land Company. As is often the case in U.S. Indian-white relations, the de-accession of the land is presented as willing and voluntary on the part of that Native people. But such willingness and legality was often not what it seemed—it was often a cover for corruption or extortion."[12]

MOVING ON TO 1826, AT WHICH TIME THE OGDEN LAND COMpany was making its first serious attempt to extinguish Indians' title to their remaining lands in New York State, Martonis steered me to an 1827 publication titled "An Exposition of the Practicability of Constructing a Great Central Canal from Lake Erie to the Hudson through the Southern Tier of Counties in the State of New York."[13] In it, the author made a case for the development of a canal running from Portland Harbor (today's Westfield, New York), by Chautauqua Lake, the little Conewango Creek, the Allegheny River, and the headwaters of the North Branch of the Susquehanna and Delaware Rivers to the Hudson River. The author never mentioned that the proposed segment on the Allegheny River would go through tribal lands. The canal's promoters failed to fulfill their objective, but their efforts demonstrate the continued interest in developing this region. At the same time, several farmers were more successful and, in the unratified "treaty" of August 31, 1826 (the same treaty that involved the sale of part of the Buffalo Creek Reservation), succeeded in "purchasing" one square mile of the southwest corner (which I cannot find on any of the maps) and seven square miles of the northern and northwestern parts of the Cattaraugus Reservation. These lands were considered to be among the richest and most valuable in western New York. (See figure 13.)

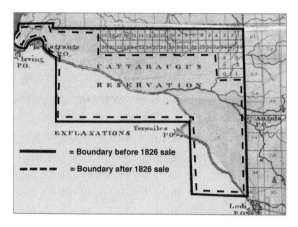

*Figure 13. Cattaraugus Reservation after 1826 sale. Courtesy of
Lionel Pincus and Princess Firyal Map Division, The New York Public
Library, "Map of the County of Erie," http://digitalcollections.nypl.org/
items/510d47da-f276-a3d9-e040-e00a18064a99,
and modified by author.*

THAT IS NOT THE END OF THE STORY OF COURSE. RECALL THAT
with the fraudulent 1838 Treaty of Buffalo Creek, the Seneca
ceded all their remaining lands in western New York, including
the Cattaraugus and Allegany Reservations. Although the Buffalo
Creek Reservation was considered to be the prize because of its
proximity to the Erie Canal and the booming city of Buffalo, a
group of New York's bigwigs also had plans for the Cattaraugus
area. A virtual who's who of New York State's financial and political
elites, the speculators included, among others, Lewis Eaton, a US
congressman from 1823 to 1825, a New York State senator from
1829 to 1832, and president of Lockport Bank; Thurlow Weed, a
prominent newspaper publisher and "boss" of New York's Whig
Party; Thomas W. Olcott, president of Mechanics and Farmers
Bank of Albany; Erastus Corning, businessman extraordinaire,
a New York State senator from 1842 to 1845 and a leader in the
organization of the New York Central Railroad; and William Kent,
a New York attorney.[14] The bigwigs combined with local investors

early in 1836 to purchase land near the mouth of Cattaraugus Creek and, on August 17, 1836, organized into the Irving Land Company. That the men had inside knowledge of the Ogden Land Company's imminent decision to buy the remaining Seneca lands is evident because William Kent, the trustee of the Irving Land Company, had a close professional and social relationship with David Ogden and Thomas Ogden. The three men were among forty-five charter members of an exclusive club organized in December 1836, the Kent Club, an association of eminent lawyers designed for the "intellectual improvement and social enjoyment" of its members.[15]

One member of the Irving Company, Henry P. Willcox, served as a spokesman for the group. Willcox, a physician, owned land in the town of Hanover. On July 5, 1837, he was hired by the Ogden Land Company and joined a select group of Buffalonians whose objective was to browbeat the Seneca into selling their lands. As an active participant in the fraudulent 1838 treaty, Willcox was paid a $10,000 salary (approximately $233,700 in today's dollars) for his services.[16] In 1837 Willcox had published the promotional brochure titled "Irving on Lake Erie." In his essay Willcox sang the praises of the harbor at Cattaraugus, noting that it was well above the ice bank that often clogged the Buffalo harbor in early spring. He advocated for the feasibility of an extension canal that linked the Allegheny River via Conewango and Cattaraugus Creeks to Buffalo. He also cited the benefits of Irving as a terminus for railroads then in the early stage of development. Presuming what he hoped would be a soon-to-be-consummated sale of the Cattaraugus Reservation, Willcox observed that the presence of the reservation had impeded local development for years, and that, with the reservation's removal, the prosperity of the port promised "a ten-fold indemnity from its convenient location, extent and variety of timber adapted to ship-building."[17]

Irving Land Company investor Lewis Eaton optimistically reported in May 1836 that "he could 'sell the whole lot out' in Buffalo in a week and at a fair profit."[18] Eaton described the advantages of the place, including the expected termination of the Erie

Railroad, the extension of the Erie Canal via Conewango, and the congressional appropriation to improve the harbor at Cattaraugus. But by 1840 the city of Dunkirk had won the battle for the Erie Railroad terminus, and the government had lost interest in continuing to develop the Cattaraugus harbor.[19] Considering the unfavorable impact that these developments had on the future of the area, it should not be surprising that the Ogden Land Company "returned" the Cattaraugus reservation to the Seneca in the compromise treaty of 1842. The Irving Land Company, for its part, divided its holdings among the individual investors in August of 1845 when a public sale was held.[20]

BY THE END OF 2014, I FELT CONFIDENT THAT DOCUMENTARY evidence supported the idea that the land deals in 1826 and 1838 to 1842 were part of what Laurence Hauptman described as a "conspiracy of interests" to steal the Indians' land.[21] But I had resigned myself to the fact that I might never find documents to prove that the land swap between the Holland Land Company and the Iroquois consummated in the treaty of 1802 was another swindle. I put the problem to rest. But as Yogi Berra famously said, "It ain't over till it's over."

Five years later, I decided to take another look at the problem. Lo and behold, in my initial review of correspondence between Joseph Ellicott and Theophile Cazenove, I had overlooked important details. Specifically, in a letter dated May 10, 1798, Theophile Cazenove, agent for the Holland Land Company, asserted to surveyor Joseph Ellicott that Captain Israel Chapin, agent of the federal government to the Six Nations, and William Johnston, "the first permanent white settler of Buffalo," spoke "on behalf of the chief Indians of Kadaragras [*sic*] and of Buffaloe [*sic*] creek" who "requested that their reservation should be more compact than it has been stipulated by them in the last treaty."[22] Johnston, of course, is the same man who traded away the valuable part of the Buffalo Creek Reservation that included the future Buffalo harbor.[23] The letter suggests that the Cattaraugus deal was another aspect of William Johnston's betrayal of the Indians. Further, the date of the letter, May 10, 1798, is noteworthy in that it preceded the June 21–22, 1798, council at Buffalo Creek at which Cornplanter and Red Jacket asserted that the land exchange was in the interest of the Indians. Expressing caution, Cazenove acknowledged that written proof of the Indians' purported request would be required.[24]

Later, in Ellicott's letter dated September 25, 1798, to Theophile Cazenove (the same letter in which Ellicott mentioned "desultory conversations" with William Johnston about the Buffalo Creek Reservation), Ellicott wrote that he "proceeded back to Cattaraugus village and agreed upon the alteration of their reservation which is to their and the satisfaction of the Nation. And will be finally Established at their general meeting when they receive their annuity and Presents. All the Sachems & Chiefs will then sign a relinquishment to the lands in their old reserve excepting such parts as are included in the New."[25] Were these "Presents" a part of the typical transactions with the Indians? Or something in addition to that?

Also, in his official 1798 report concerning the state of the survey of the Genesee lands, Ellicott wrote about Cattaraugus: "I conceive it unnecessary to detail the circumstances attending alteration of the reserved tract. I will therefore observe they were *numerous and perplexing.*"[26] He continued: "A deed of exchange was procured and is herewith presented signed by all of the Indians that signed the Treaty or convention on the Genesee river [1797 Treaty of Big Tree]...and I presume requires nothing but the will of the President to legalize it."[27] But as noted in Cazenove's September 11, 1801, report to his bosses in Holland, the status of the deed with the "Kataraugus Indians" was still unclear even though the survey of the reservation including the boundary change had been completed.[28]

Ellicott's 1799 report offered a further clue, in particular about the so-called embarrassment surrounding the Cattaraugus Reservation survey that Turner referred to in his 1850 book. Ellicott wrote:

With my report of last season [1798] I handed you a Deed of Exchange signed by the Indians, whereby they relinquish such parts of the old location as had not fallen in the new, or the one actually surveyed; but in consequence of a want of form in Said Deed of Exchange it was conceived an improper instrument. I was therefore furnished with another, annulling and rendering Void the original one, to be executed by the Indians; but this Deed was never Executed, as a sufficient number of the Indian Chiefs had not been collected upon any occasion during my residence in the Genesee Country last season, whose signatures were necessary in order to render the instrument Valid....I therefore left the said deed of Exchange with Captain Israel Chapin, Agent of Indian affairs who promised me he would attend to it, *and have it carried fully into Effect* when he assembles the Indians together.[29]

By most accounts Ellicott was an honest, reputable man. At the same time, he was not unaware of the designs of his employer, the Holland Land Company. And he had a personal financial stake in the Cattaraugus land, as noted by Martonis: "As soon as the 1802 treaty was signed, David Dickinson purchased 640 acres *from Joseph Ellicott* (an 1803 document)."[30] It would seem that Ellicott was up to his eyeballs in this ugly business.

With the caveat that there is much we may never know—were promises made to the Indians that their fishing and hunting rights would continue on land they no longer owned, and did Johnston, Cornplanter, and Red Jacket get some kind of payoff?—it seems probable that something nefarious happened between May 10 and June 21–22, 1798, that prompted the Indians to support the land swap at Cattaraugus. Moreover, judging from the kerfuffle that transpired between 1798 and 1802, it is not unlikely that the Indians experienced a period of seller's remorse at that time.

ALTHOUGH THE SENECA WOULD FACE MANY LEGAL BATTLES IN the future, in 1842 their right to live on the Cattaraugus Reservation was ensured. In any event, I think that there is ample evidence to support the argument that the land exchange confirmed in the treaty of 1802, the partial sale of Cattaraugus in 1826, and the sale and eventual return of the Cattaraugus Reservation in the treaties of 1838 and 1842, respectively, was made not in the Seneca's interest, but rather to satisfy white men's greed.

CHAPTER 10

SOLDIERS OF FORTUNE

John Woodside and Maria Woodside Novinger were less adventurous than their brother, Jonathan. They remained in the Lykens Valley throughout their lives, and like many Lykens Valley residents, they had several children. By my count, a family gathering involving John, Maria, and their children and grandchildren would include about 150 people. Thus it was fortunate for the burgeoning population that the United States Confederation Congress passed the Northwest Ordinance in 1787. The ordinance provided that as America grew, additional states would be admitted to the Union rather than expanding the existing states. The ordinance also prohibited slavery in the Northwest Territory, thereby establishing the Ohio River as the boundary between slave and free territory, east of the Mississippi River. Of no less importance to the Woodside family, and of greater importance to the nation, was Thomas Jefferson's purchase of the Louisiana Territory. That purchase, of course, doubled the country's size. But it also set the stage for the existential sectional dispute between northern and southern states over the issue of slavery. And the debate over the extension of slavery into newly annexed territories intensified in the wake of the 1846–1848 war with Mexico.[1]

In what reads like an episode of palace intrigue, the war with Mexico began on May 13, 1846, under the pretense that the Mexican army had invaded US territory north of the Rio Grande when, in fact, control of the territory between the Rio Grande and the

Nueces River was in dispute.[2] (See figure 14.) The war was well underway when president James K. Polk requested Pennsylvania to raise one regiment of volunteers on November 16, 1846, and a second regiment on December 14.[3] The Pennsylvania regiments were part of General Winfield Scott's army, the objective of which was to capture Mexico City. Two members of the Woodside family responded to the call to arms.

Figure 14. Map of major campaigns in Mexican War. Courtesy of the US Army Center for Military History, https://history.army.mil/ brochures/Occupation/Images/Map1.jpg, and modified by author; accessed October 21, 2020.

Hiram and George Novinger, descendants of Maria Woodside Novinger, volunteered in Captain Edward C. Williams's Cameron Guards, Company G, Second Regiment of Pennsylvania Volunteers, with Colonel William Roberts commanding.[4] They left Harrisburg the day after Christmas 1846 and went by way of Pittsburgh and the Mississippi River to New Orleans. There they encamped on the historic battlefield where Andrew Jackson defeated the British in 1815. The unit departed New Orleans aboard the *General Veazie* on January 31, 1847.[5] After a rough forty-one-day passage, during which an outbreak of smallpox occurred, they arrived on February 18 at Lobos Island.[6] Located in the Gulf of Mexico between Tampico and Veracruz, the island was the staging point for General Scott's army. Unfortunately, the ship was detained upon its arrival under the yellow quarantine flag. And by the time Companies B, D, and G, which had sailed together on the *General Veazie*, arrived at Veracruz on April 11, the Mexicans had already surrendered the city to General Scott, and the bulk of Scott's army was proceeding on its march to Mexico City.[7] On April 17, the Americans won the Battle of Cerro Gordo at a strategic pass on the National Road that had been occupied by Mexican forces under the command of General Antonio López de Santa Anna.

Having missed out on the siege of Veracruz and the Battle of Cerro Gordo because of the quarantine delay, Companies B, D, and G reunited with the rest of the Second Regiment of Pennsylvania Volunteers at Jalapa on April 23, 1847.[8] Upon arrival at Jalapa, their encampment, dubbed "Camp Misery," was "a quagmire of mud and human filth," a breeding ground for disease.[9] Hiram Novinger, listed as sick during May and June, was among those afflicted. The regiment was soon relocated and assigned to garrison duty of the city of Jalapa, an assignment they fulfilled adequately. They left Jalapa for Perote, a city across the Sierra Madre mountain range, on June 19. En route to their destination, the army train, with Company G in the lead, was ambushed at the pass of La Hoya. Assisted by reinforcements that arrived from Perote, the Americans routed the Mexicans. It was Company G's, and the Novinger men's, first taste of battle.[10] (See figure 15.)

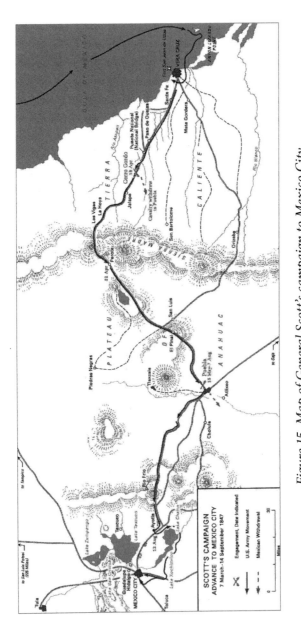

Figure 15. Map of General Scott's campaign to Mexico City. Courtesy of the US Army Center for Military History, https://history.army.mil/brochures/Occupation/Images/Map3.jpg, and modified by author; accessed October 21, 2020.

General Scott's Mexico City campaign continued. By September 11 the army was at Mexico City's doorstep preparing for an assault on the formidable fortress at Chapultepec located on the western outskirts of the city. The Second Regiment of Pennsylvania Volunteers, assigned to General John Quitman's division, played an important role in the battle that followed. (See figure 16.)

Figure 16. Fortress of Chapultepec. N. Currier, View of Chapultepec and Molino del Rey, after the Battle, City of Mexico in the distance, c. 1847 (New York: Published by N. Currier), Courtesy Library of Congress, https://www.loc.gov/item/2002698124.

On the morning of September 13, General Quitman's and General Gideon Pillow's divisions were ordered to storm the fortress from the south and west, respectively. During the battle, "by Quitman's order the New York and Second Pennsylvania regiments left the Tacubaya causeway, under a heavy fire waded the ditches on the left and rear to the redan [an arrow-shaped embankment that forms part of a fortification], and charged through the opening in the wall."[11] The commanders of the New York and Pennsylvania regiments were wounded, but the troops kept on. In the battle, six men from Company G were wounded in action, one of whom died later of his wounds. In the end, the Americans carried the day. And

Captain Edward C. Williams of Company G, as documented in Major William Brindle's official report of September 15, 1847, had the honor of raising the first American flag over the fortress. The story about the flag, if true, challenges current scholarship about the history of the Betsy Ross flag. Major Brindle wrote:

> Captain E. C. Williams...soon after we entered the Fortress, ascended to the top of it, with the first American flag made by Betsy Ross, of Philadelphia, which was presented to General Washington just before the Battle of Trenton, during the Revolution of 1776, which Captain Williams had obtained from the State Library at Harrisburg, PA, and carried with him to Mexico, with the purpose of raising it over the enemy's works at every opportunity, and which he raised over the Fortress of Chapultepec about the same time that a sergeant of one of the old infantry regiments raised a blue regimental flag over it.[12]

Having secured Chapultepec, Quitman's division proceeded under brutal enemy fire along the causeway leading to Mexico City's Garita de Belen. They halted at dusk, expecting a renewal of the fighting at dawn. But during the night, Santa Anna's army evacuated the city, and in the morning of September 14, 1847, a city official appeared carrying a white surrender flag. The Second Pennsylvania Regiment was ordered to guard the fortification at the Garita de Belen, and from there they watched as the rest of Quitman's division, including the United States Marines, paraded into the city's Grand Plaza and took possession of the National Palace, which the soldiers called "the Halls of Montezuma." Attesting to their participation in the fight to take Mexico City, ninety-seven members of the Second Pennsylvania Regiment were wounded or killed in battle. Of those, nine were members of Company G, the Cameron Guards.[13] After the battle, George Novinger was detailed to the regimental hospital in Mexico City on September 16. He rejoined his company by December 31 and was promoted to first corporal on January 1, 1848.[14]

The Mexican War ended on February 2, 1848, with the signing of the Treaty of Guadalupe Hidalgo. The treaty, largely dictated by the United States, ceded 525,000 square miles of valuable territory to the United States in exchange for $15 million. The area included parts of the modern-day states of Colorado, Arizona, New Mexico, and Wyoming and all of California, Nevada, and Utah. The remaining parts of what are today the states of Arizona and New Mexico were later ceded under the 1853 Gadsden Purchase for an additional $10 million.

The brave soldiers of Pennsylvania's Second Regiment served with honor. It should be noted that the number of men in Company G who were killed in battle (two) pales when compared to those who died of disease (eighteen).[15] Hiram Novinger was among them. He died while on a march at Beraugas on July 3, 1847. George Novinger was mustered out at Pittsburgh on July 20, 1848. Nothing beyond his service in the Mexican War is known about George. Like so many others, he appeared in the historical record only once—but indeed, it was a shining moment.

———————

WHILE HIRAM AND GEORGE NOVINGER SOUGHT GLORY IN A foreign land, other family members migrated to Ohio and Missouri. James Woodside, John and Margaret Woodside's eldest son, served in the Pennsylvania militia during the War of 1812 under the command of Captain Jacob Dietrich in Colonel Adam Richard's Regiment.[16] He was among the soldiers who helped reinforce the city's defenses after the Battle of Baltimore (September 12–15, 1814). He was discharged on December 5, 1814, and paid $6 for his service.[17] James married Sarah Shive. Their nine children were born in Dauphin County, Pennsylvania, prior to their move to Crawford County, Ohio, sometime before 1835.

Crawford County, Ohio, was named after Colonel William Crawford, who had been captured, tortured, and killed by Indians including the Wyandot during the Revolutionary War. The Wyandot are a nation with a legendary history, and settlers like the Woodsides would have been familiar with accounts of the Indians' recent past.[18] During the War of 1812 the Wyandot nation was divided. Some of the Indians joined with General William Henry Harrison in pushing the British back into Canada. Others followed Wyandot Chief Stayeghta (the Bark Carrier), generally known as Roundhead, in an alliance with Tecumseh (the Shooting Star). Tecumseh was the inspired leader of the Shawnee of Ohio who had forged a pan-Indian alliance among the Indians living east of the Mississippi.[19] Tecumseh's vision, as stated at an August 1810 meeting with William Henry Harrison, was that "the lands belong to all and were not to be gobbled up piecemeal in illegal treaties with individual tribes."[20] Tecumseh suffered a setback when Harrison defeated him at the 1811 Battle of Tippecanoe. After the loss, Tecumseh, joined by his second-in-command Chief Roundhead, regrouped his forces and, in a "brief but brilliant alliance" with the Canadian hero Major General Sir Isaac Brock, won several early battles in the War of 1812.[21] However, both Indian leaders died in the fall of 1813—Roundhead of an illness, and Tecumseh in the October 5 Battle of the Thames. Tecumseh's dream "of a united and independent state east of the Mississippi" died with him.[22]

After the war, the Wyandot Indians who had remained loyal to the United States were "given" a twelve-square-mile reservation at Upper Sandusky where they gradually adopted the lifeways of their white neighbors. Following the Indian Removal Act of 1830, the Wyandot held out until 1843 when they were removed to Kansas in yet another trail of tears.[23] They were the last tribe to leave Ohio as a group. Being their neighbors, James Woodside and his family would have witnessed the Indians' sad departure. Following the Indians' removal, the Ohio government authorized the creation of Wyandot County, named in honor of the Wyandot Indians.

ISAAC NOVINGER WAS THE FIRST OF MARIA WOODSIDE Novinger's descendants to move away from the valley. With a

Lykens Valley send-off including five hundred people wishing him Godspeed, he pulled up stakes and in 1847 moved to Missouri, settling in Adair County. Upon his arrival in Missouri with his wife, Christina Shoop, and their seven children, Isaac initially lived with his brother-in-law Jacob Shoop. The following year Isaac's parents, Jonathan Collier Novinger and Christiana Werfel, also moved to Adair County, and the family was joined in 1851 by Isaac's brother John C. Novinger and his wife, Sarah Schott, with their children. Later, John C. laid out the town that bears the family name. The Novingers figured prominently in the town of Novinger as large landowners, merchants, a mayor, and a county judge. During the Civil War several of the Missouri Novingers served in the Union army (as did Novingers who lived in Iowa and Pennsylvania).[24]

FOREIGN WARS AND WESTERN MIGRATION NOTWITHSTANDING, many of the Woodsides and Novingers stayed in the valley and surrounding region where they intermarried with other early settlers. One of those who stayed in the valley was Maria Woodside's grandson Joseph Novinger, who married a young lady named Anna Eisenhower. Anna was the daughter of Frederick Eisenhower, the great-grandfather of president Dwight David Eisenhower. Frederick had moved to the Lykens Valley in 1830 with his wife, Barbara Miller. They had six children: Polly, Anna, John David, Catherine, Samuel Peter, and Jacob Frederick, the president's grandfather. Jacob Frederick lived in a nine-room brick house on a hundred-acre farm that would later be part of Elizabethville, two miles away from the Woodside and Novinger farms; and it was in that house that the president's father, David Jacob Eisenhower, was born.[25] Joseph and Anna Eisenhower Novinger, then, would be a great-aunt and great-uncle of the future president. The fact that such an estimable leader as President Eisenhower had his roots in the Lykens Valley is a tribute to the character and values of the valley's hardworking people.

JONATHAN WOODSIDE, THE THIRD SON OF JOHN WOODSIDE AND
Margaret McMullen Woodside, married Elizabeth Schell, and
they had six known children including their daughter Mary Ann.
As the son who stayed on the family farm, cared for his father in
old age, and administered his father's estate, Jonathan was the
anchor of the third generation of Woodsides. Under his care, the
farm expanded when he warranted 427 acres in 1810. Jonathan
probably used the land, which was mostly hillside, for firewood
and timber. In the War of 1812 he served in the militia from
September 2, 1812, to December 18, 1812, in Captain Philip Fetterhoff's company attached to the Pennsylvania Second Regiment
commanded by Colonel Adam Richard. Making it a family affair,
Jonathan's three cousins—Isaac, Jesse, and John Novinger—were
also privates in Fetterhoff's company, and Jonathan's younger
brother Thomas served as the company's lieutenant.[26] The company passed its time of service encamped at York, Pennsylvania,
and never saw actual battle. Nevertheless, Jonathan was awarded
a pension for his service.

By 1850 Jonathan Woodside was the second wealthiest farmer
in Upper Paxton with the farm valued at $6,000. He had three
horses, two milk cows, one other cattle, and ten swine. In 1850
the farm produced 200 bushels of wheat, 100 bushels of rye, 250
bushels of Indian corn, 150 bushels of oats, 60 pounds of potatoes, $10 worth of orchard produce, and 20 tons of hay. He, or
more likely his wife, Elizabeth, produced 260 pounds of butter.
Jonathan was the last of the Woodsides to farm the land that
the family had accumulated for three generations. Beginning in
1862 until his death on August 7, 1869, Jonathan sold portions
of his landholdings. Seemingly he used the farm as a land bank
to support himself in old age. Some of what remained was later
sold by his son Benjamin.[27]

THOMAS WOODSIDE, THE FOURTH SON OF JOHN WOODSIDE AND Margaret McMullen Woodside, married Mary Yeager on December 29, 1812. As noted above, he served during the War of 1812. Thomas Woodside seems to have been a somewhat contentious character. For some reason he was the recipient of ill will from his father-in-law, Mr. John Yeager. In his last will and testament, Mr. Yeager emphatically ensured that his daughter Mary's portion of his estate would be untouched by Thomas. Thomas was also at odds with his older brother Jonathan. Jonathan was the administrator of John Woodside's estate, and in that role Jonathan was continually challenging Thomas to settle disagreements. It is unknown what Thomas did for a living, but prosperity apparently eluded him. In 1850 the value of his real estate was a mere $400. Thomas died on January 8, 1872.[28]

In succeeding generations, Thomas and Mary's most notable descendant was Robert Elmer Woodside (1904–1998), a lifelong resident of Millersburg, Pennsylvania. Robert dedicated his life to public service—first as a state legislator, later as a judge, and later still as the attorney general for the Commonwealth of Pennsylvania. The Pennsylvania legislature honored Judge Woodside in awarding a posthumous proclamation of gratitude to his widow and children. Judge Woodside was active in the Republican Party, and in his book *My Life and Town* there is a picture of him standing beside President Eisenhower.[29] One wonders if the judge was aware that he and President Eisenhower were united not only by political philosophy but also through kinship and place of origin.[30]

JANE WOODSIDE WAS JOHN AND MARGARET WOODSIDE'S ELDEST daughter. Like all of the women in the family, little is known about Jane. She married Simon Sallade, who was unquestionably the most remarkable person of the third generation. Simon's story follows in the next several chapters. Jane died September 3, 1854 and is buried in Elizabethville.[31]

THESE ARE A FEW OF THE DESCENDANTS AND RELATIVES OF THE Woodside and Novinger families. Strong in mind and body, they endured interminable labors. Of resourceful and adventurous spirit, they overcame their challenges with unyielding courage. They pledged their lives to a young nation and fought to get her born. We can never know what they looked like, what made them laugh or cry, or what family secrets they kept. Farmers, millers, carpenters, wheelwrights, blacksmiths, coopers, merchants, wives and mothers, and soldiers. Most died in obscurity, weatherworn inscriptions on their gravestones alone giving testament to their meaningful lives.

Part II

SALLADE

Though there no lordly castle throws,
O'er moor, or plain its shadow,
From where the Susquehanna River flows
Through mountain gap and meadow,
To where the Juniata's tide
Its tribute wave delivers;—
The streams that bound on either side,—
The land between the rivers.

—G. CARY THRAP,
"The Land between the Rivers"

CHAPTER 11

A MAN OF HIS TIME

---◆---

"Nothing should be attempted in a State, but what the citizens might be prevailed on to admit by gentle means, and that violence should never be employed." So wrote Simon Sallade in his daybook a few weeks before he died.[1] His comment was a fitting reflection for a man who had dedicated his life to his community and state, was valued for his many accomplishments, and was loved for the way he achieved them. He was, in fact, so respected by the people of the Lykens Valley that half a century after his death he was still regarded as the most spectacular man who had ever lived there. Because he focused his efforts on local rather than national issues, however, his life story has escaped the attention of modern historians. And yet, it is men like Simon Sallade whose work underpins development in the early years of America's industrial expansion. He represents the hundreds of backbench state legislators who grappled with the often mundane and occasionally riveting issues of his day. And as a nuts-and-bolts general contractor, he typified the thousands of men who struggled to build America's first great transportation system. What makes Sallade's story especially compelling is that his service in the Pennsylvania legislature (1819–1820, 1820–1821, 1836–1837, and 1854) coincided with pivotal developments in American history. Moreover, in his work as a contractor, he had firsthand experience coping with the conflicts inherent in the intermingling of politics, finance, and technological progress during Pennsylvania's canal-

and railroad-building period. But Sallade's story is more than a period tale. It is also a story about the people he knew: his family and friends, his business partners and fellow politicians, and near the end of his life, his adversaries.

Little has been published about Sallade beyond what was recorded toward the end of the nineteenth century in a few sketches in William Egle's *Notes and Queries*. Those colorful accounts mark the milestones of Sallade's life and present an intriguing image of a man resembling an iconic "Jefferson Smith," who somehow got trapped inside the body of an awkward Ichabod Crane.[2] Egle described Sallade as "a man of peace and of infinite jest."[3] A few examples illustrate.

> Although a man sparing in words, he was as you say of a decidedly sociable turn. He rarely missed a public meeting, a festival, a vendue or a dance. Many a time the writer has danced in the same set with him when he was verging on sixty, and certainly a more ungainly or awkward dancer it has never been his lot to see than was the old Colonel. In the spirit of mischief, probably, he would sometimes run wrong, swing wrong, mistake his partner and grasp somebody else, throwing the set into ludicrous confusion. Many a hearty laugh has been had over his efforts to set things aright. We judge men from appearances, but in this respect, Mr. Sallade was a puzzle and a paradox.[4]

And speaking of appearances, when he first went to the state legislature in 1819, he was playfully characterized as one of the three homeliest men in the state.

> George Kramer at that period carried a large gift knife, given him, as he said, because of his looks. With this knife he also carried a condition, to wit: That when he found a man uglier than himself, his duty was to pass it on. Judge Burnside refused to take it, and my father suggested he

bestow it on Mr. Sallade. To this Mr. Kramer demurred. Said he: "I have looked Mr. Sallade all over and in my opinion he is not as consistently ugly as myself. Whilst he beats me a little on the nose, mouth and legs, his makeup is a failure and a mistake. He has the shoulders of a Hercules and the eyes of an Apollo."[5]

Considering the foregoing vignettes of Simon Sallade's life, it should be easy to understand why I became captivated by the man's story. Unfortunately, Sallade was not a man of letters: the few surviving documents written by him primarily refer to personal business dealings and technical details about various construction projects. To some degree, the legislative record, various corporate documents, family history records, and biographies of his associates compensate for this shortcoming. But there are gaps, especially about his family life. In spite of these limitations, Sallade's story offers a fascinating chapter in my narrative about how this middle-class family was shaped by and had an impact on major historical events. Simon was, it seems to me, the quintessential engaged citizen in the years between the War of 1812 and the Civil War.

BASIC DETAILS OF SIMON SALLADE'S EARLY LIFE WERE SUMMArized in the *Commemorative Biographical Encyclopedia of Dauphin County, Pennsylvania*.[6] He was born on March 7, 1785, near Gratz in Dauphin County. His father was John Sallade of French Huguenot descent. John was born in Bosel on the Rhine in 1739, emigrated with other members of the family, and was among the first settlers on Wiconisco Creek. In what would later become Lykens Township, John warranted two tracts of land: one for 117 acres in 1789 and an adjacent tract of 130 acres in 1796. (It was common at the time for a settler to reside on a piece of land prior to filing a warrant. Further, at the outbreak of the Revolutionary War, the land office ceased to function, and it was not reconstituted until 1781.) In 1771 John married Margaret Eberhardt, who was born in Berks County in 1747. An often repeated legend claims that she was taken captive by the Indians in the French and Indian War. Despite efforts to chase down its origin, the story has not been verified.[7] John and Margaret Sallade had (as best I can tell) five sons and two daughters, Simon being the second youngest. Simon married Jane Woodside, granddaughter of James Woodside.

In some ways Simon's childhood was not much different from his parents'. Transportation in rural Pennsylvania had not improved much. There were more roads, but they were often muddy and impassable. Farm life had changed but little. Although more land had been cleared, agricultural methods remained primitive, relying on horse-drawn plows, hand tools, and homegrown labor. Children, of course, were expected to carry their own weight, performing chores that were suited to their age and gender. Family legend, as reported by Simon's great-grandson James D. Bowman, has it that Simon "was naturally an intelligent but wild boy. Like all boys he evaded work. He very frequently sat in the rye field with his favorite violin discoursing music to the delighted reapers."[8] Educational opportunities were limited in his rural community. For the lack of schools, Simon was initially instructed by his parents. An avid reader, he read and reread the few books that were available in those days. Later, probably between the ages of twelve and sixteen, he and several young men in the neighborhood hired a teacher in neighboring Mahantango. The boys would have scrambled over the hills into what was then Berks County to benefit from their teacher's instruction.[9]

But in other ways Simon enjoyed a freedom that his parents had been denied in their youth. Being born after the revolution, he grew up honoring homegrown heroes, George Washington and Thomas Jefferson most of all. As the wilderness receded in his neighborhood, attacks by predatory panthers and wolves were no longer a threat. The menace and fear of Indian ambush were history. Because of the population boom, childhood companionship supplanted the feeling of isolation that his parents had sometimes endured. He also had plenty of opportunities to engage in social activities with his friends and family. At community gatherings he would have overheard his elders reliving the defining moments of their lives, centered on the American Revolution and particularly Pennsylvania's role in it. Being naturally curious and an embryotic politician, he may have taken part in conversations about current events. Indeed, what with the proliferation of partisan newspapers, notably Philadelphia's *Aurora General Advertiser* and *Porcupine's Gazette*, discussions of unsettling political events by the valley's civic-minded citizens would have been hard to avoid.[10]

AS THE EIGHTEENTH CENTURY DREW TO A CLOSE, THE PEOPLE of the Lykens Valley found themselves in the eye of yet another political hurricane when two Federalist laws, the Direct Tax and the Sedition Act, stirred up opposition in nearby towns. Both laws were signed by president John Adams in 1798 on the anniversary of France's Bastille Day, July 14, clearly sending a symbolic message to America's Francophile republicans.[11] The direct tax levied on houses was intended to pay for enlarging the army and navy and was deemed necessary because Federalists believed at the time that war with France was inevitable. A keen observer, the young Simon Sallade couldn't help but notice the fierce local reaction to the tax. Although opposition to the tax was strongest among the German Lutheran and German Reformed farmers in nearby Northampton and Bucks Counties, support for the farmers was widespread. In eastern Dauphin County, for example, liberty poles were raised in the communities of Lebanon, Myerstown, and Jonestown, not far from Simon's home. According to historian Paul Douglas Newman, the poles were intended to explain that the law was a "repudiation of the republican and democratic values" enshrined in the Constitution.[12] Federalists' efforts to tear down the liberty poles didn't stop people from putting them up again. In referring to what came to be known as Fries' Rebellion of 1799, Federalist sympathizer Alexander Graydon cried, "Another insurrection ran in a vein through the counties of Berks and Dauphin, spreading the infection by means of liberty poles, successively rising in grand colonnade from the banks of the Delaware to those of the Susquehanna."[13]

Simultaneously, Sallade, the avid reader, likely came across the writings of Thomas Cooper, an Oxford-educated Englishman who had moved to the United States in 1794. Cooper had settled in the village of Northumberland, a few miles north of the Lykens Valley. From there, between April 20 and June 29, 1799, precisely when the controversy over the Direct Tax was reaching its peak in nearby counties, Cooper wrote essays in the *Sunbury and Northumberland Gazette*, a small newspaper that circulated locally. In the essays, he critiqued President Adams's administration. In Cooper's farewell editorial of June 29, he specifically took issue with the increase in the size of the army and navy and the Alien and Sedition Acts. He encouraged Americans to resist these measures by first discussing the issues and then by replacing the responsible officials using the constitutional electoral process. Cooper's farewell editorial was reprinted in the July 12, 1799, issue of Philadelphia's *Aurora*, the leading voice of Jeffersonian Republicans. Thereby, Cooper became a target of the sedition law.[14]

In a topsy-turvy courtroom proceeding, Cooper was convicted of sedition and sentenced to prison. Rather than being silenced, however, Cooper became a martyr in the cause of freedom of speech and the press. To this end, he exploited his celebrity by publishing, under the byline "Prison of Philadelphia," an account of his trial. In its preface Cooper spared no words in warning the citizens of the country that if "they mean to consult their own peace and quiet, they will hold their tongues, and refrain their pens, on the subject of politics; at least during the continuance of the Sedition Law; a Law, which I do not think 'the powers that be,' will incline to abolish…[Ask yourself] whether the Men who can sanction these proceedings, are fit objects of re-election."[15]

Whether it was the direct tax, Cooper's writings, or the Federalists' overzealous prosecution of him and others that had the greatest impact on the thinking of Dauphin County's farmers is difficult to tell. But it is undeniable that they changed their allegiance from the Federalists to the Republicans: in 1796, voters in Dauphin County favored Adams's Federalist electors over Jefferson's Republican electors by a two-to-one margin (464–233), and by 1804, they chose Republican presidential electors over Federalists with a near unanimous vote (569–24).[16]

Were these political developments Simon Sallade's primary concern? Perhaps not at the time. But as time marched on, the impression that his interest in politics had its genesis in the upheaval of his coming-of-age years would be affirmed when he ran for public office at the age of thirty-three. Until then, however, Sallade would be preoccupied with getting his start in life, establishing his career, and raising a family.

AT ABOUT THE AGE OF SIXTEEN, SALLADE BEGAN HIS APPREN-ticeship as a millwright under the direction of a Jacob Berkstresser of Bellefonte, Centre County. Typical skills and temperament of a millwright of the early nineteenth century were described by William Fairbairn. "An itinerant engineer and mechanic of high reputation," it was said of those early millwrights that "there probably never existed a more useful and independent class of men than the country millwrights. The whole mechanical knowledge of the country was centered amongst them and...they were generally looked upon as men of superior attainments and of considerable intellectual power."[17] Millwrights of this period were also recognized for "the kindly feeling and generous sympathy which generally belonged to them."[18] It was "in acts of charity and good will to those in want that the millwright of all times has shown his native goodness."[19] The trade required skills such as an aptitude for math and mechanics, physical strength, and a good eye. Millwrights were responsible for choosing the best site for a mill at a given location. They had to decide what type of waterwheel to employ, "what size it should be, how to design the paddles or buckets, where and how to build the dam and raceways, what gearing was necessary to power the mill itself. Then the millwright oversaw the construction. Thus millwrights might well combine the skills of carpenter, joiner, mason, stonecutter, blacksmith, wheelwright, and surveyor."[20] And of course most of the work was done by hand. Assuming an apprenticeship lasted for about four years, Sallade would have completed his in about 1805.

His apprenticeship completed, in 1806 Simon Sallade married Jane Woodside, the daughter of John Woodside and Margaret McMullen. Together Simon and Jane would have eight known children: Margaret, Jonathan, George, Jacob, Ann, Jane, Joseph, and Simon. As a father providing for his growing family, Sallade traveled the backroads of the region plying his trade. It was in this phase of his life—the early 1800s to the 1820s—that he built, often with his own hands, most of the sawmills and gristmills within forty miles of his home.

AT THE SAME TIME THAT SALLADE WAS FOCUSED ON HIS CAREER and family, the world around him was changing at breakneck speed. In April 1803, under the direction of president Thomas Jefferson, Robert M. Livingston and James Monroe had negotiated with France for the Louisiana Purchase. Even earlier, in January 1803, Jefferson had sent a secret letter to Congress in which he requested funding for an expedition to the Pacific Ocean via the Missouri River. Lewis and Clark's Corps of Discovery left St. Louis on May 14, 1804, and returned two and a half years later on September 23, 1806. As early as 1807, *A Journal of the Voyages and Travels of a Corps of Discovery* written by Patrick Gass, a sergeant in the corps, was widely read, and probably found its way into Sallade's hands.[21]

New states entered the union: Ohio in 1803, Louisiana in 1812, Indiana in 1816, Mississippi in 1817, Illinois in 1818, and Alabama in 1819. As western expansion proceeded, the need for better communication and transportation to the new states and territories created a sense of urgency. In 1807 Robert Fulton's steamboat the *Clermont* completed a round trip between Albany and New York, and by 1811 the *New Orleans*, the first steamboat on the Mississippi, was making its way downstream from Pittsburgh. In the same year, the federal government began work on the National Road at Cumberland, Maryland; it would be opened to Wheeling, Virginia, in 1818. In New York State, the legislature approved funding for the Erie Canal in 1817, sparking an intense competition among the eastern states to secure the fastest and cheapest trade route to the West.

Meanwhile, beginning at least from the inauguration of Thomas Jefferson in 1801, the relationship between the United States and Great Britain steadily deteriorated, eventually leading to the War of 1812.[22] In Pennsylvania, support for the War of 1812 was evident in the response to governor Simon Snyder's call for volunteers to answer the threat of British attacks in Philadelphia and cities situated on Chesapeake Bay.[23] Leading up to the war, the embargo of 1807 had a favorable impact on Pennsylvania's developing economy, in particular its farming and manufacturing sectors.[24] Once peace returned, however, American domestic manufactures were unable to compete with a flood of cheap foreign goods.

Complicating the postwar economic situation, in 1814 Pennsylvania's legislature overrode Governor Snyder's veto and passed an act regulating banks, derisively referred to as the forty-one bank bill.[25] According to historian Philip Klein, most of the horde of state banks established under the ill-advised law "began a course of banking malpractice which soon had the business of Pennsylvania in turmoil."[26]

In 1816 the Second Bank of the United States was chartered by Congress in order to restore fiscal and monetary stability to the country. "The essential function of the Bank was to regulate the public credit issued by private banking institutions through the fiscal duties it performed for the US Treasury, and to establish a sound and stable national currency."[27] Contrary to the bank's mandate, its first president, William Jones, launched an easy money policy that encouraged speculation and even led to a $3 million fraud by the directors of the bank's Baltimore branch. Acknowledging the errors, the bank's board of directors replaced Jones in 1818 and abruptly enacted a stringent contraction policy. The problem with that policy, as historian Sean Wilentz observed, was that "just as the Bank intensified its deflationary pressure, commodity prices for American staples on the world market collapsed," and "the freefall of agricultural prices prevented [mismanaged and corrupt Pennsylvania] state banks from either collecting from their debtors or meeting their obligations to the Bank of the United States—leading [in turn] to a tidal wave of bank failures, business collapses, and personal bankruptcies," later known as the Panic of 1819.[28]

Coinciding with the downturn in the economy was the rise in a movement to democratize the selection of candidates for political office. Pennsylvanians were no longer willing to yield to the quaint notion that only the "better sort" were destined to rule. In its place they embraced the idea that a man's opportunities should be limited only by his talent and his enterprise. By 1817 this metamorphosis in political thought centered on denouncing the method by which candidates were selected for political office, the caucus system. In the caucus system, incumbent legislators nominated candidates for future office, and thereby it tended to keep political power concentrated in the hands of the "better sort." Thus, challenging the caucus system and replacing it with a more democratic convention system became the centerpiece in the move toward more egalitarian elections.[29] The Pennsylvania group promoting change was unsuccessful in 1817 when their candidate for governor, Joseph Hiester, was defeated by William Findlay. Nevertheless, the movement opened the door for self-made men: a few great men such as Abraham Lincoln as well as hundreds of lesser lights such as Simon Sallade.

CHAPTER 12

YOUNG POLITICIAN

⸺◆⸺

S imon Sallade first ran for political office in 1818 and was
defeated in his bid for Dauphin County commissioner.[1] Undis-
couraged, he ran successfully in 1819 for a seat in the Pennsylvania House of Representatives in which Dauphin County had two
members. He and his running mate, William Rutherford, defeated
both of the incumbents, William Irvine and Isaac Smith. Illustrating the turmoil of the political party system at the time, Irvine and
Smith had been identified as Republicans when they were elected
in 1818 and as Democrats when they were defeated in 1819. Sallade
and Rutherford, in the 1819 election, were identified as Old School
Democrats in one newspaper and as Independent Republicans in
others, but in the 1820 election, they were both listed as Federalists.
As historian Philip Klein observed, "In county after county the
old party groups were being broken up and mixed together. If you
asked a man what party he belonged to, he could do nought but
answer, 'For what office do you mean?'"[2] And so, whether as an
Independent Republican, an Old School Democrat, or a Federalist,
in early December 1819 Sallade proceeded to Harrisburg, made
arrangements for his lodging, and settled in among his peers for
the three-month-long legislative session.

Sallade's first meaningful vote in the Pennsylvania House of
Representatives dealt with a historic national issue, the Missouri
Compromise. The compromise originated in the US Congress on
February 15, 1819, when the US House of Representatives voted

79–67 to incorporate James Tallmadge's amendment into the Missouri statehood bill. The Tallmadge amendment proposed to prohibit slavery in the territory of Missouri as a precondition to statehood. It was the most profound attack on American slavery since the Northwest Ordinance had been adopted in 1787, and it provoked an intense backlash especially in the southern states. Reacting to backlash against the amendment, legislators in Pennsylvania's House of Representatives introduced a bold resolution that instructed Pennsylvania's congressional delegation to vote against admission of any territory as a state unless the territory agreed that the further introduction of slavery would be prohibited. In part, the resolution read, "The senate and house of representatives of Pennsylvania...are persuaded that to open the fertile regions of the west to a servile race, would tend to increase their numbers beyond all past example; would open a new and steady market for the lawless vendors of human flesh; and would render all schemes for obliterating this most foul blot upon the American character, useless and unavailing."[3] The resolution was unanimously adopted by both the Pennsylvania House and Senate and approved by the governor.[4]

Afterward, a divisive debate proceeded in Congress. The US Senate added another amendment that would have removed the slavery restriction (the Tallmadge amendment) from the bill. On March 2, 1820, when a vote was taken on whether the US House would concur with the Senate amendment, Pennsylvania's delegation voted 21–2 against that amendment. As it was, the final vote in the Senate amendment was 90–87, and the Missouri Compromise was adopted. Had David Fullerton, representing Pennsylvania's Cumberland, Franklin, and Adams Counties, and Henry Baldwin, representing Butler and Allegheny Counties, honored the unanimous request of the Pennsylvania General Assembly and the governor and also voted no, the measure would have failed on a vote of 88–89.[5] One can only imagine what would have happened if the Tallmadge amendment had been adopted into law.

Pennsylvania's legislature was not finished with the issue, however. Since the final congressional vote on the admission of

Missouri was postponed to the next session of Congress, a "hope still remain[ed] that the wide spreading progress of slavery may be stayed," and on March 22, 1820, the Pennsylvania House voted 43–35 in favor of a resolution to request Congress at its next session to vote against the admission of Missouri unless slavery should be excluded.[6] But then, following a motion to defer the resolution to the next legislature, the House inexplicably voted 81–10 to do so. Sallade was with the majority in both votes.[7] In the 1820–1821 Pennsylvania legislature, the issue never came up, and Missouri was admitted to the Union as a slave state on August 10, 1821. The Missouri Compromise of 1820 would remain the law of the land until 1854 when it was superseded by the Kansas-Nebraska Act. As if by strange accident, Sallade's political career would be bookended by these two consequential events.

Even though Pennsylvania's resolution about the Missouri Compromise failed to achieve its goal, another act of the 1820 Pennsylvania legislature, "an act to prevent kidnapping," was approved in the legislature on a voice vote (votes of individual legislators were not recorded) and became law on March 27, 1820.[8] Introduced by William J. Duane, the law made kidnapping of any "negro or mulatto" a felony and was aimed directly at the national Fugitive Slave Act of 1793.[9] Punishment for violation of the anti-kidnapping law was a fine of $500 to $2,000 and imprisonment for seven to twenty-one years. The law became the first in the United States that prohibited state officials from enforcing the federal fugitive slave law. The law set in motion events that led to the passage of Pennsylvania's Fugitive Slave Act of 1826 and eventually to the famous 1842 Supreme Court case of Prigg v. Pennsylvania.[10] In that case, "Justice Joseph Story delivered the opinion of the Court that the 1788 and 1826 Pennsylvania laws contradicted Article IV, Section 2 of the Constitution and the Fugitive Slave Law. The Supremacy Clause ensured that federal laws prevailed over the state laws. The decision did not wholly end asylum across state lines for slaves. Story granted that the state laws put in place by slave states to recapture slaves in free states only had to be enforced by federal officials, and not state magistrates."[11]

Arguably, the 1820 act to prevent kidnapping was the session's most historically significant law. But it was not the leading concern of the 1819–1820 Pennsylvania legislature. Instead, what to do about the distressed state of the economy, precipitated by the Panic of 1819, commanded the attention of citizens and legislators alike. Early in the 1819–1820 session, committees were appointed in both the Senate and House to inquire into the cause, effect, and legislative remedies for the economic crisis. The House committee was chaired by William J. Duane.[12]

William J. Duane (1780–1865) was the son of William Duane, the inspired, uncompromising, and hot-tempered editor of Philadelphia's *Aurora*. In spite of and because of President Jefferson's support, the elder Duane had been relentlessly attacked by his numerous enemies. The younger Duane, a lawyer, shared the political ideals of his father, but he had not inherited his father's penchant for getting into fistfights, costly personal legal battles, and chronic indebtedness. The son was elected to the Pennsylvania legislature in 1809, 1812, 1813, and 1819, the same year as Sallade. An old-school Democrat, Duane was one of the leaders in the 1819–1820 legislature. He was appointed to the judiciary and banking committees in addition to the select committee concerned with investigating the causes of the downturn in the economy.[13]

The select committee proposed five resolutions: the committee opposed the creation of a loan office to relieve indebted property owners, arguing that such a measure would be unjust and inadequate; they requested a resolution be sent to Congress, encouraging congressmen to protect the domestic economy with tariffs; they promoted public improvements, arguing that such public works would benefit the state as well as relieve the unemployed; they recommended that the commonwealth procure a loan to fund the improvements; and finally, they recommended that a plan for educating the "rising generation" for preventing future "evils and distress as are now suffered."[14] A motion was made to print the report, but Duane's opponents made a motion to postpone the question until the next Monday. That motion was agreed to, 49–40. Sallade voted with Duane's group not to postpone, indicating that he agreed with the report. On February 1, the select committee's resolutions came under consideration again, but Mr. Henry Jarrett (a Republican representing Northampton, Wayne, and Pike Counties) presented a stinging rebuttal to Duane's report and proposed alternative resolutions. In the end, neither Duane's nor Jarrett's resolutions were adopted, but both reports were printed. Notably the act to create a loan office failed to pass on a tie vote, Duane and Sallade voting to defeat the law.[15]

Meanwhile, in the state senate, Condy Raguet chaired the special committee that studied the economic collapse. Raguet's committee interviewed representatives from every district in the state. The Dauphin County representative questioned by the senate committee was Simon Sallade, and the testimony he gave leaves no doubt as to his opinion on the distressed state of the economy. For example, Sallade noted that in his district seven out of ten people were affected by the downturn. Specifically, the price of good improved land in 1809 was $16 to $24 per acre; in the spring of 1816 (the peak), it sold at $25 to $45 per acre, and in 1819, no more than $12 to $15 per acre. Further, Sallade's short and to-the-point responses to the state senate's questions offer a glimpse into his personal beliefs, especially about banks and banking. He was asked several questions related to the infamous forty-one bank bill of 1814. When asked, "What advantages do you conceive have been experienced by your section of the country from the introduction of the banking system, particularly as related to internal improvements?" he replied, "None at all." When asked, "Do you consider that the advantages have outweighed all the evils attendant upon the banking system?" he replied, "I do not." And when asked, "What was the motive which led to the establishment of so many banks?" he replied, "I believe the principle motive was speculation."[16]

In addition to interviewing representatives from every district in the state, the senate committee collected detailed statistical information from county prothonotaries (similar to county clerks) and sheriffs as well as the state auditor. The senate committee's report also showed the effect of the postwar downturn on the manufacturers in Philadelphia. For example, 1,761 people were employed in the cotton industry in 1814 compared to 149 people in 1819. Likewise, in a report from Pittsburgh, which was already emerging as an industrial center, the number of people employed in steam engine factories dropped from 290 in 1815 to 24 in 1819.[17] After completing its thorough investigation, the senate committee proposed resolutions such that the state subsidize loans to inhabitants upon landed security, that the commonwealth appropriate funds for internal improvements, and that the commonwealth limit the power of banks incorporated by the act of March 1814 (the forty-one bank bill).

A CONSIDERABLE PART OF THE 1819–1820 LEGISLATIVE AGENDA WAS dedicated to addressing the transportation needs of the state's citizens. Sallade was appointed to the Committee on Roads and Inland Navigation with William Lehman (1779–1829) of Philadelphia serving as chairman. Lehman, working in concert with a group of prominent Philadelphians led by Mathew Carey, was an ardent promoter of internal improvements. Among his numerous other engagements, Lehman was a member of a Philadelphia-based "Committee of Five," a group dedicated to reviving interest in construction of a crucial waterway connecting the Delaware and Chesapeake Bays. Another member of the Committee of Five of interest to my story was Simon Gratz (1773–1839); more on Gratz later.

With thirty-five members representing all the state's legislative districts, the Committee on Roads and Inland Navigation was the House's largest committee. Working on this committee clearly gave Sallade an opportunity to build relationships with legislators throughout the state. The committee had much work to do because all petitions (and there were hundreds of them) and all business relative to roads and inland navigation were referred to this committee. In addition, the committee was directed to prepare a report on the parts of the governor's message that had to do with roads and rivers. In the report, submitted by Lehman on January 26, 1820, the committee recommended that the state assist in the development of critical waterway communications and major turnpikes that would benefit the entire state, and forgo projects that would have only a sectional impact. The report spoke to the importance of these projects because they would bind the people of the state socially and commercially, in addition to its political union. The "first and foremost object" was "the completion of the projected canal between the rivers Susquehanna and Schuylkill."[18] Further, the committee cited the "laudable efforts" of neighboring states as a threat to Pennsylvania's heretofore dominance of the inland trade.[19] They were referring, of course, to New York's Erie Canal, then under construction, and Maryland's work on the Chesapeake and Ohio Canal. Moreover, to fund the projects, the committee proposed that the state borrow $2 million and create a sinking fund into which the revenues of the various projects would flow and which "in about twenty years would be adequate to the payment of interest, and the redemption of the principal."[20] In the end, after considerable discussion and legislative logrolling, the House approved a bill titled "An Act for Improvement of the State" on a 66–28 vote.[21] It is unknown whether Sallade concurred with the committee's proposed legislation because he did not vote. The Pennsylvania Senate, however, voted to postpone the bill, thereby killing it for the session.[22] Despite the loss of Lehman's bill, however, dozens of smaller projects were approved in the session.

THE 1819–1820 SESSION WAS DISTRACTED BY FACTIONALISM THAT took the form of appointing a special committee to inquire into possible corruption on the part of Pennsylvania's governor William Findlay. Findlay had drafted the banking act in 1814 that created forty-one banks, the creation of which the Old School Democrats blamed for the depressed state of the economy. The inclusion of seven representatives in the investigating committee selected from throughout the state and professing a variety of political persuasions probably served to neutralize what was clearly a partisan witch hunt. The final vote on the governor's conduct was not a straightforward call on whether to impeach. Instead, the legislature voted on a resolution as to whether the committee should be discharged from further consideration of the subject. In a clearly partisan vote, Sallade stood with Duane and others who opposed the governor. In the end no decision was made except to print the committee's reports and let the people decide in the next election whether Governor Findlay should continue to serve.[23]

THE 1820 GUBERNATORIAL ELECTION, A REPEAT OF THE CONTEST between William Findlay and Joseph Hiester, generated wide interest among voters and a controversy over the results. In Dauphin County, voter turnout had increased considerably from about 2,255 in 1819 to about 3,304 in 1820. Sallade and Rutherford were both reelected by a wide margin, carrying about 58 percent of the votes compared with 52 percent in 1819.[24] According to the November 18, 1820, issue of the *Oracle of Dauphin* (Harrisburg), the 1820–1821 House included forty-eight Democrats, thirty-five Federalists, eleven Old School Democrats, and three Binnites, a gain for Hiester's supporters.[25] The election for governor in Dauphin County showed a similar result: whereas Hiester had eked out a victory in 1817 with a margin of twenty-one votes, in 1820 he smashed Findlay with an overwhelming seven hundred vote margin.[26] Statewide, however, the results were close, and no sooner had the General Assembly convened than petitions contesting the election were brought before the Senate, thereby getting the 1820–1821 legislative session off to a bad start.[27] A really bad start.

The session opened with a dirty fight over who won the gubernatorial election. The contest was referred to a special committee of the General Assembly. While the outcome was still in doubt, however, a bill titled "An Act Reducing the Salaries of the Governor and the Secretary of the Commonwealth" was passed in the Senate and referred to the House on December 12. A nasty piece of work, the bill was a clear shot, a poison pill, aimed directly at Joseph Hiester, the incoming governor. The votes in the House on the bill on December 15 are interesting because they demonstrated what kind of parliamentary maneuvers Hiester's supporters used in an attempt to defeat the bill, and they clearly showed who was on which side of the partisan divide. In spite of delaying tactics, the House passed the bill 53–42, Sallade voting nay.[28]

Soon, on December 18, the results of the election were certified by the House and Senate in favor of Hiester. Then, on the same day, outgoing Governor Findlay delivered his final vengeful blow to his successor, his approval of the law that reduced Hiester's salary. Hiester's supporters weren't finished with the matter, however. On December 22 the members who had opposed the bill that reduced the governor's salary took the unusual step of submitting a protest. Citing their opinion that the act violated the Pennsylvania constitution, they closed their statement with the accusation that if the law "should be considered constitutional and legal…that the choice of a people electing a chief magistrate would be but mockery, inasmuch as the Legislature may deprive him of his salary, which would in effect deprive him of his office. We do therefore consider it a duty we owe to ourselves, to our contemporaries and to unborn generations, to protest against the passage of said bill."[29] The statement had no effect on the outcome, but it showed that the signers were men of principle, Simon Sallade among them.

The partisans were just getting warmed up. One of the most important tasks assigned to the legislature was the election to replace Jonathan Roberts, whose term in the US Senate expired on March 4, 1820. To fulfill their obligation, the House and Senate met in joint session on the afternoon of December 12, only a few hours after the obnoxious bill that proposed to reduce the incoming governor's salary had been introduced. The body failed to reach a decision after two votes, a majority being required to elect. Sallade cast his two votes on that day for Roberts. The session was postponed until January 16. In the second session, Sallade voted with a coalition of Federalists and Old School Democrats for Isaac Wayne. But the legislature remained deadlocked, and the special joint session adjourned sine die. Rather than compromise, the legislature was willing to leave Pennsylvanians without their full representation in the US Senate.[30] The House adjourned on April 3, 1821, and it was not until December 1821 that a newly elected legislature quickly elected William Findlay to fill the vacant Senate seat.

For his two years in the legislature, Sallade undoubtedly became more aware of state, national, and international issues. Further, he made contact with other government officials, businessmen, and lobbyists. The contacts that he made and the reputation that he developed as a conservative and thoughtful legislator during these years would serve him well in the future.

A year after Sallade returned home to his family, tragedy struck when his two oldest sons, Jonathan, age thirteen, and George, age eleven, passed away in August 1822.[31] To be sure, the family felt the pain of the losses as strongly as we would today. What was different was that childhood deaths were so common then that the community's rituals for commiserating and condoling the bereaved were well rehearsed. When a friend would say something like "I know how you feel," it probably meant that the friend had suffered a similar loss. The affected family grieved and usually moved on, enduring the emptiness in their hearts.

Considering the death of his two oldest boys, I can't help but wonder if Sallade was trying to run away from his grief when, in the fall of 1822, he was again nominated for the assembly and ran as a Federalist or Federalist Republican. This time, however, he was defeated, coming in last among the four candidates.[32] For a while at least, Sallade would remain close to his own hearth and home. Fifteen eventful years would pass before he would be elected to the legislature again. In the meantime, Sallade's career took an interesting turn.

CHAPTER 13

A PROJECT FROM HEAVEN

I n 1825 coal was discovered in Dauphin County. The coal fields were the western extensions of the Southern Anthracite coal field, which projected into the county in a fishtail-like configuration: the upper aspect of the tail was located on ridges within the confines of the Lykens Valley, while the lower aspect of the tail was located between the Second and Third Mountains, called the Stony Creek region. (See figure 17.) By broadening the economic base of the valley beyond farming, the discovery had an immediate and far-reaching effect on nearly everyone in the region, including Simon Sallade. Further, the potential for economic development attracted not only enterprising local investors but also influential Philadelphia merchants.

The first element of change involved a rush to buy all the unclaimed lands in the area, lands that had previously been considered worthless. The most aggressive local buyer was Thomas Elder of Harrisburg, who, between 1826 and 1830, swooped up at least nine thousand acres encompassing most of Dauphin County's coal lands. Elder, a son of Reverend John Elder—noted for his association with the Paxton Boys' massacre of 1763—was an attorney, businessman, and president of the Harrisburg Bank. Another large purchaser was Joseph Barnet, a descendant of one of Hanover Township's early settlers. Other local men who bought large parcels included Conrad Fry (or Frey), Joel Ferree, Henry Sheaffer, and Henry Schreiner. Sheaffer and Schreiner would become actively engaged in the coal business.

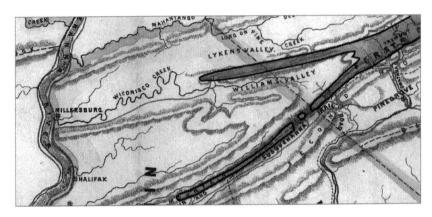

Figure 17. Map showing the extent of coal fields in the Lykens Valley, shown here as the Lykens-Williams Valley. William Lorenz, Map of the Canals and Railroads for Transporting Anthracite Coal from the Several Coal Fields to the City of New York; Drawn under the Direction of J. Dutton Steele, C. E. by W. Lorenz, Asst. Eng. (Baltimore, 1856), courtesy Library of Congress, https://www.loc.gov/item/98688361, and modified by author.

Last but not least among the local buyers was Simon Sallade. Beginning in December 1826 and continuing through October 1830, Sallade warranted twelve tracts of land scattered throughout several townships. Totaling 1,485 acres, his land was suitable for a variety of uses. Some parcels were speculative coal lands. One tract at the foot of Berry Mountain, later referred to as "Sallade flats," was on the path of the future railroad. He also acquired timberland and parcels located on Powell Creek: seemingly Sallade foresaw the coming demand for milled timber, both to shore up mine shafts and to build a railroad.[1]

One of Sallade's neighbors, Simon Gratz (1773–1839), was one of two Philadelphia merchants who bought property in the area. Adding to land he had inherited in the Lykens Valley, Gratz purchased one tract of 196 acres in Wiconisco Township and one of 306 acres in Jackson Township.

AMONG PENNSYLVANIA'S LEADING FAMILIES, THE GRATZES figure prominently in Pennsylvania history. Their story illustrates how people were often closely connected during the colonial period and the years of the early republic. Simon Gratz's father, Michael Gratz (1739–1811), and Simon's uncle Barnard Gratz (1730–1801), arrived in America in 1759 and 1754, respectively. As young men, they established themselves as trade merchants. Their businesses extended to North American and Caribbean ports and to the Indian trade on the frontier. Their initial contact with the Indian trade was through Joseph Simon (1712–1804), Michael's father-in-law and Simon Gratz's grandfather. Joseph Simon arrived in Lancaster, Pennsylvania, in about 1740. He established himself as a merchant, supplying local settlers with trade goods in exchange for their farm products. As one of Pennsylvania's leading "merchant venturers," he engaged with the Indians on the Pennsylvania frontier in the deerskin and peltry trade.[2] It was through their association with Mr. Simon that the Gratz brothers met George Croghan (c. 1718–1782). Croghan was the preeminent English trader and intermediary between Pennsylvania merchants and Ohio Valley Indians. Because of his command of the Iroquois and Delaware languages and his knowledge of Indian culture, he was appointed in 1756 as deputy Indian agent, with chief responsibility for the Ohio region, by Sir William Johnson, British superintendent of Indian affairs for the northern district. The Gratz brothers became Croghan's land agents, primary suppliers, creditors, friends, and eventually executors of his will. While dealing in the Indian trade, Croghan, the Gratz brothers, and Joseph Simon became involved in several speculative land ventures throughout the Indian country. One such deal, as an example of the magnitude of their purchases, included a grant of land that embraced the current southern half of Illinois.[3] However, many of the acquired lands came with clouded titles. After Croghan died in 1782, the task of clearing up the tangled web of financial transactions fell to the Gratz brothers, and after Michael Gratz died intestate in 1811, resolution of these problems landed in the lap of Simon Gratz and his brothers.[4]

Simon Gratz was also the "adopted" son of Aaron Levy (1742–1815). Levy was born in Amsterdam, Holland, and came to America in 1760. He speculated in land and Indian trading and soon became a prominent merchant in Northumberland County, which at the time included most of northern Pennsylvania. During the Revolutionary War he worked with Robert Morris, furnishing supplies to the colonial troops and loaning money to the Continental Congress. In 1778 Levy became a partner with Joseph Simon of Lancaster. It was there that he mentored the young Simon Gratz, who had begun his business career working as a clerk in his grandfather's firm. Having died in 1815 without an heir, Levy willed his estate including his landholdings to Simon Gratz, whom he named in his will as an adopted son.[5] Included in the inheritance were several tracts of land in the Lykens Valley, including a three-hundred-acre parcel on which Simon laid out the town of Gratz in Lykens Township. (See figure 18.)

By the time coal was discovered in the Lykens Valley in 1825, Simon Gratz was a well-established businessman. In 1798 he partnered with his brother Hyman in expanding the family business. Not only did he have responsibility for managing the family's vast landholdings, but Simon also had his own bank, the Schuylkill Bank; his own ships; and an expansive network of associates. Since transporting goods cheaply and quickly enhanced the profitability of his business, it was only natural that Mr. Gratz would be an advocate of improving Pennsylvania's transportation network. To this end, he was on the board of the Philadelphia and Pittsburgh Transporting Company and two other turnpike companies. Gratz also engaged in philanthropic activities. He was one of the founders of the Pennsylvania Academy of Fine Arts and a director of the Pennsylvania Botanical Garden. Gratz was also a trustee of Philadelphia's small but influential Congregation Mikveh Israel.[6]

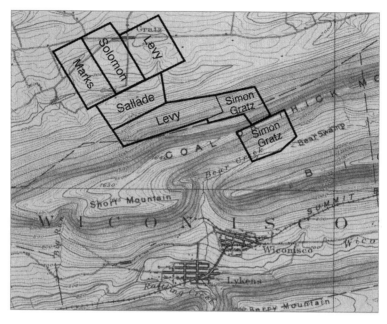

Figure 18. *Map showing approximate location of Sallade's original property relative to his neighbors, the Lykens Valley coal fields, and the borough of Gratz. Foreground: author drawing based on RG-17, Copied surveys, 1681-1912, (series # 17.114), Pennsylvania Historical and Museum Commission, Pennsylvania State Archives; Background: Lykens-Wiconisco topo- US Geological Survey, J. W. Powell, Director, Lykens, PA, 1892, (1898 ed.), https://ngmdb.usgs.gov/topoview/viewer/#*

How the history of the Gratz family and its landholdings relates to the story of Simon Sallade becomes crystal clear if one considers the proximity of Sallade's property to that under the purview of Mr. Gratz.[7] The original Sallade properties were nearly surrounded by properties controlled by Simon Gratz and his family's associates. Interestingly, two of the names on the warrantee township map never came up in the history of the Lykens Valley, and I wondered who the men were. Three hundred acres had initially been warranted to a Levy Marks (1737–1781), and an additional three hundred acres had been warranted to a Levi Solomon. (It is unknown who owned the properties in 1825 when coal was discovered.) As it turns out, Levy Marks, Levi Solomon, and the Gratzes were all affiliated with the Congregation Mikveh Israel. Levy Marks and Levi Solomon were in fact members of the congregation's initial governing body in 1773. Also on the governing body in that year were Simon Gratz's father, Michael, and Simon's uncle Barnard, who served as president of the board of directors.[8] Known as "the Synagogue of the American Revolution," the Congregation Mikveh Israel is the oldest continuous synagogue in the United States.[9] Considering his extensive landholdings in the Lykens Valley, it is no surprise that Simon Gratz would become involved with the developing coal trade and, further, that he would forge a close if not intimate relationship with his multitalented neighbor Simon Sallade.

Simon Gratz was not the only prominent Philadelphian to invest in the coal lands of the Lykens Valley. Thomas P. Cope (1768–1854) acquired 1,600 acres in the Bear Valley extending from the end of Short Mountain nearly to the Bear Creek Gap.[10] Perhaps Cope's purchase was facilitated by his Philadelphia associate, Simon Gratz. At the least, both men were involved with the construction of the Chesapeake and Delaware Canal: Gratz was one of Mathew Carey's 1821 Committee of Five activists charged with reviving interest in the stalled construction project, and Cope was a member and sometime president of the board of directors that oversaw its completion.[11]

Born in Lancaster County, Cope moved to Philadelphia in 1786. In 1790 he began his own mercantile business. During the yellow fever epidemics of 1793 and 1797, Cope remained in Philadelphia, where he ministered to the needs of the destitute. In 1807 he built his first ship, the *Lancaster*, and in 1821 he established the first packet line between Philadelphia and Liverpool, England. In addition to his business interests, Cope was active in the community. In 1807 he served in the Pennsylvania legislature. He was largely credited with bringing the construction of the Chesapeake and Delaware Canal to completion. He was among the founders of the Philadelphia Board of Trade and served as its president. He also helped establish and remained actively involved with the Mercantile Library Company. While still alive, Cope was referred to as a "merchant, enterprising, liberal, successful;—as a philanthropist, self-denying and devoted;—as a man, upright, respected, beloved."[12]

Mr. Cope's diary was published by Eliza Cope Harrison in 1978, but unfortunately, he did not make any entries between October 1820 and March 1843, the years of his involvement in the Lykens Valley coal trade. However, an interesting entry dated September 16, 1843, expresses a sentiment remarkably similar to the one written by Simon Sallade near the end of his life. To wit, Mr. Cope wrote, "When will men learn that more is gained by moderation, charity and persuasion than by acrimony, intemperate zeal and splenetic personal abuse? A man is not readily convinced by the calling of harsh names."[13] It appears that Mr. Cope and Simon Sallade were of one mind in their approach to life.

Both Gratz and Cope had experience organizing large-scale construction projects and seeing them through to completion. They were knowledgeable about new technologies regarding internal improvements, namely roads, turnpikes, and canals. They were aware of developments in a promising new means of transport: railroads. They had contacts with engineers. And they had deep pockets. Simon Sallade brought needed attributes to the table. He was an experienced legislator. He had knowledge of the local terrain and sound construction techniques. He knew local suppliers, craftsmen, and laborers, many of whom he had grown up with and counted as friends. It appears that these men, possessing complementary skills and committed to a levelheaded, fair-minded approach to business, were destined to succeed.

INITIALLY, BECAUSE COAL WAS ACCESSIBLE VIA CUTS IN THE terrain made by Bear Creek, it was mined in what were called drifts, a horizontal or nearly horizontal passageway running through the vein. There was no need to pump water, dig shafts, or employ new technology. Basically, mining the coal was a pick-and-shovel operation. The chunks of coal were then sold locally. By 1830 the extent of the Lykens coal field and the high quality of the coal was widely known. The fact that the field was close to markets in Baltimore, Lancaster, and other cities along the lower Susquehanna offered additional incentive to bring the coal to market. The problem the investors faced was how to transport the coal from the mines to the Susquehanna River, sixteen miles away. At some point between the time when the marketability of the coal was acknowledged and the spring of 1830, the group of men got together with the object of solving the problem.

Weighing their options, together these practical, knowledgeable men decided that a railroad would be the best means of transporting the coal. But they acknowledged that this technology was in its infancy. Indeed, in 1830 there were only about seventy miles of railroad functioning in the entire country, and most of those were motivated either by gravity, horsepower, or in the case of steep grades, by stationary engines that pulled the cars uphill. Although about a dozen railroads had been recently chartered in Pennsylvania, only three short lines in the Commonwealth and none in Dauphin County were in operation by 1830.[14] Domestic manufacture of locomotive engines was on the horizon, but the Baldwin Locomotive Works of Philadelphia would not complete its first locomotive engine, Old Ironsides, until November 23, 1832. Thus, the railroads of the 1830s were a far cry from the behemoths that would later be identified with the nineteenth-century transportation revolution. The men involved in the early phase of the transformation faced challenges inherent in adapting existing road-building methods to a new technology: how to construct a suitable roadbed, how to manufacture and lay the rails, how to construct and power the trains, and how to finance the project.

IN HIS MASTER'S THESIS, CHARLES L. SHEETZ INCLUDED INFORMA-tion from several primary sources including the original minute books of the Lykens Valley Railroad and Coal Company and corporate letters of patent. The company was incorporated by special act of the legislature of Pennsylvania on April 7, 1830. Men named as corporators in the act included Henry Sheaffer, Simon Sallade, Samuel Faunce, Daniel N. L. Reutter, Simon Gratz, John Barber, and James Buchanan.[15] Letters patent, which were required before the company could commence operations, were issued on December 18, 1830. In all, there were 109 people who subscribed to the initial sale of 519 shares of stock. Among the list of shareholders, Thomas P. Cope bought 150 shares, Simon Gratz and his family purchased 100 shares, Henry Schaeffer purchased 22, Henry Schreiner purchased 15, and Simon Sallade purchased 10. Along with the corporators, the familiar names of longtime Lykens Valley homesteaders appeared— Bowman, Gerhart, Woodside, Deibler, Lebo, Hoffman, Bickel, Fry, Unholtz, and Schott. Many of the locals bought only one or two shares, but the fact that the project had the support of the community as well as the financial backing of Philadelphians augured well for the success of the enterprise. Curiously absent among the stock buyers was Thomas Elder, the man who controlled the largest portion of the coal lands. And in a surprising entry, Simon Cameron (1799–1889), future US senator and secretary of war under Abraham Lincoln, bought ten shares of stock.[16]

Getting down to business, the election of officers took place at the company's first board meeting, held on January 19, 1831, in Millersburg. The board included president Thomas P. Cope; secretary John Paul Jr.; and managers Simon Gratz, Henry Schreiner, Henry Schaeffer, Simon Sallade, Samuel Faunce, Henry Kuntzelman, and Daniel N. L. Reutter.

I haven't found any information on Kuntzelman and Reutter. Samuel Faunce (1792–1856) was born in Cecil County, Maryland, and came to Dauphin County in 1826. At various times he engaged in construction, milling, farming, and merchandizing, and he owned a line of stages and canal boats. He was elected sheriff of Dauphin County in 1842. His son John E. was a member of the state legislature for many years, serving as speaker of the House of Representatives in 1883.[17] John Paul Jr., a talented craftsman, mathematician, inventor, carpenter, cabinetmaker, and surveyor, served as secretary of the Lykens Valley Railroad until 1855.[18] Noting that Paul's name appears alongside Sallade's in various ventures throughout their adult years, it seems that the two men were probably good friends.

With its leadership team in place, the project moved forward quickly. At a meeting on February 15, 1831, Simon Sallade was appointed superintendent of the project. His responsibilities included "attending the engineer at the survey and location and give attendance in making the whole of the road and that every man performs his duty well."[19] Sallade would be compensated at the rate of $1.50 for each day on duty. Considering that the Lykens Valley Railroad was among the first railroads in Pennsylvania, the prospect of being in charge of its construction must have been exciting for Sallade. Not only would he apply construction skills he had been practicing for years, but he would also organize the project into discrete, manageable elements; solicit bids; hire workmen; and troubleshoot problems.

On April 4, William Hamlin was appointed engineer to survey and lay out the railroad. Subsequently the route was adopted. Land was purchased from Thomas Elder and Jacob Haldeman at the western terminus of the railroad where coal would be transferred to arks, which would in turn carry the coal across the Susquehanna to the Pennsylvania Canal.[20]

While the company's minute book reveals the business aspect of the construction of the railroad, it is newspaper articles that capture the enthusiasm generated by the discovery of coal. An excerpt from an article originally published in the *Lancaster Journal* in early 1831 captures this optimism:

The engineers are now engaged in exploring a route for the rail road, which may occupy two or three weeks, when active operations will commence. We understand it is intended to divide the road into short sections from Millersburg to the mouth of Bear Hole Gap in the Short Mountain, and place sufficient force upon it to complete the whole line during the present year.... There are several sawmills contiguous to the line of the rail road, and others are about being erected. A brick yard on an extensive scale has been commenced. A new town contiguous to the mines has been laid out, called "Oak dale"...and another town will be laid out...for the accommodation of miners, mechanics, store-keepers and those who intend to enter into the coal trade.[21]

Of course the newspaper article was unrealistic in its hope that the railroad would be completed within the year. After all, the complicated project was the first of its kind for nearly everyone involved. Materials including suitable rock, timbers, rails, and fencing had to be procured. Railroad "cars" had to be built. Arrangements had to be made for transferring the coal across the Susquehanna to the Pennsylvania Canal. Living arrangements for the workers had to be secured. Nevertheless, progress continued apace, and construction began about November 1831.

As originally conceived and built, the Lykens Valley Railroad was a far cry from what we know today as a railroad. Rather, like many of its sisters, it would more correctly be described as a road with iron rails on it. Essentially, the "railroad" consisted of a pair of continuous large oak timbers on which a strip of iron was laid. The timbers rested on sleepers four feet apart. Great care was taken to ensure that the roadbed was structurally adequate to support the intended weight. A horse path in the center of the rails was topped with two inches of gravel. The project itself was built in sections, with about thirty such sections along the fifteen-mile route. Each section was built by local men who contracted with the company. In spite of a shortage of funds that required legislation so that the company could increase its capital, construction was completed in late 1833 or early 1834. According to Sallade, the total cost of the railroad was $69,838.02 (about $1.75 million in today's dollars), paid for by means of 2,025 shares of stock at $20, totaling $40,500; 101 part-shares, totaling $942; and loans payable in 1845, totaling $27,871.50.[22]

In April 1834, the first horse-drawn wagon containing forty-three tons of coal arrived at Millersburg and was shipped across the Susquehanna to the canal lock at Mount Patrick. It required two days to make the trip from the mines to Millersburg. An article from *Poulson's American Daily Advertiser* from late 1834 describes the rapid change that had taken place in four years. The mines were fourteen in number, and since they were divided by Bear Creek, they were equivalent to twenty-eight.

> The town of Wiconisco is very pleasantly situated. It consists of a large brick building, agent's residence, a large tavern house, kept by Mr. Sheaffer, whose table is well supplied with fresh salmon and rock, trout, and pike fish; with pheasants and venison;…a store, twelve miner's houses, saw mill, smith's shops, stables &c. The situation of the town is quite agreeable—is in the vicinity of a dense population—the extended and fertile valley called Lykens—this town must increase greatly—the first house was built in 1830–31.[23]

The railroad would continue in operation until 1845 by which time it was completely worn out. Between 1845 and 1848 the road was rebuilt to accommodate locomotive operation. In the biographical sketches about George McEliece, who arrived from Ireland in 1838, he is credited with working on the Lykens Valley Railroad. Most likely he was involved with maintaining the original railroad and, later, with its reconstruction.

Simon Sallade was among the class of men who laid the foundations for the great American railroad systems of the late nineteenth century. Today, fancy illustrated volumes have been dedicated to such colossi as the Pennsylvania and Reading Railroads.[24] But nostalgia for the good old days of railroading is nothing new. In the early twentieth century, men looked back with fondness to honor the pioneers of the industry, Charles Frederick Carter among them. About the early railroad men, he wrote, "These men built their railroads without the technical training needed to solve the profound engineering problems involved, without material to work with or money or credit to buy it, and even without a remote conception of what a railroad should be."[25] A giant, real-life, three-dimensional puzzle, their railroad was built with minimal directions and no picture to go by. In spite of these handicaps, or maybe because of them, the men involved with the construction of the Lykens Valley Railroad rose to the challenge and succeeded. Motivated primarily by a hope of financial gain, their success was due in large part to the abilities and harmonious relationships between Cope, Gratz, Sheaffer, Sallade, Paul, and others. Not only did they build a railroad, but they also created a management structure that utilized and enhanced each person's inherent strengths.

The Lykens Valley Railroad was extended about five miles to Williamstown in 1865. It continued to operate until after World War II, at which time it was controlled by the Pennsylvania Railroad through ownership of a majority of the stock. Sometime after that the railroad was abandoned and the tracks torn up. Today, a nonprofit group, Lykens Valley Rail Trail, is engaged in a multi-year commitment to build a trail along the route of the old Lykens Valley Railroad.

CHAPTER 14

BANK WARS AND LOGROLLING

———◆———

hile Simon Sallade was building the Lykens Valley Railroad, other Pennsylvanians were hardly sitting still. In Sallade's backyard, from Duncan's Island to the town of Northumberland, the state had completed a lateral extension of the Pennsylvania Canal. Authorized by the legislature in 1826, the Pennsylvania Canal began as a straightforward project intended to secure trade with the West and, ultimately, to connect with Lake Erie. As soon as the legislation was adopted, however, the need to obtain additional funding for the project was complicated by the need to secure votes from regions that would not directly benefit from the project. Therefore, in 1827 a process of legislative logrolling began that resulted in the state committing to building canals and railroads that covered the length and width of the state. Unfortunately, the state's plan to finance the projects lay somewhere between ridiculous and nonexistent. Consequently, by 1836 the state had amassed loans of $29 million without having made a realistic plan for meeting its obligation for payment of interest or principle.

Meanwhile, interstate and intrastate competition to secure the best railroad routes to the West was heating up. In New York, the New York and Erie Railroad, authorized to connect the Hudson River with Lake Erie at Dunkirk, had begun construction in 1836. In Maryland, the B&O was also being built. Yielding to competitive pressure, Pennsylvania, in its 1836 legislative session, had committed funds to survey three potential routes for a railroad across the Allegheny Mountains to either Pittsburgh or Erie. To finance this and other infrastructure projects, Pennsylvania's legislature approved a Faustian scheme.

Nicholas Biddle is most famous, of course, as the antagonist in president Andrew Jackson's Bank War, the losing fight to recharter the Second Bank of the United States. Less well known, perhaps, is what happened after the bank's charter expired in 1836. Well, the bank did not simply go away. Rather, a new charter, the Bank of the United States of Pennsylvania, was granted under the state's jurisdiction. Signed by governor Joseph Ritner on February 18, 1836, the bill had been introduced by Thaddeus Stevens, the chairman of the Committee on Inland Navigation and Internal Improvements in the state's House of Representatives. Lionized in history for his advocacy of the abolition of slavery and free public education, Stevens's role in Pennsylvania's chartering of the bank was anything but high-minded. On the contrary, as railroad historian Albert Churella observed, Stevens saw "the rescue of Biddle's bank as a mechanism to extort internal-improvement funds from the harried financier."[1] Coordinating his efforts as chairman of the internal improvements committee with Biddle's well-funded "militia" of lobbyists, Stevens scattered improvement monies throughout the state, thereby securing votes of wavering legislators for Biddle's bank bill. The bill—titled "An Act to Repeal the State Tax on Real and Personal Property and to Continue and Extend the Improvements of the State by Railroads and Canals, and to Charter a State Bank to be Called the United States Bank"—eliminated state taxes and wedded Biddle's bank to the funding of Pennsylvania's massive public works system.[2] By terms of its charter, the bank was required to pay a cash bonus to the state of $4.5 million, make a loan to the state of $1 million at 4 percent for a period not to exceed one year, invest $6 million in Pennsylvania stocks, and subscribe $675,000 to railroad and turnpike stocks. From that point forward, for better or worse, for richer or poorer, "the survival of the United States Bank of Pennsylvania and that of the Pennsylvania system of public works were inextricably tied to one another."[3]

The infrastructure/bank bill having been approved, activists in Erie sought to build support for a railroad route between Erie and Sunbury. They extended an invitation to leading citizens of several counties in which they recommended that a convention be assembled at Williamsport, Pennsylvania, on November 16, 1836. From Dauphin County, Simon Sallade and Simon Cameron were among the selected delegates. In Philadelphia, Nicholas Biddle and fifteen others, including Simon Gratz, organized a meeting to select that city's delegates.[4]

By the time the railroad convention assembled, however, Biddle's newly issued bank charter was already in jeopardy. Vigorously reacting to the bank bill, Democrats successfully used the unpopular law as a rallying cry in the October 1836 election, thereby increasing their membership in the Pennsylvania House of Representatives from thirty-one to seventy-two. Thaddeus Stevens was one of the casualties of the election, and Simon Sallade, elected as a Democrat, was among the legislators swept in on the anti-bank tide.[5]

Immediately before taking office, Sallade traveled to Williamsport, where he joined railroad supporters from sixteen counties for the railroad convention. At its first session, Biddle was chosen as chairman of the convention. Sallade was among those appointed to the committee "to report proceedings for the action of the convention."[6] The committee offered several resolutions for the consideration of the assembly, all of which were adopted. In hindsight, the resolutions reveal a conflict between the dreams of the conventioneers and the reality of the state's financial situation. Specifically, the pie-in-the-sky resolutions called for legislation to incorporate a railway between Erie and Sunbury, for aid from the state in the form of a subscription to fund the project, for the state to attend to the railways between Sunbury and Philadelphia and Sunbury and Harrisburg, for an extension of the west branch of the canal, and for a connection of the west branch canal to the Allegheny River and Lake Erie.[7] The delegation from each county was requested to sign a memorial, procure signatures from their constituents, and lay the petitions before the legislature. Then the convention adjourned. Historically unimportant in itself, the railroad convention mirrored the unrealistic thinking that prevailed at the time. I wonder if Sallade, an advocate of internal improvements and an opponent of the Bank of the United States of Pennsylvania (BUSP), recognized the tension between the two goals. As a member of the state legislature, he would have no choice but to come to grips with two mutually exclusive objectives.

When the 1836–1837 House convened on December 6, committee assignments were announced. Sallade was appointed to three: Domestic Manufactures, Lands (of which he was chairman), and Inland Navigation and Internal Improvements. Sharing the honors with Sallade on the Internal Improvements committee was Joseph McIlvaine of Philadelphia, who succeeded Thaddeus Stevens as committee chairman. In fact, prior to being elected to the legislature, McIlvaine had been one of Biddle's principal lobbyists during the previous session in which the bank won its Pennsylvania charter. In the current session, McIlvaine would continually report his activities to Biddle, and he would use his position as chairman of the committee to manipulate the provisions of an internal improvements bill, thereby ensuring that any hostile action toward the bank would be defeated. Simply put, the game was rigged at the outset. And Sallade was blessed with a front-row seat to watch the game play out.

Before he got sucked into the vortex of the struggle between the anti-bank men and Nicholas Biddle's militia, however, Sallade tended to the usual business of the legislature. On December 12 he followed through on his commitment to muster support for the incorporation of the Sunbury and Erie Railroad by submitting three petitions from Dauphin County inhabitants "to make a railway from Erie to Sunbury, and for the extension of the Susquehanna and little Schuylkill railway from Catawissa to the West Branch and for the construction of a railway from Sunbury to Harrisburg, and for aid to the said works."[8] Other petitions of like purpose were submitted by legislators from around the state, and on April 3, 1837, a bill titled "An Act to Incorporate the Sunbury and Erie and the Pittsburgh and Susquehanna Railroad Companies" was signed by Governor Ritner. (In spite of the efforts of the railroad's supporters, the newly granted Sunbury and Erie Railroad charter would gather dust, and construction of the Sunbury and Erie Railroad would not begin until 1852.) During the session Sallade also assumed responsibility for some of the legislature's typical business, and dozens if not hundreds of issues were adroitly managed by the legislature.

Successes notwithstanding, it was the war between Biddle and his anti-bank foes that dominated the session. Historian Charles M. Snyder, in a colorful chapter titled "Nourishment for the Monster," details how the war played out.[9] On February 8, 1837, a bill intended to clip the bank's wings—"an act to prevent the president, directors and company of the Bank of the United States, from subscribing to or holding stock in any railroad company or other internal improvements of this commonwealth"—was passed in the House.[10] The bill passed 57–32, Sallade voting with the majority. The bill would have amended the terms of the original bank charter, but it died in the Senate. (By 1839 nearly one-sixth of the BUSP's earning assets would be in stock accounts that would have been prohibited if this bill had become law.[11])

In other action, John Hill of Westmoreland County fired a salvo against the BUSP when he introduced a resolution "that a committee of seven be appointed to inquire into the mode, manner and means by which" the bank law had been enacted in the previous session.[12] After the resolution was approved by a vote of 82–11, McIlvaine and his sycophants sprang into action and managed to organize the committee so that its members lacked both legislative "experience and legal talent."[13] Further, in engineering the committee's proceedings, McIlvaine ensured that "the investigation was limited to the testimony of a handful of witnesses, made up for the most part of members of the previous session" who were friendly to the BUSP.[14] Ex-legislator and Biddle's buddy Thaddeus Stevens was the star witness.[15]

McIlvaine did not rely solely on influencing a committee over which he did not have direct control. He also used his post of chairman of the internal improvements committee to "carefully nurture the improvement bill so as to keep its progress parallel" with the investigation of the BUSP.[16] His bill, No. 311, "an act further to continue and promote improvements of the state," swelled to include appropriations totaling $3,031,943 in order to appease anti-bank men.[17]

By this time, 1836–1837, momentum was building to extend the canal system in order to accommodate the burgeoning coal industry along the Susquehanna from Wilkes-Barre down to Lykens Valley. The coal fields in the Lykens Valley had proved to be extensive. It was asserted that "in less than ten years, that such an amount of coal will pass down the Susquehanna, that more sloops will be loaded at its mouth, than are now employed in the coasting trade of the whole Union" and that in "Lykens Valley, only eighty miles from tide…are fortunes to be made."[18] Undoubtedly, the prospect of securing state funds to build a canal on the east side of the Susquehanna from the mouth of Wiconisco Creek to the lock at Duncan's Island seemed to be a realistic idea when Sallade was elected to the Pennsylvania General Assembly. Coal had been transported from the Lykens Valley mines to the Susquehanna since April 1834. But the transfers from the trains to barges, and then from barges to coal chutes near the Mount Patrick lock (on the opposite side of the river), and then to canal boats were clumsy and costly. In the milder months of the year, and especially in the summertime, the low flow of the river sometimes prevented the crossing. So the managers of the coal mines and the managers of the Lykens Valley Railroad collaborated in proposing the Wiconisco Canal.[19]

On March 21, Sallade moved to amend McIlvaine's improvement bill by inserting the following words: "That the canal commissioners be authorized and required to locate and contract for the construction of a navigable feeder of dimensions not less than those of the Pennsylvania canal with the works appurtenant, that is to say, from the canal at Clark's ferry, up the eastern side of the Susquehanna river, to the mouth of Wiconisco Creek, and that of the Lykens Valley rail road, towards which the sum of forty thousand dollars is hereby specifically appropriated."[20] The amendment was narrowly approved, 46–45.[21]

The internal improvement bill passed the House and the Senate and was sent to the governor for his signature only a few hours before the committee investigating the BUSP made its report. But last-minute turmoil ensued on March 24 when George Espy, representative from Venango County, "offered an amendment to the [investigating] committee's report which instructed the Judiciary Committee to bring in a bill repealing the charter of the bank."[22] The amendment put the anti-bank men in a tight spot. If they voted in favor of the amendment, would they thereby risk losing appropriations for their pet projects? After a disruption, the amendment failed on a vote of 31–60, Sallade voting with the majority. In voting against the repeal of the bank charter, Sallade revealed that his desire to obtain funding for the canal project was his highest priority.

But the drama was not over yet. On April 3 Governor Ritner sent a veto message on the improvement bill to the assembly. An attempt to override the veto won a majority, Sallade voting in favor, but the vote failed because a two-thirds majority was necessary to override a veto. Immediately thereafter, McIlvaine offered a well-crafted resolution that amounted to a watered-down improvement bill. That McIlvaine's resolution had been prepared in advance there can be little doubt. It points to the probability that he had been apprised of the governor's intent to veto the original improvement bill, and it raises the question of whether Biddle, McIlvaine, and Ritner had been playing a game of rope-a-dope all along. In any event, the watered-down improvement bill, which excluded a provision for Sallade's pet project, the Wiconisco Canal, failed on a vote of 34–57, Sallade voting with the majority.[23]

The governor's veto of the improvement bill, combined with legislators' failure to stand firm in their opposition to the bank, put

Sallade and other anti-bank men out on a limb. Now they had to return to their constituents empty-handed. Worse, they had voted against the Espy amendment to repeal the charter of the BUSP. Hoping to salvage their reputations and neutralize criticism by their constituents, twenty democrats, including Sallade, submitted for the record an explanation of their vote against the March 24 Espy amendment. While the claims they made in the explanation are credible, the timing of releasing the statement—soon after the demise of the improvement bill was certain, and too late in the session for the legislature to take action—suggests that, now that all hope was lost, the men had nothing to lose in disavowing their vote against the Espy amendment. They proclaimed their belief that "in truth and sincerity" the existence of the bank was "inimical to the well-being of society, if not to social and political liberty."[24] Although the statement got buried in the *House Journal*, it was subsequently published in *Niles' Weekly Register*, one of the most widely circulated magazines in the United States at the time.[25]

Sallade's performance in the 1836–1837 session was mixed. While he apparently functioned well in his role as chairman of the lands committee and on other incidental duties to which he was assigned, he failed to secure funding for projects important to his constituents—the Wiconisco Canal and the railroad between Sunbury and Harrisburg. I wish he had kept a diary because it would be interesting to know what he thought about the session and his role in it. Was he disillusioned with the legislative process? Was he embittered by the manipulations carried out by Nicholas Biddle and his followers? Was he concerned about Pennsylvania's faltering financial situation? Was he worried about the reception he would receive when he returned home? The answers are impossible to know. By all accounts Sallade was an even-tempered man and not inclined toward gloomy thoughts. Chances are he shrugged his broad shoulders, acknowledged his defeats, defended his votes, and continued to fight for the interests of the people in his district—especially for the elusive Wiconisco Canal.

CHAPTER 15

A PROJECT FROM HELL

In spite of the failure to win a grant for the Wiconisco Canal during the 1837 legislative session, Simon Sallade persisted in his effort to secure funding for the project. Fortunately for Sallade and his associates, 1838 was an election year for Pennsylvania governor. At the time, the most reliable way to win votes was through a calculated use of the state treasury, and in Pennsylvania the subsidies were inseparable from the State Works, its publicly funded infrastructure. Thus, on April 14, 1838, Governor Ritner, the Anti-Masonic Party candidate who hoped to win a second term, signed an improvement bill that revived many of the projects that were lost when he vetoed the improvement bill of the 1836–1837 session. Included in the $1,952,344 bill were appropriations of $20,000 for the Wiconisco Canal and $10,000 for construction of an outlet lock at Duncan's Island. To oversee the spending, Governor Ritner appointed three of his most stalwart allies to the Canal Commission: Elijah F. Pennypacker, John Dickey, and Thaddeus Stevens, who was elected as the commission's chairman. The Wiconisco Canal project was about to become a pawn in the Ritner reelection campaign.

Historian Charles M. Snyder continued to follow this tumultuous period in Pennsylvania history. Under the direction of Stevens, he wrote, the commission "set to work to transform the improvements into a gigantic political machine for the cause of Antimasonry."[1] But the methods employed by Ritner's supporters were not revealed until 1839—after Ritner had lost the election.

Read on June 15, 1839, before the Pennsylvania House of Representatives, the "Report of the Committee Appointed to Investigate the Conduct of the Late Board of Canal Commissioners" was a scathing indictment of the canal commissioners' misuse of public funds.[2] Among its numerous allegations, the report disclosed that contracts on the Wiconisco Canal project, awarded August 8, 1838, at Halifax, had been given only to men who supported Governor Ritner in the upcoming gubernatorial contest. Further, it was alleged that Stevens had directed John Rutherford, superintendent of the project at the time, to require the successful contractors to contribute to a "missionary" fund.[3] The missionary fund was to pay for "handbills, circulars, and for other electioneering purposes," and worse yet, the engineer (Rutherford) was to allow the cost of this contribution in the construction estimates.[4] In other words, the Ritner reelection campaign would be funded by the state's taxpayers. Sallade was among the witnesses in the investigation. Avoiding political commentary, he testified that the cost of the contracts on the Wiconisco Canal would have been $20,000 less if rejected bids had been accepted.[5] (Sometime in the 1838 session, additional funds must have been appropriated to the Wiconisco Canal project.)

The minority on the investigative committee (Ritner's supporters) offered a strong rebuttal. Among other items, the June 24, 1839, minority report included John Rutherford's sworn affidavit in which he denied the charges against him. The report also elaborated on Sallade's testimony. To wit, on questioning by Thaddeus Stevens, Sallade acknowledged that he considered "some of the contracts let at a fair price and some of them low enough" and he didn't "consider any of them extravagant."[6]

Were it not for another report submitted to the House, the conflicting majority and minority reports on corruption of the late canal board would be inconclusive. But on June 18, 1839, the hammer came down when James R. Snowden, chairman of a committee appointed to enquire into the causes of the disturbances at the seat of government (Harrisburg) in December 1838, read his report about the Buckshot War, another notorious incident in Pennsylvania's political history.[7]

In retrospect, accounts of the Buckshot War, in which government officials attempted to subvert the electoral process, read like a tale from a corrupt banana republic. Despite the efforts of Ritner's supporters, he lost the gubernatorial election to David R. Porter. Unwilling to concede defeat, his supporters, including representatives at the highest level of government as well as local judges and officials, hatched an elaborate scheme to overrule the vote of the people and retain control of the House of Representatives. As reported by Snowden's committee, the difficulties

> had their origin in a fraud concocted by certain federal return judges in the county of Philadelphia, with the advice and co-operation of William B. Reed, the Attorney General of the Commonwealth, and John G. Watmough, sheriff of the city and county of Philadelphia, by which the regularly elected members of the House of Representatives, were iniquitously attempted to be deprived of their seats; a fraud which Thomas H. Burrowes, secretary of the Commonwealth under Governor Ritner, and Thaddeus Stevens, one of his canal commissioners…attempted to consummate— the former [Burrowes], by suppressing the legal election returns of said county; and the latter [Stevens], by attempting to organize the legislature in a manner unknown to the constitution and laws.[8]

For his part in the upheaval, Governor Ritner abused his power as commander in chief of the state militia by calling up troops—first from Philadelphia, later from Carlisle Barracks—to suppress what he falsely claimed to be an insurrection.

The ringleader of the fracas in Harrisburg was none other than Thaddeus Stevens. It was under his direction that John Rutherford and the so-called Halifax bullies took command of the state arsenal at Harrisburg. The Halifax bullies, it was said, were the toughest men in the county. They included Wiconisco Canal contractors James McCoy, John P. Leebrick, James Martin, and others.[9] Eventually both the civil and the military coups d'état failed. The civil coup fell apart when three Whigs abandoned the illegal scheme for taking control of the legislature, and the military coup failed when officers declined to obey Ritner's illegal orders. For his part in the troubles, Rutherford lost his job as superintendent of the Wiconisco Canal project, and Sallade was named in his place on February 13, 1839.

Cleaning up the political mess would be a manageable challenge for Sallade, who had an engaging yet commanding demeanor. His ability to organize and supervise a construction project had already been proven during the construction of the Lykens Valley Railroad. He had also done contract work for the state on the Swatara feeder canal, a branch of the Union Canal that connected the Schuylkill and Susquehanna Rivers. But political issues and construction work were the least of Sallade's problems. The biggest obstacle he faced involved negotiating the troubled waters of Pennsylvania's financial crisis—a problem that would take many years to resolve.

PENNSYLVANIA'S FINANCIAL CRISIS IN THE YEARS BETWEEN 1839 and 1843 is legendary. In 1835 the interest payment on the state's $25 million debt was $1,169,455, nearly twice the toll revenue of $684,357. In 1836 the state got a reprieve when the Bank of the United States of Pennsylvania (BUSP) paid the state its charter bonus of $2 million. And in 1837 the state got more help when it received its share of a distribution of the federal surplus amounting to $2.9 million.[10] Rather than apply the windfall to its outstanding debt, however, the state went on another construction binge. Benefitting from an artificially low interest rate when the BUSP extended a line of credit worth $6 million, the state started borrowing again: $15,000 in 1838, $6,289,000 in 1839, $3,754,000

in 1840, and $3,159,000 in 1841. The state's total debt in 1841 was
$36,366,000.[11]

By 1841 the BUSP was no longer in a position to help the flail-
ing state. In his desperate attempt to keep the bank afloat in the
aftermath of the Panic of 1837, Biddle had transformed the bank
from a conservative institution to a speculative entity. Rather than
restricting investments to high-quality, short-term commercial
paper, the bank engaged in risky transactions including investment
banking, international borrowing and merchant banking, and
commodity speculation.[12] After its investments turned sour, the
BUSP suspended specie payments in October 1839 because of a
run by New York and Boston banks.[13]

In response to the looming financial crisis, the state also
resorted to desperate measures. Although the legislature in 1840
had belatedly adopted a tax bill that included levies on both personal and real property, revenue generated from the tax would
not be sufficient to meet the state's expenses for several years. In
February 1841 the state attempted to force the BUSP to resume
specie payments, whereupon the bank went out of business. As a
result, the state was forced into the regular credit markets, causing the yields on Pennsylvania bonds to rise from 6.01 percent in
January 1841 to 9.5 percent just three months later. By the fourth
quarter of 1841, its rate stood at 11.42 percent—that is, junk bonds.
In November 1841, "Pennsylvania announced that it would require
a loan from all banks in the state equal to 5% of their capital."[14]
Word on the street was that Pennsylvania was "carrying out its
threat to make the banks sustain the state credit through forced
loans."[15] And in February 1842, "the state precipitated a banking
panic in Philadelphia when it attempted to withdraw funds from
the Bank of Philadelphia necessary to cover the interest payments
due that month."[16] However, when the state finally made it clear
in April 1842 that it would not force more loans upon the state's
banks, the crisis was over.[17] Pennsylvania finally faced its problem
when the state was unable to sell its bonds at any price, when its
revenues fell far short of its expenses, and when its golden goose,

the BUSP, closed its doors. The state defaulted on its loans in August 1842. Other states that defaulted subsequent to the Panic of 1837 included Indiana, Florida, Mississippi, Arkansas, Michigan, Illinois, Maryland, and Louisiana. Some of the states, including Pennsylvania, eventually resumed payment on their debt; others repudiated their debt entirely.[18]

Although the ill-advised chartering of the BUSP was intimately intertwined with Pennsylvania's financial problem, the root of the problem lay in Pennsylvanians' aversion to taxation of any sort and their delusions about their beloved public works. As historian T. K. Worthington aptly concluded late in the nineteenth century:

> A Pennsylvanian always lost his common sense when the public works were mentioned, and the public men lost their wits—or pretended to—more completely than anyone else. It was one of the most marked influences of the public works, that the people were infected with an intense conviction that, in the near future, they would return enough revenue to pay the cost of their construction, with interest, to support the common schools, to provide for the expenses of government, and, in some mysterious way, to convert the state into a paradise.[19]

Thus, Simon Sallade's timing relative to building the Wiconisco Canal could not have been worse. Between the time when the initial canal bill was passed in 1838 and the time when Pennsylvania defaulted on its debt in 1842, a total of $304,837 had been appropriated for the Wiconisco Canal. Whether the entire amount had been expended is unclear. In the Canal Commission's report dated November 1839, state engineer A. B. Warford reported that "should funds sufficient be provided, it may be completed by the next fall."[20] In the report for November 1840, it was said that

> this work is in such a state of forwardness as to render its completion practicable by August next [1841], if the nec-

essary appropriation should be made for the purpose. The appropriation of last session [1840] was exhausted on the 15th of August, and the usual notice of the fact was given to the contractors. Most of them, however, on the presumption that the Legislature would make an early appropriation, have since been prosecuting their respective contracts with their own means and on their own responsibility, so that there is now due them $58,083.[21]

On February 13, 1841, John C. McAllister was appointed as superintendent of the project, succeeding Sallade. On November 30, 1841, it was reported that "no appropriation having been made the last session [1841] to prosecute the work, the contractors have done very little during the season," and the engineer reported that "the cost of making this canal will doubtless be considerably increased in consequence of its remaining in its present unfinished state; for the materials delivered for the mechanical work will probably be injured, the embankments will be washed down by the rains and floods, and some of the jobs it is supposed will be abandoned. An early appropriation would enable us to complete it by next fall."[22]

But the well had run dry, and no appropriations were made. In response, Sallade and others successfully petitioned the legislature, and by Act No. 113, signed into law on July 13, 1842, the Wiconisco Canal Company was authorized to incorporate. The commissioners for the act were a diverse group including many of the canal's contractors, local coal land owners, and individuals from the city of Philadelphia and the counties of Lancaster, York, Lycoming, and Bucks. Authorized to sell five thousand shares at $20 each, the commissioners—probably due to the state's default, the depressed state of the economy, and a competing need for cash to rebuild the Lykens Valley Railroad, or a combination of the three—failed to organize the corporation.[23] Construction of the Wiconisco Canal, for the time at least, was abandoned.

Meanwhile, during the years since the Lykens Valley Railroad had been completed in 1834, Lykens Valley coal had been transported more or less continually. In 1840 alone, the Lykens Valley Coal Company had sold 5,200 tons of coal at a value of $15,207. By 1841 the superstructure of the railroad was wearing out and would soon need to be replaced with T-rails, fit to bear trains powered by locomotives. Further, the railroad needed to be regraded and straightened. Sallade, who had continued through the years in his role as one of the directors of the Lykens Valley Railroad, estimated the cost of the needed repairs at $98,963.[24] The railroad hobbled along, doubtlessly requiring increasing resources for maintenance, until 1845 when its use was discontinued. Sallade supervised the reconstruction of the railroad between 1846 and 1848.[25]

By February 1845, the property tax that was legislated during the financial crisis had generated enough revenue for the state to resume interest payments. The general state of the domestic economy had also recovered. It was at this time that Sallade and others petitioned the state for a second time for a charter to incorporate the Wiconisco Canal Company. Most of the commissioners named in the act had an obvious interest in the success of the canal company.[26] The act, No. 100, signed by Governor Shunk on March 13, 1845, authorized the corporation to sell three thousand shares at $20 each. The leading shareholders were the Gratz family, 897 shares; George H. Thompson, 200 shares; and Thomas Elder, 194 shares. As with the Lykens Valley Railroad, the members of the local community endorsed the project with their purchases of one to ten shares, Sallade buying five shares.[27] The state was generous to the company, allowing it to take possession of the canal and building materials at no cost to the company and with limited provisos. Specifically, the company had to begin construction within two years and complete construction within three years, and the state retained the right to resume possession of the canal after January 1, 1853.[28] Stock in the company sold quickly, and the canal was completed.

Finally, by 1848, with the Wiconisco Canal completed and the Lykens Valley Railroad rebuilt, coal and other products of the Lykens Valley moved efficiently to markets. But the troubles were not over yet. In an article in which he considered the economic importance of the canal to Upper Dauphin County, geographer Paul G. Marr brought to light some of the technical details surrounding the construction project. One of the problems had to do with the water supply. He wrote, "Unfortunately, during periods of drought or low flow, the creek could not supply enough water to operate the canal" and "fully loaded boats were having an increasingly difficult time using the canal."[29] The solution decided on was to construct a waterwheel at Millersburg to raise water to the canal from the Susquehanna River. "The wheel was constructed and put into operation in 1849."[30] Sadly, a dispute arose between the Wiconisco Canal Company and the Lykens Valley Coal Company, which had funded the project. The dispute was eventually resolved in favor of the canal company. I do not know if Sallade was involved in this construction activity and its resultant litigation. It appears that control of the Wiconisco Canal Company at that time was in the hands of Edward Gratz, Elder, and Thompson, the largest shareholders.[31]

According to the Historic American Engineering Record, the Wiconisco Canal continued to carry Lykens coal for several years. However, "years of marginal returns and costly repairs meant but meager dividends for the original investors....Because yearly returns seldom exceeded $3,000, it is not surprising that in November 1871 control of the Wiconisco was taken over by the Pennsylvania Canal Company, a subsidiary of the Pennsylvania Railroad....A flood in May 1889 destroyed much of the canal; it was closed in 1890 and not reopened."[32] Today, the most enduring structure of the canal, the aqueduct over Powell Creek, is part of State Route 147 and is listed on the National Register of Historic Places. (See figure 19.)

*Figure 19. View looking northwest at Wiconisco Canal
Aqueduct No. 3, spanning Powell Creek at State Route 147, Halifax,
Dauphin County, Pennsylvania. Courtesy of the Library of Congress,
https://www.loc.gov/resource/hhh.pa3667.photos/?sp=1.*

How different were Sallade's experiences in working on the Lykens Valley Railroad and the Wiconisco Canal. The former, with its opportunity for innovation, solid planning and execution, and an effective management team, was a project made in heaven. The latter, with its political and financial headaches, frequent work stoppages, changes in management, and corporate feuds, was a project straight out of hell. Above all, both projects illustrate the kinds of challenges that men like Sallade faced on a daily basis. And they highlight the importance of those middlemen—neither business titans nor laborers—who engineered and built America's first transportation system.

CHAPTER 16

SEASONED POLITICIAN

B etween his work on the Lykens Valley Railroad and the Wiconisco Canal, Simon Sallade had dedicated at least eighteen years of his life to building vital infrastructure in his community. But there was much more to this man than his work-a-day life. Although his pocket memoranda are faded and barely legible, his personal involvement with the people in his neighborhood is clearly indicated in his notes chronicling transactions from 1846 through 1848. Whether serving as executor of various estates, transacting financial business with his neighbors and business partners, selling products from his farm, or keeping financial accounts for the local school district, his notes reveal a man with a variety of interests. In 1846, while serving as treasurer for the Washington School District in Dauphin County, he recorded an income statement. On February 4, 1847, he "made a bargain with Christian Orendorff [sp?] for a field of land joining his other land."[1] In one of several transactions dealing with farm produce, on April 28, 1847, he sold four bushels of oats and one-half bushel of Long John potatoes to Cyrus Buffington for $1.81.[2] He was not averse to lending money to people in the neighborhood. On March 2, 1847, he received of M. Novinger $300 toward payment of a note at Harrisburg Bank.[3] On April 10, 1847, he loaned $51.66 to Isaac Flak [sp?] and on April 1, 1848, he loaned his friend John Paul Jr. $233.17.[4] Sallade was also entrusted with the administration of several estates. Specifically mentioned in the Sallade-Bickel Papers are John Deiterich, Philip Haman, and Edward Bickel.[5]

Simon and Jane became grandparents. Their daughter Margaret married John Bowman, descendant of one of Lykens Valley's early settlers. Their children were John F. Bowman, born January 2, 1841; Simon Sallade Bowman, born October 10, 1842; and Levi B. Bowman, born December 14, 1846. The couple suffered a devastating loss when Margaret gave birth to triplets on September 24, 1844; the infant son and two daughters died on the same day. Anna Sallade married Edward Bickel, and by 1850 they had two children, Simon Bickel, born circa 1842, and Matilda Bickel, born circa 1846. Jane Sallade married David K. Smith, and they had three children by 1850: Charles W., born circa 1846; Sarah F., born circa 1847; and Oliver, born circa 1849. It's easy to imagine Simon and Jane helping the young families, shamelessly indulging their little grandchildren with special treats and enjoying the gleeful pandemonium of family gatherings.

In 1848 Simon Sallade was nominated at the Dauphin County Democratic Convention to run for a seat in the state legislature.[6] Whether he lost the election or declined the nomination is unclear, but by then Dauphin County's electorate overwhelmingly supported the Whigs.

In 1853, a year in which "no burning issues or spirited races, national or State, enlivened [the] campaign," Sallade, at the age of sixty-eight, ran for and was elected to the Pennsylvania House of Representatives for the fourth time.[7] When the session convened in January 1854, Sallade was appointed to the agriculture and the domestic manufactures committees. Issues of particular interest to him that were approved in the session included a bill to allow the Wiconisco Canal Company to increase its tolls and a bill to incorporate the Lykens Valley Mutual Fire Insurance Company.[8]

After the legislative session concluded, the insurance company was organized on June 3, 1854, and Sallade was elected as its first president in which office "he applied his wisdom and ability during the formative months of the company."[9] Coincidentally, one of the first policy holders was Jacob Frederick Eisenhower, grandfather of President Eisenhower. Sallade purchased his own policy on the same day as Jacob Eisenhower and is listed immediately above Eisenhower in a copy of the first policy register, which was written by John Paul Jr. with a goose quill pen. Could it be that Sallade and Eisenhower were next-door neighbors?[10]

The Wiconisco Canal and insurance company acts were among several uncontroversial laws approved in the 1854 session. But true to form, Pennsylvania politics were never dull. At the time, a contest raging in New York, Ohio, and Pennsylvania over control of railroads passing through Erie, Pennsylvania, had turned violent when the people in Erie repeatedly tore up the tracks wherever they crossed the city's streets, a conflict that came to be known as the "Erie War of the Gauges." Historian Donald H. Kent observed that "the immediate cause of the Erie war was the attempt to eliminate the break or difference in railroad gauges between the two east-west lines which connected at Erie."[11] Erieites wanted to retain the difference in railroad gauges because Erie's businesses profited when passengers were forced to transfer between trains. Passengers often missed their connections and consequently had to purchase meals and lodging in Erie. Likewise, cargo had to be transferred, thereby offering employment for several men. If a standard gauge was adopted, the Erie economy would take a hit. Kent continued: "The underlying cause of the Erie war lay in the struggle for commercial leadership and economic advantage" in controlling trade with the Midwest.[12]

A sign of future railroad battles, in the Pennsylvania House of Representatives, the War of the Gauges debate centered on bills relating to the Franklin Canal Company; the Cleveland, Painesville, and Ashtabula Railroad (CP&A); and the Sunbury and Erie Railroad. (In 1851, influential citizens revived the Sunbury and Erie Railroad project, which lay dormant since it had been organized after the 1836–1837 legislative session.) Briefly, by an act approved on January 28, 1854, Pennsylvania had revoked the charter of the Franklin Canal Company and leased the railroad that the Franklin

Canal Company had built—from Erie to the Ohio state line—to the CP&A, an Ohio company. Later in the session, Governor William Bigler approved an act on May 5, 1854, titled "An Act Relating to the Sunbury and Erie Railroad Company, and the Cleveland, Painesville and Ashtabula Railroad Company." Among charges of bribery and corruption and intense lobbying by both the state of Ohio (on behalf of the CP&A) and supporters of the Sunbury and Erie Railroad, the act reeked of backroom deals. The act awarded the disputed line between Erie and the Ohio state line to the CP&A. But it also required the CP&A to grant certain advantages to the Sunbury and Erie Railroad—not the least of which was a requirement for the CP&A to subscribe to $500,000 of Sunbury and Erie stock. In its effect, the act "sounded the death knell for the Sunbury and Erie's share in large part of the rail traffic of the Midwest."[13] Sallade's involvement in the railroad debate is not documented, but it is difficult to imagine that he did not weigh in on the issue in the interest of the Sunbury and Erie. Specifically, an entry in his field book on August 9, 1852, pinpoints the earliest date of Sallade's involvement in the revitalized project. His survey notes include comments about the junction of the Sunbury and Erie Railroad with the proposed Susquehanna and Erie Railroad at Sunbury. Sallade also acted as the Sunbury and Erie Railroad Company's commissioner of damages from November 1852 to February 1853.[14]

ANOTHER ISSUE THAT WAS A SUBJECT OF HEATED DISCUSSION in the 1854 legislature had to do with temperance laws. The temperance movement, which had been gaining momentum since the 1840s, reached a peak after the passage in 1851 of a prohibitory liquor law in the state of Maine. While legislators agreed that excessive alcohol consumption was harmful, they disagreed over how to regulate the problem. Early in the session a controversial temperance bill modeled after the Maine law was introduced. The more restrictive provisions of the bill included a prohibition on the sale of spirituous liquors except for medicinal, chemical, mechanical, or sacramental purposes and a very strict licensing procedure for both the sale and manufacture of liquor, including a detailed description of punishment for violating the laws. The person authorized to sell liquor was required to keep record of each sale—the amount sold and to whom—and the books were to be subject to inspection by any person who so desired. The law was silent about allowing the home manufacture of spirituous beverages for domestic use. A rather humorous provision, humorous today anyway, was a restriction on the sale of liquor "in any tent, shanty, hut…or near the grounds of any cattle show, agricultural exhibition, military muster, political or religious meeting."[15] The bill was defeated in the House. In its place, the House introduced a bill that would put the issue of temperance before the voters in an October 1854 plebiscite.

Sallade's idea for a moderate temperance law was written in his daybook but apparently was not submitted to the legislature. It included provisions that a limited number of licenses should be granted to operate a tavern to accommodate the traveling public, that those licenses would be granted only after the potential tavern owner submitted a petition from a dozen freeholders in the vicinity of the proposed tavern, and that the tavern owner was prohibited from selling spirituous drinks on the Sabbath.[16] On the temperance bills that came before the legislature, Sallade consistently opposed amendments that imposed excessive regulation. In the end, the vote to approve a plebiscite was approved, Sallade voting no. In so doing, he put a target on his back.

CHAPTER 17

A Know-Nothing Episode

⸻ ◈ ⸻

W hile talk of railroads and liquor created a big fuss within the halls of Pennsylvania's state capitol, the people outside the walls were aroused by activity in Congress. The Kansas-Nebraska Act, by letting the residents of the newly created territories of Kansas and Nebraska decide whether they would allow slavery, repealed the Missouri Compromise of 1820, which had prohibited slavery north of the 36°30′ parallel. On January 23, 1854, US senator Stephen A. Douglas introduced the bill in the Senate. On March 3 it was approved by the Senate with a vote of 37–14, causing the people of Harrisburg to pour into the street. A rally was called together by the state's Democratic administration to endorse the bill. But the organizers of the meeting were put to rout, and after discussion, strong resolutions in opposition to the bill were carried by an overwhelming majority.[1] The ensuing debate over the bill in the US House of Representatives was raucous, ending with a final vote on May 22 in favor of the bill, 113–100. Northern Democrats split in favor of the bill by a narrow 44–42 vote, while all 45 northern Whigs opposed it. In the South, Democrats voted in favor by 57–2 and Whigs by a closer 12–7. The act to organize the territories of Nebraska and Kansas was signed into law by president Franklin Pierce on May 30, 1854.

On May 22 Stephen Miller, editor of Harrisburg's *Morning Herald*, published a condemnation of the "Traitors to Pennsylvania"—the state's Democratic congressmen who voted in favor of the

Nebraska bill.[2] But Miller was merely warming up for a season of unbridled attacks on anyone who opposed his agenda. A grandson of German immigrants, Miller was born in Perry, Cumberland County, Pennsylvania, in 1816 and was educated in the common schools. In 1834 he went into business as a clerk in a store in Harrisburg, and in 1837 he became a forwarding agent. Between 1849 and 1852 he served as prothonotary of Dauphin County. Between 1853 and 1855 he was part owner and editor of Harrisburg's Whig newspapers, the *Telegraph* and *Morning Herald*.[3]

In Pennsylvania, furor over passage of the Kansas-Nebraska Act was to some extent overshadowed by mounting hostility toward the increasing political participation of foreign-born citizens. In particular, conspiracies about a Catholic invasion of America caused disaffected American-born Protestants to join the Know-Nothings.[4] But when Know-Nothingism appeared in Dauphin County in 1854, it came with an interesting twist. As documented by historian Gerald G. Eggert, Catholics were not really a threat in Harrisburg. They were few in number, and the pastor of the Catholic Church worked hard to earn the respect of the community. Further, the Know-Nothings in Harrisburg did not formally organize their nativist group, the Guard of Liberty, until June 24, 1854, and the group never became large.[5] By contrast, as historian Mark Voss-Hubbard argues, Harrisburg's temperance movement was well organized in its efforts to advocate for the prohibitory Maine liquor law as early as 1852.[6] The fact that a plebiscite on the liquor law was on the October 1854 ballot added momentum to the already popular temperance issue. The by-products of intemperance—pauperism, brawls, violence—were often associated with foreigners, especially with Irish and German Catholic immigrants.

Seeing an opening, Stephen Miller brought the issues of nativism and temperance together in one voice, aiming his venom at any politician who failed to fall in line with his nativist, anti-Catholic, pro-temperance agenda. Miller obviously failed to recognize the incongruence between his antislavery rhetoric and his nativist views, an incompatibility that was explained by no one less than

Abraham Lincoln in a poignant 1855 letter to his friend Joshua Speed. Lincoln wrote:

> I am not a Know-Nothing.…How can anyone who abhors the oppression of negroes, be in favor of degrading classes of white people? Our progress in degeneracy appears to me to be pretty rapid. As a nation we began by declaring that "all men are created equal." We now practically read it "all men are created equal, except negroes." When the Know-Nothings get control it will read "all men are created equal, except negroes, and foreigners, and Catholics." When it comes to this I should prefer emigrating to some country where they make no pretense of loving liberty—to Russia, for instance, where despotism can be taken pure, and without the base alloy of hypocracy [*sic*].[7]

As editor of the *Morning Herald*, Miller whipped up "a steady froth of nativist agitation."[8] He was the attack dog who "maintained a steady flow of squibs against immigrants and the Catholic Church.… Neutral or sympathetic…items on Know-Nothingism appeared in almost every issue."[9] Invariably he expounded against obnoxious, noisy German beer gardens. And "any Irishman arrested for drunkenness or brawling was guaranteed notice" in Miller's paper.[10] Laying the groundwork for the October gubernatorial and legislative election, Miller began his campaign soon after the Pennsylvania legislature adjourned on May 3, 1854. And Simon Sallade, because of his moderate political views concerning the Maine liquor law, found himself in Miller's crosshairs.

At the Dauphin County Democratic Convention, Simon Sallade was nominated for the fifth time to fill a seat in the state House of Representatives. However, because his wife, Jane Woodside Sallade, died of an unknown cause on September 3, 1854, Sallade, on September 8, informed the county Democratic committee that "owing to unforeseen circumstances—the recent death of my wife, and the severe illness of other members of my family—I am now compelled to decline the nomination."[11] The county Democratic committee met on September 14 to consider its options and unanimously passed resolutions in which it appealed to Sallade to retract his resignation. Citing the sense of duty to the party they represented, the committee avowed that Sallade's declination would cause universal regret and impair the strength of the whole ticket. Assuring Sallade that the action of the committee reflected the universal sentiment of the entire party in the county, the committee affirmed its approval of his course in the previous legislature. Acknowledging his "recent heavy bereavement," the committee also released him of any obligation for canvassing the county if he withdrew his declination.[12] After receiving many private letters, Sallade recalled his letter of resignation and agreed to "cheerfully abide the will of the people," and he added, "If re-elected to the legislature, I will endeavor to serve the people honestly and faithfully."[13]

The campaign would be the most bitter of his life.[14] Focusing on Sallade's stand against intrusive regulation of spirituous liquors, the assault on him began in earnest in a September 21 *Morning Herald* item. Stephen Miller's essay satirized an article in the *Democratic Union* in which the editor of the Democratic paper "compliments Mr. Sallade for 'the high position he has taken against fanaticism and tyranny'—denounces the temperance men as 'fanatical ruffians' and appeals to the whiskey manufacturers, sellers and drinkers to rally for '[Governor] Bigler, Sallada, Liberty and the sixty thousand dollar distillery!'"[15]

The immediate provocation for Miller's attack was Sallade's response to a query addressed to the candidates for the legislature by a local temperance committee. The query to Sallade was dated September 3, and he probably received it the same day his wife died. Basically, the questionnaire asked the candidates if they would secure passage of laws related to temperance in the next legislature. Sallade's response to the questionnaire, initially printed in the *Democratic Union* on September 20 and reprinted in the *Morning Herald* on September 23, is as follows:

Elizabethville, Sept. 16th, 1854

To Charles C. Rawn, Esq., Chairman of the Temperance Committee, Harrisburg

Sir: Your letter of the 4th of September, inst., propounding to me certain interrogatories, in regard to my course on the prohibitory and other temperance questions, should I be elected to the next legislature, is now before me.

In reply, I have to say that I am a republican and I believe in the capacity of the people to govern themselves morally as well as politically.

I am opposed generally to all laws curtailing the liberty of our citizens, except for the absolute commission of crime. I am also opposed to the passage of any law which might interfere with the rights of property or injure the market for the produce of the soil. You know what my course has heretofore been; I should not deviate from it if again elected.

If it should be the will of the people to send me once more to the legislature, I would endeavor in all respects faithfully to perform my duty to my constituents. In a word, sir, I am opposed to the passage of the Maine Liquor law, because I consider it a direct invasion of the liberties of the people.

Yours, very respectfully, Simon Sallada.[16]

On September 23 Miller continued his invective. In reporting on a meeting of the temperance committee, he quoted Charles C. Rawn, chairman of the committee and principal signatory of the questionnaire: "Rawn showed up the kind of 'flat-footed liberty' that Mr. Sallada is so very fearful of 'invading'—the 'liberty' to get drunk and wallow in the gutter, and starve and abuse helpless women and children."[17] Miller didn't stop there. In a second column he preached: "Sallada and Liberty. This is now the battle cry of the Democracy and their rum-selling allies. Liberty to sell whiskey

and lager beer and make men drunk according to law. Mr. Sallada
and the *Democratic Union* will soon discover that a majority of the
people of Dauphin County are not in favor of that kind of 'liberty,'"
and "Enjoying his Liberty—We saw a fellow lying on the pavement
in Third street last night, feeling upward for the ground. He had
evidently been to a lager beer shop, luxuriating on the delectable
beverage which the *Democratic Union* classes among the 'good
things of God,' and was enjoying the 'liberty' which Simon Sallade
thinks it is wrong for the legislature to 'invade.' This poor fellow
fell and an awful hard fall it was in the glorious cause of 'Sallada
and Liberty.'"[18]

The assault on Sallade was relentless. In a September 24 article
again titled "Sallade and Liberty," Miller likened the liberty to
"the 'liberty' to make and sell bad whiskey, the 'liberty' to poison
men and ruin them temporally and eternally, the 'liberty' to
degrade and impoverish men, desolate hearthstones, crush the
hearts of women and 'rob the orphan of its crust of bread,' the
'liberty' to fill our poorhouses, prisons and penitentiaries, and
crowd the gallows with victims, the 'liberty' to tax the people for
the support of paupers, made such by intoxicating liquors. Such
is the 'liberty' that SIMON SALLADE and the *Democratic Union*
are in favor of."[19]

And the next day, Miller wrote, "We denounce Simon Sallade
as an unscrupulous demagogue, and arrant tyrant; a supple tool
of Geo. M. Lauman: who, in order to perpetuate the streams
of desolation and death, that flow out of the 'Big Distillery,' has
promised to set at defiance the popular will lawfully expressed at
the ballot box."[20]

Sallade's friends had not been idle. They distributed throughout
the county a circular, written both in German and English, that
emphasized personal liberty and the economic losses that prohibition would visit upon grain farmers and innkeepers. In its October
4 edition, the *Democratic Union* made its final endorsement for
Sallade. Sallade was

a man whom God made honest, and who, therefore, needs no adventitious aids, no Maine law pledges to hold him up. He is one of your oldest citizens. He has grown gray in your own county. He is known by all of you. He has represented you three times in the legislature, and always faithfully. Will you reject an old and tried servant, familiar with legislation, a man of character and influence, merely to gratify the Maine law fanatics? Of course you will not. Friendship, principle, interest, all urge you to vote for him; and we shall be disappointed, indeed, if your votes when counted, don't tell a cheering tale for Sallade and liberty.[21]

But Miller got in the last lick, saving his cruelest personal attack on the bereaved Sallade for the October 6 edition of the *Morning Herald*:

Sallade and Liberty

We learn that Mr. Sallade attended a vendue at a tavern in the upper end of the county, several days ago, and held a "levee" in the back room, where he "entertained" the crowd with as much whiskey as they could drink. Among the "guests" present on the occasion enjoying their "liberty," was Mr. Sallade's own son, who imbibed until he became so intoxicated, that he fell from his chair in a drunken fit. A number of Democrats present were so disgusted with Sallade's twaddle about "rights" and "liberties," while the son lay on the floor a victim of his father's cause, that they avowed their determination to vote against him. "Sallade and Liberty." The advocates of such a man and such a cause should hang their heads and blush for shame.[22]

Acutely concerned about the rise of Know-Nothingism, Sallade had accounted for their numbers in his daybook, estimating supporters of the movement in Pennsylvania to be forty-two thousand, including, he claimed, eighteen thousand Democrats. He also named individual adherents including Miller. And Sallade's opinion of the cause was made clear by what he wrote: "I had timely notice of the movement of Knownothing [*sic*] in Dauphin County if I had chosen to join them. I made up my mind Not to do it at all—Hotheads—Sooner Lose the Election."[23]

And he did. Resoundingly. Nowadays people constantly complain about negative political campaigns. But the fact is, they work. They work today, and they worked in 1854 when Sallade was defeated. Of twenty-nine election districts in Dauphin County, Sallade won only seven. (Two assemblymen were elected in Dauphin County.) Tellingly, his Democratic running mate for assembly, Dr. John Stehley, who had pledged his support for the prohibitory liquor law, carried all but two districts. In the gubernatorial contest the county went for the Whig candidate, James Pollock, over the incumbent Democrat, William Bigler, by an almost 2–1 margin. And in a counterintuitive development, the plebiscite for the prohibition law carried only six Dauphin County districts, four of which were in Harrisburg. Locally, the law was defeated in the county by a wide margin, 2,475 in favor of the law and 3,448 against.[24] Statewide, the prohibition law was narrowly defeated with 158,318 voting for the law and 163,457 against it.

Perhaps it was because of the stresses of the summer and fall of 1854—his new role as president of the Lykens Valley Mutual Fire Insurance Company, the death of his wife and illness in his family, the demoralizing reelection campaign—or perhaps it was his age that got the better of him. Simon Sallade died at his home in Elizabethville on November 8, 1854. The cause of his death is unknown, but given his age and the absence of an obvious illness, a good guess would be that he succumbed either to a stroke or a heart attack. His passing was noted in the *Democratic Union* on November 16, 1854:

DEATH OF SIMON SALLADE

Col. Simon Sallade, of Washington township, Dauphin County, departed this life on Wednesday last, full of years and full of honors. He represented this county three several [*sic*] times in the legislature, at intervals of seventeen years, and filled other minor offices with credit to himself and benefit to the people. He was a man whose honesty and sterling worth endeared him to all who knew him, and his death is sincerely lamented by hundreds who were proud to call him friend.

SALLADE'S ANTAGONIST, STEPHEN MILLER, BENEFITTED FROM his support of the Whigs. Earning the spoils of victory, he was appointed by Governor Pollock as flour inspector for Philadelphia in 1855. In 1858 he moved to St. Cloud, Minnesota, where he engaged in the real estate and mercantile business with Henry Swisshelm.[25] Perhaps needless to say, it didn't take long for Miller to involve himself in local politics. Swisshelm, as it turns out, was the brother-in-law of Jane Grey Swisshelm, the noted journalist, abolitionist, and advocate for women's rights who edited the *St. Cloud Visiter* and, after that newspaper's press was destroyed and tossed into the Mississippi River by her political opponents, the *St. Cloud Democrat*. The destruction of the press created quite a kerfuffle in St. Cloud. Responding to the incident, and armed only with her pen, Mrs. Swisshelm crushed the good old boys who dared to try to put her out of business.[26] Clearly, this well-spoken woman was no damsel in distress. Nevertheless, the recently arrived Stephen Miller penned a letter of support for Mrs. Swisshelm.[27] Not long after that, Miller emerged as the chairman of the newly organized local Republican committee.[28] In 1860 he served as a delegate to the Republican convention that nominated Abraham Lincoln. During the Civil War he fought first with the Army of the Potomac. Upon returning to

Minnesota in September 1862, he was assigned to the Seventh Minnesota Volunteer Infantry Regiment and took command of the federal prison near Mankato, Minnesota, where hundreds of Dakota Indians were being held.

In the aftermath of the Dakota War of 1862—a rebellion by the Dakota Indians of western Minnesota driven by their frustration over repeated failure of the United States to live up to its treaty obligations—303 Indians were condemned to die. President Lincoln, however, upon review of trial transcripts, commuted the sentences of all but thirty-nine of the Native Americans, thirty-eight of whom were hung on December 26, 1862, at the Mankato prison, then under the command of Colonel Stephen Miller. Prior to the hanging, Colonel Miller implored the citizens to "maintain the law," saying that the "State of Minnesota must not, in addition to the terrible wrongs and outrages inflicted upon her by the murderous savages, suffer, if possible, still more fatally, in her prosperity and reputation, at the hands of a few of our misguided, though deeply injured fellow citizens."[29] To this day, this injustice remains the largest mass execution in American history. Rather than being held to account for this affront, Miller was elected in 1863 as the fourth governor of Minnesota and served in that capacity from 1864 to 1866. He is credited with advocating for generous appropriations for higher education and, in his final address to the legislature, for adoption of a black suffrage amendment to the state constitution. He died in 1881 in Minnesota.[30]

OF SIMON AND JANE WOODSIDE SALLADE'S CHILDREN AND grandchildren, I know little. There is a grave marker in Old Stone Church Cemetery in Elizabethville that bears the name of Joseph H. Sallade, deceased in 1842. The reference also gives the year of Joseph H.'s birth as 1822. I do not know if this is Simon and Jane's son, but if it is, he would have been the third son to die at a young age.[31] Another report asserts that Simon and Jane's youngest son, Simon Sallade, died on May 14, 1854.[32] If the report is correct, 1854 was an absolutely horrible year for the Sallades; young Simon would have been twenty-nine when he died.

Simon and Jane's grandson John Bowman became a physician and practiced in Millersburg and Lykens. Simon Sallade Bowman, another grandson, became a lawyer who practiced in Millersburg. In his 1940 address to the Historical Society of Dauphin County, James D. Bowman, Simon Sallade Bowman's son, recounted the following story about his father:

> My Father attended the funeral of Judge Packer at Sunbury. Simon Cameron was there. During part of the services incident to the funeral, Father spoke. He had a wealth of literature, which he could so appropriately use. After which the Senator [Cameron] came to Father and said: Well Bowman, it's funny I never heard of you. [Bowman replied] Never heard of me, you defeated me for the legislature one time. Said the Senator—Who are you? [Bowman replied] I am the grandson of Simon Sallada. What? [said Cameron] You the grandson of Simon Sallada and I defeated you for the legislature, had I known that all Hell wouldn't have defeated you.[33]

I have not found documentation for Simon Cameron running against Simon Sallade Bowman for the legislature. Perhaps Bowman ran against someone whom Cameron endorsed? Still, it's a nice story.

The Lykens Valley Mutual Fire Insurance Company celebrated its one hundredth anniversary in 1954 with the publication of a booklet about its history titled *Through the Years* by Miles V. Miller. I do not know if the Lykens Valley Mutual Fire Insurance Company was later liquidated or acquired.

America changed a lot during Simon Sallade's lifetime. When he was born, America included the thirteen original states. When he died, the nation's boundary with its territories circumscribed the modern-day contiguous United States. But the America of 1854 had become a nation encompassing two separate worlds, worlds that would collide not long after Sallade died. The hallmarks of one of those worlds, Sallade's world, were advances in industry, transportation, and communication. Sallade had been among the enterprising men, the movers and shakers, who had transformed his world from an economy based solely on agriculture to a mixed economy based on agriculture, commerce, and industry. The symbols of the other world, the world that occasionally intruded on Sallade's political life, were conquest, slavery, and expropriation of land. In that world, revolution in the manufacture of cotton cloth had caused America to look to its dark side, instigating a war of conquest, stealing land from American Indians, and enslaving millions of African Americans.

Although Simon Sallade's list of tangible accomplishments is impressive, to me his most important legacy lies not in what he did but in who he was. Even though he was acclaimed throughout his life by his friends, neighbors, business associates, and fellow politicians, he was that rare individual who never assumed the mantle of arrogance that so often accompanies fame. To the end of his life, Simon Sallade remained an honest, honorable man.

Part III

MCELIECE AND BROWN

FAR hence, amid an isle of
wondrous beauty,
Crouching over a grave, an ancient,
sorrowful mother,
Once a queen—now lean and tatter'd,
seated on the ground,
Her old white hair drooping dishevel'd
round her shoulders;
At her feet fallen an unused royal harp,
Long silent—she too long silent—
mourning her shrouded hope and heir;
Of all the earth her heart most full of
sorrow, because most full of love.
Yet a word, ancient mother;
You need crouch there no longer on the
cold ground, with forehead between
your knees;

O you need not sit there, veil'd in your
old white hair, so dishevel'd;
For know you, the one you mourn is not
in that grave;
It was an illusion—the heir, the son you
love, was not really dead;
The Lord is not dead—he is risen again,
young and strong, in another country;
Even while you wept there by your fallen
harp, by the grave,
What you wept for, was translated,
pass'd from the grave,
The winds favor'd, and the sea sail'd it,
And now with rosy and new blood,
Moves to-day in a new country.

—WALT WHITMAN,
"Old Ireland" in *Leaves of Grass*

CHAPTER 18

THE LUCK O' THE IRISH

Simon Sallade, as it turns out, was the transitional figure in the family. With his feet firmly planted in the rich agricultural soil of Dauphin County's Lykens Valley, he was in the forefront of change when America began its shift from an agricultural economy to an industrial one. He was among those who built the railroads, canals, and bridges that would open up a whole new world. George McEliece, John McEliece, and Anthony J. Gallagher were on the other end of the bridge. Each of them was a civic leader in Shamokin, a sooty town in Northumberland County's anthracite coal region.[1] What makes their stories interesting is that they were all caught up, sometimes in different ways, in the dramatic developments that disrupted the region in the late 1860s and 1870s.

ONE YEAR WHILE VISITING MY FAMILY—I LIVE ON THE WEST Coast—I decided to visit Shamokin. Starting at Rochester, I took Route 15, an old road that winds through central New York and Pennsylvania before it continues on to South Carolina. I stopped and spent the night in the town of Shamokin Dam, located on the Susquehanna River opposite Sunbury. Early the next day, I visited Sunbury to take a few pictures of the county courthouse, which was built in 1865 and is still in use. From Sunbury, the road to Shamokin winds through a gorgeous Appalachian valley. As I drove through what seemed to be an enchanted forest, I felt like I was traveling back in time. After driving about fifteen miles, a Coal Township road marker announced my arrival in coal country. A bit farther down the road, off to my left, a man operating an excavator at the base of a heap of coal proved the industry that had put the town on the map was not completely dead. After a few more miles, I reached Shamokin.

I was immediately struck by the apparent poverty of the town. It seemed to me to be a dismal place. The buildings were as they must have been when the town was in its heyday—save a layer of asbestos shingles slapped onto the aging structures. As I drove farther along, I noticed a few nice-looking old homes—perhaps they had belonged to the collieries' owners or successful businessmen. Also, well-maintained churches announced the ethnicity of their parishioners.

I parked my car on Independence Street in the central business district. Most of the storefronts were vacant, and on this particular day the street was empty. A few proprietors—a furniture store owner and a restauranteur—stood outside their businesses, and there were no customers inside. Oddly, the parking meters didn't have turnkeys. Not wanting to get a parking ticket, I dutifully dropped my quarter into the slot, and when the minute meter didn't register, I thought, Here is a town so poor that it cannot afford to remove its broken parking meters. Somewhat amused, I wondered if anyone would ever collect my quarter, or if it would be trapped in the meter forever, much as the town itself seemed to be stuck in a time warp. But despite the business district's generally shabby appearance, I could easily imagine what a thriving, bustling commercial district it once had been.

Exploring farther, I drove up Shamokin Street to the Bunker Hill neighborhood. The street ended at a brick wall, and peering over the wall and looking through trees, I could see vestiges of an abandoned coal mine. When the mine was operating at full steam, the view would have been different for the coal miners' families who lived in the neighborhood. Instead of trees, they would have viewed a mountain of mining refuge and huge industrial buildings. The air would have been laden with coal dust and dirt.

I wondered what it was like to live in the town in the 1870s. At that time, the water system was crude. Although water lines had been installed on a few streets by the effort of private citizens, it was not until 1873 that clean water was finally available in all parts of the city. Public sanitation, however, was nonexistent. Garbage was typically dumped on the outskirts of the city. And of course indoor plumbing was unknown—rarely cleaned outdoor privies serving that necessary function. In thinking about basic infrastructure, though, I have to remember that lack of public services was not uncommon for the period, and peoples' reaction to the environment would have been far different than mine. In fact, the people often treated the situation with humor, as noted in a newspaper account of a local spelling bee: "Mr. Owen exhausted his [spelling] list in reducing these [contestants] to two—Mrs. Caldwell and Miss [Belle] McEliece. The latter going down, Mrs. C. was first best for the evening, but before leaving the stage she gave us to understand she didn't know all about *ichthyology*. The Shamokin Creek is certainly a poor place to study it."[2] It was one of those you-had-to-be-there kind of jokes: Shamokin Creek, at the bottom of the hill, had at one time supported a population of trout and other species, but because of the coal boom, it ran black and acid due to untreated mining waste.

Next, I crossed Shamokin Creek to explore the other side of town, the Market Street neighborhood. Today, Market Street is a broad boulevard with a tree-lined greenway separating the traffic moving in two directions. Benches are placed intermittently along a sidewalk that runs up the middle of the greenway. The whole effect is to give this part of town a cheery, airy aspect, much nicer than the claustrophobic feeling one gets on the other side of town. The houses seemed newer too. Some were large buildings that I assumed were boardinghouses; others were single-family homes. A few even had front lawns. To my untrained eye, I guessed these houses were built in the 1890s to 1910s, when the population of

Shamokin was nearing its peak of about twenty thousand. I drove around the town for a while longer and left with a feeling that the town's physical environment had never been pleasant. But this was where George McEliece had settled, undoubtedly because of his work as a railroad man, around 1850.

FROM WHAT I HAVE LEARNED ABOUT GEORGE MCELIECE'S IRISH heritage, his voyage to America, and his arrival on these shores, he may as well have been born at Deer's Watering Place, the site of the original Woodside homestead located on the banks of Wiconisco Creek, four miles upstream from its confluence with the Susquehanna. I am aware of two of my contemporaries, both George's descendants, who traveled to Ireland hoping to find information about his family. The only clue they had to go on was what was in the old mug books: that George was born on February 22, 1819, in County Armagh; his father's name was John; and he came to America in 1838 when he was nineteen years old.[3] The family historians returned empty-handed. Stateside, documents verifying George's immigration, naturalization, his 1840 marriage to Mary Ann Woodside, and the birth of their first three children—Elizabeth, John, and Mary—are also missing.[4] When I began to write his story, then, all I knew about George's early years in America was what was written in the nineteenth-century county history books, and I had taken that on faith.

CONDITIONS IN IRELAND WERE BAD IN 1838. ALTHOUGH THE potato blight had not yet arrived when George sailed for America, the crop was unreliable. Following the coldest summer in fifty years, there had been widespread failure of the crop in 1836. Hunger followed in 1837. We will never know if George was a victim of this hardship. Whether he fled Ireland to escape hunger and poverty, traveled to America seeking adventure and fortune, or a little bit of both, remains a mystery. But he was young, bright, and ambitious, and the prospect of a better life in America must have been irresistible.

Keeping in mind that the information in the county histories was most likely provided by his son John, who was born in 1842, it makes sense that George's first employment upon arrival in America would be described as working on the Lykens Valley Railroad: John's earliest memories of his father would have been exactly that because the railroad was rebuilt between 1845 and 1848, when John was three to six years old. But John's memories are not consistent with what was happening in Dauphin County when George arrived in 1838, namely, the construction of the Wiconisco Canal. Thus, although it is possible that he was working as a day laborer on local farms or in the coal mines or maintaining the worn-out railroad, it is most likely that he was employed on the canal project precisely when Simon Sallade was the superintendent.

Canal building in the 1820s and the 1830s was America's first experience with building large public works, and it was the first time there was a need for massive amounts of labor. Contracts for the canals and appurtenances were typically awarded to local men. The actual construction was done in part by local farmhands who seasonally worked as a means of earning extra cash. But the biggest source of canal labor was from immigrants, especially Irish immigrants.

The work was backbreaking: the canals were dug by men with pick and shovel, spade and mattock, wheelbarrow and cart. Working conditions were harsh: the men worked outdoors in all seasons from dawn to dusk. They "spent much of their day in ditches, hacking at the dry earth with dust in their throats, mired in mud or up to their waists in water."[5] Disease was ever present: typhoid, malaria, and the "king of terrors"—cholera. Living conditions were primitive: several men were confined to a small shanty thrown up near the worksite. Wages, which included food, shelter, and lots of whiskey, were nominally adequate, but because the work was intermittent, there was barely enough to survive.

Amid all this, it is anyone's guess how George, the poor young Irish immigrant laborer, met Mary Ann Woodside, the great-granddaughter of one of the Lykens Valley's oldest settlers. Perhaps Simon Sallade arranged for George's lodging either at his homestead in Elizabethville or at his Woodside in-laws' sprawling farm two miles away. Maybe they met at a local celebration or holiday gathering. Mary Ann may have visited the canal construction site to help with ancillary tasks—food preparation and the like. Then again, could it be that young Mary Ann had a rebellious streak, and the couple met on the sly against her parents' wishes? Whatever happened, George and Mary Ann were married in 1840, barely two years after George's arrival in America. Something extraordinary about George enabled him to make the transition from a young Irish immigrant to a member of a well-established family in such a short time. Perhaps it was his work ethic, his intelligence, or his charm. Or maybe it was his Irish luck.

George and Mary Ann McCleese first appear in official records in the 1850 federal census when they were located in Coal Township, Northumberland County, Pennsylvania, which includes the borough of Shamokin.[6] The children in the household included Elizabeth, John, Mary, and Sarah (Annie), ages nine, seven, five, and nine months, respectively. Considering the gap between the birth of Mary and Sarah, there may have been a child who died young. Also living with the McElieces were two miners, both age twenty-four and born in Ireland. Although the 1850 census lists a person's occupation, the scribble after George's name is not legible. Herbert C. Bell's *History of Northumberland County*, however, states that George was a section superintendent working for the Philadelphia and Sunbury Railroad from 1853 to 1864.[7] Perhaps he got the job with the help, again, of Simon Sallade, who had been involved with the railroad from its inception. Nevertheless, judging from George's rise from being a probable laborer on the Wiconisco Canal in 1838–1839 to holding a position as a construction superintendent on a railroad by 1853, he likely exhibited a talent for mechanics, construction techniques, and leadership, as well as a knack for making the most of his contacts with influential people.

By the time of the 1860 census, Jane (Jennie), age seven; Isabelle (Belle), age five; and Margaret (Maggie), age two, enlivened the bustling household. John, age seventeen, was employed as a laborer, probably working beside his father. In that census, George's occupation was listed as a tender on the railroad; his real estate was valued at $500 and his personal estate at $100 (about $14,425 and $2,875 in today's dollars). After twenty years in America, George, although not wealthy, enjoyed a measure of financial stability.

Unlike many Irish immigrants, George supported the Union cause in the Civil War. He was one of Shamokin's leaders who organized a meeting to raise funds for a bounty to be paid to men who enrolled as soldiers. It is interesting that George was identified in the article about the meeting with the honorary title "Esq." The title suggests that George was well respected in the community. It is the first indication that he was among the community's civic leaders. The *Shamokin Herald* reported on July 29, 1862:

War Meeting—An Enthusiastic War meeting was held on Saturday evening in front of Weaver's Hotel. George M'Clease, Esq., [*sic*] was chosen Chairman, and speeches were made by S. John, Rev. Mr. Stevens, Rev. A. D. Hawn, Rev. J. F. Wampole, W. P. Withington, Daniel Bower, and Dr. J. J. John. After the close of the meeting a subscription was gotten up to be appropriated as a Bounty to those who volunteer from this place, and it was resolved that the town of Shamokin, pay to each volunteer, from this town the sum of Fifty dollars, upon being mustered in as a Bounty. The meeting adjourned to meet again on Monday, (last) evening.

George was probably moved to organize the war meeting in response to President Lincoln's and Pennsylvania governor Andrew Gregg Curtin's calls for troops after the Union loss in the Seven Days' battles (June 25–July 1, 1862). More importantly, George had a personal stake in the war because his only son, John, was a corporal in the Union army.[8] Little could George know that in two short weeks he would be agonizing over his son's fate when John was listed among the missing in action after the Battle of Cedar Mountain on August 9, 1862. Fortunately, that nightmare ended soon thereafter when it was reported that John was recovering from his wounds in a rebel hospital in Staunton, Virginia.

Both at home and in the public sphere, 1863 was a busy year for George. He and Mary Ann were blessed with another child, a little boy, George Francis, born May 31, 1863. (The boy, as mentioned by Elizabeth McEliece in John McEliece's pension file, died young.) George's involvement in civic affairs picked up speed. In February 1863 he was elected to the local school board.[9] George's achievement while serving on the school board was later acknowledged in an address delivered by J. J. John, one of the community's leaders.[10] George and another board member, Jonas L. Gilger, successfully negotiated a transaction to purchase a building for a high school. Not many years later, George's daughters Jane and Isabelle would be among the high school's outstanding students.

Concurrent with his service on the school board, George was elected to the board of the Coal Poor District for a term of three years. The Coal Poor District, authorized by act of the legislature, April 15, 1863, was composed of Coal Township and borough of Shamokin. The act provided for the erection of a poorhouse, its management, and the general method of alleviating the conditions of the destitute. A precursor of today's social services sector, the district's provisions were accepted by the voters of the township on June 12, 1863. In the spring of 1864, the board purchased a farm and its buildings located a mile northwest of Shamokin.[11]

Sometime around 1864 or 1865, George leased the A. S. Wolf colliery in Locust Gap, an unincorporated hamlet in Mount Carmel Township, at which he served as superintendent. In 1868 Conrad Graeber and John Kemple, under the firm name of Graeber & Kemple, acquired the leases of the A. S. Wolf and Locust Gap collieries.[12] At the time of the lease, Graeber, who had emigrated from Prussia in 1845, was already a successful businessman. Through the years he had operated a confectionary, a restaurant, a boardinghouse, a grocery store, and a hotel. Moreover, he had been politically active. In nearby Schuylkill County, Graeber had at various times been elected as a constable, school board member, and representative of the county in the state legislature.[13] Thus, with similar backgrounds, including affiliations with both the Democratic Party and the Catholic Church, it's not surprising that Graeber and George would strike up a friendship and that Graeber would then team up with George to manage the colliery. George would soon quit the coal business, however, and pass responsibility for managing the colliery to his son, John, then about twenty-eight years old.

When the 1870 census was taken, George was living in Shamokin. His real estate was valued at $4,000 and his personal estate at $800 (about $82,000 and $16,000 in today's dollars). He was employed as Northumberland County's treasurer, having won election to the office as a Democrat in the fall 1869 contest. The children still living at home included Annie, who was a teacher in Mount Carmel Township; Jane; Belle; and Maggie.[14] Elizabeth's whereabouts at the time are unknown.[15] John, living at Locust Gap, was married to his second wife, Ann Ellen Lukens.[16] Daughter Mary was married to Anthony J. Gallagher, a teacher, bookstore owner, and aspiring politician.

Absent from the 1870 census was the "little stranger" who entered the McElieces' lives soon after George won the 1869 election. A surprising report in the *Shamokin Herald* tells what happened:

Foundling. About nine o'clock on Tuesday evening last the family of one of the successful candidates for county office were attracted by the cries of an infant to the front door, and on opening it a male child, about six weeks old, was found snugly deposited upon the step. As no one was to be found to claim the "little stranger" he was taken in and cared for. Nothing was found upon the person or clothing of the child to indicate what was expected of the family and report says they were congratulating themselves upon the possibility of them being the victims of a practical joke, when a spoon and two bottles, one of castor oil and the other of soothing syrup, were found among the wraps indicating that it had been "left to stay."[17]

The baby, named George Alfred, was christened on October 24.[18] Since the baby was not listed in the 1870 census, presumably he died soon after being adopted. What this episode reveals about the kindness of George, Mary Ann, and the rest of the family is heartwarming. But it also makes one wonder what desperate circumstances drove the baby's mother to abandon her child.

Contemporary newspaper accounts of school reports and cultural events show that the McEliece family associated with respected members of the community—Shamokin's social elite, such as it was.[19] In 1870, for example, Jennie and Belle were among only thirty-one high school students at a time when the population of the borough of Shamokin and Coal Township was 7,240. The young ladies were also members of the High School Literary Society, with Belle on occasion opening the society's meetings with a musical presentation on the school's organ. Not to be outdone by the youngsters, the grown-ups organized the Shamokin Progressive Literary Society, Anthony J. Gallagher being a prominent member. Other gatherings such as spelling bees attracted Shamokin's best and brightest, the McEliece family among them. Upon graduation from high school, Jennie was hired as a schoolteacher for one of the district's grammar schools, a position she held for two years until she married. Margaret, too, even as a youngster, participated in charity fundraising events.[20]

In 1871 George, while still serving as the county's treasurer, joined Conrad Graeber, George Ryon, and other community leaders in successfully petitioning the legislature for a charter for the Shamokin Banking Company. The company elected its first board of directors in August 1871, and George was named as one of the directors. After completion of his term as county treasurer, George remained active in Democratic Party politics, although he never again ran for office. In 1874 he was engaged in the wholesale liquor business and continued in that business until his death in 1886. His wife, Mary Ann, also died in 1886.

So reads the story of George McEliece as revealed in the old county histories, newspaper articles, and official government records. It's a classic rags-to-somewhat-fancier-rags tale similar to those that played out thousands of times in hundreds of small towns across America. In what would later be called the American Dream, George McEliece, a poor Irish immigrant, worked hard, played by the rules, accumulated some assets, and emerged as a community leader. It's a lovely story. And true. At least by half.

CHAPTER 19

THE UNDOING OF GEORGE MCELIECE

What first made me consider that George McEliece's rags-to-riches story might be incomplete was his testimony in the 1877 trial of a Molly Maguire, Patrick Hester, a resident of Locust Gap, Pennsylvania.[1] Hester was on trial for the 1868 murder of Alexander Rea, superintendent of the Locust Mountain Coal and Iron Company and the Coal Ridge Improvement Company. You can probably imagine my surprise when I discovered that George McEliece; George's son John McEliece; and his son-in-law, Anthony J. Gallagher, were all witnesses at the trial. George and Anthony were witnesses for the defense. John was a witness for both the prosecution and the defense. Anyway, what grabbed my attention was George's response to a simple opening question by the prosecution's counsel, namely: "What business have you been engaged in?" George's reply was: "I have been in the flour and feed business." Really? This reply contradicted the fact that George was engaged in the wholesale liquor business soon after the completion of his 1870–1871 term as county treasurer, and he continued in that business until his death.[2] But then, considering that alcohol *is* made from grain and, for some at least, it is food for the soul, perhaps George was just stretching the truth a bit. While under oath! Still, I suspected that there may be a darker side to the story of George McEliece, the upright community leader.

George's political career peaked when he served as Northumberland County's treasurer. Before he was elected, however, there was a hint that something was amiss. In the run-up to the 1869 election, an intriguing comment published in the *Sunbury American*, a Republican newspaper, made reference to what the editor called the "Democratic Ring of Sunbury." In the article, which was about jostling for clerkships at the county courthouse, the editor implied that some members of the Democratic Party were allied with the Molly Maguires. "Perhaps the late threats of the Molly Maguires has something to do with it [the jostling]," he wrote, continuing with, "Can't they be trusted any longer or is it feared they will trade off the other candidates to elect the Treasurer?"[3] Whatever threats the editor was referring to are unknown, but there was a suggestion that George McEliece, the Democratic candidate for county treasurer, was somehow connected to the Mollys. Only a few issues of the *Sunbury American* for the years 1869 and 1870 have been preserved, and they made no further mention of the "Democratic Ring" or the Mollys.

Nor did the democratic newspaper, the *Northumberland County Democrat*, which instead headlined the party's position as the "Democratic or White Men's ticket."[4] The party platform condemned what it described as the "HIGH-HANDED and OUT-RAGEOUS ACTION" (capitals in the original) of Pennsylvania's legislature because it ratified the Fifteenth Amendment which gave former enslaved men the right to vote.[5] McEliece endorsed this platform. Racism in the immediate post–Civil War period was multifaceted. At the time it was not uncommon for people in the northern states to oppose slavery and also believe that African Americans—as well as Native Americans and Chinese Americans—were inferior human beings.[6] Racism among newly arrived Irish immigrants was intensified, as historian Forrest G. Wood observed, by fear that radical Republicans planned to "use the Negro vote to suppress the white immigrant."[7] An explicit example of this idea is illustrated in an 1869 article promoting McEliece's candidacy for county treasurer. (See figure 20.)

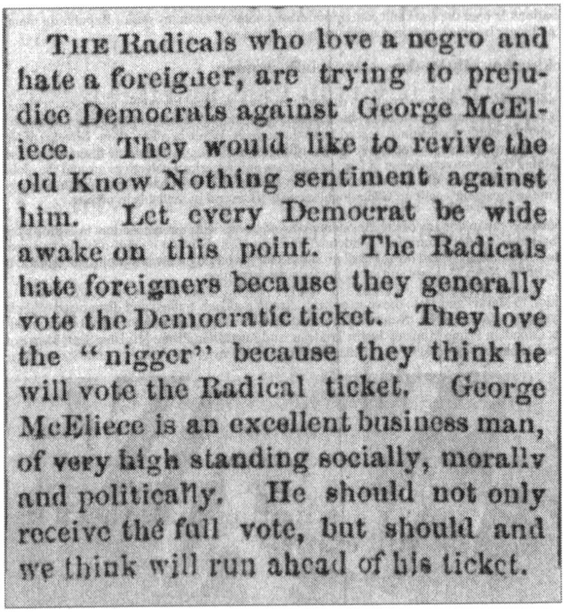

> THE Radicals who love a negro and hate a foreigner, are trying to prejudice Democrats against George McEliece. They would like to revive the old Know Nothing sentiment against him. Let every Democrat be wide awake on this point. The Radicals hate foreigners because they generally vote the Democratic ticket. They love the "nigger" because they think he will vote the Radical ticket. George McEliece is an excellent business man, of very high standing socially, morally and politically. He should not only receive the full vote, but should and we think will run ahead of his ticket.

Figure 20. Article depicting racist comment in Democratic campaign promoting George McEliece. Northumberland County Democrat, September 3, 1869, p. 2.

In any event, by 1871 the coverage of local politics dominated many editions of the *American*. How do I tell the story about what happened to George McEliece and his son-in-law Anthony J. Gallagher amid the tangled web of Northumberland County politics in the year of 1871? Do I start by telling how hard I tried to cram the facts into a sensational crime story that would have involved McEliece and Gallagher in a secret society of murderous Irish thugs? Or with my surrender to the evidence that pointed to something altogether different—that what happened in Northumberland County in 1871 was a story that revealed how a nation's xenophobia, combined with its deep-seated fear of Catholicism, its concern about newly organized labor unions, and its anxiety about widespread corruption, had penetrated a little county in central Pennsylvania? And how a zealous newspaper editor exploited those worries in order to defeat his political foes? And how a few small-town politicians got caught in the cross fire? Where do I begin? One place to start, I suppose, is to introduce the principal antagonist, the editor who played a crucial role in the story.

Not much is known about Emanuel Wilvert, editor of the *Sunbury American*. He was born in Lykens Township, Dauphin County, in 1830. While a printer's apprentice, he lived with the Henry Masser family of Sunbury in the 1850s. Under Masser, who established the *Sunbury American* in 1840, the paper had been Democratic until Lincoln was elected in 1860. Thereafter, it became a staunch Republican paper. Wilvert secured an interest in the paper in 1864. After Masser's retirement in 1869, Wilvert became the sole proprietor and remained involved with the paper until 1887.[8] How he came to be bitterly opposed to everything having to do with Irish Catholic Democrats and labor unions is unknown, but the vitriol he dished out to his adversaries in 1871 made the venom that Simon Sallade endured at the hands of Stephen Miller in 1854 seem mild by comparison. Wilvert's crusade is interesting not only because of its effectiveness in defeating his political opponents, but by bringing together an unlikely cast of characters, his campaign offers insight into a small town's reaction to, and the editor's exploitation of, concurrent events in the early years of the gilded age.

The story of the George's undoing, which involved several Democratic activists, began quietly enough with a legitimate critique about Northumberland County's finances, as revealed in the county's auditors' report for the year ending on December 31, 1870, George's first year as county treasurer.[9] In addition to claiming that the county's expenditures were excessive—a perennial target for any and all government entities: local, state, and federal—Mr. Wilvert took particular offense with the fact that the county was paying interest on its indebtedness while, at the same time, tax receipts were left in the hands of tax collectors. The reason that the shadowy Courthouse Ring allowed this practice to continue—so the accusation went—was that the tax collectors, thus enriched, would campaign to ensure that members of the Ring would win the fall 1871 election.[10] Throughout the spring, the editor of the *Sunbury American* continued to drive home his points about the Courthouse Ring's financial misdeeds.[11] Incidentally, Anthony J. Gallagher was one of the county's auditors.

THERE IS NO BIOGRAPHICAL SKETCH OF ANTHONY, AND HE LEFT no manuscript collection behind. However, when I was looking for stories about George and John McEliece in old newspapers, Anthony's name kept popping up—sometimes in stories about community events, but more often in reports and opinion pieces about his political aspirations. Anthony was born in 1841 near Pottsville, Schuylkill County. He was educated in the common schools. By 1867 he was a teacher in Mount Carmel Township. It seems probable that he met and married Mary McEliece, the second oldest daughter of George and Mary Ann McEliece, at this time. Mary may have been a teacher, although there is no record to prove it. Mary's sister Annie (Sarah) did, in fact, teach in the Mount Carmel district at the same time that Anthony did.[12]

At least by 1868 Anthony was involved in local politics. He was elected as justice of the peace in the borough of Mount Carmel in 1868.[13] He was elected as a county auditor and served in that position for the years 1869, 1870, and 1871. He was also among the most prominent members of the Workingmen's Benevolent Association from its first organization.[14] The WBA, as it was called, was the first union of anthracite miners. It was organized in St. Clair, Schuylkill County, in the spring of 1868 by John Siney. Soon thereafter, the WBA of Northumberland County was organized on September 23, 1868.[15] In April 1870 Gallagher was elected as business agent for the *Anthracite Monitor,* the WBA's newspaper. As business agent of the *Monitor,* at the general council of the W.B.A., held in Centralia, Pennsylvania, on June 23, 1870, Gallagher asked the organization to get more accurate reports of the condition of the coal trade for use in its publication.[16] By August, however, Gallagher had resigned his position at the *Anthracite Monitor,* saying that "my private business will not permit a continuance of my stay with the gallant little vessel of the M. & L. B. A., without suffering."[17] Gallagher was possibly instrumental in arranging a visit of Siney and Richard Trevellick to the area in the following month. Trevellick was president of the National Labor Union, the first national labor federation in the United States. First stopping in Mount Carmel, Siney and Trevellick addressed over one thousand people. In Shamokin "they found an audience of 1,500 and a miners' band awaiting them."[18] Based on his involvement in local government and his empathy for workingmen, it's not surprising that on June 3, 1871, Gallagher was nominated as the Democratic candidate for the state assembly at the local Democratic convention.[19]

By early June, Wilvert's editorial emphasis shifted to what he described as fraud by the Democracy.[20] Under the headline "The Democratic Convention—The Ring Successful—Heavy Returns from the Coal Regions—Honest Democrats Sold—Independent Candidates in the Field," Wilvert described a suspicious voting pattern in the local Democrats' June primary election.[21] Pointing out that 1,200 votes cast in the four districts of the coal region (the borough of Mount Carmel, Mount Carmel Township, the borough of Shamokin, and Coal Township) inexplicably exceeded the 600 votes cast in the same districts for the 1870 Democratic congressional candidate, he accused the Ring of stuffing the ballot box.[22] As anecdotal evidence, the editor offered a statement by an observer: "So intent were the Irish on his [Gallagher's] nomination that small boys, slate pickers from the coal breakers, were allowed to vote," and when a boy of fourteen years of age who attended the primary election in Shamokin was asked how things went, he answered that "Mr. Gallagher seemed to be doing all the voting himself, for in the hour that he [the boy] was at the polls he saw him [Gallagher] voting five times."[23] Moreover, observing that none of the Ring's candidates won a majority, the editor alleged that an alliance had been formed between the Ring and "Pat Hester & Co." to place in nomination numerous candidates, thereby dividing the vote and ensuring that the Ring's favored candidates would win.

Countywide, for example, Gallagher won 41 percent of the vote compared to 89 percent in the coal districts.[24]

Patrick Hester plays an important part in this story. Born in County Roscommon, Ireland, on May 4, 1825, he immigrated to America in 1846, eventually settling at Locust Gap Junction, a hamlet located midway between Locust Gap and the borough of Mount Carmel. There, near the railroad, he opened a hotel and tavern. He married Catherine O'Rourke, and the couple had four daughters, each of whom was at one time a teacher.

Hester was a man about town, popular and influential. He was a tax collector for Mount Carmel Township for about sixteen years.[25] He had served as overseer of the poor and as school director for several years. In February 1868 he was elected Mount Carmel Township supervisor. In that capacity, he received an order from Northumberland County court to put two expensive roads through Mount Carmel Township. As Hester later explained, "In 1871 there was a strike of the miners, and I put the men to work on the roads and I gave orders to storekeepers for provisions, and I kept them at work for the town until the operators in coal made a favorable proposition to the men and coal production set them to work again. Because I gave the men good wages—as high as $10 per week—the capitalists were down on me and have been spiteful ever since."[26] Hester was indeed a supporter of the National Labor Union's president, Richard Trevellick. Hester was also Northumberland County's leading figure in the Ancient Order of Hibernians (AOH), an Irish Catholic benevolent society that was characterized at the time as what we would call today a terrorist organization. With his extensive involvement in community affairs, there can be no question that Hester was among Northumberland County's leaders.

But Hester was hardly a saint, and he had the record to prove it. In 1864 he appeared in Northumberland County court as the prosecutor (accuser) in two cases of assault and battery. In both cases the charges were dismissed, and Hester was ordered to pay the court costs, suggesting that he had made a false accusation and implying that he was probably equally at fault for the altercation.[27]

Scattered in the record are other signs that Hester was less than an honorable citizen. There is the matter of his illegal still, hidden in the woods near his Locust Gap Junction tavern.[28] Not to mention the charge, albeit by the newspaper editor who despised him, of electoral fraud.

THROUGH EARLY JULY, WILVERT'S EDITORIAL COMMENTS continued in the same vein, complaining about inept management of the county's finances and assailing the crookedness of the Democratic primary election. But in an effort to gin up his anti-Catholic, anti-Irish campaign, he exploited reports on national and worldwide events, beginning with corruption in New York City.

On July 8, 1871, the *New York Times* led with an explosive headline:

MORE RING VILLAINY, Gigantic Frauds in the Rental of Armories...Thousands of Dollars Paid for Bare Walls and Unoccupied Rooms, Over Eighty Per Cent of the Money Stolen.[29]

The *Times'* reporting marked the beginning of the end for William M. Tweed—the corrupt boss of Tammany Hall, the lord of lords of New York City Democratic politics. Tweed, along with New York City's mayor A. Oakey Hall, comptroller Richard "Slippery Dick" Connolly, and parks commissioner Peter Sweeny, were prominent members of the notorious Tweed Ring. Born in 1823, Tweed was elected to the New York County Board of Supervisors in 1858, the year that he became the head of the Tammany Hall political machine. He is most remembered for his profligate fleecing of New York City's treasury, a feat that has earned him a place—along with such luminaries as Huey Long and Spiro Agnew—in a gallery of the ten most corrupt politicians in American history. Tweed died in prison in 1878.[30]

A few days after the exposé of Tammany Hall began, New York City's residents awoke to another alarming headline:

A TERRIBLE DAY—The City in a State of Siege Yesterday—
Armed Mobs of Men in Possession of the Streets—Prompt
Action of the Police—The National Guard Heartily Sustain-
ing Them—Several Expeditions Made Against—Incipient
Outbreaks Suppressed—How the Hibernians Prepared for
the Struggle.[31]

On Orangemen's Day—which commemorates the July 12, 1690,
victory of Protestant King William of Orange over Catholic King
James II at the Battle of the Boyne—the streets of New York literally
exploded in violence. What started out as a parade to celebrate the
occasion erupted in a deadly clash among Irish Protestants (the
Orangemen), Irish Catholics, the New York City Police Department, and the New York State National Guard. In all, over sixty
civilians and three guardsmen were killed, and over 150 people
were wounded. Blame for the incident fell on Tweed, Mayor Hall,
and other members of the Tweed Ring for not controlling their
Irish Catholic "mobsters."[32]

While these events were enough to light a fire under Wilvert, a
short article that appeared in *Harper's Weekly* on July 15 and was
reprinted in the *Sunbury American* added a bucketful of bullets to
the blaze. The article, "A Mask Removed," was a critical response to
two essays published in the August 1871 issue of *Catholic World*.[33]
The first essay in *Catholic World*, "Infallibility," was written by
Father Isaac Thomas Hecker, the founder in 1858 of the Missionary
Society of St. Paul the Apostle (the Paulists). In 1869–1870 Hecker
attended the First Vatican Council, at which the church issued the
dogma of papal infallibility. In his *Catholic World* essay, Hecker
declared that the Catholic Church was infallible—incapable of
being wrong—and he explained why he thought that the pope, as
head of the church, was also infallible.[34]

The second essay in *Catholic World*, "The Secular Not Supreme,"
was written anonymously. It was a reactionary and internally
inconsistent piece inspired by a fear that Protestantism would
suppress the Catholic Church in America. In the article, the author

attempted to persuade readers that the Catholic Church posed no real threat to American government. But it seems to me the author's argument would heighten rather than calm any fear. He wrote that "the state divorced from the church and wholly separated from religion is separated from morality, and a state separated from morality cannot stand."[35] He continued with "there is no hope for our republic under Protestantism" and "whatever hope there is for our republic is in the growth and predominance of the Catholic Church" and "shall the state be informed by the infallible and holy church of God or by the synagogue of Satan?"[36]

The Tweed Ring and corruption, Irish Catholic mobs and violence, and the threat of Catholic dominance of political institutions were all brilliantly captured in one of Thomas Nast's famous cartoons, "The American River Ganges." (See figure 21.)

Figure 21. Thomas Nast's "The American River Ganges: The Priests and the Children" cartoon, originally published in Harper's Weekly on September 30, 1871. Courtesy of the Library of Congress, https://www.loc.gov/item/2004670394.

With St. Peter's Basilica in the background, the cartoon pictures Tweed and Co. up on the cliff, where some men are brawling and others are feeding little children to the Catholic bishop-crocodiles that lurk on the shoreline below. A Protestant minister, with his hand on the Protestant bible, is attempting to protect the little children from the jaws of the crocs.

FOR THE REPUBLICAN EDITOR OF THE *SUNBURY AMERICAN*, THE New York City debacle was a disaster made in heaven. And the flurry of religious propaganda played right into his hands. The enterprising Wilvert was quick to exploit the crisis. For the rest of the summer and into the fall, Wilvert engaged in a sustained attack on Northumberland County's Courthouse Ring, comparing its hapless foibles to the grandiose schemes of Tweed and Co. He implied that what occurred in New York City was a harbinger of what would surely occur in Northumberland County if the candidates favored by the Irish Catholic voters of the coal district prevailed in the fall election. Vicious attacks on the Roman Catholic Irish would plainly show that anti-Catholic sentiment was never far below the surface in nineteenth-century America, and was alive and well in Northumberland County. In any event, no one escaped the editor's wrath. E. G. Scott, the Democratic candidate for president judge; George Ryon, the candidate for district attorney; and Anthony J. Gallagher, the candidate for assembly, were all targeted. George McEliece was attacked as the county's treasurer.

Wilvert began his campaign in earnest in the July 22 edition of the *Sunbury American*. Atypically, he used his front page, which was usually reserved for poems and short stories, to reprint a complete copy of the *New York Herald*'s account of the Orange Day riot. Also, in his leading editorial, Wilvert set the stage for what was to follow in the coming months, an unrestrained assault on Catholicism. He began with a quotation from the *Williamsport Standard*: "A little hanging would not be much out of the way in the case of the New York Militiamen who fired without orders upon inoffensive civilians. The act was simply murder—no more, no less."[37] Then Wilvert spoke his mind:

> "Inoffensive citizens" indeed! Ignorant and bigoted rowdies, mostly foreign Irish Catholics, led by designing politicians who call themselves Democrats, and who swore weeks before, that Irish Protestants would be shot if they attempted to parade and exercise the rights of freemen. But the "inoffensive citizens" are the voters that make up the Democratic majority in New York, and fired upon their brother Irishmen from the windows, simply because they were Orangemen or Protestant Irishmen, and did not support the Pope and the Democratic party. Some of them at least have learned that liberty does not mean Roman Catholic Supremacy.[38]

Next, a reprint of a satire originally published in the Buffalo *Express* made fun of the "tremendous skedaddling among the Big Injuns of the Tammany Chiefs" in the aftermath of the riot.[39] All in all, excluding advertisements, three-fourths of the copy space in the *Sunbury American*'s July 22 edition was consumed by these articles. But Wilvert was barely warming up; throughout the summer and into the fall, he hammered away at his adversaries.

On Tammany Hall being controlled by Roman Catholics, Wilvert offered a reprint from the Harrisburg *Telegraph* that claimed "every department in the city [New York] is headed by or under the control of an Irish Catholic except the office of Mayor."[40] In support of the comment, the *Telegraph*'s article listed the name, title, and religion (Roman Catholic) of thirty-two public officials including Sweeny, Connolly, and a slew of judges.[41] On August 12, in a column-length story about the New York riots titled "Real Murderers of New York," Wilvert wrote that "New York has given over to the thieves and Catholics who manage there....These men—the Halls, Sweenys, Connollys are the murderers of New York who live to look at their rosewood hog-pens and mahogany barns stolen from the people while their poor dupes fall before the military or languish in garrets or cellars, wounded and wailing death."[42]

Of course, the difference between the Tweed Ring and Northumberland County's Courthouse Ring, in Wilvert's eyes, was only a matter of degree. "The Tammany Ring of New York," the editor wrote, "is composed principally of Irish Catholics who fleece the city annually of their millions. The Court House Ring of Sunbury is more moderate. The Irish Catholics who are now seeking to control the county...will not be as moderate as the Ring is now, and the taxes will increase accordingly."[43]

Amplifying criticism of Roman Catholicism, he printed these condemning words: "The conclusion is inevitable that the doctrines of the Roman Catholics, as promulgated by the head of the church, are inimical to civil and religious liberty or a Republican form of government,"[44] and "Father Hecker asserts in the church paper and on all public occasions that before the end of this century this great nation of ours will be as much under Roman Catholic rule as Rome was till lately made free."[45] And there was this innocuous little piece:

The Great Danger! Our free Republic passed through three terrific wars....The greatest danger of all is now coming forth upon us. A powerful and mighty church that claims to be above all human government...asserts that it is above and higher than our government and that all its members owe their highest allegiance to the Pope....The first victory of the Pope and his church is in New York City....This fearful church, by political power, we must meet and curb in this country or it will put down the Republic and all free religion, free thought, free press and free speech. This is the great danger that now threatens us and our liberty....Let us meet it at the ballot box in whatever shape it appears.[46]

All that was left to do was to show that the treacherous Irish Catholics from the coal region were conspiring to take over the county just like the Irish Catholic rioters took over New York City.

More than any of the Democratic candidates, Wilvert took aim at E. G. Scott, candidate for president judge. Scott was educated at Yale and upon graduation studied law in Sunbury under his uncle, William I. Greenough. Scott traveled extensively to Europe and Canada; he was a frequent contributor to the *Atlantic Monthly*; and he was the author of several books, some of which were accepted as textbook authority in the legal profession. He was a candidate for Congress in 1870 but was defeated by Republican John Black Packer of Sunbury. He died in 1919 in Wilkes-Barre.[47]

In his opening salvo against Scott, the editor proclaimed that "we should not allow the temple of justice of Northumberland County to be converted into a house of debauchery and intrigue."[48] What he was referring to became clear in several columns in which the editor claimed that Scott had promised, if elected, that he would "award my friends and my enemies must beware."[49] And again,

> it is an undeniable fact that the corruption of the judiciary in New York City, who are elected solely through the rowdy and Irish Catholic element…has brought one of the highest and most responsible offices into disrespect.…The late disgraceful row in the Democratic county convention, in this place, in regard to the nominee of that party for the judgeship [E. G. Scott] in which it was proven beyond a doubt that over four hundred fraudulent votes, or repeaters, were given for him in the Irish Catholic districts furnishes an example of the prostituting and corrupting influences that will be resorted to to [sic] secure a nomination.[50]

Despite the fact that Scott was a lay deputy in Sunbury's St. Matthew's Episcopal Church, Wilvert falsely claimed that Scott was a Catholic—just like those Tweed Ring fellows.[51] "Every person knows that it was the Irish Roman Catholic votes in the Coal region that placed him on the ticket…there cannot be found in Shamokin a man who will not tell you that he is a member and goes to the priest whenever he is in Shamokin. Everybody knows that Pat Hester, George McEliece and James Malone, the three leading Roman Catholic spirits of Northumberland County, are Mr. Scott's right-hand men. That he sits with them, sips with them and smokes with them as often as they meet together everybody can see for themselves."[52] Roman Catholic spirits—E. G. Scott, George McEliece, and Pat Hester!

Likewise, Anthony J. Gallagher was attacked because he was a Catholic. In a letter, a writer claimed that Gallagher, after obtaining a common school education, began teaching in the townships that were controlled by Catholics, thereby implying that Gallagher was an exemplar of a feared Catholic takeover of American schools. "Now the life of American institutions is threatened by the hordes of Irish Catholics who are flocking to our shores and congregating together in numbers large enough to obtain and hold the offices in their possession and to work everything towards the downfall of Protestant usages of free press, free speech and free bibles."[53] At the time, the Protestant translation of the Bible, the King James Version, was widely taught in many public schools, and there was a raging debate about its use. Catholics condemned the present system of education as sectarian. They argued that a portion of the public taxes should be reserved according to the number of children that the Catholics educated in their own schools. Protestants contended, in an argument that I suppose made some sense in 1871, that if "they closed the free schools and chained the Bible, that they would soon be so Papalized as to be prepared to invite the old grand-dame of the Vatican to our shores."[54]

Wilvert also found fault with Gallagher because he was supportive of labor unions, and even though the editor's criticism of labor unions was comparatively restrained, it was persistent. Richard Trevellick made a return visit to Northumberland County, speaking in Sunbury on July 25, 1871, with Gallagher and Hester in attendance.[55] In Wilvert's mind, Trevellick's "whole address was tinctured with Tammany Democracy."[56] He wrote, "The people generally have seen enough of the late New York City riots to convince them why the Irish Catholics are so favorable to the union and why the order [the union] is principally composed of that class of laboring men who are in league with the Tammany Ring of New York City in whose services Mr. Trevellick is now travelling."[57] Further describing Trevellick's speech, Wilvert wrote that "it was highly tinctured with modern democracy and his whole argument was similar to that of the Commune of Paris—*A division of property on Saturday night, feast and riot on the Sabbath and nothing left on Monday.*"[58] So now, based on the editor's point of view, it was not only Catholics who were in cahoots with Tammany Hall and the Tweed Ring, and Tammany Hall in league with the National Labor Union, but the National Labor Union was spouting the gospel of the Commune of Paris. Thus, with his connections to the Catholic Church and labor unions, not to mention his alleged fraudulent nomination, Gallagher was doomed on three counts.

Compared to his treatment of other members of the Democratic ticket, Wilvert's attacks on George Ryon, the candidate for district attorney, were rather mild. Ryon was born in Tioga County, Pennsylvania, in 1839. He was educated at the Genesee Wesleyan Seminary in Lima, New York, and at Eastman's Commercial College in Rochester, New York. Upon completion of his education, he was employed as a civil engineer but later began the study of law under his uncle, Judge James Ryon of Schuylkill County. He was admitted to the bar in 1864 and practiced law in Tioga County until he moved to Shamokin in 1869. In 1871 he drafted the charter for the Shamokin Banking Company and remained involved with the bank for several years.[59] Wilvert accused Ryon of being the prime mover "in getting up the fraudulent votes in the coal region."[60] Proof of this was that "Mr. Ryon has been sitting in the same buggy with Mr. Gallagher driving through the Irish districts soliciting the Irish votes."[61] Furthermore, Ryon was involved with the labor union. Otherwise, "how could he benefit them by delivering their address, in which 'he stated that in every issue between capital and labor, he would be found on the side of labor, and that he favored high wages,' if he was not acquainted with their workings?"[62]

While Wilvert's objections to the Courthouse Ring's financial mismanagement had some basis in facts, he wasn't about to forgo an opportunity to compare it to the Tweed Ring's thuggery. Without mentioning George McEliece by name, the editor continued to take aim at the county's finances. "THAT $94,000!" headlined several midsummer articles in which Wilvert made an obvious attempt to equate the Courthouse Ring with the Tweed Ring. Mentioning New York City's comptroller Richard "Slippery Dick" Connolly and Mayor Hall, and referring to the $2.87 million paid to one New York City plasterer in 1870, Wilvert wrote that "plastering in New York pays, and the ring here might have adopted the same plan instead of leaving the surplus funds in the hands of collectors to gain their good graces to keep them in office."[63] Repeating the same headline in the next issue, the editor suggested that the Northumberland County treasurer (McEliece) was burying unlawful expenditures in legitimate accounts.[64] By late summer, however, attacks based on the April 1871 auditor's report were old news.

For his closing argument on the eve of the election, Wilvert chose to publish a satirical treasure that added a Northumberland County exclamation point to Thomas Nast's memorable cartoon.[65] The seven-thousand-word essay, "A Dream," described a preposterous extravaganza, a lavish ox roast celebrated in the forest between Mount Carmel and Locust Gap. In attendance were denizens of New York City: Tweed and his cronies, the Irish Catholic rioters, and Father Hecker were joined by Jim Fisk, Robert Bonner, and Horace Greeley.[66]

In "A Dream," this notorious cast of characters arrived on a special New York train "ornamented with rare engravings in gold, and frescoes of beautiful design and finish."[67] The men and women came to celebrate the success of E. G. Scott, Anthony J. Gallagher, George Ryon, and Pat Hester for bringing electoral fraud, corruption, high taxes, labor unions, the rule of Irish Catholics, and "Universal Liberty, without Law and Order, or stint, or limit" to Northumberland County.[68] While Wilvert's earlier appeals to the voters were serious, even though they were hyperbolic, his final plea intended to turn the candidates into laughingstocks. The essay must have humiliated the candidates. Lucky for him, George McEliece was not mentioned by name.

As I consider what happened in Northumberland County in 1871, a worn-out platitude comes to mind. The fact that 150 years later Americans are still talking about electoral fraud, the place of religion in public schools, the role of labor unions in a capitalist economy, corruption in government, and fear of foreigners and an unpopular religion proves that the more things change, the more they remain the same. Moreover, Wilvert's antics and editorials clearly illustrate how the media influenced public opinion, just as it does today. In the end, Wilvert's strategy of using bigotry and fearmongering was successful. All the Democratic candidates were defeated in the fall 1871 election. And for some of Wilvert's targets, the undoing of 1871 was a life-changing event.

———— ◆ ————

PATRICK HESTER RAN INTO TROUBLE WITH THE LAW. A LARGE, burly man, he was clearly not a person to sneak up on in a dark alley or, if you were a Catholic priest, in broad daylight. On May 26, 1872, Hester and others forcibly entered St. Edward's Cemetery in Shamokin to bury their friend in defiance of Father J. J. Koch's refusal to allow the burial. The deceased was a member of the Ancient Order of Hibernians, which was condemned by the archbishop of Philadelphia as well as several pastors in the coal region, including Father Koch. A ruckus ensued, the men buried their friend, and for the deed, the men were charged with riot. For being the instigator in that little melee, Hester ended up in Pennsylvania's Eastern State Penitentiary for two years and seven months.[69] Of course the worst fact about Hester is that in 1877 he was tried, convicted, and executed—albeit on flimsy evidence—for the 1868 murder of Alexander Rea.

Anthony J. Gallagher, for a while at least, continued to teach.[70] He discontinued his book and stationery business.[71] In 1875 he was considered for the position of county superintendent of public schools but was not selected.[72] By 1877 he had moved to Ashland in Schuylkill County.[73] By 1880 he was located in Wilkes-Barre, working as a newspaper reporter. His children, Stella and George, were seven and three years old at the time.[74] At a later date, Gallagher was employed as a high school principal in Wilkes-Barre.[75] He died in 1898. His wife, Mary McEliece, died in 1896. Neither of them lived long enough to meet their grandson John Frank Gallagher (1918–2010). A son of George Gallagher and his wife, Julia, John Frank had a distinguished career in publishing. He first achieved prominence at Harcourt Brace in the 1950s and later headed the Michigan State University Press and the college departments at T. Y. Crowell and St. Martin's Press. In the course of his publishing career, he worked with such distinguished authors as Robert Penn Warren, Loren Eiseley, Abba Lerner, A. J. Ayer, Isaac Asimov, Gwendolen Carter, George Gaylord Simpson, Cleanth Brooks, and Jacques Barzun.[76]

For George McEliece, the fallout became manifest on March 23, 1872, three months after he completed his term of office, when a grand jury reported that "we are also informed that our ex-Treasurer of the county, when he gave up his office to his successor, removed all the deposits to Shamokin."[77] Wilvert's reaction was swift.

> The last Grand Jury gave the late County Treasurer rather a hard hit when they state that "when he gave up his office to his successor, removed all the deposits to Shamokin." This rather looks as though the Ring intended to follow in the footsteps of Boss Tweed, and go into the Banking business. Had the people submitted last fall and elected the full Democratic ticket, all this trouble would have been avoided, and a large Banking institution might have been established by the Ring, when in comparison to the York county frauds would have been nowhere. We don't wonder at the Ring becoming vexed at the honest people for spoiling their contemplated speculations whereby all might have become rich at the expense of the taxpayers.[78]

When the auditor's report for 1871 was published on April 13, 1872, it revealed that "the former Treasurer's account exhibits a deficit of $7,910.62 and, as Mr. McEliece cannot account for the whole amount, he has filed exceptions to the audit, although he had the report examined previous to its approval by the court.…Since the auditors met, a collector of Coal township exhibited a receipt of $700 from McEliece that is not on the books, which will increase McEliece's indebtedness to $8,610.62 [about $186,000 in today's dollars]."[79] The next relevant event came in 1873 when the court, in Northumberland County v. George McEliece, issued a judgment against McEliece and ordered him to reimburse the county in the amount of $6,898.70.[80] Considering that the salary of the county treasurer was $1,500 per year and that George's personal assets as of the 1870 census totaled $800, the amount was hardly chump change. Although it took many years, McEliece eventually paid it back. The auditor's report for 1873 shows that George made a payment of $2,160.[81] In 1877 he made a payment of $2,213, and in 1883 he made a final payment including principal and interest of $2,640.[82]

Was George McEliece an embezzler? It is worth noting that the county's judgment against him in 1873 did not include a prison sentence. So what happened? Hints appear in later newspaper articles. In 1874: "Mr. Henrie has had the promise of the [County Commissioner] office by the Ring two-years ago to make amends to the coal region for fleecing Geo. McEliece while in the Treasurer's office."[83] And: "McEliece was elected because we could not get out of it. But what makes matters worse, when he got out of office he was plundered by the Ring at the Courthouse, and sent home ruined and penniless."[84] On March 6, 1874, the Northumberland County Democrat newspaper reported: "A suit has been brought in the Court of Common Pleas of this county by ex-treasurer [George] McEliece against John Farnsworth, Esq., his late deputy treasurer, whom he accuses of appropriating funds. Hon. Jno. B. Packer is McEliece's attorney."[85] Unfortunately, the official court record of that case does not include the court's decision. The issue was not quickly forgotten. In 1877 the *Sunbury Gazette* reported:

The county accounts have been examined very closely by experts since 1871, whose opinion is that Mr, McEliece can never get his money back unless he can get those who surrounded him while in office to disgorge. It is well remembered that the "Ring" that existed then was in a low state of funds, were watched very closely, and as they had little chance to steal from the county, they commenced robbing their own members of the party. To create another extra expense to feed the "ring" now, when everybody is satisfied that Mr. McEliece was robbed by his own party, is adding insult to injury. Suppose our neighbor at the *Democrat* would advocate the disgorging of his friends to make Mr. McEliece whole?[86]

And in his 1886 obituary, it is clear that the matter remained a sore point: "About fifteen years ago he was elected treasurer of this county, and believing others as honest as himself, entrusted considerable of the business of the office to members of his own party, who robbed him and he came out a defaulter."[87]

What, in the end, were George's and Anthony's ties to the Molly Maguires? It's hard to say. Without question, George and Anthony associated with Patrick Hester, and Hester, by virtue of his leadership role in the Ancient Order of Hibernians, was identified at the time as a Molly leader. However, in a newspaper edited by a confirmed nativist, having a few random mentions included in the same paragraphs as the word *Molly* hardly serves as proof of anything. Indeed, although some alleged members of the Molly Maguires were politically active, Hester among them, the movement is more frequently linked to violence in the coal regions, and there is not a shred of evidence to suggest that either George or Anthony engaged in violence.

But it was George's son John McEliece who lived in the midst of that Molly mayhem. John McEliece's life could not have been easy. It began in earnest during the Civil War.

CHAPTER 20

JOHNNY'S GONE FOR A SOLDIER

*When unborn generations shall admire the bravery of the
46th Pennsylvania regiment, and justly, more particularly
Co. K., then shall the children and children's children of
that patriotic band feel their hearts swell within them as
they say "I am the offspring of that noble company."*

—*SHAMOKIN HERALD*, AUGUST 19, 1862

John McEliece's adult years unfolded under the dark cloud of the Civil War and its aftermath. The son of George McEliece and Mary Ann Woodside was born in 1842 in Dauphin County's Lykens Valley. Presumably, his childhood and adolescence were typical of the time—doing his chores, attending school, and playing with his cousins and neighbors. He may have helped with farmwork on his grandfather Jonathan Woodside's farm, especially at haying time. Being the only boy in a family that included six girls, he undoubtedly formed a strong bond with his father. By the age of fourteen, he was probably working beside his father on the railroads, performing tasks suited to his size and ability.

John's transition to adulthood was abrupt: when the Civil War broke out, he was eighteen years old. In early April 1861, prospects for the preservation of the Union appeared dim. Efforts were being made by both of Virginia's United States senators and former vice president John C. Breckinridge to induce Virginia to secede and join the other states of the Confederacy. The fear prevailed that if Virginia left, then Maryland would also go, and with those two states the capital at Washington could go with the South too.[1] Then, on April 12, Fort Sumter was attacked, and President Lincoln, in office little more than a month, quickly issued his famous call for seventy-five thousand troops. Five days later the Virginia convention voted to secede.

Shamokin's boys, the so-called three-month soldiers, responded enthusiastically. Stores were closed, church bells rang, and the coal breakers stopped. Among wild cheering the young men marched through the streets of the town. Cyrus Strouse prepared a membership roll, and within an hour, 103 names were put down. Possibly at work with his father somewhere on the railroad, John missed this early call. But Shamokinites had rallied to organize and fight to save the Union.[2] The young men boarded the Shamokin Valley and Pottsville Railroad and headed west for Sunbury, then on to Harrisburg, on April 22. They were mustered in at Camp Curtin as Eighth Regiment, Company A, Pennsylvania Volunteers. Aside from a brief foray into Virginia as guard to an advancing battery, the company spent their time posted near Williamsport, Maryland, to guard the fords along the shore of the Potomac. But just as their three-month tour of duty was almost up, the troops—and the Union—were sobered by news of defeat at the hands of the rebel army at Manassas Junction on July 21. The three-month recruits were mustered out on July 29.[3]

When the full force of the defeat of the Union forces at Manassas was realized, people were awestruck. But they responded quickly. For the second time a call for service arose in Shamokin. Many of the three-month soldiers reenlisted, and they were joined by several new recruits, among them John McEliece. On the day the Shamokin Guards departed, August 20, the street along the train depot was blocked with a dense mass of people—among them mothers, fathers, wives, daughters, brothers, sisters, and sweethearts. I can imagine John McEliece waving out the window as the train pulled away, his mother and father stoically returning his salute, his sisters holding back their tears. The boys arrived in Sunbury and transferred to the Northern Central Railroad, where they were joined in their travels by the Sunbury Guards.[4] Arriving in Harrisburg, they marched to Camp Curtin, where they were organized as Company K of the Forty-Sixth Pennsylvania Regiment on September 1, 1861, under the command of Colonel Joseph Knipe. The troops were mustered in on September 4, at which time the regiment was awarded its colors by Governor Curtin.

Considering that John served for a little over one year, in which only two days involved major battles, his Civil War story is not all that remarkable. Nonetheless, because his story is my family's story, I wanted to see what he saw during his tour of duty. So a few years ago, my brother and I went on a road trip following the Civil War trail through Pennsylvania, Maryland, and Virginia. Before we departed, I tried to figure out where John had been at any given time during the war. My idea was to try and get a sense of what it was like for John.

During John's service, Joseph Knipe's Forty-Sixth Pennsylvania Regiment, while under the overall command of General Nathaniel Banks—first in the Shenandoah theater of war and later in the Army of Northern Virginia—was at various times under the brigade command of General George H. Gordon, General Alpheus S. Williams, Colonel Dudley Donnelly, or General Samuel Crawford: that's four different brigade commanders in little over a year.[5] General Gordon's memoir of the war was published in 1885.[6] Letters from Williams to his daughters were published in 1959.[7] Both sources offer colorful personal accounts that are not included in the official record. The official records of the war have been digitized at HathiTrust.[8] Articles in the *New York Times* archives and contemporary Northumberland County newspapers offer additional insight. What is missing is John's diary of the war, which, according to my second cousin Robert McEliece, was handed down through John's daughter Isabell McEliece Campbell. We are still looking for it but have had no luck so far.

Continuing with John's story, on September 17 the regiment left Harrisburg, and their train slowly made its way south to Columbia where it crossed the Susquehanna to Wrightsville, then moved through the York County countryside on its way to Baltimore and eventually arrived in Washington, DC.[9] In the evening of September 18, John gathered with his companions around the army's campfire to celebrate his nineteenth birthday.

With little time for basic training, the regiment soon began its march to an encampment at Muddy Branch near Darnestown, Maryland. Passing through Rockville, some of the soldiers got drunk, and one of the drunken soldiers, John Lanaghan (possibly Lanehan or Lanahan, Company I), got in a quarrel. As punishment, he was tied to the rear of a wagon by Major Arnold Lewis. But Lanaghan somehow got loose, took a loaded musket from one of his comrades, and swore he would shoot the major. The major, learning of the disturbance, returned to the scene and ordered the soldier to surrender the gun, whereupon Lanaghan shot the major through the heart, killing him instantly.[10] The September 22 murder undoubtedly sent a shudder through the recently organized regiment.

A few days later, on September 26, the Forty-Sixth Pennsylvania, the Fifth Connecticut, the Nineteenth and Twenty-Eighth New York, the Second Massachusetts, and a Rhode Island battery were assigned to a brigade commanded by Colonel George H. Gordon, commander of the Second Massachusetts. Upon his initial visit to the Forty-Sixth, Gordon was unimpressed. He wrote, "I found one sentinel sitting down on his post; while another, as I galloped towards him, whipped his musket across both shoulders and dashing up and down, imitating quite creditably my horse's gallop, but with such a great grin of fun and good-nature that I laughed without control."[11] The men quite obviously were still raw recruits.

About the same time, Gordon discovered a young woman about eighteen years of age enrolled as a soldier in the Forty-Sixth Pennsylvania, and promptly ordered her to be discharged. The woman, Hatty Robinson of Auburn, New York—enrolled as Charles

D. Fuller, of Company D—was recruited at Dauphin County on September 2. Subsequent to her discharge, she was arrested by the provost police in Baltimore on October 5. She claimed that all the officers of the regiment were aware of her sex and that she was induced by Colonel Knipe to go with him to Washington. Although it is impossible to know if her story is true, the reporter opined that the woman's comments reflected poorly on the officers of the Forty-Sixth Pennsylvania.[12] Barely one month into its service, the regiment had suffered through two scandals. But that was the end of it; from that point forward the regiment would earn praise for the performance and bravery of its soldiers and officers.

On October 13 Gordon relinquished command of the brigade to General Alpheus S. Williams. Besides Colonel Knipe of the Forty-Sixth Pennsylvania Regiment, the regimental commanders included Colonel Gordon, Second Massachusetts; Colonel Ferry, Fifth Connecticut; Colonel Donnelly, Twenty-Eighth New York; Major Ledlie, Nineteenth New York; and Captain Tompkins, Company A, Rhode Island Battery; in all about five thousand men.[13] Encamped at Muddy Branch, a tributary stream of the Potomac located in Montgomery County, Maryland, Williams's brigade was charged with guard and outpost duty along the upper Potomac. Sounds simple enough. But it actually involved quite a bit more than standing around and shivering while glaring at the rebels on the opposite side of the river who were, likewise, standing around and shivering. As General Williams wrote, picket duty "was hard duty, as the poor fellows are not allowed fires and the weather has been very inclement. Still they go with wonderful cheerfulness."[14]

Around camp, the days were taken up with fatigue duty (domestic chores), drilling, and practicing battle maneuvers—the stuff that turned raw recruits into battle-ready soldiers—and after only a few months in service, the brigade performed their drills with the regularity of veterans. General Williams observed, "They trot off with knapsack packed, canteen and haversack and cartridge box, with forty rounds of ball cartridges, as if nothing was on their backs."[15]

THE FORTY-SIXTH'S FIRST MILITARY ENGAGEMENT CAME IMME-diately after the October 21 Battle of Ball's Bluff. Fought near Leesburg, Virginia, the Battle of Ball's Bluff was an unintended and poorly executed conflict in which a reconnaissance mission to the Virginia side of the Potomac resulted in a demoralizing Union defeat.[16] There were 1,002 Union casualties, many of whom drowned in the cold waters of the Potomac while attempting to escape under a withering enemy fire. The battle was already over when General Williams's brigade got its orders to march. By eight o'clock in the evening of October 21, the men were all on the move, and the head of the column reached Edwards Ferry between three and four o'clock in the morning on October 22.[17] (See figure 22.)

Figure 22. After the Battle of Ball's Bluff,
the Forty-sixth Pennsylvania was stationed at Edwards Ferry,
across the Potomac from Goose Creek. Photo by author.

Edwards Ferry is a beautiful spot, and when my brother and I visited, it was a gorgeous fall day—sun shining, clear skies, peaceful—which made it nearly impossible for me to imagine what it must have seemed like to John on a dark and stormy night when he had his first encounter with the fallout of war. While marching to their destination, the soldiers came upon the "first droppings of disaster: dark figures standing by the roadside muttered…about entire defeat in a fight that had lasted all day…men half-naked, hatless, shoeless, hastening in the pouring rain towards Poolesville."[18] The men decried: "We had to take to the water and swim, and they shot us while swimming; many men are drowned."[19] The relief column, "wearied with fatigue and shivering with cold, unsheltered from the pitiless rain that continued to fall in torrents, saw the wretched daylight break upon a closing scene over which the elements themselves seemed to brood in sympathy."[20]

After the main Battle of Ball's Bluff, skirmishes continued opposite Edwards Ferry for two more days. At daylight on October 22, Williams's brigade was supposed to cross over to Virginia and waited until two o'clock when orders came to bivouac. Around four o'clock came the sudden rattle of small arms and the booming of big guns from over the river. Williams's brigade was ordered under arms again but after some delay was ordered back for the night. Williams reported, "The day following [this would be October 23] was a furious gale, so strong that only one or two boats crossed. There was a furious popping of skirmishers all day and we could see bodies of their troops on the hills behind. My brigade was taken down to the ferry, my artillery embarked on the boats, and after dark I was ordered back again to remain in readiness to embark during the night."[21] During the conflict, the Forty-Sixth Pennsylvania had occupied the tow path opposite Harrison's Island, three and a half to four miles upriver from Edwards Ferry, with orders to hold the island unless driven out.[22] There they stayed for two or three days guarding the Potomac, and on October 26 at nine o'clock in the morning, they returned to their encampment at Darnestown. Thus, John's first taste of war turned out to be more about slogging through mud and hurrying up to wait rather than fighting the fight he had signed up for.

As the days grew shorter and the nights colder, Banks's division was relocated from Muddy Branch to an encampment near Frederick, Maryland. It was decided that topography and facilities in the new campground—well-drained soil, adequate supply of timber, buildings suitable for hospital purposes, access to paved roads, railways, and the Chesapeake and Ohio Canal—were favorable to setting up a winter camp. On December 4, Williams's brigade moved into winter quarters about three and a half miles west of Frederick.[23] It was there, on December 23, that the entire brigade stood in a rain-drenched field to witness the hanging of Private Lanaghan, the soldier who had killed Major Lewis three months earlier.[24]

Meanwhile, on the other side of the Potomac, in a lead-up to his Valley Campaign, Confederate General Stonewall Jackson launched an operation in western Virginia aimed at disrupting the Union's supply route from the west. His first attempt involved breaching Dam #5 on the Potomac at Williamsport in order to flood the Chesapeake and Ohio Canal. The rebels were also massing south of the Potomac in order to repel Union takeover of the B&O Railroad as it passed through northern Virginia between Harpers Ferry and Cumberland.[25] On January 5, as part of his campaign, Jackson opened fire on Hancock, Maryland, which was then under the command of Union General Frederick Lander.[26] General Williams was ordered to Hancock to relieve Lander on January 6, with the Forty-Sixth Pennsylvania ordered to delay at Williamsport while awaiting further orders. By January 8, it appears that Williams's entire brigade was stationed at Hancock.[27] The weather was miserable, and the Union troops witnessed "the horrors of this war in its worst form"—cold, starving refugees, scores of poor people who would struggle to survive the winter.[28] Through the winter Williams's pickets patrolled along the B&O line between Hancock and Cumberland, on the extreme right wing of the Army of the Potomac.[29] The brigade left Hancock on March 1, 1862, for Williamsport where they crossed the Potomac.

TYPICALLY, WHEN ONE SPEAKS ABOUT CIVIL WAR ACTIVITY IN the Shenandoah Valley, discussion ignores the fact that General Banks enjoyed tactical successes in the early months of 1862. Indeed, the standard map of Stonewall Jackson's Valley Campaign fails to show that Banks's army had initially driven Jackson's forces all the way up the valley (the Shenandoah flows northward, so a person going up the valley is heading south) to Gordonsville and Keezletown Crossroads. It was only after Banks's force was considerably reduced in size that he was ordered to withdraw to Strasburg. And even then, on May 16, after he was ordered to send two regiments to guard the railroad between Strasburg and Front Royal, Banks informed the secretary of war that his force was too small to defend his position at Strasburg.[30] Thus, although Banks shouldered the blame for the loss at the May 25 Battle of Winchester, the fault really belonged further up the chain of command.

For John and his regiment, the Valley Campaign involved labor on fieldworks and repairing bridges, a few skirmishes with the rebels, and a lot of marching, all of which preceded the First Battle of Winchester. Throughout March, April, and May, the Forty-Sixth chased the rebel army up, down, and around the Shenandoah Valley. They supported General James Shields in the First Battle of Kernstown.[31] They captured a company of the enemy's cavalry at Columbia Furnace.[32] By the end of April they had progressed beyond Harrisonburg.[33] But on May 17 the division began a retrograde movement to Strasburg due, probably, to the overextension of the troops and the long supply line.[34] On May 18 it was reported that no rebel infantry was in the valley.[35] But by May 21 Jackson's force was again near Harrisonburg.[36] And on May 22 Banks was preparing to be attacked, with the rebel enemy massing in greatly superior numbers.[37] (See figure 23.)

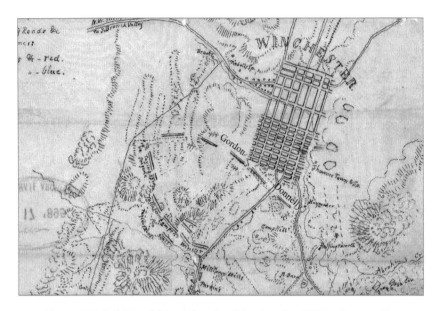

Figure 23. Jed Hotchkiss, Sketch of the Battle of Winchester, Va.,
Courtesy of National Archives, RG-109: War Department
Collection of Confederate Records, 1812-1927; Series: Confederate Maps,
1861-1876; File Unit: Virginia. Names and approximate location of
Union commanders Donnelly and Gordon added by author.
The Forty-sixth Pennsylvania was in Donnelly's brigade.
https://catalog.archives.gov/id/70653180, and modified by author.

There's no telling when Johnny first realized that he was about to be
on the front line in his first major battle of the war. Unbeknownst to
General Banks's command, on May 23, Generals Stonewall Jackson
and Richard Ewell, with an overwhelming force, made a surprise
attack at Front Royal, nearly wiping out the Union garrison, the First
Maryland, stationed at that place. (Ironically, it was the Confederate's
First Maryland regiment that led the attack.) Jackson's objective was
nothing short of capturing Banks's entire force of about five thousand
officers and men. After initially doubting the alarming reports that
came in from Front Royal, and resisting the efforts of members of his
staff to act with haste, Banks finally ordered his troops to make an
orderly retreat toward Winchester and the Potomac on the morning
of May 24. In a running fight involving several skirmishes and a major

battle, the May 25 Battle of Winchester, Union troops retreated to the Maryland side of the Potomac. Northumberland County's newspaper, the *Sunbury American*, published an account of the important role that the Forty-Sixth Pennsylvania, especially Company K, John's company, played in the action (see appendix A). Because Company K was in the thick of the fight, and noting that Johnny was promoted to corporal soon after the battle was over, it is fair to assume that he exhibited leadership and bravery during the battle.

Soon after abandoning the valley after the Battle of Winchester, Banks was ordered to reoccupy the "sacred ground." And so, on May 31, they did, with the Forty-Sixth Pennsylvania "cheering and singing as they marched, many of them singing John Brown's Body...without fear of the chivalric sons of that deluded state."[38] By June 3 General Crawford had replaced Colonel Donnelly as commander of the First Brigade—not due to any want of talent by Donnelly, but because Crawford outranked him.[39] Throughout June, General Banks's army was cooling its heels, holding down the fort in the Shenandoah Valley. On June 29–30, the Forty-Sixth Pennsylvania, with other regiments, completed a successful reconnaissance mission to Luray and back.[40]

AT THE SAME TIME, ACROSS THE BLUE RIDGE, UNION GENERAL George B. McClellan and Confederate General Robert E. Lee were thrashing it out in the Seven Days' Battles near Richmond (June 25–July 1). And in Washington on June 26, by the order of President Lincoln, all of the "stray and loose armies within the theater of our operations" were placed under the command of General John Pope.[41] Pope's 70,000-man Army of Northern Virginia included three corps—the first led by Franz Sigel, the second by Banks, and the third by Irvin McDowell. Banks's corps included two divisions. The First Division, commanded by General Alpheus S. Williams, included two brigades: the First Brigade, which included the Forty-Sixth Pennsylvania, was under the command of General Crawford; the Third Brigade was under the command of General

Gordon.[42] The field officers of this division—Williams, Gordon, Colonel Donnelly, Colonel Knipe, Colonel George Chapman, Lieutenant Colonel Edwin Brown—were dedicated to the men who served under them.[43] Their dislike of General Pope, combined with empathy for the soldiers, no doubt helped ameliorate the dispiriting effect that Pope had on the troops. The dislike had to do with Pope's orders, with his demeaning communications with General Banks, and with the seemingly pointless movements of the army.

If nothing else, soldiers have always found a way to express their discontent. Sometimes they do so overtly; at other times, the soldiers manage to find ingenious ways to get under a commander's skin. The following amusing story, originally told by General Gordon, reveals how they did it to General Pope. The occasion was an inspection of the army where it was amassing near Warrenton, Virginia.

> As the General rode in turn in front of each brigade, he was to be received by each regiment in the orthodox style of the regulation,—three ruffles from the drum, the march, the colors drooped, and a present-arms. Now when Pope was receiving these regulation tokens of respect from the left regiment of the brigade in my front, what did that incorrigible Twenty-seventh Indiana do, on the left of my line, but put the whole paragraph, of ruffles, marches and droops in, and all in the wrong places,—the colonel commanding looking on meanwhile as blandly as did Pickwick when he awoke in the pound as a trespasser upon the lands of the fierce Captain Boldwig. My feelings [Gordon's] were indescribable. I fancied Pope looked like Captain Boldwig....He let out in censure with such vigor, that if words had been missiles our army would never have failed for want of ammunition.[44]

That wasn't all. If there was an increase in the use of cuss words among the rank and file, the field officers not only tolerated them but also matched and possibly exceeded the common soldiers. Colonel Gordon agreed.

I think General Pope's freedom of speech infected his command with a general mania for discussing men and measures. It was not an uncommon event for generals and colonels to meet at my tent, and express their views in words stronger than those generally used in war councils—"cuss words" of such vigor, when they fell from the lips of our division commander, [A. S. Williams] that all were appalled into silence, save Colonel Knipe of the Forty-Sixth Pennsylvania; and when he began, Williams was silent. Ordinary words being totally inadequate to express one's feelings, swearing became an epidemic.[45]

WEATHER HAS ALWAYS PLAYED AN IMPORTANT ROLE IN WAR. Eventually the rain stopped, only to be replaced by a summertime Virginia heat wave. Clueless, Pope issued Order No. 18 on August 6, providing that "hereafter, in all marches of the army, no straggling or lagging behind will be allowed. Commanders of regiments will be held responsible that this order is observed, and they will march habitually in the rear of their regiments."[46] Never mind that the temperature on August 7 reached 92°F and for the preceding six days the lowest temperature at two p. m. had been 88°F.[47]

And so it was on August 9—hot, humid, and dusty—when Union and Confederate armies clashed at the Battle of Cedar Mountain. Strategically the battle had little bearing on the outcome of the war, but for my story it is uniquely important because it is where John was wounded and captured by the rebels. Naturally, the visit to the battle site was the highlight of our road trip. I wondered if, when I got there, I would experience some profound or eerie feelings. I didn't. But my brother and I tried to figure out where we thought John had been wounded.

Robert Krick, in *Stonewall Jackson at Cedar Mountain*, used several sources to piece together the details of how the battle unfolded. (See figure 24.) His sources included, among other documents, historical accounts of the New York, Connecticut, and Wisconsin regiments but unfortunately no particular account from the Forty-Sixth Pennsylvania because, I suppose, most of the officers who could have written that account were killed or wounded in the battle. Thus, if John's diary were to be discovered, it might reveal not only what happened to him in particular but also new information about the role of the Forty-Sixth in the battle.

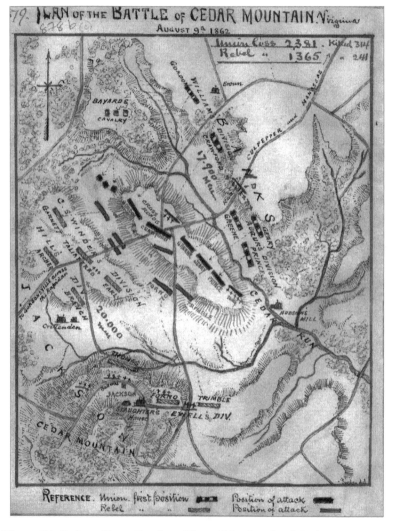

Figure 24. Robert Knox Sneden, Plan of the Battle of Cedar Mountain, Virginia, August 9th. The Forty-sixth Pennsylvania was in Crawford's brigade. Courtesy of Library of Congress, Geography and Map Division, https://www.loc.gov/item/gvhs01.vhs00057/, and modified by author.

The battle unfolded in several stages. First there was some cannon-ading, next an attack by the Union army through a cornfield, fol-lowed by a Union attack through a wheat field, and later a successful counterattack by the rebels, who, at the end of the battle, controlled the field. According to Krick, Crawford's brigade of Williams's division was lined up in the woods on the edge of the wheat field, in order from left to right, the Fifth Connecticut, Twenty-Eighth New York, and Forty-Sixth Pennsylvania. Further, one of General Williams's staff officers had ordered six companies of the Third Wisconsin—of General Gordon's brigade—to join the line on the right of the Forty-Sixth Pennsylvania. Opposite the brigade, on the Confederate side, were two Virginia brigades. One was lined up in three rows in the woods on the opposite side of the wheat field directly in front of Crawford's brigade. The other was hidden in a brushy field near Crawford's right flank. Which means to say that when Crawford's order came to fix bayonets and charge across the wheat field, the Forty-Sixth Pennsylvania and the six companies of the Third Wisconsin were targeted by rebels from two sides. As Crawford's brigade advanced across the wheat field, the Fifth Connecticut and Twenty-Eighth New York led the way and were closely followed by the Forty-Sixth Pennsylvania. The Forty-Sixth, once it reached the woods held by the rebels, split into two wings: one wing joined the Connecticut and New York regiments as they charged toward the rebels' cannons located near a gate; the other wing charged straight ahead into the woods, where it overwhelmed the Tenth and Twenty-Seventh Virginia regiments.

Because John was captured, we know that he was behind enemy lines. Was he wounded in the initial charge across the wheat field and captured only when the rebels retook the field? Was he wounded and captured in the woods during the initial assault? I can only speculate. But his wounds in the left hand (a Minié ball shattered the first metatarsal bone and was not properly set, and the hand remained deformed throughout his life) and left shoulder (a bullet lodged at the top of the shoulder and was extracted) suggest that he was shot while in the act of shooting. And because, as Krick describes, the fighting in the woods was more likely with fists, bayonets, and the butts of their rifles, my guess is that John was shot during the initial charge across the wheat field and captured later in the day when the rebels retook the field. If my guess is correct, the implication is that he lay among the dead and wounded under the glare of the sun on that scorching hot day for several hours before he was captured. But, as Krick reported, the rebel soldiers were humane in their treatment of the Union captives and soon-to-be captives. Later in the day, when a truce was arranged so that the Union men could bury their dead, they found that each wounded Union soldier had been given a canteen of water by their rebel opponents. Following the battle, the *Shamokin Herald* reported on the battle (see appendix B).

John survived, of course. He was located in a rebel hospital at Staunton, Virginia, until he was discharged on September 16, the day before the Battle of Antietam. (Perhaps the Confederates anticipated the impending need for hospital beds.) For the remainder of September 1862 and into November, John was located at Fort McHenry, Maryland, which was at the time a Union prisoner-of-war camp.[48] By December he had rejoined his regiment, which was located across from Harpers Ferry at Maryland Heights, at the confluence of the Shenandoah and Potomac Rivers, at which place he was discharged with the rank of sergeant on December 6 on account of the wounds suffered at Cedar Mountain. (See figure 25.) And so, our Johnny went marching home, at least for a while.

Figure 25. John McEliece was discharged at Maryland Heights, opposite Harper's Ferry. View of Harpers Ferry from the Maryland side of the Potomac River. On the left is the Shenandoah River. On the right is the Potomac. Photo by author.

JOHN'S SECOND TOUR OF DUTY DURING THE CIVIL WAR WAS mentioned in his official pension file. He volunteered in the Thirty-Sixth Pennsylvania Emergency Volunteer Regiment for about six weeks in the summer of 1863, coincident with Confederate General Robert E. Lee's invasion of Pennsylvania. On June 16 President Lincoln issued a call for 100,000 six-month federal troops and governor Andrew Gregg Curtin followed up by requesting 50,000 men from Pennsylvania. Accordingly, on Saturday, June 20, the *Sunbury American* announced on page 2: "The miners and other citizens of Shamokin to the number of 120 men came in on Wednesday [June 17] and proceeded to Harrisburg…accompanied by a company from this place." The troops, including John, had responded to Curtin's call. But as documented in Samuel P. Bates's *History of Pennsylvania Volunteers*, the men were not mustered in until July 4, the day after the conclusion of the battle at Gettysburg.

Why the two-week delay, especially considering the urgency of the moment? Puzzling, to be sure.

Untrained as many of them were, some of the Pennsylvania emergency troops were involved in construction of fortifications above the approaches to the three bridges crossing the Susquehanna at Harrisburg; others were ordered to guard the Columbia-Wrightsville Bridge, which connected Adams and Lancaster Counties. But not John's Thirty-Sixth. In fact, as I later discovered on page 3 of the June 20 edition of the *Sunbury American*, "the Shamokin Company returned this (Friday) morning [June 19], and in the same train some of our hands—None but six-months men are wanted." So John's company, for whatever reason, passed the crucial weeks leading up to the bloodiest battle of the Civil War biding its time in Shamokin. And it wasn't only the Shamokin men who dawdled. The initial response to Lincoln's and Curtin's calls for volunteers was lukewarm for several reasons: rumors circulated that there was no actual invasion; workers were busily engaged on their farms and in other well-paying jobs; the terms of service and pay were not clearly spelled out; men worried that, once they were mustered in, the army would find a reason to extend enrollment beyond six months. In any event, a desperate Governor Curtin issued another proclamation on June 26 calling for sixty thousand men for the defense of the state, for a period of ninety days, unless discharged sooner. Pennsylvanians did respond to the late call with about twenty-four thousand troops, but not in time to halt the rebel advance.

<hr>

By June 26 confederate forces under Major General Jubal Early had entered Gettysburg and demanded a ransom—that they did not get—and Confederate Lieutenant General Richard Ewell was on the verge of capturing Carlisle, a mere twenty-five miles west of Harrisburg. On the next day, the city of York surrendered to Early, who then attempted to seize the Columbia-Wrightsville Bridge, which was burned by Union militia as a defensive tactic. On June

28 Confederate forces occupied Mechanicsburg, four miles west of Harrisburg, and were planning to capture Harrisburg on July 1.

But on June 28 General Lee, with his army scattered, had learned that the Army of the Potomac, now under the command of Major General George Meade, was on his flank. Lee issued orders for his army to consolidate. The Union army rushed to intercept the rebels, and as we know, the confrontation at Gettysburg began on July 1. Just as the battle got underway, the Shamokin men, for the second time, passed through Sunbury on their way to Camp Curtin.[49] One can only imagine what it was like for the raw volunteers who were stuck in Harrisburg, anxiously awaiting news of the battle, wondering when they would be mustered in and what their assignment would be. What relief they must have felt on July 4 when news arrived not only of the Union victory at Gettysburg but also of the capture of Vicksburg on the Mississippi.

It was truly a memorable Fourth of July for the men who were mustered in as the Thirty-Sixth Pennsylvania Emergency Volunteer Regiment under the command of Colonel H. C. Alleman: John was a sergeant in Company K. Presumably the regiment passed the next two days, July 5–6, organizing, procuring supplies, and practicing basic maneuvers. On July 7 they were ordered to Gettysburg. They left Camp Curtin, traveled via the Cumberland Valley Railroad to Carlisle, and marched five miles to Mount Holly, where they encamped. And then it started pouring.[50] The rain drenched the soldiers, flooded streams, and washed out bridges. Finally, after a circuitous thirty-five-mile slog, the regiment arrived at Gettysburg in the afternoon of July 9.

As they made their way to their encampment along the Baltimore Pike south of the village, some of the men, bug-eyed, took in the gruesome scene: "death in its ghastliest and most abhorrent forms everywhere. Festering corpses at every step...a hideous and revolting sight."[51] Others, protecting themselves from the sight, kept their eyes glued to the ground. But there was no escaping the smell of death. As the honored journalist Daniel Pearl wrote in 2001 concerning the aftermath of an earthquake in Gujarat,

India: "It smells. It reeks....Even if you've never smelled it before, the brain knows what it is, and orders you to get away. After a day, the nose gets stuffed up in self-defense. But the brain has registered the scent, and picks it up in innocent places: lip balm, sweet candy, stale breath, an airplane seat."[52] Pearl spoke of hundreds of decaying bodies, whereas at Gettysburg there were 7,500 dead soldiers, many of whom—especially Confederate soldiers—were still unburied when the Thirty-Sixth arrived. Not to mention the carcasses of at least 1,500 horses and mules rotting in the July heat.

But the men had a job to do. Clean up the immense battlefield. The task was made more difficult because thousands of people immediately descended on the place. Some came in search of loved ones; others came simply to gawk and collect souvenirs. Indeed, a half dozen citizens from Northumberland County paid a hurried visit to the battlefield, noting that a number of the dead rebels were still unburied, which, together with hundreds of dead horses, made the air "redolent with fetid smell"—lofty words for a big stink.[53]

During their tour of duty, the men of the Thirty-Sixth performed a variety of tasks. The first day's work was to gather arms and accoutrements. "In his official report Colonel Alleman gives the following figures in detailing this branch of the work: There were brought in not less than 26,664 muskets; 9,250 bayonets; 1,500 cartridge boxes; 204 sabers; 14,000 rounds of small-arm ammunition; 26 artillery wheels; 702 blankets; 40 wagon loads of clothing; 60 saddles; 60 bridles; 5 wagons; 510 horses and mules; 6 wagon loads of knapsacks and haversacks."[54] The men supervised groups of rebel prisoners who buried their dead comrades in arms. They burned dead horses. The soldiers helped transport injured soldiers from field hospitals, barns, and homes scattered around the battlefield to Camp Letterman, a large temporary general hospital. Some of the troops got a lucky break when they were assigned to accompany rebel prisoners to Baltimore.

In all, I think the men of the Thirty-Sixth Pennsylvania Emergency Volunteer Regiment had one of the most difficult tasks of the war, certainly one of the ugliest. But it was a task without glory. Unlike the effusive tribute the Shamokin men received in the *Shamokin Herald* after the Battle of Cedar Mountain, there was not a single word in that newspaper when their men returned from Gettysburg. The *Sunbury American* hardly did better, not even mentioning the difficult duties that the men performed:

On Wednesday last, Company F., Capt. S. P. Wolverton, of this place, and Company K., Capt. A. R. Fiske, of Shamokin, of the Thirty-Sixth Regiment of the three months troops, after a service nearly two months, reached this borough. They were brought to this place in an extra train. The Shamokin Company left for home via Shamokin Valley and Pottsville Railroad on the same day. They were mustered out of service and paid at Harrisburg on Wednesday last. The men enjoyed excellent health with but a few exceptions while absent, and made considerable progress in drill and discipline under their officers.[55]

One month after his return from Gettysburg, John celebrated his twenty-first birthday. There is no evidence that he suffered lasting mental trauma from his experience, but then again, shell shock, battle fatigue, and PTSD would not replace the notions of cowardice and melancholia until World Wars I and II, Vietnam, and later wars. After the war, John joined the Grand Army of the Republic, the veterans' organization of the time. He also joined the less famous Union Veterans' Union, whose membership was restricted to those who had served in combat. John endured his physical infirmity. He applied for an invalid pension in 1874. In 1879 "he received a lump-sum payment of $683.83 (about $19,000 in today's dollars) for arrears of pension from the time of his discharge in 1862. Thereafter he received amounts varying from $5 to $10 a month. At a young age, he had already seen more death and misery than most people witness in their entire lives. But he had also appreciated the value of friendship and camaraderie born of shared experience. It was the latter that seemed to motivate his life.

CHAPTER 21

A CASE AGAINST THE MOLLY MAGUIRES

⸺◆⸺

After John McEliece completed his military service, he was employed by the Northern Central Railroad, first as a brakeman and later as an engineer. In 1864 he married Lydia Adams, a young lady from Danville, Pennsylvania. But five months after their marriage, pregnant Lydia contracted smallpox; she went into premature labor, and both she and her baby died in May 1864. The tragic scene was described by John's sisters and a lifelong family friend in separate affidavits in John's pension file. Both Elizabeth and Sarah (Annie) McEliece recalled that Lydia and her baby were buried in the middle of the night without benefit of a funeral, a precaution against the communicable disease. Sarah added that she and her father, George, arrived too late for the burial. The McElieces' lifelong friend wrote that her sister Jane had been nursing Lydia, but when Lydia came down with smallpox, the woman abandoned Lydia.[1] Consequently, as Annie wrote, Mary Ann Woodside came to care for her daughter-in-law.

Sometime around 1865 or 1866, the McElieces moved to Locust Gap, an unincorporated community in Mount Carmel Township, Northumberland County, located about twelve miles from Shamokin. Living near them was the family of Michael Lukens, who worked as a clerk at a colliery. Michael's eldest daughter, Ann Ellen, and John McEliece were married August 21, 1867, and their first child, George, was born three months later on November 10,

1867. Given the facts that Ann Ellen recorded her marriage date in the family Bible as August 21, 1866, and that the family made the same claim decades later in what I presume was the interview leading to the biographies in the old history books, it is obvious that the shotgun wedding was a source of embarrassment. Indeed, I wonder if the out-of-wedlock pregnancy caused Michael Lukens to disown his eldest daughter: noticeably absent in the first and middle names of John and Ann Ellen's six male children is the name of their maternal grandfather, Michael.

Ann Ellen Lukens McEliece died in 1908. My generation knew very little about her family's background. Indeed, Ann Ellen's father, Michael Lukens, was orphaned at the age of thirteen, and it's probable that he himself was unaware of his forebears' past, which made the discovery of the important role that Ann Ellen's ancestors played in Pennsylvania's colonial period all the more startling.[2] She was a descendant of Johannes Cassel (1639–1691), one of the founders of Germantown, Pennsylvania, and John Cadwallader (1676–1742) of Horsham Township, a prominent Quaker missionary. She was also a descendant of Jan Lucken (1650–1744), who arrived from Krefeld, Germany, aboard the *Concord* on October 6, 1683. Lucken was among the thirteen original settlers of Germantown. And in an interesting coincidence, Lucken was also an ancestor of John Lukens, surveyor general of Pennsylvania from 1761 to 1776 and 1781 to 1789—the man who had signed, in 1765, the surveys of James Woodside's tracts identified as the Deer's Watering Place and the Indian Encampment. But without question, the most prominent descendant of Jan Lucken is president Theodore Roosevelt, who would be Ann Ellen's fifth cousin.[3]

John's move to Locust Gap opened a new and, to me, confusing chapter in his life. Confusing because a haunting spirit, the ghost of Molly Maguire, wanders now and again through his story, often overshadowing the most salient factor that influenced John's life, namely, the complexity of managing a colliery at a time when the struggle between free market capitalism and workingmen was just beginning to come into focus. In order to understand John's work-a-day life, then, I had to sort out what impact the reported Molly violence had on the everyday lives of the people of Northumberland County, generally, and John McEliece, particularly.

As shown in table 1, Northumberland County was not immune from trouble. Katherine Jaeger's listing of Molly Maguire incidents included those crimes that could be verified by newspaper articles or court records. Several of the crimes were labor related, many were robberies, a few involved family quarrels, some had to do with retributive justice, and the list was rounded out by drunken brawls, arson, and random acts of violence.[4]

TABLE 1. MOLLY MAGUIRE INCIDENTS IN NORTHUMBERLAND COUNTY

Year	Number of Molly-related crimes in Northumberland County
1866	1
1867	4
1868	2
1869	3
1870	7
1871	0
1872	3
1873	0
1874	5
1875	5
1876	1

Source: Jaeger, "The Molly Maguires of Northumberland County, Pennsylvania."

Even though Jaeger's list may not be exhaustive and focuses on so-called Molly crimes, one could argue that a community that experienced what amounts to an average of 3.1 violent Molly-related offenses per year over a ten-year period and, in the worst year of 1870, a rate of 0.17 per one thousand residents, is not exactly a hotbed of crime.[5] Indeed, considering the 2018 United States' violent crime rate of 3.689 per one thousand residents, the characterization of crime in Northumberland County during this period as being out of control is contrary to the evidence, especially when one considers that the community was experiencing a lag in public services and policing due to rapid growth.[6] Moreover, as will be shown in the next chapter, the harm to families caused by Molly criminal activity pales when it is compared to the suffering that resulted from injuries and deaths in the coal mines. Thus, the brouhaha, then and now, about crimes of the Mollys, at least in Northumberland County, is overstated. And I would not be surprised to discover similar results if the actual Molly-related crime rate were tallied for neighboring Schuylkill County, the center of Molly activity.

Nonetheless, criminal activity in the Locust Gap area propelled John McEliece to act. It wasn't long after he moved to Locust Gap that, on October 17, 1868, Alexander Rea, an agent for both the Locust Mountain Coal and Iron Company and Coal Ridge Improvement Company, was murdered in cold blood on the road between Centralia and Mount Carmel. As described in the local newspaper at the time, "that he was murdered for money, there is little doubt, as he was generally liked, and not known to have a single enemy."[7] Although there is no evidence to support the assertion, a family legend claims that John was involved in the initial chase to find the killers. Not long after the murder, three men—Thomas Donohue, John Duffy, and Michael Prior—were arrested, tried, and acquitted of the murder. A fourth man, none other than Patrick Hester, turned himself in to the authorities, but he was later released for lack of evidence. After the acquittals and dismissal, the murder case went cold for nearly a decade. Notably, contemporaneous reports about the murder in the *Miners' Journal* and the *Columbian and Democrat* make no mention of the Molly Maguires.[8]

Soon after the 1868 Rea murder, John organized and equipped a military company, initially numbering sixty men, to guard against further acts of violence.[9] The Washington Rifles, with John as its captain, had few qualms about meting out a sort of vigilante justice, as illustrated by the following incident in Locust Gap that happened sometime in early 1870 and was described in detail in 1876:

> [John] Mahan is the man who, in company with Bear Dolan and Taylor Dolan, several years ago went into a house at Locust Gap, locked themselves in, and almost beat to death an old man and old woman [a Mr. and Mrs. Burk]. Capt. McEliece's company, who were drilling at the time, heard the cries of the old people and broke into the house when a desperate fight ensued. Bear Dolan, in attempting to shoot one of the soldiers missed his aim and shot Mahan in the head. *Mahan was also badly beaten by the soldiers who left him for dead* and pursued Bear Dolan who succeeded in getting away. When they returned they found Mahan still alive and, keeping him in charge until next morning, brought him to Shamokin.[10]

Presuming that John had been a witness in the Dolan and Mahan trials, I was eager to read his testimony. At the Northumberland County courthouse—built in 1865—I was directed to case numbers John Mahan, #31, August 1870; and Patrick Dolan, #3, January 1873.

The county's original court records, dating back to 1772 when the county was erected, were stored in numbered metal boxes that were organized on floor-to-ceiling shelves along a long wall. There was a big book listing all the cases by year and what number box the files were in. It didn't take long to find what I was looking for. To retrieve the boxes, there was a long pole with a box-grabber gadget on the end—similar to the window openers they used to have in schools. The gadget on the end of the pole hooked into a corresponding gizmo on the metal box so you could bring the heavy box down without getting clobbered. Each box contained about ten bundles tied with ribbons, and each bundle included ten slightly yellowed and surprisingly supple documents of original court records. The first file, six pages long, Commonwealth v. John Mahan, included an explanation of the charge against Mahan, handwritten by the district attorney, but nothing else. The second file, two pages, Commonwealth v. Patrick Dolan alias Bear Dolan, was a motion to quash the bill of indictment, which had been handed down on November 6, 1872. I was disappointed that there were no witness lists, much less trial transcripts. However, newspaper accounts revealed the disposition of both cases. Mahan was sentenced to two years in the Eastern State Penitentiary.[11] Dolan was sentenced by the court to five years and three months in the Eastern State Penitentiary.[12] As was the case in the 1868–1869 reporting on the Rea murder, early reporting in the *Shamokin Herald* about the assault on Mr. and Mrs. Burk did not mention the Mollys.

In any event, the Washington Rifles were clearly a force to be reckoned with when they encountered the criminal element. But those occasions were rare. The militia was also a social group. The men were liberally entertained at Weaver's Hotel by Shamokin's leading citizens. They marched in parades, and they turned out for military displays, one observer noting that "the Washington boys behaved admirably, and not a man was intoxicated."[13] The militia was initiated into the Pennsylvania National Guard, first in 1873 as part of the Eighth Division and later in 1874 as Fourth Division, Seventh Regiment, Company A, at which time it included eighty-two men.[14]

In addition to organizing and commanding a local militia group, John served as justice of the peace for Mount Carmel Township. First elected in 1870, he was granted his commission by the Commonwealth on September 5, 1870, and continued to serve for fifteen years. The office of justice of the peace is unusual today, but in the late nineteenth century it was still an important element of the judicial system in remote communities. Although untrained in the law, the justice of the peace had considerable authority. In criminal matters, Pennsylvania's justices of the peace were authorized to issue warrants for arrest, arrest offenders, subpoena witnesses, administer oaths, and conduct preliminary hearings similar to a grand jury proceeding. Based on evidence presented in the hearing, the justice could either discharge the accused, bail him if the case was bailable, or commit him to jail pending trial before a judge. In civil actions, duties of a justice of the peace were constrained by several Commonwealth statutes, including one that limited suits to those not exceeding one hundred dollars.[15] As justice of the peace, John also performed administrative tasks such as witnessing last wills and testaments. It is amazing to me that so much power would be conferred on an individual with no legal training. What it says about John is that the people who repeatedly elected him to office respected him for his judgment and common sense.

EVEN THOUGH THE VIOLENCE AROUND LOCUST GAP WAS APPARENTLY contained by this makeshift system of law and order, the uproar in the press persisted and was amplified. Throughout the early 1870s, desultory reports of Molly Maguire activity appeared in the *Shamokin Herald* and the *Sunbury American*. In 1875, the year of a long, bitter coal miners' strike, reports of acts of violence in the coal regions were sometimes conflated with Molly Maguireism. Typical were the types of crimes one would associate with the labor dispute: train derailments, dumping loaded coal cars, property damage, and threatening strikebreakers (known at the time as blacklegs). That said, in a major exception, in Schuylkill County six murders were committed by Irishmen and were attributed to the Mollys. And in the spectacular trial that followed in 1876, Commonwealth v. John Kehoe et al., the prosecution, led by Franklin Gowen, the president of the Philadelphia and Reading Railroad, deliberately and maliciously conflated the Mollys with the Ancient

Order of Hibernians, characterizing the AOH as the most villain-
ous and murderous fiend that had existed since the world began.
Afterword, the proceedings of the trial were promptly printed in a
262-page book.[16] (In a curious historical footnote, Jack Kehoe was
granted a full pardon by governor Milton J. Shapp in January 1979.)

And so the outrage about Molly "outrages" had itself become
outrageous, with stories reaching an audience as far away as the
Hawaiian Islands.[17] In Pulaski, Tennessee, the editor of the local
newspaper opined that Pennsylvania authorities should "send
for [General Phillip] Sheridan," who at the time was engaged
in murderously subduing the Plains Indians.[18] Moreover, Molly
Maguireism had become synonymous with protests of all kinds. In
Chicago the "coal heavers" went on strike and were "performing the
Molly Maguire role—going about intimidating non-union workmen and making things generally unpleasant."[19] And according to
a ridiculous statement by an indignant Indiana physician who had
been expelled from a medical society for inserting an advertisement
in a local newspaper, the members of that society were nothing
short of "Medical Molly Maguires."[20] Further, a new dimension
entered the discussion: anticipating our enduring national phobia
about communism, the National Industrial Congress, a precursor
of the Knights of Labor, was characterized as the "Communistic
Congress" and tied to the Mollys; it was feared that an element
in its platform adopted at Indianapolis—that the military should
be prevented from interfering with just protests of the "toiling
masses"—would lead to Molly Maguire outrages.[21]

By the time Patrick Tully, Peter McHugh, and Patrick
Hester (Hester for the second time) were arrested in 1876 for the
murder of Alexander Rea, readers no longer questioned the merit of
inflammatory headlines. On November 29, 1876, the *Williamsport
Sun and Lycoming Democrat* announced: "MURDER WILL OUT.
Molly Maguires Arrested for a Crime Committed 12 Years Ago." At
the trial in 1877, Commonwealth v. Patrick Hester, Peter McHugh,

and Patrick Tully, John and George McEliece and Anthony J. Gallagher and several other reputable citizens testified on behalf of the defense that the Commonwealth's chief witness, Dan Kelly, alias Kelly the Bum, was a liar and not to be trusted. A low-life criminal, Kelly turned state's evidence after he was guaranteed immunity from prosecution as one of the murderers. Strangely, John was also summoned to testify on behalf of the prosecution. In that part of his testimony, John corroborated a part of Kelly's story having to do with Kelly's whereabouts on the day after the murder. Illustrating one of the peculiar moments in the trial, John's testimony included the following exchange:

Cross examination by Mr. Ryon (for the defense)

Q (Ryon): How was Kelly dressed that day
A (McEliece): I do not recollect—I think he was dressed about as he was always dressed that I saw him—in fact he was never dressed very well
Q: Always dirty?
A: Yes about that way all the time
Q: He never combed his hair, did he?
A: It did not look like it
Q: But face generally dirty
A: Well—I don't know about his face—he was very red looking in the face always
Q: Did he look any different that day from the way he usually looked?
A: I think he did. I noticed it particularly
Q: Were his clothes very dirty
A: I could not say as to his clothes
Q: Was his face dirty
A: The appearance of his countenance, not the dirtiness attracted my attention
Q: Did he look very pallid?
A: No I do not think he was
Q: Redder?

A: Redder he was I think. He was generally pretty red
      but I thought he was redder then
Q: He did not try to hide from you?
A: No Sir[22]

That a person recalled, nearly ten years after the fact, that a man's
face on a particular day was redder than usual seems to me to be
just plain weird. But there were many aspects of this sensational
trial that challenged the boundary of justice. In any event, Kelly the
Bum's questionable testimony was sufficient to convince a biased
jury that Hester, Tully, and McHugh were guilty.

After the men were convicted, the February 28, 1877, headline
of the *Williamsport Sun and Lycoming Democrat* shouted: "Murder
in the First Degree; Hester, Tully and McHugh, the Molly Maguire
Assassins, Convicted at Last; Alexander Rea's Death to be Avenged;
Thrilling Scene in Court on the Rendition of the Jury's Verdict on
a Nine Years' Old Crime; Fifteen Mollys Waiting for Halters."[23] In
big-city newspapers, headlines were even more sensational. On
February 10, 1878, not long before Hester was to be hung from a gal-
lows in Bloomsburg jail yard, a *New York Times* headline screamed:
"CRIMES OF THE MOLLYS; KEHOE AND HESTER'S BLOODY
WORK; APOSTLES OF ASSASSINATION—NO VILLAINY
TOO DARK OR DESPERATE—A TERRIBLE DISGRACE TO
MODERN CIVILIZATION—A DETECTIVE'S THREE YEARS'
WORK—THE MURDERERS FINALLY BROUGHT TO JUSTICE."
And so it went.

But why so much Molly Maguire hullabaloo? In his comprehensive work, *Making Sense of the Molly Maguires*, Kevin Kenny
explored the Mollys' origins in the Irish countryside, history of
violence and retributive justice, response to oppressive working
conditions in the anthracite coal regions, relationship to early labor
unions, and portrayal as evil incarnate by a nativist, free-market
loving press—notably by Benjamin Bannan in the *Miners' Journal*.
Kenny concluded, in part, that, while not denying their existence
"as a group of Irish immigrants who assassinated their enemies,...

their existence was put to all sorts of ideological uses."[24] In short, their misdeeds were magnified by a hostile press using sensationalized stories.

Anthony F. C. Wallace, in his sociological study, *St. Clair: A Nineteenth-Century Coal Town's Experience with a Disaster-Prone Industry*, had a slightly different take. He described Molly activities as "a mechanism for Irish Catholics to achieve retributive justice in a hostile world."[25] He noted that the attacks were proportionate to the alleged offenses. For example, "killing an Irishman and being acquitted by the court" was a capital offense, "whereas verbal threats justified no more than a severe beating."[26] Another function of the Mollys "was to help members get out of trouble with the law," often by providing an alibi or by offering funds for legal defense.[27] Why a hostile press mischaracterized and exaggerated the Molly crimes, according to Wallace, rested with anti-Catholic sentiments and, more venally, with the "tradition of placing the blame for the problems of the coal trade on forces outside the trade itself."[28] That tradition of blaming outside forces—Irishmen, immigrants, papists, commies, anarchists, and union leaders—would become an oft-repeated strategy during the violent struggles between capital and labor in the late nineteenth century.

Not only was the Molly Maguire episode a harbinger for what was to come vis-à-vis labor relations, the story has staying power. As recently as 2014, the Historical Society of Pennsylvania published an account of the Mollys that included full-page glossy images.[29] In popular culture, in the 1970 movie *The Molly Maguires*, Sean Connery played Jack Kehoe, the king of the Mollys, and Richard Harris played James McParland, the Pinkerton Agency's spy and agent provocateur whose testimony sealed the fate of Kehoe and others.

Clearly, the Molly episode has the elements of an exciting story: strong, colorful characters; an intriguing plot; a dramatic setting. Another reason for its endurance, I think, is embedded in American culture. To be sure, we honor our George Washingtons, Abraham Lincolns, and Martin Luther Kings. But we are enthralled by tales of rugged individualists who tamed the wild Wild West—embodied in the exploits of the fictional cowboys and Indians such as Larry McMurtry's characters in *Lonesome Dove* and in real-life legends like Kit Carson and so many others. At the same time we are intrigued by the crimes of rascals and rogues such as Jesse James, Al Capone, and John Gotti. What these men have in common, of course, is that they spit in the eye of authority and bucked the system, all the while taking care of their own.

Truth be told, the violence in the coal region was a hodgepodge of domestic violence, inter- and intra-ethnic conflict, labor disputes, and rank criminality that will probably never be disentangled. And so it has remained with the legend of the Molly Maguires: larger than life, dwarfing the everyday existence of the men and boys who worked the mines. But in Northumberland County the violence was controlled. Thus liberated, at least in my own mind, from the distraction presented by Molly Maguireism, I am able to look at John McEliece's situation with a clearer eye.

CHAPTER 22

Down in the Coal Mine

O nce upon a time I passed a summer as a high school exchange student in Colombia. While visiting Bogotá, a tour of the old Salt Cathedral of Zipaquirá was among the many unique adventures I shared with my companions. Back then, the cathedral was located six hundred feet underground inside an ancient salt mine.[1] Our bus sped through what seemed to be miles of one-lane underground tunnels that had clearances of mere inches. We careened around sharp curves, now and again pulling into a turn-out to allow an oncoming vehicle to pass. It was a harrowing ride.

The Salt Cathedral, inaugurated on August 15, 1954, and dedicated to Our Lady of the Rosary, patron saint of miners, was an incredible structure. Carved from the inside out, it sprawled for over an acre and was four hundred feet in length and seventy-five feet high. It included three naves and had a capacity of eight thousand people.[2] Icons of saints, the stations of the cross, and the Virgin Mary were all carved from salt. The magnificence of the site notwithstanding, I felt as though I was entombed in a massive sepulcher, and I was relieved when we emerged from the mine to be again beneath a broad, unending sky. The tunnels and roads and caverns in the salt mine perhaps compare to the gangways and breasts of an underground coal mine.

When I was twentysomething years old, I went on a spelunking adventure in Kentucky's Mammoth Cave National Park. At the time only a few of the park's thousands of visitors were permitted to go on the Wild Cave Tour. Guided by a park ranger, we crawled through long passageways and tiny openings. We ate our lunch in a drippy underground dome where our guide pointed out tiny stalactites hanging from the ceiling. After lunch, the ranger instructed our group, which was gathered in a tight circle, to turn off our headlamps. Total and complete darkness. In darkness, our eyes adjust, and our pupils dilate to admit more light. But here in the depth of the caves, there was no light. I put my hand in front of my face and could not see it. It was like being in another world. That foray into the caves gave me a sense of the closeness, total darkness, dank atmosphere, and penetrating cold of an underground environment. Clearly, though, nothing in my experience remotely compares to what it was like for the men and boys who worked in the coal mines of Pennsylvania's anthracite country.

AS THE BASIS OF ECONOMIC ACTIVITY, COAL MINING WAS THE principal (almost exclusive) employer in Locust Gap, a coal patch located about twelve miles from Shamokin in Mount Carmel Township. Locust Gap was a noisy, dirty, industrial place. Machinery constantly clanked in the background. Train whistles and colliery whistles cut through the air. Clouds of coal dust spewed forth from the breakers, soiling the laundry hung out to dry. Fog—from the boilers that generated the steam that powered the machinery—dimmed the sky. Housewives, many dressed in mourning black—many children died in infancy of communicable diseases— visited with each other while caring for their babies and toddlers and tending their little vegetable gardens. Young boys and all the girls attended school while the men, and many of the older boys, labored in the coal mines and breakers.

But in spite of the gloomy setting, the community was literally bursting with life and youthful energy. How could it not be? Based on 1870 census data (see table 2), 40 percent of Mount Carmel Township's population of 2,350 were age ten and younger; 60 percent were age twenty and younger. And among the adults, those age forty-one and older made up a mere 11 percent of the population.

TABLE 2. MOUNT CARMEL TOWNSHIP
POPULATION BY AGE GROUP, 1870

Age	5 and under	6–10	11–20	21–30	31–40	41–50	51 and over
Number	575	366	454	367	318	163	107
% of population	24.4	15.6	19.3	15.6	13.5	6.9	4.6

Source: Ninth Census of the United States, 1870, National Archives and Records Administration, RG-29, Pub. No. M593, Roll No. 1385.

The people in Mount Carmel Township were entirely of European descent. A majority of the residents, comprising 59 percent of the population, were born in the USA. (That number included about six hundred children whose parents were born in Ireland.) Irish-born residents formed the next largest group, at 22 percent, followed by those who heralded from Great Britain, at 12 percent. Based on the age of their American-born children, many of the immigrants who hailed from the British Isles had arrived in earlier decades. A newly arrived contingent from Poland, at 5 percent, and a smattering of people from the German states, less than 1 percent, rounded out the population. Judging from the order of the census enumerator's survey, the English- and German-speaking groups intermingled, but the Poles, many of them single men, lived apart from the others in a cluster. Moreover, with the exception of the Polish people, the ratio of unskilled to skilled workers was proportionate to the population of the various ethnic groups.

Most of the families lived in company-owned housing. The few people who owned real property included hotel owners, grocers, and dry goods merchants, occasionally a mine operator, a teamster, or a "gentleman." Some of the families had accumulated personal savings, but it was rare for someone to possess more than $500; the amounts cited by most of the families were $100 and $200. John and Ann Ellen McEliece lived in company housing and had $150 in savings (about $3,000 in today's dollars). In sum, Mount Carmel Township was a vibrant working-class neighborhood.[3]

It was in Locust Gap that John McEliece worked first as an engineer under his father and, after 1870, as superintendent of the Locust Gap and A. S. Wolf collieries for about fifteen years.[4] The operator of the collieries where John was employed was the Graeber & Kemple Company. The landowner was the Locust Gap Improvement Company until 1873, after which it was sold to the Philadelphia and Reading Coal and Iron Company, a subsidiary of the Philadelphia and Reading Railroad.

The Locust Gap Improvement Company was chartered in 1854 when the coal fields in the Shamokin area were first opening up to large-scale development. The company acquired more or less two thousand acres in Locust Gap, divided equally between timberland and undeveloped coal land.[5] Abraham Simon Wolf (1809–1880), a Philadelphia businessman, was president of the company. Wolf was a member of the Congregation Mikveh Israel, where he was an active trustee, and in an odd coincidence, he succeeded Hyman Gratz as treasurer, serving in that capacity from 1856 to 1861.[6] Hyman Gratz, of course, was the brother and sometime business partner of Simon Gratz, who owned property in the Lykens Valley and had worked alongside Simon Sallade.

IN 1870 THE LOCUST GAP COLLIERY WAS A COMPARATIVELY simple operation. It consisted of a drift opening on the north side of the Mammoth vein. A drift mine was the least complicated of the types found in anthracite country. (See figure 26.) It was worked directly into the mountainside and, because it inclined toward the mouth of the drift, did not require pumps to remove water. The gangway (main passageway) of the mine was in 1,850 yards, working three breasts (individual chambers that miners worked in) in twenty-six feet of solid coal. Ventilation was effected by the action of the atmosphere and was judged by the mine inspector to be inadequate. A small locomotive engine was used to convey the coal to the breaker, and one steam engine ran the breaker; the engines' combined power was 40 horses. The employees included 137 men and boys. Fifteen mules and sixty wagons were in use. For the year 1870, the colliery shipped 38,286 tons of coal.[7]

Figure 26. Coal drift mine. Reproduced from Bowen, "Coal, and the Coal-Mines of Pennsylvania," Harper's New Monthly Magazine 15 (1857): 461, https://catalog.hathitrust.org/Record/008919716, and modified by author.

In 1873 the Locust Gap colliery had a new owner, the Philadelphia and Reading Coal and Iron Company, and Graeber & Kemple continued as the operator/lessee. The drift mine had been abandoned, and a slope mine was expected to begin operations in 1874. (See figure 27.) The new mine consisted of a double-track slope in coal twenty-feet thick and was under water level. One slope was for hoisting coal; the other was for pumping water. There was also a roadway for the workmen. Power to operate the mine included a double engine of 120 horsepower for hoisting and a 90-horsepower engine for pumping water. In addition, there was a 40-horsepower engine to run the coal breaker. In all, 250 horsepower generated by twelve steam boilers provided the power to operate the mine.[8] In 1874, its first year of full operation, 192 men and 45 boys mined, prepared, and shipped 22,825 tons of coal.[9]

Figure 27. Interior plat of a coal slope mine. Reproduced from Bowen, "Coal, and the Coal-Mines of Pennsylvania," Harper's New Monthly Magazine 15 (1857), 462, https://catalog.hathitrust.org/ Record/008919716, and modified by author.

Upgrades at the colliery continued apace. In 1878 the two slopes had been sunk to 140 yards on an angle of forty degrees with east and west gangways. East gangway was driven 1,500 yards, with seventy-eight breasts opened, seven breasts working. The vein on the east side was from twenty-five to thirty feet thick. The vein on the west gangway split into two veins; No. 8, driven 700 yards, with thirty-nine breasts opened; and No. 9, driven 710 yards, with forty-three breasts opened. The colliery employed 212 men and boys who worked 165½ days during the year and shipped 63,970 tons of coal. There were twelve boilers, four engines yielding 265-horsepower, sixty-two mine cars, twenty-six mules, and a mile of track.[10]

BY THE 1870S, THEN, GETTING COAL OUT OF THE GROUND WAS more complicated than it had been when the men of Simon Sallade's generation discovered and developed Pennsylvania's anthracite coal fields. In the 1830s and 1840s, the coal was found near the surface. Technology was fairly simple, and as noted by Grace Palladino, "the miners and operators had worked together as producers to develop the trade."[11] As time passed, the cost of capital increased dramatically. For example, the coal breaker, that funny-looking monstrosity of a building unique to Pennsylvania's anthracite region, was invented in 1844 and came into general use. The relationship between coal operators and workers had also changed. Now, a layered economic and social structure prevailed. At the top of the order were the landowners who generally controlled large tracts of land. Manning (or "boying") the colliery operation required a variety of workers. These thousands of worker bees "generally comprised a property-less and subordinate wage-earning class."[12] Wage slaves, as some would put it.

Belowground there were door boys, often only twelve years old, who sat in the dark all day long and opened and closed doors whenever a mine car passed by; the doors were an integral part of the ventilation system. Mine car drivers, mostly teenage boys, guided the underground mules hauling mine cars to and from the various breasts. The stable boss cared for the mules, which lived underground and rarely saw the light of day. Contract miners were skilled independent businessmen who contracted with the mine operator to work a specific breast: their wage varied with the amount of coal they mined; they hired their own helpers and paid for their own supplies—blasting powder, blasting caps, fuses, lamp oil, and tools. Company miners were regular employees who were paid a weekly wage; they were often hired to do so-called dead work such as extending gangways or digging tunnels between different levels of the slope.

The management team included the fire boss, who was the first person to enter the mine at the beginning of the workday. He inspected the mine for noxious gas, especially highly explosive methane, which, because it is lighter than air, would accumulate near the roof of a breast. Only after the fire boss completed his rounds could the day's work begin. In some collieries the fire boss reported directly to the superintendent; in others he reported to the inside boss. The inside boss had overall responsibility for the often-conflicting objectives of maximizing productivity of the mine and minimizing the risk of explosions and other hazards; he reported to the colliery superintendent.

Aboveground workers included slate pickers—the iconic breaker boys—the slate-picker boss, numerous unskilled laborers who performed a variety of tedious tasks, and in charge of it all, the outside boss, who reported to the superintendent. In addition the colliery employed or contracted with highly skilled craftsmen: blacksmiths, engineers, machinists, carpenters, and teamsters. The superintendent reported to and typically had a close relationship with the mine operator who held the lease to the mining operation.

Needless to say, John McEliece was in charge of an impressive operation. Keeping the colliery running smoothly was a demanding task that involved training and managing the workforce, ensuring that complicated machinery functioned properly, interacting with inspectors and others, and coordinating building projects with construction contractors. And to think that John was only twenty-eight years old when he assumed this responsibility speaks to his maturity, his technical expertise, and his overall management skills. Not to forget that he was simultaneously commanding the local militia, serving as justice of the peace, leading relief efforts when disasters struck (such as "the Great Hailstorm" of 1871), serving on committees such as the county's agricultural committee (really, how did he get stuck with that job?), and last but certainly not least, helping Ann Ellen raise a large family. Thus, on any ordinary day, John had his hands full. Often, however, events were beyond his control. The vagaries of the market for coal, the weather, labor disputes, and accidents—all of these added an element of uncertainty to the coal business.

As colliery superintendent, John maneuvered his way through a variety of complex situations. One of the more challenging problems involved labor relations. Coal miners and laborers endured long hours, low wages, seasonal unemployment related to a drop in demand for coal, and unemployment related to miners' labor strikes. By 1867 the coal operators had reduced wages to below 1857 levels, thereby making it difficult for laborers to provide for the most basic needs of their families.[13] Counteracting this trend, the Workingmen's Benevolent Association, a miners' union established in the anthracite coal region in 1868 by John Siney, enjoyed some initial success. But at the same time that the miners were organizing, Franklin Gowen, the president of the Philadelphia and Reading Railroad, was laying the groundwork to establish America's first union-busting cartel.[14]

Most historical accounts of labor relations during this period focus on chaotic events that transpired in adjacent Schuylkill County, probably because that is where Siney and Gowen, as well as the editor of the *Miners' Journal*, Benjamin Bannan, rose to prominence. However, judging from a survey of the weekly column in the *Shamokin Herald* titled "Coal Department" authored by Dr. J. J. John between 1868 and 1875, there was far less acrimony and violence in the Shamokin district than in other parts of the coal region. Because Dr. John's objective reporting transcended political and social boundaries, it is a reliable source of information.

To be sure, the miners and coal operators in Northumberland County faced off in tense negotiations. There were strikes and occasional labor-related violence. But unique characteristics of the Shamokin area helped blunt destructive forces. For one thing, Shamokin was served by both the Northern Central Railroad and the Philadelphia and Reading Railroad. Consequently, when Gowen raised the P&R's shipping rate as he did in 1871 as part of his union-busting strategy, Shamokin's coal operators shipped their coal to western markets via the Northern Central. This, in itself, allowed the coal operators to remain profitable and thereby stick to the wage agreement reached with the miners. Also, some of Shamokin's coal operators employed nonunion miners, which effectively limited the union's bargaining power in the district. Moreover, although Shamokin was a boomtown, it was a cohesive community. The men sitting on opposite sides during labor contract negotiations also attended church together, shopped in the same stores, and sent their children to the same schools. It seems that personal relationships between the negotiating parties probably eased tensions. For example, one Michael Pepper represented the local miners at the negotiation table. Pepper had served as a witness at John and Ann Ellen's wedding, and, as first lieutenant of the Washington Rifles, he was John's right-hand man in the militia. Sitting across the table from Pepper, representing the coal operators, was Conrad Graeber, John's boss.[15]

Which is not to say that everything was all right in the district. Because it wasn't. The casualty rate was sky-high. Day after day, month after month, year after year, the number of deaths and life-altering injuries to men and boys mounted. The inspectors' reports and local newspapers revealed—often in gruesome detail— the place, nature, and cause of mining accidents.

PENNSYLVANIA HAD ENACTED A COMPREHENSIVE MINE SAFETY law in 1870 in response to public outcry after 110 men and boys had been killed in a devastating accident at Avondale colliery, located in Luzerne County. Among its provisions, the law required the owners, superintendents, lessees, and operators to furnish adequate ventilation for controlling noxious gases, notably firedamp—that is, methane. It also required collieries to construct more than one means of egress from the mine. The 1870 law called for three inspectors for Luzerne and Carbon Counties and three for Schuylkill, Dauphin, Northumberland, and Columbia Counties. The mine inspectors were required to file an annual report to include, among other things, type of mine—drift, slope, tunnel, or shaft—equipment and structures, number and type of employees, number of days worked, tons of coal shipped, and most importantly, a casualty list.

For the year 1870, among seven thousand mine workers in Northumberland County, fourteen workers were killed—a rate of 2.0 per one thousand workers—and an additional thirty-five suffered serious injuries, including some traumas that permanently maimed the victims.[16] Moreover, despite safety regulations implemented by the 1870 mining law, the situation was worse in 1883 when sixty-four among 14,588 workers in the Shamokin district were killed—an astounding rate of 4.38 per one thousand workers. (See table 3.) For perspective, the mining fatality rate for the entire United States in 2014 was 0.14 per one thousand workers. Further, the casualty rates for the years between 1876 and 1883 far exceeded the Molly Maguire-related crime rate in 1870 of 0.17 per one thousand Northumberland County residents. Plainly, when weighed against the realistic and deep-seated fear that a husband, father, brother, or son may never come home for supper, the antics of the Molly Maguires measure up as little more than a distraction, inconsequential in the daily lives of the coal miners and their families.

By and large the people who were killed were young: the average age of those killed in 1883, for example, was thirty, one-fourth of whom were in their teens.

Table 3. Casualties in the coal mining district of Shamokin

Year	No. killed	Average age	No. of teens killed	No. injured	No. employed	Days worked	Fatality rate per 1,000
1876	37	33.7	5	61	10,652		3.47
1877	28	33.1	4	68	10,857		2.58
1878	47	31.4	11	128	11,106	157	4.23
1879	46	31.3	7	103	11,094		4.14
1880	34	34.1	5	124	11,616	174	2.93
1881	48	30.9	9	147	11,875	217	4.04
1882	44	31	10	182	12,973	216	3.39
1883	64	30	17	170	14,588	206	4.38

Source: Pennsylvania Annual Report of Mines by Year: 1870–1979, PennState University Libraries.

Such numbers are daunting, but the suffering of the families living in the coal mining district cannot be understood by looking at a bunch of statistics. Even today, reading the newspaper accounts and reports of the inspectors of mines is heartbreaking. The *Shamokin Herald* of August 18, 1870, fairly represents what was reported weekly.

MINING CASUALTIES Samuel Swan, miner employed by the Hickory Swamp Colliery, was severely injured internally by a fall of coal, on the 5th last. He is attended by Dr. Kreighbaum.

On Thursday morning last, Henry, son of Washington Hoffman, aged about 12 years, met with a frightful accident at the Gap mines which resulted in his death. He was employed as a driver on the dirt road, and in some way fell in front of

the car, the wheels passing over him and frightfully lacer-
ating his left side. Dr. Kreighbaum was summoned but the
unfortunate boy's injuries were of such a nature as to render
medical aid of no avail, and he died the next morning.

On Saturday last Jno. Kane, Jr., employed at the Excelsior
colliery, received severe contusion of the back and internal
injuries while engaged in loading a car by a breaking of a
door of one of the coal bins, which caused a large amount
of coal to be let down upon him. He is being attended by
Dr. Kreighbaum.

On the same day Thomas Steele, inside boss at the Luke
Fidler Colliery, was badly burned about the face and arms
by an explosion of fire-damp. He is under the care of Dr.
E. S. Robins.[17]

In 1878, of approximately sixty-five collieries operating in the
Shamokin district, roughly 40 percent experienced fatal accidents
and about half had nonfatal accidents. Some collieries were worse
than others. Potts colliery had five fatal and twelve nonfatal accidents.
Locust Spring colliery had three fatal and six nonfatal accidents.
Henry Clay shaft #1 had one fatal and ten nonfatal accidents; this is
the same colliery where an explosion killed ten men and boys in 1873.[18]

Drilling down to the data in the reports for McEliece's collieries,
the Locust Gap and A. S. Wolf, I discovered that the number of
injuries sustained over the years was about average for a colliery of
its size. Although there were no catastrophic events involving great
numbers of workers, the record is clearly nothing to be proud of.
Specifically, I tallied ten fatal injuries and forty serious, nonfatal
injuries in the years between 1870 and 1884.[19] Clearly, anthracite
coal mining was a dirty, dangerous business, a fact that makes it
all the more alarming that little children were put to work in this
environment. Which brings me to the most difficult part of my
story—the need to confront the fact that my great-grandfather
employed young children in a deadly industrial setting.

CHAPTER 23

THE BITTER CRY OF CHILDREN

I n the initial stage of what has turned out to be a complicated history project, I was stunned when I read accounts in Pennsylvania's records that described the savagery between Indians and settlers during the colonial and Revolutionary War periods. Equally horrifying, but in a different way, was what happened to young boys who worked in and about the anthracite coal mines, a practice that continued for more than half a century. My great-grandfather John McEliece was among those who employed children in this deadly industry.

At the start of this venture, I reacted to Lewis Wickes Hine's photograph of a breaker boy at work (see figure 28).

Figure 28. Close-up of breaker boy. National Child Labor Committee collection, Lewis Hine photographs. Courtesy of Library of Congress, https://www.loc.gov/resource/nclc.01127/, and modified by author.

Hopefully the boy in the picture survived and went on to live a healthy and happy life. Many boys didn't. The following selected stories illustrate extreme cases, but they reveal how gruesome the accidents could be. An article in the *Shamokin Herald* on May 24, 1866, described the fate of one poor boy:

> Shocking Death—John Gagin, a young man who fed the rolls at Smith's New Breaker, at Locust Gap, was on Saturday last caught in the machinery and carried through with the coal. He was completely mashed and torn to pieces. From what we can learn it seems no one was near him at the time, and that the first intimation his fellow-workmen had of the terrible event was in seeing the parts of his body come out with the coal. He was of Irish descent, about sixteen years old, and was followed to the Catholic burying ground in this place on Sabbath afternoon by a large concourse of people.

Included among the coal inspectors' reports were these two accounts:

> December 6, 1878. George Zimmerman, slate picker, aged thirteen years, caught in monkey rolls at Franklin colliery. Zimmerman and a boy named Reifsnyder were "cutting up" with each other, when the former jumped from a window, where he was, across fly wheel of monkey rolls to the roller box, and from there jumped around to where his seat was, which he missed, landing on the sheet iron in chute, on which he slipped. The rollers catching his left foot, drawing it in up above the knee. The injuries received caused death to ensue on 15th December.[1]

> April 21, 1883. John O. Straw, driver, age eleven years, killed in Big Mountain colliery by a gangway collar falling on him. At time of accident deceased was employed on night shift, helping his brother drive mule. About half-past three o'clock, A. M., both were going toward plane or inside slope. Deceased went to repairman's box, which was on turnout about four or five yards inside of gangway which leads to inside slope. After filling his lamp with oil he was on his way towards inside slope; while passing slope where inside slope gangway intersects the turnout, a large mass of coal and slate fell, one end of the collar in falling caught and instantly killed him.[2]

Why was an eleven-year-old working at all when the mine law of 1870 prohibited anyone younger than twelve from working inside the mine? And at three o'clock in the morning?

The mine inspectors' reports show that at the Locust Gap and A. S. Wolf collieries, where McEliece worked as superintendent, the accidents involving children were all aboveground, none within the mine, most involving mishaps with mine cars. No children died during John's tenure as superintendent. And there was a stretch of about seven years when no incidents involving children were reported. However, a few youngsters did get mangled.[3]

August 26, 1871. James Wood, legs crushed in the rollers;

August 25, 1874. M. Miller, boy, severely injured, run over by wagons;

March 24, 1882. Aaron Kelfer, slate-picker, leg broken by being thrown down by two other boys who were quarreling;

October 25, 1882. Frank Boschee, dirt bank boy, fell off and right foot run over by locomotive, amputated afterward on same day [The report doesn't say what he fell off of; it was probably a dirt wagon.];

April 18, 1883. Wm. Ruffle, slate-picker, leg broken; plank broke and precipitated him a distance of thirty feet.[4]

CHILDREN HAVE ALWAYS WORKED, BUT IT IS DIFFICULT TO pinpoint when children began to work in the collieries. While it is possible that the practice began soon after the coal breaker was invented in 1844, it seems likely that the number of children employed increased dramatically during the Civil War. The demand for coal—both to fire the iron smelters that produced war matériel and to fuel the trains that moved men and weapons—increased. As men marched off to war, the labor supply dwindled, and young boys were available to fill the gap. By the time John McEliece arrived on the scene at the Locust Gap collieries in about 1866, boys aged sixteen and under were an essential part of the workforce.

Frankly, it takes little imagination to understand why John and other men in supervisory positions went along with the system of employing children: it was part of their job. But I am left to wonder what John thought of the system. Did he grasp the enormity of the change that was taking place on his watch? Could he not see that the boys in his employ were mere cannon fodder for the industrial revolution? Perhaps as the years passed by, and as he bore witness to the harmful effect that mine labor had on young boys, he would begin to see the light.

But besides employers, I have to ask what the parents of these little boys—sometimes as young as eight, nine, or ten years old—were thinking. What motivated them to send their children off to work in a cold and drafty building or, in the summer, a sweltering, airless workplace clouded with coal dust, where the sound of the machinery was deafening, where little boys sat perched on hard wooden benches, stooped over a chute, picking pieces of dirt and sharp-pointed slate out of coal for ten or twelve hours a day, six days a week? Was their decision to send their children to the coal breakers entirely a consequence of extreme poverty? Could it be that the parents were simultaneously perpetrators and victims in a heartless system? Or was it something else?

The men and women who subjected their children to this toxic environment were ordinary people. They were John and Ann Ellen McEliece's friends and neighbors. Their families played and worked and prayed together. They were bound together by a shared history and by their hopes for the future—which for them was tied to the vicissitudes of the coal industry. Not yet recovered from the trauma inflicted by the bloodiest war in American history, the men and women of this generation were just beginning to grapple with the benefits and burdens of the industrial revolution. It was a period of turmoil and unprecedented change. Life was complicated, and so were their decisions.

In my twenty-first-century mind, the only possible justification, and a weak one at that, for a parent to allow this to happen to their child would be the threat of a family's survival driven by extreme poverty, a likely situation given the absence at the time of a robust social service system. But financial hardship was not always present. To be sure, wealth eluded the coal miners and their families, and there were cases in which widows and invalids found themselves in dire straits. But based on data derived from the 1870 and 1880 censuses for Mount Carmel Township, and at the risk of seeming to blame the victims of a horrible practice, it appears that employing boys in the collieries was the community norm. (See table 4.)

TABLE 4. MOUNT CARMEL TOWNSHIP CHILDREN
AT WORK AND SCHOOL, 1870

Age	Number in census tract	Work only	School only	Work and school	No work, no school	% working (total)	% attending school only
10	40	1	23	7	9	20.0	57.5
11	34	2	17	10	5	35.3	50.0
12	25	4	6	12	3	64.0	24.0
13	33	5	5	22	1	81.8	15.2
14	30	7	2	18	3	83.3	6.7
15	27	9	3	13	1	81.5	11.1
16	23	11	0	11	1	95.7	0.0
Total	212	39	56	93	23	62.3	26.4

Source: Ninth Census of the United States, 1870, National Archives and
Records Administration, RG 29, Pub. No. M-593, Roll-1385.

The data for 1870 shows that approximately 62 percent of boys ages ten to sixteen worked in the coal breakers, with a trend toward increased employment as children got older. The data also revealed the prevalence of illiteracy, even though most of the children attended school at some point during the census year. (Many of the parents were also illiterate.)

I especially wondered what prompted the eight families of the nine- and ten-year-old boys, included in the following list, to send their sons to work in the coal breakers.[5]

- Winnie Keniffe, age forty, born in Ireland, apparently was a widow. She had five sons, all born in Pennsylvania, ranging in age from seven to seventeen. She sent her oldest boys—ages ten, thirteen, fourteen, and seventeen—to work in the coal breakers. None of the boys attended school. Neither the boys nor their mother could read or write.

- John Ryan, age forty-five, born in Ireland, was an invalid. His wife, age thirty-five, also born in Ireland, kept house. Both were unable to read or write. Their eight children, ranging in age from eight months to fourteen years, were all born in Pennsylvania. The oldest boys—ages nine, eleven, and fourteen—worked in the coal breaker. But they also attended school and were able to read and write.

- Anthony Manly, age forty-nine, a recent immigrant from Ireland, worked in the breaker. His wife, age thirty, was also born in Ireland. Neither could read nor write. They had two children: a boy, age ten, who worked in the breaker and attended school, and a little girl, age three. Both of the children were born in Ireland.

- Michael Muir, age fifty-two, born in Scotland, worked in the breaker. His wife, age forty, also born in Scotland, kept house. Both could read and write. They had eight children, five boys and three girls, ranging in age from one month to twenty years old. The oldest two children were born in Scotland, the rest in Pennsylvania. The oldest boys—ages ten, twelve, fourteen, and eighteen—worked in the breaker. All but the eighteen-year-old attended school. They all could read and write.

- Charles Emery, age twenty-four, born in Maine, was a carpenter. He could read and write. It is unclear what his relationship was to the thirty-two-year-old female who kept house. Considering Emery's age, he was probably not the father of the children in the household. Perhaps he was the younger brother of a widowed sister. She was born in Pennsylvania, and she could not read or write. Five boys, ranging in age from six to thirteen, were born in Pennsylvania. The two oldest boys—ages ten and thirteen—worked in the breaker and attended school. One nine-year-old boy had a different surname.

- Patrick Rennian, age fifty-four, worked in the coal mine. Neither he nor his wife, age forty, both born in Ireland, could read or write. They had six children, two girls and four boys, ranging in age from one to sixteen, all of whom were born in Pennsylvania. The oldest boys—ages ten and thirteen—worked in the breaker and went to school.

- John Honimarch, age forty-six, was born in England and worked in the coal mine. His wife, age thirty-two, was also born in England. Both could read and write. Their four children, two boys and two girls, were all born in Pennsylvania. The two oldest boys—ages ten and twelve—worked in the coal breaker and attended school.

- J. N. Evans, age forty-five, was born in Wales. He worked in the coal mines. His wife, age forty, was also born in Wales. Both could read and write. They had seven children, three boys and four girls, ranging in age from two to eighteen years. The four oldest children—ages eight, ten, fifteen, and eighteen—were born in Wales, and the younger children—ages two, four, and six—were born in Pennsylvania. The oldest boys—ages ten and fifteen—worked in the breaker and attended school.

Clearly, Winnie Keniffe's and John Ryan's families found themselves in desperate circumstances and did what they needed to do to ensure their families' survival, the Keniffe family going so far as to avoid schooling. Charles Emery's family may also have been in trouble. The remaining families—Manly, Muir, Rennian, Honimarch, and Evans—were headed by men who were foreign born. Perhaps tradition in their native countries played into their decision to engage a child in wage work at such a young age. Even so, these foreign-born parents—whether literate or illiterate—brightened the future prospects for their children by sending them to school.

For comparison, I considered the situation of a few other families, selected from the same census, for no other reason than they happened to catch my eye.

- William Mimbleby, age forty, born in Pennsylvania, was a railroad engineer. His wife, age forty, also born in Pennsylvania, kept house. Both of their parents were also born in America. Both could read and write. They had seven children, three boys and four girls, ranging in age from three to seventeen years, all born in Pennsylvania. The oldest boy—age seventeen—worked as a railroad fireman. The next oldest boy—age thirteen—did not work and attended school. All the older children could read and write.

- Charles Brislon, age forty-four, born in Ireland, worked in the coal mine. He was able to read and write. His wife, age thirty-six, also born in Ireland, kept house. She could read but not write. They had ten children, six boys and four girls, ranging in age from one to seventeen years, all born in Pennsylvania. The oldest boy—age sixteen—worked as a clerk in a store. The next oldest boy—age fifteen—was an apprentice to an engineer. The third oldest boy—age eleven—did not work, and he attended school. All except the youngest children could read and write.

- Thomas Morgan, age fifty-one, born in England, was a breaker boss. His wife, age thirty-eight, born in Wales, kept house. Both were unable to read or write. They had five children, four boys and one girl. The oldest boy—age

twenty-two—born in Wales, worked as an engineer at the
mines and was able to read and write. The rest of the children were born in Pennsylvania. The second oldest boy—
age nineteen—worked in the breaker and was unable to
read or write. He was followed by two boys—ages eleven
and sixteen—who worked in the breaker, did not attend
school, and could read but not write.

The Mimbleby family represents an established native-born family.
The Brislons, by placing their boys in promising situations and committing to their education, suggests an upwardly mobile family of
foreign origin. The Morgan family, also of foreign origin, is puzzling.
Although they lived in the country for almost twenty years, the
family appeared to generally eschew education and, consequently,
seemed to sentence the younger generation to a life of hard labor.

If anything, what review of these eleven families shows is that
each family had its own story; that decisions about their children's
roles were based in varying degrees on the individual family's values
and financial situation. Moreover, their decisions were not made in
a vacuum; rather, they were influenced by community norms.

The data from the 1870 census is, in some respects, at odds with
the reports presented at the turn of the century by Owen Lovejoy
of the progressive National Child Labor Committee (NCLC).[6]
Specifically, the idea that the coal breakers were staffed by boys
and old men—"once a miner, twice a breaker boy" was the popular
characterization—was apparently not the case in 1870 in Mount
Carmel Township. (See table 5.) The age of those listed as "works
at breaker" shows that boys ages sixteen and younger composed
40.7 percent of the workers in the breakers. But the majority of
workers were ages seventeen and up. The average age was 27.4
years. In other words, the boys were working in close proximity to
adults. The data suggests the possibility that the market for child
labor in the collieries was in transition from a farm-based model
in which children were closely supervised by adult members of a

family to the more egregious form of exploitation later described by the progressives at the NCLC. One possible problem with the data, however, may be that the classification "works at breaker" in the 1870 census may have included all those people who worked above the ground and was not limited to the so-called slate pickers.

TABLE 5. MOUNT CARMEL TOWNSHIP AGE
DISTRIBUTION OF MEN AND BOYS
WORKING IN BREAKERS, 1870

Age	Average age	Number	% of workforce	% of workforce aged sixteen and under
9		1	0.3	
10–12		36	11.0	
13–16		96	29.4	
17–19		30	9.2	
20–29		42	12.8	
30–39		49	15.0	
40–49		30	9.2	
50–59		28	8.6	
60 and over		15	4.6	
Total	27.4	327		40.7

Source: Ninth Census of the United States, 1870. National Archives and Records Administration, RG 29, Pub. No. M-593, Roll-1385.

Another point of diversion from the NCLC observations relates to the employment of boys inside the mines. The NCLC observed that teenage driver boys worked inside the mines and that door boys as young as twelve years old worked all day inside the mines.[7] This may have been true in the 1890s and early 1900s. But according to the 1870 census data for Mount Carmel Township, only one sixteen-year-old boy worked inside the mine as a laborer. Which is not to dismiss the possibility that some youngsters may have accompanied their fathers or older brothers into the mines, working as unlisted and unpaid laborers. Since the wages of contract miners depended on output, bringing children along to perform simple tasks would make sense in what has been described by Hugh Hindman as a family wage system.[8]

BY 1880 THE SITUATION HAD CHANGED SOMEWHAT. (SEE TABLE 6.) The increased commitment to educating children is the most prominent feature observed in the 1880 census data. Even though many of the children attended school only part of the time, the percentage of children attending school full-time among the youngest children—ages ten and eleven—increased dramatically. Among those aged twelve and thirteen, the rate increased slightly, and among those aged fourteen, the rate nearly doubled. A trend toward decreased full-time school attendance among the older boys—ages fifteen and sixteen—probably reflects a lack of educational opportunities in the town. As noted in Bell's 1891 *History of Northumberland County*, the Mount Carmel schools offered only three primary grades, two grammar school grades, and one high school grade. That limitation was exacerbated by the fact that attendance was irregular. Moreover, as late as 1887 there were only four high school graduates in the Mount Carmel school district. In the 1890–1891 school year, among 1,600 students enrolled in the school district (which encompassed both the borough of Mt. Carmel and Mount Carmel Township), only about twenty-five attended high school.[9] Thus, it would appear that for parents of the older boys, the choice was to either send their sons to work or have them do nothing. In examining the employment of the fathers of the boys aged thirteen and older who attended school only, three (including John McEliece) were colliery foremen, one was an engineer, one was a railroad agent, four were miners, and two were laborers (four were undetermined).[10] Although the lines were not rigid, this suggests a bit of an emerging class structure.

TABLE 6. MOUNT CARMEL TOWNSHIP CHILDREN
AT WORK AND SCHOOL, 1880

	Number in census tract	Work only	School only	Work and school	No work, no school	% working (total)	% attending school only
10	43	0	39	3	1	7.0	90.7
11	48	3	36	8	1	22.9	75.0
12	42	4	13	25	0	69.0	31.0
13	43	5	10	28	0	76.7	23.3
14	33	5	4	24	0	87.9	12.1
15	41	5	1	35	0	97.6	2.4
16	39	6	0	33	0	100.0	0.0
Total	289	28	103	156	2	63.7	35.6

*Source: Tenth Census of the United States, 1880,
National Archives and Records Administration, RG-29,
Pub. No. T-9, Roll 1164 Part 1 and Roll 1164 Part 2.*

By 1880 the absolute number of boys aged sixteen and under working in and about the coal mines had increased from 132 to 184, suggesting that the problem worsened on John McEliece's watch. The increase, however, was in rough proportion to the overall increase in population, and the percentage of boys working remained nearly constant: 62.3 percent in 1870 compared to 63.7 percent in 1880. The trend toward increased work participation relative to age was, by 1880, more clearly defined.[11]

There is also a problem with comparability of the data in the 1870 and 1880 censuses. Specifically, at a time when the coal business was growing, the 1880 census indicated that 189 people worked in the breakers, compared to 322 in 1870. Also in 1880 workers older than sixteen years composed 2.6 percent of the workers in the breakers compared with 59.3 percent in 1870. Only five people older than the age of sixteen (three seventeen-year-olds, one twenty-two-year-old, and one sixty-five-year-old) were listed as working in the breakers in 1880. Further, the average age of people who were listed as working in the breakers in 1880 (14.1 years old) had decreased dramatically from the average age in 1870 (27.4 years old). Possibly, the method used to track employment had changed. It could be that some of the workers listed as laborers in the 1880 census were actually working aboveground in the breakers doing something other than picking slate out of the coal.

As with 1870, I was curious as to why the parents of the youngest boys—one eight-year-old, three nine-year-olds, and four ten-year-olds—sent their children to work in the breaker; they are included in the following list. Also included in the ranks was one fourteen-year-old girl.[12]

- Patrick Daniel, age thirty-eight, born in Pennsylvania, was a mine boss. His wife, age twenty-eight, was born in Ireland. They had six children, three boys and three girls, ranging in age from three months to ten years old, all born in Pennsylvania. The oldest boy, age ten, worked in the breaker for six months and went to school.

- Bridget Logan, age twenty-nine, was a widow, born in England. She lived with her son, age eight, born in Pennsylvania, who worked in the breaker for six months and attended school.

- Patrick Gribbons, age forty-six, born in Ireland, was an engineer, probably in the colliery. His wife, age forty, was also born in Ireland. Their seven children, five boys and two girls, ranged in age from one to eighteen. The oldest child was born in New York, the rest in Pennsylvania. The two oldest boys, ages twelve and ten, worked in the coal breaker and attended school.

* Katherine (illegible), age twenty-nine, born in Ireland, was married, but the husband was not present in the household. Living with her were her three sons and two daughters, ages three through nine, all born in Pennsylvania. Her oldest son, age nine, worked in the coal breaker and did not attend school.

* Lewis Bezowski, age thirty-five, born in Poland, was a miner. His wife, age forty-four, was also born in Poland. Neither could read nor write. Given the ages of the four boys and three girls, from one to nineteen, this was probably the second marriage for Mrs. Bezowski. The four oldest children were born in Poland; the rest, beginning with a seven-year-old daughter, in Pennsylvania. The two oldest boys, ages seventeen and nineteen, worked as laborers. The oldest girl, age fourteen, worked in the coal breaker for eight months and went to school; she was the one and only girl in the township to be thus employed. In Europe it was common at the time for girls to work in mines.

* Henry Rifer, age forty-seven, born in Prussia, was a blacksmith. His wife, age fifty-five, was also born in Prussia. Three children, one girl, age thirteen, and two boys, ages ten and eleven, were born in Pennsylvania. Both boys worked in the coal breaker and attended school.

* Francis Pepper, age sixty-five, born in Ireland, worked in the coal breaker. His wife, age sixty-five, was also born in Ireland. Living with them were two grandchildren, surname Coyle, both born in Pennsylvania—a boy, age nine, who worked in the breaker and did not attend school and

a girl, age seven. The grandfather was the only adult male in the township who was listed as being employed at the breaker. Living next door in household #302 was Henry Coyle, age twenty-six, a miner, born in England. His wife, age twenty-seven, was born in Ireland. Living in this household were three children, twin three-year-old girls and an eight-month-old boy. It seems likely that these two households were all of one family. Did Grandpa and his young grandson traipse off to work together?

- John Givitz (sp?), age fifty-five, was a laborer, born in Poland. His wife, age sixty, was also born in Poland. Two boys, listed as sons but possibly grandsons, were also born in Poland. The oldest boy, age thirteen, worked in the breaker and went to school. The younger boy, age nine, worked in the coal breaker for eight months and did not attend school.

With the exception of two households headed by women who demonstrated financial need—one was a widow, the other a married woman whose husband was not present in the household—there was no obvious pattern as to why the families sent such young boys to work. Again, each individual family had its own story and made its decisions for reasons known only to them.

IN ADDITION TO LACK OF EDUCATIONAL OPPORTUNITIES AND financial and value-based elements, other trade-specific factors may have played into and alleviated concerns about sending a child to work in the coal breakers. For one, little or no thought seems to have been given to the fact that inhaling coal dust–laden air would damage developing lungs. Historian Alan Dickerson described the long fight to get coal dust recognized as a causative agent of black lung disease. Incredibly, as he wrote, some medical practitioners actually asserted that inhaling coal dust immunized a person against tuberculosis. "In 1904, the *Coal Trade Journal* announced that the disinfective power of coal dust had prompted a proposal… to erect a sanitarium at the mines."[13] Also gaining little notice was the idea that performing tedious work for long hours would have a negative impact on young minds and bodies. Further, at least in 1870, before accumulated casualty rates in the coal inspectors' reports proved otherwise and became widely publicized, working in the breakers was not thought to be all that dangerous. The reported data for 1871 plainly shows that most of the accidents occurred inside the mine and not in the breakers. For example, of forty-three persons who lost their lives in the Shamokin coal district in 1871, nine were caused by a fall of coal, three by fall of rocks, eight by wagons, one by explosion of powder, nine by explosion of gas, one by suffocation of noxious air, one by pump rods, one by breaking of a slope chain, one by breaker machinery, two by dirt falls, three by discharge of blasts, and four by falls of slate. Only one fatality happened in a coal breaker (age of the deceased not given).[14]

Another element may have weighed on people's minds—the fact that early childhood death by communicable diseases was an everyday occurrence. The number of children injured in the collieries' breakers was small when compared to the many who succumbed to childhood disease. As revealed in the death notices in the local Shamokin newspaper, children's names usually outnumbered those of old people. The following list in the September 1, 1870, edition of the *Shamokin Herald* was typical:

Agnes Gertrude Gray, infant child of William and Sarah Gray, aged 2 months and 11 days.

Jacob Norman, Twin child of M. F. and A. Gardner, aged 1 month and 23 days.

Charlie Albert, son of Henry and Anna Amelia Moser, aged 8 months and 21 days.

Mrs Catherine Whary, aged 64 years, 3 months and 29 days.

Emmerson Rumberger, infant son of Jacob and Harriet Rumberger, aged 2 months, 1 week and 5 days.

The census data is also telling. Many families were large. Having a baby every two years or so during a woman's childbearing years was common. Noticeable gaps in the ages of children within a family often imply that a child had died. John and Ann Ellen's experience is typical. A son, Francis, was eight months old when he died on May 1, 1872. Cause of death is unknown, but it coincided with a smallpox outbreak in the area. A double tragedy followed four years later when six-year-old Mary Elizabeth McEliece died on April 4, 1876, one day after her little brother, eighteen-month-old John Edgar, passed away, both of diphtheria. I cannot begin to imagine their sorrow and grief. Or how they managed to plod through the days. And to think that a great many, perhaps most, of the families shared the same fate. Could it be that men and women had learned to cope with adversity by seeing tragic events, even when they happened to children, as a normal part of life? Compounding that idea, I cannot forget that the mothers and fathers of these children were members of the Civil War generation, that it had been only five years since they bore witness to that horror.

━━━━◆━━━━

BEYOND THE LOCALIZED SITUATION IN THE COAL REGIONS, additional societal forces played into the decision to employ child laborers. As reformer Florence Kelley observed in 1889, "The data afforded by the records of statutory legislation show that the wage slavery of children not only now is, but for half a century has been, a legally accepted American institution; in fact, ever since the development of machinery, and the production of commodities on a large scale, for sale and profit, made child labor profitable."[15] According to Edith Abbott—an outstanding economist, social worker, educator, and author—exploitation of children in the labor market became nearly inevitable when a set of sociocultural, economic, and legal forces converged in the early years of America's industrial revolution. "The colonial attitude toward child labor and the Puritan belief in the virtue of industry and the sin of idleness" led to a mind-set by which child labor was held to be a righteous institution.[16] In the preindustrial era this idea was realized on family farms, in indentured servitude of poor children, and in apprenticeships. Without any acknowledgment that circumstances had changed, this attitude toward children's work carried over to the factory system.[17] Also, in the early years of the republic, enthusiasm for development of a robust manufacturing sector in combination with the introduction of the economic theory of division of labor ensured that little children would work in factories and mines for long hours and meager wages. It was the patriotic thing to do! Early legislation that intended to protect these children failed to include effective enforcement provisions, thereby allowing desperate parents and greedy mine owners to skirt the law. Meanwhile, the courts were slow to adapt when the child labor market changed from an apprentice-based system (in which a contract was between a parent and a master) to something akin to a "free" labor system (in which the child was an employee).

ALTHOUGH POVERTY OF WORKERS AND GREED OF COAL OPERA-tors played a role in the exploitation of children in the anthracite coal industry, they were not the only factors. Individual circumstances, fixed societal beliefs, unprecedented and rapid economic change, entrenched bureaucratic institution, post–Civil War dynamics, a primitive sociomedical environment, and community norms all had an impact on a family's decision to send their child to work. But despite these explanations, it remains difficult to understand how parents could fail to protect their children from danger.

Early on, in 1870, when the employment of children in coal mines was beginning to take off, perhaps there was little recognition that there might be a problem. Later, as the system worsened and became entrenched, the prospect of correcting it became more difficult. Eventually, the situation became so egregious, and so pervasive, it took decades to fix. The members of the National Child Labor Committee and other progressives would lead the reform effort that continued well past the years of FDR's New Deal. But decades before Edith Abbott, Owen Lovejoy, Florence Kelley, Lewis Wickes Hine, and other reformers brought their combined forces to bear on the disgrace of child labor, prominent leaders were, perhaps unwittingly, planting the seeds of reform. John McEliece, in his small way, took part in those early efforts to change.

But before I move on to tell the story of Kehler v. Schwenk, I would like to share an insight I had while preparing this chapter. As I was struggling to find answers to my questions related to child labor in Pennsylvania's anthracite coal mines, I was rudely interrupted by news reports of yet another school-shooting inci-dent—the thirteenth such happening in a year that had barely begun. It struck me that the questions I asked myself about child labor exploitation in the years between 1870 and 1880—how could this nightmare have happened? When did it begin? How long did it continue? And where were the helpers?—applied equally to the tragic situation our society faces today. And it made me wonder if people in 150 years will be asking of us, What were they thinking? Tellingly, today's crisis demonstrates how difficult it is and how long it takes to solve an entrenched societal problem. Hopefully, the leaders who are fighting today's deadly epidemic will soon prevail.

CHAPTER 24

SEEDS OF REFORM

⸺⸻◆⸻⸺

The accident rate among employees of the anthracite coal companies of Pennsylvania was incredibly high for both men and boys. Long before the great reformers of the progressive era achieved success, however, Pennsylvania's mine inspectors were reacting to the problem on a daily basis. Consider, for example, the comments of inspector William S. Jones (Luzerne and Carbon Counties, Eastern District) in the case of William Van Buskirk, a thirteen-year-old slate picker who was killed when his head was crushed in the pony screen on February 9, 1878. The boy had been sent into the "hopper" to scrape out the culm that had accumulated during the day.[1] While the boy was in the hopper, the engine was started by the engineer. The boy's head got caught against a timber, fracturing his skull and killing him instantly. Jones wrote, "On examining the case, I felt that there was great blame laying somewhere," and so he ordered an inquest.[2] Disgusted with the inquest jury's mealymouthed verdict, which stated that there was "a certain amount of carelessness and negligence, on the part of some of the superintendents," Jones reported: "As there is only one superintendent at the breaker, we must conclude that he is the party referred to."[3] He continued, "It is very evident that the boys were afraid to go into the dangerous trap, and that they went only because the penalty for refusing to go was a summary discharge. Two boys had been discharged, and the little fellows knew that the same penalty would be visited on them also, if they dared to disobey the inhuman order of their cruel boss. And all this tyranny and cruel oppression was exercised, where there was not the least shadow of necessity for it."[4]

In 1879 inspector T. M. Williams (Luzerne and Carbon Counties, Middle District) suggested a minimum of twelve years of age be set for boys in aboveground work and that the minimum for belowground work should be raised to fourteen years. He also proposed that a standard for education should be required before employment could be granted.[5]

Leaders in the community were acutely aware of the problem as it related to interference with a child's education. Northumberland County's representative in Pennsylvania's Assembly, Dr. J. J. John, had introduced a compulsory education bill in 1876. Proving the maxim that a stopped clock is correct twice a day, my least favorite newspaper editor, Emanuel Wilvert, while not failing to allow his contempt for the people in the coal region to shine through, commented favorably on Dr. John's bill.

> The bill is a fair one, and will prove very beneficial if passed. In our coal regions particularly it will have a good effect. Many of the children in those localities never see the inside of a school house and grow up in entire ignorance. As soon as they are able to work they are put at a breaker to pick slate, where they are kept until they can enter a mine. They, in consequence of ignorance, are thrown into the lowest society, and grow up depraved and become vicious; whereas, if educated, many brilliant minds would become developed and a better state of society would exist in the black diamond region.[6]

Inspector Samuel Gay (First District) in 1881 addressed the problem of coal dust in the breakers and the effect it had on the health of boys "in age from seven to sixteen years" who were "impelled to breathe it ten hours a day from two hundred to three hundred days in the year."[7] Because correcting the problem would cost a lot of money, he proposed that legislation was needed to compel the coal operators to fix the problem. He also suggested that the state establish a minimum age for working aboveground. He wrote, "I sincerely hope some of our legislators will give this subject their attention at the next session, whereby these objects of pity will be protected."[8]

Pennsylvania, acting on the recommendations of a committee formed in 1883 to propose changes to the mine law of 1870, enacted a new mine safety law in 1885.[9] The act included several provisions specific to children. The age of boys allowed to work inside the mines was raised from twelve to fourteen and a minimum age of twelve was set for boys working outside the mine. Only authorized persons, not less than fifteen years of age, were to run or sprag cars on gravity roads.[10] And the accumulation of coal dust injurious to the health of those in the breakers was prohibited.[11]

In his 1882 report, inspector James Roderick (Luzerne and Carbon Counties, Southern District) reviewed an inquest jury's verdict on one of the fatal accidents in his district. A twenty-one-year-old driver was fatally injured by being crushed between mine cars and a door on the gangway. There were four doors (part of the ventilation system) in the gangway. In violation of the law that required each door be attended by a door boy, the company had only two boys, one to run ahead of the mine car and open the doors, the other to follow the mine car and close the doors. In the fatal accident the boy who ran ahead had not had time to secure the door properly before the mine cars arrived. But the cars kept coming on, crashed into the door, and crushed the driver "in a shocking manner."[12] Even though the company had violated the law, the inquest jury—all of whom were miners—concluded "that deceased came to his death through the neglect of the door boy, but advised the company in the future to put boys to attend each main door."[13] There was a decided tendency to exonerate the company and instead put the onus on a worker who, in this particular case, was a boy.

In the same report, Roderick turned his attention to the social disaster that the situation left in its wake. He discussed the fate of young injured workers and the need for a means of support for widows and orphans. "The attention of all fair-minded people is called to the great necessity of providing education and suitable trades for the young men and boys that are daily incapacitated to earn their bread."[14] He continued: "There is an army of these cripples in the several districts of the anthracite coal fields of Pennsylvania, some minus a hand, others a leg or foot, and exceptional cases are to be found wanting both an arm and a leg. They are pitiable objects, indeed, when seen before the break of day, on winter mornings, on the road to the several breakers."[15] These young men are "as bright and intelligent as any class," he observed, and he recommended a system of education that would prepare them to "hold any position in life that does not require manual labor."[16]

Roderick observed "that the widows and orphans are tolerably cared for, for a few months. Something being given by the operator, a little by the miner's friends; and relatives, too, are kind and sympathetic, but in a few months all these feelings cool off, and the widow and her orphans are forced to realize the stern reality that they are left all alone in the world."[17] He gave credit to the few operators that continued to support widows but noted that this was rare. He proposed that the German system was worth studying so that a law could be made to "answer the need of this class of sufferers."[18]

What the mine inspector was referring to was Germany's Employers' Liability Law of 1871, which provided limited social protection to workers in dangerous industries. Later, in 1884, Germany adopted a workers' accident insurance law, the first modern system of workers' compensation. However, in spite of Roderick's plea that humanity demanded "something be done to relieve them, and that as speedily as possible," the seeds of reform he and others planted would have to wait thirty years to bear fruit.[19] Shamefully, Pennsylvania was one of the last industrialized states to adopt a workmen's compensation law. Eventually, the Commonwealth created the Bureau of Workmen's Compensation within the Department of Labor and Industry, which was to administer the Workmen's Compensation Act of 1915.[20]

Destitute and left to their own devices, one would think that the disabled boys and men, the widows and orphans, would turn to the courts for a remedy. Strangely, however, at a time when employees in the anthracite coal fields had suffered 9,575 fatal and an untold number of nonfatal injuries in the years from 1870 to 1899, personal injury claims were rare.[21] Based on Yale law professor John Fabian Witt's search of Westlaw, an online legal research service, only six mining-related personal injury cases were filed in Pennsylvania prior to 1900.[22] Witt speculated that the "local power of mining companies appears often to have been enough to deter the filing of lawsuits by accident victims and their families in mining communities around the country."[23] Fear of losing one's job or of being blacklisted discouraged both victims and potential witnesses from testifying against an employer. Witt noted that, in places where "no single mining company was dominant," and "the average duration of any one mining enterprise was less than one year, employers were effectively judgment-proof; most mines would have closed down long before the resolution of any legal action."[24]

CONSIDERING THE ABOVE, IT IS AN EXTRAORDINARY COINCIdence that John McEliece was the expert witness for the plaintiff in the case of Kehler v. Schwenk, a civil suit involving an injury to a fourteen-year-old boy who was injured at the Black Diamond colliery on September 13, 1882.[25] Daniel Kehler was employed as a slate picker, and per directions his father had given to the employer, he was not to be put at more dangerous work than slate picking. Contrary to the father's direction, however, the boy was ordered to assist in hauling the cars conveying the waste dirt from the breaker out to the dump. The dirt car ran on an upgrade to the dump and was drawn by a mule hitched to it by a short chain. To obtain the momentum that would carry the car to the breast of the dump, the mule had to be driven rapidly with the load and detached quickly at some distance from the end of the track. Young Kehler was assigned to detach the mule. On account of his small size, the only way he could do the job was to step in front of the moving car and detach the hook that attached the chain to the dump car, after which the mule would step to one side out of the way of the dirt car. While in the act of detaching the mule, Kehler was caught by the car, thrown beneath it, and his right arm was crushed so that it became necessary to amputate it near the shoulder. The boy's father, Charles Z. Kehler, on July 25, 1883, initiated a case to recover damages for his minor son's injuries alleged to have been the result of negligence on the part of the operators of the colliery, William Schwenk, George Robertson, and Jacob Geise, who were doing business as Schwenk, Robertson & Co.[26]

Heartened to discover that my great-grandfather had partly redeemed himself of serving as the employer of young boys, I couldn't help but wonder why this, of all possible cases, made its way to the docket in the first place, much less how it managed to survive a journey through three trials in the Court of Common Pleas of Northumberland County and three appeals to the Pennsylvania Supreme Court. At the least, the contestants were highly motivated.[27]

The plaintiff, Charles Z. Kehler, Daniel's father, was a man of limited financial means. He was a butcher who followed that trade for some time. He lived in Eldred Township, Schuylkill County, in 1870 and relocated to Mount Carmel in 1882 where he worked as a day laborer until his death in 1898. Charles and his wife, Sarah, had seven children. At the time of his son's accident, Charles and two of his sons were employed at the Black Diamond colliery. The other son was probably Thomas Kehler, who was two years older than Daniel.[28]

The defendant, William Schwenk, was a descendant of John Schwenk, who had emigrated from Germany in 1701 and settled in Montgomery County, Pennsylvania. At various times the Schwenk family engaged in farming; they owned a sawmill, a tannery, a woolen mill, a linseed oil mill, a brick plant, and a powder mill.

They became quite wealthy. From the age of fourteen until age twenty-one, William Schwenk helped superintend the family's businesses. In 1862 he struck out on his own. He engaged in various businesses until 1871 when he began operating the Black Diamond colliery, which he continued until 1886.[29] Because employer liability insurance was unavailable in the United States until 1886, a loss in court could put a small company like Schwenk's in jeopardy.[30] But Schwenk had ample financial resources to fight a protracted battle in court.

With the case shaping up to be a classic David vs. Goliath contest pitting a poor but angry father against a wealthy businessman, it would seem that the case was doomed to fail. But it didn't because Mr. Kehler's case attracted the interest of an esteemed attorney and ambitious politician, a state senator at the time the case was filed—Simon P. Wolverton (1837–1910). Why Wolverton accepted the Kehler case is unknown. Considering that his clients included some of the largest corporations in the state, it is unlikely that he was in it only for the money, even if there was a contingent fee on the table. And while there is a possibility that he got involved for humanitarian reasons, it seems probable that he saw an opportunity to win a precedent-setting case, gain favor among the voting population, or both.

After more than a three-year delay, the case went to trial on November 8, 1886.[31] To win, the plaintiff (Kehler) had to prove that the defendant (Schwenk) was negligent. The essence of the plaintiff's case was that, because the dumper car and hitch used at the defendant's colliery was not in general use and was defective, the defendant was negligent and therefore the plaintiff was entitled to recovery. Here enters John McEliece, an expert witness for the plaintiff. Why did Wolverton pick him? Probably because he was the perfect man for the job. Not only was John, by virtue of having been involved in the coal industry for a number of years, familiar with equipment used in the business, he was also generally known to be an experienced and confident witness. Moreover, Wolverton and McEliece shared a common history. Both men came of age in the Civil War years. They had served side by side in the Thirty-Sixth Pennsylvania Emergency Volunteer Regiment cleaning up the Gettysburg battlefield mess in 1863. Both men were active in Northumberland County's Democratic Party.[32] Moreover, in 1877 Wolverton was among the defense attorneys who interrogated John in the Commonwealth v. Patrick Hester, Peter McHugh, and Patrick Tully murder trial.

McEliece's testimony went straight to the issue of the defendant's negligence. He related that the kind of equipment—the dumper car and hitch—that was used at the Black Diamond colliery was not in common use, and he described the type of equipment that was in use at the other collieries. The defendant, however, produced witnesses who claimed that the contrivance was, in fact, in common use and, furthermore, that it was the right of the defendant to choose what type of equipment he wanted to use.

But there was another challenge that the plaintiff faced. Even if the jury decided that the defendant was guilty of negligence, the charge could be neutralized by proving that the plaintiff was liable for contributory negligence. Contributory negligence is a doctrine in common law whereby failure of an injured plaintiff to act prudently is considered to be a contributory factor in the injury suffered. In the trial, Schwenk's attorneys argued that Mr. Kehler, in allowing his son to continue working in what he thought was a dangerous employment, was chargeable with contributory negligence and therefore could not recover.

There were, of course, other important elements in the trial: whether young Kehler had assumed the risks inherent in performing the task and that he, too, could be charged with contributory negligence. The law at the time presumed a boy of fourteen to be capable of appreciating danger and therefore responsible for his own negligence. Nevertheless, he was not to be held to the same degree of prudence as an adult. In the trial, Daniel Kehler testified that his boss had sent him to do the work over the boy's protest that the job was too difficult for him to perform. Also, two boys engaged in similar work testified that Daniel Kehler, because he was small for his age, was not strong enough to perform the task required of him. The defense challenged whether the admission of testimony of the boys who had obtained an actual practical knowledge of the job was proper, whether admission of John McEliece's testimony was proper, and whether the trial judge's instructions to the jury were in error. All in all, it was a more complicated case than it appeared to be on the surface.

The judgment in the initial trial in 1886 was in favor of Kehler, awarding him $500. The case was appealed by the defendant (Schwenk) to the Pennsylvania Supreme Court in 1888 (122 Pa. 67) at which the judgment was reversed and a new trial was ordered. It appears that the judgment at the second trial in Northumberland County (date unknown) was in favor of the defendant (Schwenk) because the plaintiff (Kehler) appealed the decision to the Pennsylvania Supreme Court, which, in 1891 (144 Pa. 348) reversed *that* decision and ordered yet another trial. The third and final trial in Northumberland County (date unknown) issued a judgment in favor of Kehler for $1,500 (about $43,000 in today's dollars). In 1892 that decision was appealed by the defendant (151 Pa. 505), and the judgment in favor of Kehler was finally affirmed.

Of the three separate trials and appeals, none have had negative treatment, which means they have not been overruled. Nor do they have any history, meaning there are no further rulings by a higher court on these cases.[33] In fact, the 2013 *Pennsylvania Suggested Standard Civil Jury Instructions* in regard to negligence actions cites to the 1891 Kehler v. Schwenk case (144 Pa. 348). The standard set by the case was that once a child reaches the age of fourteen, the law presumes that he or she has the capacity to appreciate danger and to exercise reasonable care and that a child of fourteen years of age or over has the burden of proof to show that he or she did not have the same capacity to appreciate danger or exercise care as other children who are the same age. The instructions quoted directly from the Pennsylvania Supreme Court opinion in stating that the age of fourteen is "the convenient point at which the law, founded upon experience, changes the presumption of capacity, and puts upon the infant the burden of showing his personal want of intelligence, prudence, foresight, or strength usual in those of such age."[34]

While the Kehler case is significant in that it is one on which Pennsylvania's current instructions to jurors is based, it is also noteworthy for what it did not do. Even though the judge in his 1892 opinion affirmed that it would be difficult for a youngster to stand up to a powerful boss, he did not consider the concept, later embodied in the mission statement of the National Child Labor Committee, that children had rights as they related to work and working. In short, the Kehler case was barely a blip on the radar screen in the cause of justice for children in the workplace. Nor did the case have an impact on the eventual adoption of workmen's compensation laws in the early twentieth century. As noted by G. Edward White, the workmen's compensation "reform signaled a recognition that workplace injuries had become so ubiquitous in certain industries, and the established doctrines of tort law had so regularly failed to address the problem in an adequate fashion, that the best policy was to remove workplace injuries from the tort system and address them though [sic] a system that emphasized a kind of bureaucratic justice."[35] (The established doctrines of tort law referred to included contributory negligence, assumption of risk by the employee, and something called the fellow-servant rule, which barred or reduced the amount of money an injured employee could recover against an employer if an injury was caused by the negligence of a fellow worker.) Commenting about workmen's compensation laws, White concluded that "no single reform of the common law of torts had previously had a comparable effect in America, and none has since."[36]

EVEN WHILE HIS CASE WAS MAKING ITS WAY THROUGH THE court system, Daniel Kehler completed high school in 1888. He then entered Schuylkill Seminary (now Albright College) and subsequently studied law. Perhaps he used the proceeds from the successful lawsuit to finance his education. He was admitted to the Northumberland County bar in 1902 and to practice in Pennsylvania's Supreme Court in 1903. In 1909 he joined in a partnership with his younger brother, attorney James Kehler. Daniel was active in the community of Mount Carmel, having been borough auditor for three years, a member of the school board, and a member and trustee of the Anthracite Fire Company. He married in 1904, and the couple had at least two children.[37]

William Schwenk pursued his business interests. In 1888 he moved to Minersville, where he became a member of the firm of Leisenring & Co., operators of the Oak Hill colliery. He was president of Mount Carmel Savings Bank since 1891, president of the Tremont Engine and Boiler Works since 1892, and a director of the Mount Carmel Water Company.[38]

Kehler's attorney, Simon P. Wolverton, continued to serve in the Pennsylvania State Senate through 1887. In 1887 he was nominated by the Democrats of the Pennsylvania General Assembly for the office of US senator but was defeated by the Republican candidate, Matthew Quay. He was among five potential candidates considered for the office of governor in 1890 but failed to win the nomination.[39] He was elected as a Democrat to the United States House of Representatives and served in the Fifty-Second and Fifty-Third Congresses (1891–1895). Wolverton's law practice was extensive and included wealthy clients: P&R Railroad Company, P&R Coal and Iron Company, Lehigh Valley Railroad, Lehigh Valley Coal Company, Cox Bros. and Company, and the Delaware, Sunbury & Schuylkill Railroad. He was among those who organized the Shamokin, Sunbury & Schuylkill Railroad and served as its president.[40]

In the great anthracite coal strike of 1902, as general counsel for the Philadelphia and Reading Coal and Iron Company, Wolverton was a hard-nosed spokesman for the large coal companies.[41] In response to the Anthracite Coal Strike Commission, a fact-finding commission set up by president Theodore Roosevelt to suspend the strike, the P&R Coal and Iron Company, in concert with the other coal companies, denied that "the children of the anthracite mine workers are prematurely forced into the breakers and mills instead of being supported and educated upon the earnings of their parents because of low wages of such parents."[42] And the company asserted that "no boys are employed in and about the mines and breakers in violation of the statutes fixing the ages of employment."[43] (It would seem that accepting the Kehler v. Schwenk case was an anomaly for Wolverton, bolstering the idea that he took the case for political reasons.) In its report, the commission judged that the miners' contention that wages were so low that boys were forced into labor prematurely was not sustained by the evidence, and consequently, the commission did not include the accusation in its findings of fact. However, the commission recommended that "while the law prescribes ages at which boys may be employed in and around the mines, it appears, from the evidence, that the age is not placed sufficiently high."[44] It also recommended that there "ought to be a more rigid enforcement of the laws which now exist."[45]

The fact that children were being killed and permanently disabled while working in the mines was no secret. By the time the strike commission convened in 1902, more than thirty years had passed since the first mine inspectors' reports had been published in 1871. Still, it was not until the strike that "publicity of child labor conditions in the industry resonated with the public."[46] The National Child Labor Committee was organized in 1904. Its first studies were conducted in Pennsylvania's anthracite coal fields. Considering the horrendous conditions reported by the committee, it is dumbfounding that the committee's recommendations faced considerable resistance from parents, employers, and government officials. Surprisingly, among the government resisters was one James Roderick, who was by then the chief of Pennsylvania's Department of Mines: this is the same man who had passionately advocated on behalf of young boys, widows, and orphans in 1882.[47]

In the end, the seeds of reform planted in the 1870s and 1880s had little effect on the elimination of child labor in the coal mines. But the accounts of the mine inspectors and actions in the legislature and the courts do show that early on, long before the reformers of the progressive era began their work, a few people—John McEliece among them—recognized the problem. Sitting in the courtroom, listening to young Kehler, John must have been struck by the injustice of a system that considered loss of life and limb to be of little consequence. I wonder if John underwent a crisis of conscience, if he realized that "but for" the particular circumstance of Kehler's injury, the person sitting in the defendant's chair could have been him. Perhaps. In any event, by the time the Kehler case was decided for the third time in 1892, John McEliece had left the darkness of the coal mines and moved into the light. Literally, he got into the light-generating business.

Since at least the 1860s, children had been working in the coal mines. By the time they were no longer found in these dangerous, dreary workplaces, more than half a century had gone by. Regrettably there is a sad coda to this story. As Hugh D. Hindman points out, while child labor has been eradicated in the United States in mining and manufacturing, trouble spots remain, especially in the agriculture sector. And one need only refer to the US Department of Education's Office of Safe and Healthy Students to begin to understand the extent of the problem of human trafficking of children in the United States. Moreover, in the world today, "there are 250 million working children under the age of fifteen in the developing nations alone" and "of these, 120 million are considered to be fully at work."[48] Clearly, there is still much work to do.

CHAPTER 25

LIGHT

—————◆—————

J ohn McEliece returned to Shamokin in the mid-1880s. During his fifteen-year absence, Shamokin's population had more than doubled, and by 1900 the town would be home to about eighteen thousand people. The economic base of the community had diversified beyond the coal industry to include bakeries, ice cream and dairy factories, a brewery, a silk mill, and dress and hosiery factories. Shamokin had emerged as a regional commercial center and offered a variety of amenities including theaters, an amusement park, and an opera house, all of which were powered by electricity.

The age of electricity began on September 4, 1882, when the Edison Electric Illuminating Company of New York lit up Manhattan's night. Soon thereafter, Thomas Edison visited Shamokin where the Edison Electric Illuminating Company of Shamokin was organized. It was a proud moment for the city when the company was incorporated, November 29, 1882, with a capital of $27,000. The electric company purchased two lots on Independence Street and commenced construction of a brick building abutting the Pennsylvania Railroad. However, Shamokin would not be the first city in Pennsylvania to be lighted by electricity.

Soon after his arrival in Shamokin, Edison also licensed an electric company with investors in Sunbury, some sixteen miles to the southeast. Using Sunbury's City Hotel as its base, the Sunbury company built a coal-fired power plant on a vacant lot at the corner of Vine and Fourth streets in just three weeks. After a three-wire line was strung to the City Hotel, Edison, on the night of July 4, 1883, switched on the current to a 100-candle power light over the City Hotel entrance, to the cheers of residents and marches played by a local brass band.[1]

The Shamokin company was hard on Sunbury's heels, however, and on September 6, 1883, the engineer at the partially completed plant "grasped the lever, gave it a twitch, and in an instant the splendidly balanced machine was running like a scared dog."[2] The oohs and aahs followed when the engineer "touched a key and presto, twenty-five of these beautiful little globes sent out their pure rays, and again, and again, and again until one hundred of them glowed with their slender ribbons of thunderbolt arched in security and magnificent splendor chasing every vestige of darkness from the unpainted and unceiled building and filling every crevice with a beautiful white light devoid of quiver or flicker to annoy the eye."[3] A short while later, on September 22, Thomas Edison visited the city and turned on the lights at St. Edward's Catholic Church, the first church in the world to be lighted with electricity. At an unknown time John was brought down from Locust Gap, and he succeeded one William Brock as superintendent of the company. And when the Shamokin Arc Light Company was incorporated on August 17, 1887, he became superintendent of that company as well. Both positions were described in the old biographical sketches as "lucrative."[4] John also remained active in public affairs, serving for a while as a selectman (a city councilor).[5]

For the first time in their lives, John and Ann Ellen became homeowners, purchasing a double-frame house on Sunbury Street. In September 1889 the house was destroyed by fire. Even though the house was insured for $700, McEliece was still out about $1,000.[6] Later he purchased a house on the Market Street side of town at 17 Gold Street. The last of their ten children, Margaret, was born in 1888: John was forty-six years old at the time, and Ann Ellen was forty-three. It was a lively household including George, Fred, Isabella, Leo, Lloyd, my grandmother Lillian, and newborn Margaret.

The time John spent in the employment of the electric light companies provided a reprieve from his years of toiling in the coal mines. But the damage to his body had been done. As the years passed, his wartime injuries troubled him more and more, causing him to repeatedly seek an increase in his military pension. He suffered from miner's asthma—black lung disease—and heart failure. At age fifty-eight, with three children still living at home, he was no longer able to work. McEliece was among those who, in the words of historian Richard White, were "dying for progress" in America's Gilded Age.[7]

But there was a difference between John and the millions of industrial workers who were crowded together in America's filthy slums. Supposedly he was among the better off in the city of Shamokin. His position as manager of the electric companies was described as lucrative. So why was John McEliece among the destitute? It may have had something to do with an incident with a minor girl. In April 1891 the *Sunbury Gazette* reported that "John McEliece, manager of the Edison electric light plant at Shamokin, was on Saturday evening held at bail for court on several charges, one of which is rape, preferred by Miss Snyder, aged about 15 years."[8] The case was settled for $3,000 (about $86,000 in today's dollars) and, as was reported in the *Sunbury Weekly News*, "That kind of amusement always comes high, but in cases like this one it is invariably higher than the ordinary, and the defendant an [sic] congratulate himself on his very fortunate escape from the penitentiary for a good long term."[9] Had I known about this incident when I began this story, I probably would have abandoned this project. Needless to say, it shattered the illusion created by the sugarcoated profiles in *Biographical Sketches* and Bell's *History of Northumberland County* that presented John as a heroic and honorable man.[10] And I am left to wonder how my great-grandmother reacted to John's betrayal. Why did she not leave?

In 1904, with no income other than his $10 a month military pension, the family applied for a pension increase to $30. The graphic report to Congress describes the misery of John's final days.

The affidavit of the beneficiary...asks Congress to come to his relief in his present lamentable condition, he having been confined to the house for about two years and not able to do any work for the last three years, suffering from heart trouble, dropsy, and asthma, unable to lie down to sleep for the last two years, and compelled to sit upon a chair, resting his head on a table; that his legs and body are swollen to an enormous size; that there is no hope for improvement whatever; that he has no means of support except a pension of $10 a month, and that his home, valued at about $2,200, is encumbered by a mortgage of $1,300.[11]

On April 8, 1904, Congress voted to increase John's pension to $30 a month. Eight days after the congressional relief measure was passed, John passed away. He was sixty-one years of age.

Perhaps in his own eyes, John enjoyed a fulfilling life. He had been blessed with a large extended family. He had loads of friends. His work was challenging. He was a community leader. But when compared to his Woodside ancestors—the men and women of the pre-industrial age who lived much longer—he was among those who sacrificed years of life to the cause of America's industrial development.

AT THE BEGINNING OF THIS RIDE THROUGH AMERICAN HISTORY, I hoped to understand how my great-grandfather John McEliece came to oversee children working in a dangerous industry. I thought, perhaps naively, that something in his family background may have predisposed him to take part in this abhorrent practice, but I found no explanation in the past. Rather, it appears that exploitation of children working in dangerous industries was part and parcel of the evils of the industrial revolution. Thus, while John's involvement in the practice could be explained away as a by-product of the time and place in which he lived, it cannot be justified. At the same time, it seems unfair to condemn John for failing to live up to a standard that was nowhere in sight until the early years of the twentieth century. Moreover, in acknowledging that the process of reforming social norms is the work of genera-tions—witness the never-ending struggle for equal rights among marginalized peoples—John should get some credit for moving the needle ever so slightly when he testified on behalf of a boy who was seriously injured while working in a coal mine. That said, does a ten-minute appearance on the witness stand absolve John for the injuries that occurred on his watch? No. John's life was defined by some of the most brutal events in American history: the Civil War, in which he served, and the Industrial Revolution. And it appears that he fit right in.

Ann Ellen McEliece, who herself was not in good health, strug-gled to pick up the pieces after her husband's death. The $30 a month pension that John was awarded by an act of Congress was dropped upon his death. On April 29, 1904, Ann Ellen filed an application for a soldier's widow's pension. It was rejected on May 9. She refiled her application with additional documents on September 26, after which she received $8 a month (about $230 a month in today's dollars). In 1907 she joined her three daughters— Isabella, Lillian, and Margaret—who had moved to Buffalo, New York, shortly after John's death. It was there that Ann Ellen passed away in January 1908.

And so, I have returned to the beginning of my story where I asked—in referring to my great-grandfather's role as an agent of cruelty to children—how can this be? But before I finish, I would like to close the circle with an uplifting story about my grandfather Dr. James J. Brown, Lillian McEliece's husband.

CHAPTER 26

HEALING HANDS

⸻◆⸻

From the moment that James Woodside set foot on American soil in 1746 until the day John McEliece passed away in 1904, my family had been caught up in the hustle and bustle of American life. But while America flourished, little heed was paid to the human cost of progress. That began to change in the late 1800s and early 1900s when activists addressed the problems associated with industrialization, immigration, and governmental corruption. Muckrakers such as Lincoln Steffens, Ida Tarbell, and Upton Sinclair penned exposés about municipal corruption, the oil industry, and the meatpacking industry. Social reformers such as Jane Addams, Florence Kelley, and Jacob Riis raised public awareness of the wretched working and living conditions of the poor. Likewise, but in his quiet way, my grandfather James J. Brown dedicated his life to helping and healing the less-fortunate inhabitants of South Buffalo, New York.

⸻◆⸻

NOT LONG AFTER JOHN MCELIECE BEGAN HIS TENURE AS SUPER-intendent of the Edison Electric Illuminating Company of Shamokin, Thomas Edison's dominance in the contest to electrify America was challenged. Remembered by historians as the War of the Currents, the struggle between Thomas Edison and General Electric, who were advocating for the use of direct current, and Nikola Tesla and the Westinghouse Company, who were advocating for alternating current, persisted from the late 1880s to the early 1900s. The "war" included a bidding competition for the privilege of electrifying the Chicago World's Fair of 1893, and in the same year, Westinghouse won the contract to generate power from Niagara Falls, and "On November 16, 1896, Buffalo was lit up by the alternating current from Niagara Falls."[1]

THE AVAILABILITY OF AN UNLIMITED SUPPLY OF HYDROELEC-tric power from nearby Niagara Falls was the crown jewel that reinforced Buffalo's already-favorable location for industry. That power, in combination with a transportation network that afforded first-rate access to railroads and Great Lakes shipping, a supply of cheap nonunionized immigrant labor, and an attractive financial package, induced Walter Scranton, president of the Lackawanna Iron and Steel Company, to relocate to the Buffalo area. Construction of "the largest steel plant in the world" in the adjacent town of West Seneca began in 1900.[2] Although Buffalonians had hoped that the steel company would hire local men to fill its managerial and supervisory positions, most of those jobs were assigned to employees who were transferred from Pennsylvania. Among them was Isabella McEliece's husband, John F. Campbell, who was employed as foreman of the company's bridge department.[3] John and Isabella were married in Shamokin on September 7, 1904, and almost immediately moved to Buffalo. Joining them were Isabella's younger sisters, Margaret and my grandmother Lillian.

AS LATE AS 1902 MUCH OF THE SOUTH BUFFALO NEIGHBORHOOD was still farmland and swamp. That began to change rapidly with the arrival of Lackawanna Steel. Among the changes, in 1902 the Sisters of Mercy established their motherhouse across from Cazenovia Park on land they purchased from the Choate family. And in a bold move two years later, the financially strapped nuns purchased a large house on Tifft Street and converted it into the "old" Mercy Hospital. The little hospital was established "to serve as an accident or emergency hospital for the reception of sick and injured from the populous and growing section near the Lackawanna Steel plant."[4] With accommodation for thirty patients, the hospital was opened on September 24, 1904. The hospital's medical and consulting staff included twenty-seven physicians. Among them was Dr. James Joseph Brown.[5]

Dr. Brown's lifelong commitment to the Sisters of Mercy began in his growing-up years in the rural community of Wellsville, Allegany County, New York. The son of Irish immigrants, John and Margaret Brown, James was born in 1870 in Wainfleet, Ontario, Canada. When James was an infant, the family was admitted to the United States, and they settled on a farm that was partly in the town of Wellsville and partly in the town of Andover. It was on the farm that James and his brother William spent their youth clearing the land. Father Bill "Mario" Brown, OFM, William's grandson, recalls that his mother was always talking about "how rough her father's hands were, and his brother's too."[6]

Deeply religious, John and Margaret Brown were steadfast members of Wellsville's Immaculate Conception Roman Catholic Church to which, on August 30, 1876, Reverend Philip Kinsella, the first resident pastor of the parish, brought the Sisters of Mercy.[7] The nuns immediately established classes in which the Brown children received their primary and secondary education. One of the Brown children, Agnes (Sister Mary Loretto, RSM), entered the sisterhood at the age of seventeen. She taught in Hornell, Corning, Batavia, and finally at St. Patrick's in Elmira where she was in charge. Sister Mary Loretto Brown died in 1895 at the age of twenty-nine.[8] She was one of three of the Brown children who entered the religious community. In the parish church in Wellsville, one of the stained-glass windows is dedicated to Rev. John Brown, Deacon Maurice Brown, and Sister Mary Loretto.[9]

Embracing the importance of education and service to the community, at great sacrifice John and Margaret Brown sent their son James to study medicine at the University of Buffalo from which he graduated on May 2, 1902.[10] (Two women were included among the thirty-eight graduates. Among them was Dr. M. Louise Hurrell, who served during World War I as director of the American Women's Hospital No. 1 in Luzancy, France.) Upon completion of his internship at Sisters of Charity Hospital, Dr. Brown joined the Sisters of Mercy as an "alternate" of the attending medical department at the Tifft Street hospital upon its opening.[11]

THROUGH THE EARLY YEARS OF THE TWENTIETH CENTURY, advances in medical science were numerous and profound: in 1895 Wilhelm Conrad Röntgen, a German physicist, discovered the X-ray; in 1901 Karl Landsteiner introduced the system to classify blood into A, B, AB, and O groups; in 1906 August von Wassermann introduced a diagnostic test for syphilis (congenital syphilis was a leading cause of intrauterine and neonatal death); in 1907 Clemens von Pirquet introduced a skin test for tuberculosis; in 1911 Paul Ehrlich tested Salvarsan, the first treatment effective against syphilis; in 1913 Paul Dudley White became one of America's first cardiologists and a pioneer in the use of the electrocardiogram; in 1921 Frederick Banting and Charles Best isolated insulin, which was first used to treat a person with diabetes a year later; in 1921–1927 the first vaccines for diphtheria, whooping cough, tuberculosis, and tetanus were developed; in 1928 Sir Alexander Fleming discovered penicillin, although it did not become available in a therapeutically usable form until 1940.

Without diminishing the importance of particular scientific contributions during the progressive era, the changes that had the longest-lasting impact on health care delivery concerned public health and medical education.[12] Perhaps the most sweeping development had to do with the general acceptance that microbes were the cause of infectious diseases. As noted by H. Burns, chief medical officer for Scotland, "Advances in our understanding of hygiene, sanitation, and pathology that followed the development of germ theory have done more to extend life expectancy and change the nature of society than any other medical innovation."[13]

In 1910 infectious diseases were the leading cause of death in New York State, with tuberculosis claiming more lives (16,516 persons) than all other infectious diseases combined (9,285 persons). Diphtheria, whooping cough (pertussis), scarlet fever, and measles exacted their toll. Among children two years and younger, diarrheal diseases were the biggest killers, accounting for more than one-fourth of the deaths in this age group. In Buffalo, as in other locations, children under the age of five suffered the highest death rate. Specifically, children under one year of age accounted for twenty-three of one hundred deaths in the city; children under five years of age accounted for thirty-three of one hundred deaths in the city.[14]

But Buffalo was fortunate in having Dr. Ernest Wende as commissioner of the Buffalo Department of Health from 1892 to 1901 and 1907 to 1910. Dr. Wende, who had done postgraduate work in Berlin under Robert Koch, "was in the vanguard of American physicians in understanding the new microbiology."[15] Wende was a "pivotal figure in bringing the latest science of his day to bear on the health challenges of one of the U.S.'s fastest growing centers of commerce, transportation, and manufacturing."[16] Among numerous other initiatives, Dr. Wende applied his near-autocratic authority to implement an aggressive campaign to regulate and require improvements to unsanitary housing.[17] Dr. Wende also placed "great importance on collection of all forms of data relating to morbidity and mortality," an approach that "could have detected linkages between environmental exposures and chronic diseases."[18] But then, during the years of Dr. Wende's service, it was infectious diseases rather than chronic diseases that were the number one killer. One measure of the success of scientific discoveries and public health initiatives is that, by 1934, the proportion of deaths among children under five years old in New York State had dropped precipitously to a little more than eight of one hundred deaths.[19]

Concerning medical education, in 1910 a survey of all medical schools, completed by Abraham Flexner under the auspices of the American Medical Association and the Carnegie Foundation, was undertaken. The resulting study "set American medicine on a course that was fueled by the energy of scientific discovery."[20] But, as Dr. Thomas Duffy opined one hundred years later, the survey failed to recognize "the primary role of physician as beneficent healers."[21] Continuing, Dr. Duffy observed that today's revisions in medical education "are reclaiming the rightful eminence of the service component of medicine" that was overlooked in the Flexner report.[22] Be that as it may, the publication of *Medical Education in the United States and Canada*—the Flexner Report—highlighted the inadequacy of many of the schools and advocated for major reform. The study recommended closure of all but thirty-one of the 151 medical schools then in operation.

As an example of the report, the University of Buffalo, where Dr. Brown was trained, did not receive high marks. "Despite the university charter," Flexner wrote, "the University of Buffalo is a fiction."[23] Entrance requirements, he observed, were based on the "Regents' Medical Student Certificate, being the equivalent of a high school education."[24] He went on to criticize the laboratory facilities; was fairly neutral about the clinical facilities at Buffalo General, County, and Sisters' hospitals; and acknowledged the "good library of 8000 volumes, current German and English periodicals, with a librarian in charge."[25] He concluded with a brutal assessment of the college dispensary, describing it as "wretched."[26] He was particularly critical of the unsystematic recordkeeping. "The work is hastily and superficially done," he wrote, "and its influence on the students, so far as it goes, must be thoroughly bad." Indeed, in his recommendation for reconstruction of medical education, Flexner advised that the school at Buffalo should "disappear."[27] So much for my grandfather's less than ideal medical education. Nevertheless, by all accounts he was an excellent physician who exemplified the subtle balance between the art and science of medicine.

And so, it was in this progressive environment that Dr. Brown built his medical practice. Typical for the period, his office was located in his home. It included two rooms—a waiting room and an examination room—and was accessed by patients through a separate side entrance. A door between the waiting room and the family dining room provided access to the living quarters.[28] (See figure 29.) On a typical day Dr. Brown arose at 7:00 a.m. With the tools of his trade—diagnostic equipment and remedies—packed in his black leather doctor's bag, he made his morning rounds, visiting those patients who were too ill to visit his office. He conducted office hours from 1:00 to 4:00 p.m., ate dinner at 5:30 p.m., followed by office hours from 7:00 to 9:00 p.m. Sunday was his only day off. After church he spent his time reading the newspaper from cover to cover. On occasion he walked across the street to the Capitol movie theater. Always sitting at the end of a row in case he was called for an emergency, he enjoyed the latest shoot-'em-up and laughed heartily at the antics of Buster Keaton.[29]

Dr. Brown's staff consisted of family members: his wife and daughters. Lillian McEliece and James J. Brown were married at Holy Family Church in 1906. As the story goes, soon after he opened his medical practice, Dr. Brown was smitten by the girl from Shamokin, saying, "When I saw her walking down the street, with those blue eyes and black hair, I *knew* she was the one."[30] How they met is unknown, but it is thought that James first laid his eyes on Lillian while visiting his dentist (who was also his nephew) whose office was located in the neighborhood where Lillian lived. However it happened, Lillian traded in her role as a seamstress for that of a doctor's and philanthropist's wife, and a mother. Mary was born in 1907; Irene, my mother, was born in 1909; and Lillian was born in 1913. Two other children, John and Grace, did not survive.

Figure 29. The Brown house and office, circa 1910. Author's collection.

Eventually Dr. Brown emerged as a leader of South Buffalo's medical community. The inadequacy of the Tifft Street hospital became increasingly clear, and in 1913 the Sisters of Mercy purchased a four-acre property on Abbott Road. The site, once a part of the Buffalo Creek Indian reservation, was adjacent to their motherhouse. Nine years later, "on March 28, 1922, Dr. James J. Brown, who was to be an ardent apostle in the building of the new Mercy and who had always been an enthusiastic supporter of anything concerning the Sisters of Mercy, presided over a lively meeting of a small group of twenty-seven men at old Mercy to discuss the prospects of erecting a new hospital."[31] Ground was broken for the new hospital on November 4, 1924, but the project soon stalled due to a lack of funds. Once again Dr. Brown and eleven other gentlemen offered their help. They proposed to raise the interest on a loan for three years if the Sisters would continue with the building.

The "twelve apostles" as these gentlemen were called proved their plan to be a sound one. They left no section "uncombed" looking for members of the Mercy Hospital Sustaining Society, as the new organization was called. Each Friday evening they met with the Sisters…"to make returns, to report on the progress made, to give and receive counsel, and, finally, to encourage each other to keep on with the good work." Their meetings were very informal; they were like "simple schoolboys" reporting on what they had been doing during the week. Sometimes they might have had two hundred dollars to turn in; other times they might have but ten…. In a few instances, Dr. Brown, after staying all night in a home where there was sickness, would take no fee but would ask instead that the family enroll in the Sustaining Society or in the case of a birth of a child would ask that the child be enrolled.

At first there was no formal Constitution. Indeed, when Dr. Brown was asked to be president of the little organization, he, who normally was even-tempered, became quite indignant and said not one of the twelve men was looking for any honor; they were there only to do what the Sisters want and not be distracted by credit or politics.[32]

The new Mercy Hospital, a seven-story structure with two hundred beds, was opened to the public on February 2, 1928. It provided space for children's cases, medical and surgical cases, a maternity ward, operating rooms, X-ray and laboratory facilities, classrooms, and store rooms. Dr. Brown served as its first chief of staff. Among his first duties, he called the staff together to draw up bylaws and regulations for the new hospital.[33]

Dr. Brown served his community in other ways. Like his parents, he was very religious. His daughter Lillian wrote, "I'm sure my father would have been a priest if he hadn't married."[34] As president of the Holy Family church conference of the St. Vincent de Paul society, he sought personal holiness by attending to the physical and spiritual needs of the poor.[35] He was also one of the doctors for Our Lady of Victory Infant Home since its founding.[36] Father Nelson Baker opened the OLV Infant Home in 1906 to house and care for abandoned babies and their socially stigmatized, unwed mothers.[37]

Upon Dr. Brown's death, in their tribute to him, the Sisters of Mercy wrote, "On February 20, 1934, the Sisters at the hospital and the community in general were saddened by the word of the death of their beloved friend Dr. James J. Brown....That the new Mercy Hospital exists today is in great part the result of his generous expenditure of effort to establish the Sustaining Society. The Sisters of Mercy will be ever mindful of this devoted friend for his unfailing and devoted assistance in furthering their work."[38] Perhaps of all my ancestors and relatives, my grandfather—whom I never met—was the most admirable. Given his prominence in the community of South Buffalo, he could have been haughty. Instead, he remained a good man, a humble man of simple tastes. Some might have called him a saint. (See figure 30.)

*Figure 30. My mother, Irene Brown Speth, and my grandfather,
Dr. James J. Brown, circa 1925. Author's collection.*

ACKNOWLEDGMENTS

I could not have completed this ambitious project without the help of historians, archivists, librarians, family, friends, and the people who turn a manuscript into a book.

The first time I made an inquiry to a historian, I was somewhat surprised to receive a prompt, courteous reply. After all, I was not a colleague or a student; just a random person with no background in history. I quickly learned this is the norm in a truly honorable profession. Many may have forgotten our exchange, but their responses provided insight, facts or direction that helped me develop the story.

Thank you to you all: Terry Bouton, Colin Calloway, Katherine Faull, Norm Gasborro, Laurence Hauptman, Wythe Holt, Jon Parmenter, Dean Snow, Mark Voss-Hubbard and John Fabian Witt. John Heiser of National Park Service, Gettysburg National Military Park, helped with information about the role of the PA 36th after the battle of Gettysbueg. Kevin Kenny read chapters having to do with the Irish diaspora, and offered useful suggestions. Vince P. Martonis, the Hanover Historian, generously shared what he knew about the history of the Cattaraugus reservation. And he knew more than anyone else. Grace Palladino offered research suggestions about child labor in the nineteenth century.

No one helped me more than Professor Matthew Dennis of University of Oregon. In 2011, referred by Colin Calloway, I asked if he would help me. Without hesitation his answer was yes. Through the years he has read many of my chapters, offered suggestions and corrections. Without his continued and unfailing support, this book would never have seen the light of day.

Working behind the scenes were a slew of librarians and archivists. Sometimes they came up empty-handed. Other times they struck what was for me a treasure trove. Thank you for your labors. Here they are: Patricia Cummings-Witter, The State University of New York at Fredonia; Christopher Damiani, Historical Society of Pennsylvania; Carol Eddleman, PA-Roots; Christy Fic, Shippensburg University Library; Ken Frew, Historical Society of Dauphin County; Caitlin Hucik, Somerset Historical and Genealogical Society; Louise Latsha, Northumberland County Historical Society; Patricia Medert, Ross County Historical Society; Betty McMahon, Ontario County Historical Society; Tal Nadan, New York Public Library; Susan O'Neill, State Library of Pennsylvania; Sister Helen Parot, R.S.M. sent a lovely package that detailed my grandfather's relationship with the Sisters of Mercy; Louise Peterson, Douglas County Public Library; Amy Pickard, Buffalo and Erie County Public Library; Mary Portelli, West Pittston Historical Society; Leigh Rifenburg, Delaware Historical Society; Jonathan Stayer, Pennsylvania State Archives; Rebecca Trook, Latah County Historical Society; Cynthia Van Ness, Buffalo History Museum; Joanne M. Weber, Diocese of Harrisburg; Glenn Wenrich, Pennsylvania Canal Society and Kris Wiley, Roseburg Public Library.

This is a story about family. The early settlers of Pennsylvania's Lykens Valley had large families, and many of their descendants intermarried. Tracing lines of descent does not appeal to me personally; fortunately, others have taken up the task. Bob Greiner sent his privately published booklet about the Woodside descendants; it was an invaluable resource in the early stages of my work. Richard Lebo answered questions about the Woodside and Schott family connections. Roger Cramer shared information on the early settlers of Lykens Valley, especially the Novinger family. John A. Gustafson sent me information about the Sallade family tree. Anna C. Woodside (1912-2013) sent me a copy of Robert E. Woodside's privately published book, *My Life and Town*.

My immediate and extended family pitched in. My talented nieces and nephews contributed their specialized talents. Patti Peet did legwork in Harrisburg. Sharon Higginbotham was my legal eagle. Kelly Speth helped me with statistics. Tom Higginbotham offered advice on the child labor chapter. My cousin Dawn Speth-White read early chapters and encouraged me to "keep writing." My brother Rick drove me around Pennsylvania, Virginia and Maryland as we followed the Civil War Trail. My sister Ginny read some chapters. Eric, my son and sun, is a genius with words, and so kind. He-who-shall-not-be-named out of respect for his privacy has been my guiding light, my north star.

Barbara McEliece, had been tracking down McElieces for quite a while. Barbara put me in touch with Robert McEliece up in the Seattle area who continues to share new information when he discovers it. M. Kerry Robinson helped with information about Jonathan Fletcher Woodside, and he directed me to the Ross County Historical Society which holds some of Jonathan F. Woodside's papers. Sarah Woodside Gallagher filled in some gaps about Anthony J. Gallagher's life.

Friends read early drafts. Janice Willms (1936-2019) read some early chapters. Playwright Kathleen Tomko was there at the beginning and I can still hear her saying, "that poor little boy." Kathy Focareta did some useful edits on the McEliece chapters. Anna Willman read some beginning chapters. Michael Schuman at the US Department of Labor Statistics read the chapters on child labor.

The copyediting of Jennifer Kepler of Cypress Editing was precise and professionally done. The staff at Luminare Press was a joy to work with. They created the cover, formatted the manuscript and so much more.

BATTLE OF WINCHESTER

SUNBURY AMERICAN, JUNE 7, 1862
THE BATTLE OF WINCHESTER
GALLANTRY OF OUR SOLDIERS
WILLIAMSPORT, MAY 27

Amid the reigning confusion at this point it is almost impossible to procure sufficient accurate information to warrant the sending of a letter. During the occurrence of Saturday and Sunday there was not a single recognized correspondent of the public press present. Several had taken advantage of the quiet and fancied security to visit their friends elsewhere; one, a person by the name of Clark, is believed to have been taken prisoner at Front Royal, and the only one in the vicinity was the correspondent of the World, who was, unfortunately, asleep in Winchester, and who was compelled to rely upon the statements of officers the next day, for material sufficient to enable him to write an epistle. Fortunately, he awoke in time to escape with the army.

The subjoined account of the movement of the Division is collected from statements of the principal officers engaged in the fight, and they may be relied upon as correct. This is really scarcely deserving of the name of a Corps d'Armee, the regiments having been withdrawn from time to time, until not more than five thousand men in all were in the command. With these were five hundred wagons; and as only a few—probably not more than fifty—were lost, it was a most astonishing retreat.

The left wing and the Forty-sixth Pennsylvania Regiment, Col. Joseph P. Knipe

The actions of this regiment are spoken of in the highest terms. Information having been received of the attack at Front Royal, an order was given to the regiment, at three o'clock on Saturday morning, to march immediately for Winchester. The regiment was then encamped on the banks of a small stream called Tom's Brook, about six miles southwest of Strasburg. The order was immediately obeyed. Tents were struck and, without breakfast, the men started on their march. The Forty-sixth, being the right of Acting Brigadier-General Donnelly's Brigade, moved in advance, followed by the Twenty-eighth New York, Lieutenant-Colonel Brown (Col. Donnelly acting as brigadier) and the Fifth Connecticut, Lieut.-Colonel Chapman. (The colonel of this regiment, Col. Ferry, is acting as brigadier-general of Gen. Shields' command.) The brigade and regimental trains, in number about one hundred fifty wagons, had been sent on immediately in advance.

About seven o'clock the brigade arrived at Strasburg, where it was joined by Brigadier-General Gordon's brigade, Donnelly's brigade taking the advance. An hour afterwards the entire force, under command of Major-General Banks, took up the line of march for Winchester. The cavalry, consisting of the First Michigan and parts of the Fifth New York and First Vermont, under General Hatch, and Hampton's Pennsylvania Battery, in the meantime remained at a point about four miles south of Strasburg, for the purpose of protecting the removal of a large quantity of commissary's stores. Finding it impossible to remove all, the soldiers were supplied, and the balance were prudently set fire to and destroyed. When the command reached Middletown, six miles this side of Strasburg, the Rebel cavalry came out from the woods on the side of the road and attacked the train in front. A stampede took place among the teamsters, and while many wagons were upset in turning short, others were set fire to and burned. Among the wagons were several belonging to sutlers and refugees.

The Forty-sixth immediately, by companies, placed their knap-sacks, blankets, and everything that would interfere with their movements, upon the roadside, loading at will, and forwarded at will double-quick up the turnpike as far as Newtown, about four mile distant, driving the Rebel cavalry ahead until they reached the village, where the Rebels took to a woods to the right. One section of a New York battery, under Lieut. Woodbury, followed, and taking position, opened fire, driving them back. At the same time two companies of the Forty-sixth, A and K, acting as skirmishers, fired, killing two and wounding one, which they left upon the field. The Forty-sixth and the battery then returned to the pike and moved on in front of the train, which was protected in the rear by the rest of the command. No Rebel interference was experienced after that, and the command reached Winchester about nine o'clock p. m. Donnelly's brigade bivouacked that night, without food or blankets, on the Front Royal road, about a mile south of the town, Gordon's brigade resting on the left of the Strasburg road. On Sunday morn-ing before daybreak, revile was sounded, and the troops were called to arms. During the night there had been constant and heavy firing between the pickets.

During the night, anticipating an attack in the morning, an order was given by General Banks that Gordon's brigade should form the right wing of the defence and Donnelly's the left. About half past four fire was opened upon the left by the Rebel batteries, about two miles distant, and almost immediately afterwards an attack was also made on the right. Our batteries then returned the fire and a general engagement ensued. A North Carolina regiment, several of the officers of which were in citizens' dress—one Captain having on a black silk hat, and who was subsequently shot in the head—made an attack on the Forty-sixth, taking them by surprise; but most gallantly was the assault met, for scarcely had they made their appearance over the hilltop and fired their murderous volley, before the rifled Minnies of the Forty-sixth had played havoc with their ranks. Bayonets were then fixed, and a charge being made, the traitors were driven from behind a stone wall where they had taken shelter. Severe fighting continued for half an hour—the firing on both sides being desperate and the loss severe. Severe fighting was also continued by the other regiments of the two brigades. Towards seven o'clock a heavy mist caused the firing to be suspended on both sides.

During this time the Forty-sixth changed their pickets to rising ground, and when the mist disappeared, which was in about twenty minutes, firing again began. A regiment of Rebel infantry now appeared in a hollow near, but failed to advance against the skirmishers. About 8 o'clock a combined attack of infantry and artillery was made by the Rebels upon Gordon's brigade—the right wing of the defence—and in such numbers that a stand was impossible. About an hour before this attack, a regiment of Rebel cavalry (Stuart's) charged down the pike into the town, thereby getting into our rear, and giving them an opportunity to cut off stragglers and sick and wounded, and the supply trains.

The batteries of the rebels are said to be well manned, and shot and shell were thrown with the greatest accuracy. Their guns were mainly rifled. Our own artillery also did most excellent execution.

The left wing, notwithstanding the unfortunate position of the right, stood firm, Gen. Banks adding to their determination by his constant presence. About half past 8 o'clock an order to retreat was given, which was made in excellent order under a heavy fire of shot and shell from the Rebel battery on the hill, many of the deadly missiles going through and riddling the houses of their own friends. The Forty-sixth, in solid column and in perfect order, marched through the street in Winchester as if on parade. As soon as the regiment entered the town the street re-echoed with the shots discharged from the windows of the dwellings. The destined attack upon our troops was evidently well known by the people of Winchester, since no sooner had the battle commenced than the windows bristled with guns and pistols.

Whenever a Union soldier was seen, there a shot was fired. Not men only, but women used with effect the deadly weapons. Accurate aim was taken not only by these female fiends, but large hand grenades were thrown by them from windows, which, as they burst, proved destructive to the lives and limbs of our gallant men. The shots were, of course, returned, and heads here and there were seen to suddenly disappear below the sash.

When the Forty-sixth arrived at a point just this side of the depot, they received a volley from a regiment of Louisiana Tigers, stationed some two hundred yards distant, but did not return the fire, from prudential motives. The retreat was then continued, Gordon's brigade being about half a mile in advance on the left, and the remainder of Donnelly's about a mile to the right, the Rebel battery which had been previously engaged against our right having taken position in the earthworks made by Johnson last summer, on the top of the hill, shelling our men as they moved forward.

About six miles this side of Winchester an order to halt was given, and the word was passed that reinforcements from Gen. Dix were within a short distance. Hearty cheers were given, and the spirits of all were revived. The Rebels themselves, who were following about two miles behind, were surprised and alarmed and came to a sudden halt. The reinforcements, however, did not come, and the retreat was recommenced, the Rebels following and shelling until within three miles of Martinsburg. About three o'clock on Sunday afternoon the command reached Martinsburg, and passing immediately through, marched up the pike to the Potomac, opposite Williamsport. The troops bivouacked on the Virginia shore that night, and on Monday crossed over in a ferry-boat and two boats formerly used for a pontoon bridge.

The Forty-sixth is now encamped one mile from Williamsport, on the St. James College road. The men are naturally much fatigued, but are anxious and determined to return at an early day to Winchester and Strasburg.

The events of Saturday and Sunday will be remembered by General Banks' command. Not only did they march sixty-five miles during the two days, without anything to eat, save what could be picked up by the roadside, but they fought one severe battle and two engagements.

To specify individual acts of gallantry and bravery would be invidious where all fought so well. The field officers of the Forty-sixth were ever in the thickest of the fray and won everlasting praise. Col. Knipe received a slight flesh wound in the shoulder, and his right pistol holder was the recipient of a ball which, glancing, passed immediately under the leg of the gallant rider. Lieut.-Colonel Selfridge made a narrow escape, a shall bursting in front of his horse, causing the animal to fall, slightly bruising Col. S's leg.

The Major, Adjutant, and in fact all, were alike cool and brave. Captain S. A. Brooks, of Company D, the color company, received a ball through the skirt of his coat. Himself and his company are referred to in exalted terms, as is, also, that of Capt. Wise, of Reading. Color-Sargeant James McQuillan behaved nobly. While bearing the colors, he was wounded by a Minnie ball, in the calf of the leg. For a moment he dropped, and then, with one hand raised above his head, cheering his comrades, and with the other waving the Stars and Stripes, he arose, and apparently forgetting his wounds, marched in the advance. The flag received two balls. Among the prisoners taken by the enemy were Captain Cyrus Strause, from Shamokin, Northumberland county, and Lieut. A. W. Selfridge, of company H, from Bethlehem. Both officers were engaged upon a court-martial at Strasburg, and in attempting to join their regiment, were cut off.

The wounded in the engagement forgot their wounds, in their patriotism. One poor fellow, belonging to company A. of the Forty-sixth, with the top of his left hand blown off by a piece of shell, walked coolly along with his musket trailing in his right, until Col. Knipe ordered him to the rear, while another, wounded in the calf of the leg, walked twelve miles before he was compelled to succumb to his pain. Col. Knipe had previously given up his horse to a wounded private, and Lieut.-Colonel Selfridge had a few moments before done likewise. Brigadier-General (acting Major) Williams was passing at the moment, and immediately dismounting, made the private take his place in the saddle, while he walked. With such sympathy, such feeling, on the part of the officers, how could men fail to fight well.

The total loss of the Forty-sixth up to the present time is as follows:

	Killed	Wounded	Missing
Company A	0	3	10
Company B	1	Not rep.	Not rep.
Company C	0	6	5
Company D	0	4	2
Company E	1	3	12
Company F	0	5	11
Company G	0	6	3
Company H	1	2	7
Company I	0	8	4
Company K	1	2	12

Two officers—the Commissary Sergeant, C. J. Rees, and Deetz of the band—are among the missing.

The most distressing sight I have witnessed hereabouts is the care, worn anxious appearance of the hundreds of refugees—black and white, male and female—who have been compelled to flee with our army from Strasburg, Winchester, Martinsburg, and other sections of Virginia. The hotels here and at Hagerstown are filled with them, as are also many private houses, while along the turnpike for a mile or two, they may be seen reclining in the fields. Wealth and position were naught when weighing the scales against personal safety. A number has returned to Virginia with our army and had, with the little they had saved from the Rebels recommenced business or restored their private dwellings to at least partial comfort.

BATTLE OF CEDAR MOUNTAIN

SHAMOKIN HERALD, AUGUST 19, 1862

Co. K, 46th. Regiment P. V.—From all accounts yet received concerning the battle of Cedar Mountain, Company K, the Shamokin boys, behaved most gallantly. The principle newspapers speak in the highest terms of praise of this Regiment, and the New York Journals, who have always been parsimonious of their praise of Pennsylvania bravery, say it was so badly cut up that it can no longer be called a regiment. It will be recollected that some time ago the Captain of this company [Cyrus Strouse] was taken prisoner and has been kept a prisoner in North Carolina ever since. The boys were determined to avenge themselves, and this, together with their undaunted bravery, led them to battle with the full determination to stand by their flag and never surrender their position, though it was held at the fearful sacrifice of nearly every man in the company. We learn through the Major of the regiment [Major J. A. Matthews was wounded but survived. He had been promoted from Captain of Company I after Major Selfridge was shot and killed by Private Lanahan.] that when they were ordered to make a charge on a rebel battery, they responded with alacrity, but before they reached the battery, an awfully terrific fire from concealed rebels literally mowed them down, and for a moment the regiment seemed to falter. It was then, the brave, courageous, and much lamented Lieut. W. Caldwell, unsheathed his sword and rushed in advance of the company calling upon his comrades, "Follow me in the charge," and in this act, we are told he fell, with his face toward the enemy, sealing his devotion to his country with his life's blood. But the bravery of the men, is as undoubted as that of the officers, and years hence, when the veteran soldier shall recount the deeds of valor and noble examples of bravery, of the second war of American Independence, he will dwell with emphasis on the bloody battle of Cedar Mountain, and when that story shall be told, when unborn generations shall admire the bravery of the 46th Pennsylvania regiment, and justly, more particularly Co. K., then shall the children and children's children of that patriotic band feel their hearts swell within then as they say "I am the offspring of that noble company."

From the most reliable information we gather the following list of casualties:

KILLED—Lieut. W. Caldwell, James Haas, A. Totsworth, J. Urfeltz.

WOUNDED—Corporal John McEliece, wounded (not heard from,) John Coder, on the lower part of the leg, Thomas Caldwell, wounded slightly, Orderly Gilger, wounded in the shoulder, Corporal James Shipp, wounded, (not heard from,) Corporal Shuck, Corporal J. W. Young, wounded in the arm, F. Arter, wounded in four places, Benson Bird, in arm and knee, Patrick Donoven, wounded, John Gilger, wounded in two places, John Knipe, wounded slightly, John Medlicot, prisoner, John Neifer, wounded, L. Paul, wounded, Wm. C. Roth, wounded, in the thigh, D. Snyder, wounded, W, Tharp, wounded in the groin.

CASUALTIES AT LOCUST GAP MINE

—————➤◆⧐—————

1870. August 30, John Reed, found dead at mine. October 1, Adam Campbell, thigh lacerated, run over by a dirt car.[1]

1871. October 5, John Smith, died from injuries received on August 12; his arm was crushed by a wagon. October 17, James Mangan, killed between wagons and chute. June 16, Michael Troy, severely injured by a fall of coal. July 2, Anthony Godfrey, severely injured by a fall of coal. July 2, Dan Foley, arm severely cut by a fall of coal. August 23, Isaac Thomas, leg broken by prop timbers. August 26, James Wood, legs crushed in the rollers.

1872. September 27, James Dooley, mortally injured by a fall of coal at the A. S. Wolf colliery. October 25, Hugh Hogan, killed by a fall of coal.[2]

1873. April 10, a miner, legs broken by fall of coal. April 10, Theo Ginter, ribs broken, crushed between timbers and wagon. November 27, Benj. Moyer, arm broken by breaking of signal wire.[3]

1874. November 23, James Mangan, killed by a fall of gangway slate. April 14, Thomas Rowland, dangerously injured by a fall of slate while working. June 2, Chas. Dougherty, hand crushed by a wagon. June 30, James Roach, John Stulfox, and Thomas Churchill, severely burned by firedamp, which had been ignited in the east gangway, forcing it to where the men worked with safety lamps—the careless act of other persons. August 25, M. Miller, boy, severely injured, run over by wagons. August 25, Thomas Platt, slightly hurt by a fall of coal. August 25, A miner, leg broken by a fall of coal. October 21, a Pole, legs cut and crushed by cars.[4]

1875. September 8, Frank Barlow, terribly injured by a fall of coal.[5]

1876. August 2, Wm McCafferty, injury not specified. November 14, James Car, injury not specified.[6]

1877. October 23, Adam Zeigler, age thirty-five, killed. The deceased and his partner were working in a breast, under a piece of top coal and slate, which appeared dangerous. They both examined it and concluded it was safe. The deceased then resumed work for a short time when the partition, slate, and coal fell on him, fatally injuring him; he died a short time later. April 12, Thomas McHale, injured by a fall of coal. May 3, Michael Moran, leg broken by a fall of coal.[7]

1878. August 19, Josiah Gross, miner's laborer, age twenty-three, killed, slip of coal while loosening a prop. January 18, James McBride, collar fell on him. October 23, Anthony Sinto, fell from trestling.[8]

1879. No casualties reported.[9]

1880. December 24, Michael O'Neill, struck by coal from blast, head and shoulder injured.[10]

1881. June 25, Thomas Horan, age fifty-five, killed by a premature blast. The deceased was working at night in a breast with a man by the name of Bernard Cannon. About three o'clock on the morning of the accident, they had two holes drilled and tamped. Cannon fired his first. Shortly after, Horan went up to the heading to fire his and had been gone but a short time when the blast went off. Cannon hurried up from the heading and found him about eight yards down the breast from the face, lying on his back, bleeding from the forehead and back of the head. He was fearfully cut about the head and face. When he was found, there were no signs of life. He left a wife and six children. April 18, Michael Kellagher, miner, seriously injured by fall of coal.[11]

1882. September 29, Nicholas Schwade, miner, age thirty-seven, killed by a rush of coal, slate, and rock. He left a wife and four children. By the evidence elicited at inquest, deceased and another man by the name of John Linenbach were robbing pillars in No. 9 vein, west gangway. On the day of the accident, they were engaged in drawing out some loose coal that had been left in breast No. 46. After going into work in the morning, they loaded three cars. After loading the cars, both men went up, Linenbach to the first cross heading, the deceased up the manway about thirty yards to a point where the loose stuff in the breast was blocked. He took a hatchet up along with him to chop out some slabs or planks that were on the manway, which prevented the coal from running into and down it. While in the act of chopping, the loose stuff in the breast started and rushed with such force as to break in the manway on him, thereby killing him instantly. March 23, James Woods, rock bank man, leg injured by being kicked by a mule; March 24, Aaron Kelfer, slate picker, leg broken by being thrown down by two other boys who were quarreling. May 9, George Storey, miner, leg broken by a prop falling on it.

June 26, Frederick McGrady, laborer, injured about body, fell off breaker trestling. July 14, James Deneen, laborer, arm broken by uncoupling railroad cars outside. October 25, Frank Boschee, dirt bank boy, fell off and right foot run over by locomotive, amputated afterward on same day.[12]

1883. June 13, Thomas Pendergast, driver, age twenty-one, single man, fatally injured by being crushed between loaded mine cars while uncoupling them. He died same evening. About between the hours of two and three o'clock in the afternoon, he was, with his mule, hauling two loaded cars from the west to the east side of the slope. When about opposite the slope bottom, and while attempting to uncouple the last car from the first, his head was crushed between the bumpers, fracturing his skull; he died in about six hours. April 18, Wm Ruffle, slate picker, leg broken; plank broke and precipitating him a distance of thirty feet. September 8, Jacob Dietz, miner, leg broken by a fall of coal. November 15, Philip Huntzinger, jig attender, arm broken and elbow dislocated—caught between jig bell and wheel. December 19, James Cunippe, miner, leg bruised by a fall of top coal.[13]

1884. November 12, John Burke, miner, died of injuries received by a fall of coal on September 15. Deceased was working by night, robbing the east gangway Mammoth vein at the time of the accident; he was standing on the gangway partly under a collar when the coal fell, striking him and fracturing his collarbone, together with a compound complicated fracture of the right leg above the ankle joint, which, according to the testimony of the resident surgeon, necessitated the amputation of the limb about three or four inches above the ankle joint; he died, however, on day named of the injuries received.[14]

1885. John was no longer superintendent. He had moved on.

NOTES

INTRODUCTION

1 An overseer of the poor was a township official whose responsibilities included providing relief for the poor, protecting the township from vagrants, and finding apprenticeships for children of the poor.

2 *Book of Biographies: Biographical Sketches of Leading Citizens of the Seventeenth Congressional District, Pennsylvania* (Buffalo, NY: Biographical Publishing Company, 1899), 368. A colliery is a coal mine and the buildings and equipment associated with it.

3 Sisters of Mercy, *Annals Mercy Hospital* (Buffalo, NY: Sisters of Mercy, Buffalo Archives, 1934), unpaginated document included with correspondence from Sister Helen Perot to author, November 25, 2008.

4 David Brooks, "What Holds America Together," *New York Times*, March 19, 2018.

CHAPTER 1: CLASHING CULTURES

1 I say this tongue in cheek.

2 Joe Beine, comp., "Passenger Ships from Ireland to America 1732–1749," March 2004, http://www.genealogybranches.com/irishpassengerlists/ships.html. There is no definitive proof that the James Woodside listed in the ship record is the James Woodside in the story.

3 David Hackett Fischer, *Albion's Seed: Four British Folkways in America* (New York: Oxford University Press, 1989).

4 James Graham Leyburn, *The Scotch-Irish: A Social History* (Chapel Hill: University of North Carolina Press, 1962); Kerby A. Miller, *Emigrants and Exiles: Ireland and the Irish Exodus to North America* (New York: Oxford University Press, 1985).

5 Wayland F. Dunaway, *The Scotch-Irish of Colonial Pennsylvania* (Chapel Hill: University of North Carolina Press, 1944), 13–27, 38; Donald E. Jordan, *Land and Popular Politics in Ireland: County Mayo from the Plantation to the Land Wars* (Cambridge: Cambridge University Press, 1994), 43.

6 Peter Kalm, *Travels into North America; Containing Its Natural History, and a Circumstantial Account of Its Plantations and Agriculture in General,*

with the Civil, Ecclesiastical, and Commercial State of the Country, the Manners of Its Inhabitants, and Several Curious and Important Remarks on Various Subjects (Warrington, England: William Eyres, 1700), 10–11, https://archive.org/details/travelsintonorth01inkalm.

7   Leyburn, *The Scotch-Irish*, 174.

8   George W. Neible, "Account of Servants Bound and Assigned before James Hamilton, Mayor of Philadelphia," *Pennsylvania Magazine of History and Biography* 32, no. 3 (July 1908): 358, https://archive.org/details/pennsylvaniamaga32hist.

9   Karl Frederick Geiser, "Redemptioners and Indentured Servants in the Colony and Commonwealth of Pennsylvania," Supplement, *Yale Review* 10, no. 2 (August 1901): 72, https://archive.org/details/redemptionersind01geis.

10   Johann Casper Stoever, *Records of Rev. John Casper Stoever: Baptismal and Marriage, 1730–1779* (Harrisburg, PA: Harrisburg, 1896), 64, https://archive.org/details/recordsofrevjohn01stoe.

11   William Henry Egle, ed., *Commemorative Biographical Encyclopedia of Dauphin County, Pennsylvania, Containing Sketches of Prominent and Representative Citizens, and Many of the Early Scotch-Irish and German Settlers* (Chambersburg, PA: J. M. Runk, 1896), 13–14, https://archive.org/details/cu31924028852668. James Woodside is listed in the early assessment list for 1758 in Paxtang but is not on the list for 1756. Tax lists were typically drawn up in the year prior to the date on the list. So the 1758 list would have been made in 1757. Generally, people moved in the springtime in order to sow their crops. Therefore, James probably moved to Paxtang in the spring of 1757.

12   Arthur C. Lord, "The Pre-Revolutionary Agriculture of Lancaster County, Pennsylvania," *Journal of the Lancaster County Historical Society* 79, no. 1 (1975): 23–42, specifically 29.

13   Kalm, *Travels into North America*, 69.

14   Dunaway, *The Scotch-Irish of Colonial Pennsylvania*, 189.

15   Warp and weft are the two basic components used in weaving to turn thread or yarn into fabric.

16   Dunaway, *The Scotch-Irish of Colonial Pennsylvania*, 172.

17   Dunaway, *The Scotch-Irish of Colonial Pennsylvania*, 165–79.

18   The complex world of Indian-white and Indian-Indian relations during the period is artfully described in Richard White, *The Middle Ground: Indians, Empires, and Republics in the Great Lakes Region, 1650–1815* (New York: Cambridge University Press, 2011).

19   The Delaware Indians were both protected and controlled by the Six Nations. They were not allowed to sell land or wage war without approval

of the Six Nations. "Uncle" is how the Indians described the relationship.

20 See, for example, Colonial Records of Pennsylvania, Volumes 6, 7, 8, and 9, and *Pennsylvania Archives*, First Series, Volume 3, all of which are available at several websites including the HathiTrust Digital Library. Ben Franklin's *Pennsylvania Gazette* offers a steady stream of reports of atrocities as they came in from the frontier. See also Paul A. W. Wallace, *Conrad Weiser: Friend of Colonist and Mohawk* (Philadelphia: University of Pennsylvania Press, 1945; repr., Lewisburg, PA: Wennawoods, 1996). C. Hale Sipe's *The Indian Wars of Pennsylvania* (Harrisburg, PA: Telegraph Press, 1929; repr., Lewisburg, PA: Wennawoods, 1999) is a compilation that contains graphic descriptions of atrocities, but the author does not consistently cite his sources.

21 "Since our last several Letters have been received in Town from Lancaster County," *Pennsylvania Gazette*, September 1, 1757, p. 3, describes the murder and scalping. The rest of the story comes from two sources. In William Henry Egle, *History of the Counties of Dauphin and Lebanon in the Commonwealth of Pennsylvania* (Philadelphia: Everts & Peck, 1883), 423–26, the author writes that the story of the Mackey boy came to him by way of a letter from the late Samuel Barnett (1790–1869) of Springfield, Ohio. Samuel was born in Hanover Township and was related to Joseph Barnett, who was taken captive together with the Mackey boy. The quotation "my father's pretty hair" is from *Report of the Commission to Locate the Site of the Frontier Forts of Pennsylvania* (Pennsylvania: State Printer, 1896), 1:42, https://catalog.hathitrust.org/Record/007702197.

22 David A. Copeland, "How Newspapers Covered the French and Indian War," accessed September 12, 2020, https://www.varsitytutors.com/earlyamerica/early-america-review/volume-2/how-newspapers-covered-the-french-and-indian-war.

23 Egle, *Commemorative Biographical Encyclopedia of Dauphin County*, 13.

24 Egle, *Commemorative Biographical Encyclopedia of Dauphin County*, 13–16. I did not include the category "freemen" in the tabulation.

25 "Extract of a letter from Reading," *Pennsylvania Gazette*, July 7, 1757, p. 3; "Since our last an Express came to Town from Hanover Township, in Lancaster County," *Pennsylvania Gazette*, October 6, 1757. p. 3; "By a letter from Hanover Township, in Lancaster County," *Pennsylvania Gazette*, October 13, 1757, p. 2; "We have Advice from Paxton, in Lancaster County," *Pennsylvania Gazette*, October 27, 1757, p. 3; "Extract of a letter from our Correspondent at Fort Herekheimer [sic]," *Pennsylvania Gazette*, November 3, 1757, p. 2.

26 Robert C. Greiner, *Descendants of James Woodside of Dauphin County*,

PA (Laurel, MD: Robert C. Greiner, 1994), a private publication. In James Woodside's will, Jonathan is listed as the eldest son. He is also listed in several deeds, including #5-97, dated October 18, 1808, in Somerset County. According to https://www.findagrave.com/memorial/19226990/jonathan-woodside, the transcription of the letters on a gravestone in Younkin Cemetery in Somerset County is "In memory of, JONATHAN WOODSIDE, Deceased 8th of July 1800, aged 52 yrs." The last digit on the weatherworn gravestone appears to be a 9 rather than a 0. Jonathan purchased property in the area as late as 1808. Thus, Jonathan would have been born in about 1758.

27 Greiner, *Descendants of James Woodside.*
28 White, *The Middle Ground,* 257.
29 White, *The Middle Ground,* especially chap. 6 and 7.
30 For a discussion on scalping, see James Axtell and William C. Sturtevant, "The Unkindest Cut, or Who Invented Scalping," *William and Mary Quarterly* 37, no. 3 (July 1980): 451–72, https://www.jstor.org/stable/1923812; and George A. Bray III, "Scalping during the French and Indian War," *Early America Review* 3, no. 1 (Spring/Summer 1998), https://www.varsitytutors.com/earlyamerica/early-america-review/volume-3/scalping-during-the-french-and-indian-war.
31 "At a Council held at Philadelphia, on Friday, the 6th of July, 1764," Pennsylvania Colonial Records, vol. 9, 188–92, https://catalog.hathitrust.org/Record/000540855. Pennsylvania also offered bounties for Indian scalps in 1756 and 1780.
32 John Elder to John Penn, December 16, 1763, *Pennsylvania Archives,* 1st ser., 4:148–49, HathiTrust Digital Library, https://catalog.hathitrust.org/Record/003912969 (hereafter cited as *PA*).
33 John Elder to John Penn, December 27, 1763, printed in Francis Parkman, *The Conspiracy of Pontiac, and the Indian War after the Conquest of Canada* (Boston: Little, Brown, 1902), 2:345, https://catalog.hathitrust.org/Record/100730923.
34 "A Narrative of the Late Massacres, [30 January? 1764]," Founders Online, accessed June 10, 2019, https://founders.archives.gov/documents/Franklin/01-11-02-0012.
35 John Gottlieb Ernestus Heckewelder, *A Narrative of the Mission of the United Brethren among the Delaware and Mohegan Indians* (Philadelphia: McCarty & Davis, 1820), 77–80, https://archive.org/details/narrativeofmissi00heck.
36 Matthew Smith and James Gibbon, *A Declaration and Remonstrance of the Distressed and Bleeding Frontier Inhabitants of the Province of Pennsylvania,*

Presented by Them to the Honourable the Governor and the Assembly of the Province, Showing the Causes of Their Late Discontent and Uneasiness and the Grievances under Which They Have Laboured, and Which They Humbly Pray to Have Redress'd (Philadelphia: W. Bradford, 1764), https:// archive.org/details/declarationremon00smit.

37   Alexandra Mancini, "The Paxton Boys and the Pamphlet Frenzy: Politics, Religion, and Social Structure in Eighteenth-Century Pennsylvania," *Concept* 30 (November 2006), https://concept.journals.villanova.edu/ article/view/278; Kevin Kenny, *Peaceable Kingdom Lost: The Paxton Boys and the Destruction of William Penn's Holy Experiment* (Oxford: Oxford University Press, 2009); Peter Silver, *Our Savage Neighbors: How Indian War Transformed Early America* (New York: Norton, 2008); Patrick Griffin, *American Leviathan: Empire, Nation, and Revolutionary Frontier* (New York: Hill and Wang, 2007); David Dixon, *Never Come to Peace Again: Pontiac's Uprising and the Fate of the British Empire in North America* (Norman: University of Oklahoma Press, 2005).

38   Dixon, *Never Come to Peace Again*, 168–70, 184–98.

CHAPTER 2: A FINE VALE

1   Stephen A. Runkle, *Native American Waterbody and Place Names within the Susquehanna River Basin and Surrounding Subbasins*, Publication 229 (Harrisburg, PA: Susquehanna River Basin Commission, September 2003), 28, https://www.srbc.net/our-work/reports-library/technical-reports/229-native-american-names/.

2   William C. Reichel, ed., *Memorials of the Moravian Church* (Philadelphia: J. B. Lippincott, 1870), 1:82, https://archive.org/details/memorialsofmoravoo0reic.

3   Reichel, *Memorials of the Moravian Church*, 1:82–86.

4   John Bartram, *Observations on the Inhabitants, Climate, Soil, Rivers, Productions, Animals, and Other Matters Worthy of Notice Made by Mr. John Bartram in His Travels from Pensilvania to Onondago, Oswego, and the Lake Ontario, in Canada* (London: J. Whiston and B. Write, 1751), 12, https://archive.org/details/cihm_11915.

5   Bartram, *Observations on the Inhabitants*, 10–20.

6   A. G. Spangenberg, "Spangenberg's Notes of Travel to Onondaga in 1745," *Pennsylvania Magazine of History and Biography* 2, no. 4 (1878): 427, https://www.jstor.org/stable/20084365.

7   John Christopher Frederick Cammerhoff and John W. Jordan, "Bishop J. C. F. Cammerhoff's Narrative of a Journey to Shamokin, Penna., in the Winter of 1748," *Pennsylvania Magazine of History and Biography* 29, no.

2 (1905): 160–79, http://www.jstor.org/stable/20085277.

8   Paul A. W. Wallace, *Conrad Weiser: Friend of Colonist and Mohawk* (Philadelphia: University of Pennsylvania Press, 1945; repr., Lewisburg, PA: Wennawoods, 1996), 186. In the colonial period, *treaty* referred to the negotiation process, similar to a summit meeting of today.

9   Wallace, *Conrad Weiser*, 190.

10   Wallace, *Conrad Weiser*, 191–92; *Minutes of the Provincial Council of Pennsylvania from the Organization to the Termination of the Proprietary Government* (Harrisburg, PA: Theo. Fenn, 1851), 4:706–7, bracketed text appears in original, https://catalog.hathitrust.org/Record/011262481. The entire proceedings of the June 22 to July 4, 1744, treaty, as translated by Weiser, offer insight into Indian-white relations at that time.

11   Witham Marshe, *Journal of the Treaty at Lancaster in 1744 with the Six Nations* (Lancaster, PA: New Era Steam Book and Job Print, 1884), 25, https://archive.org/details/lancasterin1744j00mars. Marshe was the secretary to the commissioners of Maryland at the 1744 Treaty of Lancaster.

12   Wallace, *Conrad Weiser*, vii.

13   "Currency Converter: 1270–2017," National Archives, accessed March 2, 2020, http://www.nationalarchives.gov.uk/currency/results.asp#mid.

14   "An Act for Opening the Land Office," in *Laws of the Commonwealth of Pennsylvania, Republished under the Authority of the Legislature, with Notes and References* (Philadelphia: John Bioren, 1810), 2:119, https://catalog.hathitrust.org/Record/008596137.

15   "An Act for Opening the Land Office," in *Laws of the Commonwealth of Pennsylvania*, 2:126.

16   William Henry Egle, ed., *Commemorative Biographical Encyclopedia of Dauphin County, Pennsylvania, Containing Sketches of Prominent and Representative Citizens and Many of the Early Scotch-Irish and German Settlers* (Chambersburg, PA: J. M. Runk, 1896), 55–56, https://archive.org/details/commemorativebio00jmru.

17   Thomas M. Bonnicksen, *America's Ancient Forests: From the Ice Age to the Age of Discovery* (New York: Wiley, 2000), 259–69.

18   "Records of the Land Office: Warrantee Township Maps," RG-17, Pennsylvania Historical and Museum Commission, Pennsylvania State Archives, http://www.phmc.state.pa.us/bah/dam/rg/di/r17-522WarranteeTwpMaps/r17-522WarranteeTwpMapMainInterface.htm. Trees were often used as boundary markers on the original warrantee township maps. I plotted these trees on a topographical map to determine the location of various tree species.

19   Donald Culross Peattie, *A Natural History of Trees of Eastern and Central North America*, 2nd ed. (Boston: Houghton Mifflin, 1966), 196.

20   Peattie, *A Natural History of Trees*, 221.

21   Peattie, *A Natural History of Trees*, 233.

22   Thomas Pownall, *A Topographical Description of the Dominions of the United States of America*, ed. Lois Mulkearn, 2nd ed. (Pittsburgh: University of Pittsburgh Press, 1949), 167–68, https://catalog.hathitrust.org/Record/000600774.

23   Copy of original document, East Side Application #2695 and #2696, Pennsylvania State Archives, RG-17, author collection; Robert C. Greiner, *Descendants of James Woodside of Dauphin County, PA* (Laurel, MD: Robert C. Greiner, 1994). It was common to settle on a piece of land and make improvements on it prior to applying for a land warrant.

24   George Korson, *Black Rock: Mining Folklore of the Pennsylvania Dutch* (New York: Arno Press, 1979), 156.

25   Ruthven Deane, "Abundance of the Passenger Pigeon in Pennsylvania in 1850," *The Auk* 48, no. 2 (April 1931): 264–65, https://sora.unm.edu/sites/default/files/journals/auk/v048n02/p0264-p0265.pdf.

26   Henry W. Shoemaker, *Extinct Pennsylvania Animals: Part I, The Panther and the Wolf* (Altoona, PA: Altoona Tribune, 1917), https://catalog.hathitrust.org/Record/008595561.

27   This passage was inspired by Conrad Richter's *The Trees* (New York: Alfred A Knopf, 1940), 293–99, and the author's personal experience in clearing land.

28   Greiner, *Descendants of James Woodside*. The will was executed in 1796, and in the will the "beloved wife" is also identified as John's mother, so we know she was still alive in 1796.

29   "Records of the Land Office: Warrantee Township Maps," Pennsylvania State Archives.

30   Greiner, *Descendants of James Woodside*.

31   Arthur C. Lord, "The Pre-Revolutionary Agriculture of Lancaster County, Pennsylvania," *Journal of the Lancaster County Historical Society* 79, no. 1 (1975): 23–42.

32   T. H. Breer, *The Marketplace of Revolution: How Consumer Politics Shaped American Independence* (New York: Oxford University Press, 2004).

33   Greiner, *Descendants of James Woodside*.

34   George W. Cain, transcriber, "A Biographical Sketch of Isaac Novinger and His Family," 1889, Dauphin County Geneology Resource Center, accessed May 21, 2010, http://maley.net/DAUPHIN/OnlineData/collections/isaac-novinger.htm.

35   "Richard Alan Lebo Geneology," accessed February 28, 2010, http://aqua.dev.uga.edu/~lebo/novinger-da_geno.html.

36   William Henry Egle, *History of the Counties of Dauphin and Lebanon*

in the Commonwealth of Pennsylvania: Biographical and Genealogical (Philadelphia: Everts & Peck, 1883), 443, https://archive.org/details/historyofcountie01egle.

37   Richard Alan Ryerson, *The Revolution Is Now Begun: The Radical Committees of Philadelphia, 1765–1776* (Philadelphia: University of Pennsylvania Press, 1978), 250.

CHAPTER 3: FLYING CAMPS

1   "The Hanover Resolves," *PA*, 2nd ser., 13:271.

2   Wikipedia, s.v. "Continental Association," last modified September 11, 2019, at 20:37 (UTC), https://en.wikipedia.org/wiki/Continental_Association.

3   I. Daniel Rupp, *History of Lancaster County: To Which Is Prefixed a Brief Sketch of the Early History of Pennsylvania* (Lancaster, PA: Gilbert Hills, 1844), 384, https://archive.org/details/historylancas00rupp. For a fascinating story about how the minutes of the Lancaster County committees landed among the Peter Force papers at the National Archives, see Francis F. Fox, "The Minutes and Papers of the Revolutionary Committees in Lancaster County, 1774–1777," *Pennsylvania History: A Journal of Mid-Atlantic Studies* 71, no. 2 (Spring 2004): 213–25, http://www.jstor.org/stable/27778602. The Peter Force papers and collection can be found at https://lccn.loc.gov/mm80020990.

4   Rupp, *History of Lancaster County*, 392–403. In the following year, 1776, Upper Paxton's representatives to the committee were Samuel Taylor, James Murray, and Lykens Valley's Adam Wert.

5   Richard Lee Baker, *"Villainy and Madness": Washington's Flying Camp* (Baltimore: Published for Clearfield Co. by Genealogical, 2011), 9, 14. *Flying camp* is a literal translation of the French *camp volant*, defined in eighteenth-century military terminology as "a strong body of horse or foot…which is always in motion to cover its own garrisons, and to keep the enemy's army in a continual alarm."

6   *Provincial Conference of Committees, of the Province of Pennsylvania; Held at the Carpenter's Hall at Philadelphia* (Philadelphia: W. & T. Bradford, 1776), http://www.ushistory.org/pennsylvania/birth3.html#page4; James E. Gibson et al., "The Pennsylvania Provincial Conference of 1776," *Pennsylvania Magazine of History and Biography* 58, no. 4 (1934): 312–41, http://www.jstor.org/stable/20086878.

7   *PA*, 5th ser., 7:16, lists Captain William Brown's company among those companies that marched in the Jersey campaign in August 1776. William Henry Egle, *History of the Counties of Dauphin and Lebanon in the Com-*

monwealth of Pennsylvania: Biographical and Genealogical (Philadelphia: Everts & Peck, 1883), 92, https://archive.org/details/historyofcountie01egle, lists Brown's company among those included in Timothy Green's battalion, but Jonathan's name is not listed in the muster roll provided.

8   In the end, I integrated evidence from the *PA* and Peter Forces's *American Archives* with my research about Lykens Valley residents to create what I think is a probable scenario. See Peter Force, *American Archives*, 4th and 5th ser. (Washington, DC: M. St. Claire Clarke and Peter Force, 1837–1853), https://catalog.hathitrust.org/Record/000346548 (herafter cited *AA*). Berryhill to Chairman of Upper Paxton Township Committee, August 13, 1776, *AA*, 5th ser., 1:948; and *PA*, 5th ser., 7:17–20, give an overview of the Lancaster County Flying Camp of 1776, including the names of its officers. Among the officers, Timothy Green was captain of the Eighth Company, and one of that company's officers was wounded at Long Island. *PA*, 5th ser., 7:343, lists men of Captain John Reed's company who lost equipment at Long Island. *PA*, 5th ser., 7:347–48, lists Captain Albright Deibler's muster role of March 14, 1776, and states that a portion of the command was captured at the Battle of Long Island. *PA*, 5th ser., 7:353, submitted by Captain James Cowden and signed by James Burd, includes a list of money paid to men of Captain James Murray's company for a loss of equipment at the reduction of Fort Washington on November 16, 1776. The list repeats some of the names in the list on p. 1142, including Captain Deibler, James Woodside, and others. Deibler had been wounded and later died from his wounds at the Battle of Long Island, so he obviously could not have lost his gun in November. Further, there is no evidence that Murray's company was among those who were at the reduction of Fort Washington. *PA*, 5th ser., 7:1142, includes a list of money paid to men of Captain James Murray's company for a loss of guns including James Woodside and several men who were listed in Captain Diebler's muster roll of March 14, 1776.

9   *PA*, 5th ser., 7:353.

10   *PA*, 5th ser., 7:347–48.

11   Douglas S. Freeman, *George Washington* (New York: Scribner, 1951; repr., Fairfield, NJ: Augustus M. Kelley, 1981), 4:248n, notes that the list of Pennsylvania's Flying Camp officers taken prison at Fort Washington included Michael Swope, Frederick Watts, William Montgomery, and ___ Baxter. Neither James Cunningham, commander of the Lancaster County flying camp, nor Colonel Hays is listed.

12   "Pennsylvania Convention, August 10, 1776," *AA*, 5th ser., 2:19; "Letters from Colonel Dickinson and General Mercer," August 12, 1776, *AA*, 5th ser., 2:40. *PA*, 5th ser., 7:971–72, shows how only four men in Captain Samuel Boyd's company were in the Flying Camp. *PA*, 5th ser., 7:1073, shows how only

three men in Captain Andrew Graff's company were in the Flying Camp.

13 David Hackett Fischer, *Washington's Crossing* (New York: Oxford University Press, 2004), 387; Francis E. Devine, "The Pennsylvania Flying Camp, July–November, 1776," *Pennsylvania History* 46, no. 1 (January 1979): 59–78, https://www.jstor.org/stable/27772569; "Return of the officers present and absent of the First Regiment of the Flying Camp from Lancaster County," *AA*, 5th ser., 2:873–74; "Major General Sullivan's Orders, Camp on Long Island, [*Colonel Little's Order Book*]," in Henry P. Johnston, *Memoirs of the Long Island Historical Society, Vol. 3: The Campaign of 1776 around New York and Brooklyn* (Brooklyn: Long Island Historical Society, 1878), part 2:27–29, https://archive.org/details/campaignaroundn00john-goog. Sullivan's order lists Colonel Hays's regiment, among others. *PA*, 5th ser., 7:1078, shows that then Major Willian Hays was in command of Colonel James Cunningham's battalion at Long Island.

14 "Lord Stirling to General Washington, 29 August 1776," *AA*, 5th ser., 1:1245; "Colonel Samuel J. Atlee's Journal," *AA*, 5th ser., 1:1251–55; "Extract of a letter from an officer in the army to his friend in the country, dated, Turtle-Bay, September 6, 1776," *AA*, 5th ser., 2:198–99; various letters describing the Battle of Long Island, *AA*, 5th ser., 1:1194–96, 1232; Johnston, *The Campaign of 1776 around New York and Brooklyn*, part 1:148, 159–60.

15 John Ewing to Judge Yeates, September 14, 1776, in Johnston, *The Campaign of 1776 around New York and Brooklyn*, part 2:51–52.

16 Douglas S. Freeman, *George Washington: A Biography* (New York: Scribner, 1951; repr., Augustus M. Kelly, 1981), 4:166.

17 *PA*, 5th ser., 7:17–18; Devine, "The Pennsylvania Flying Camp, July–November, 1776," 66n30.

18 Fischer, *Washington's Crossing*, 95; Christopher Ward, *The War of the Revolution*, ed. John Richard Alden (New York: Macmillan, 1952), 226.

19 "General Return of the Army in the Service of the United States of America, at King's Bridge, September 21, 1776," *AA*, 5th ser., 2:449–51; "Return of Officers in Colonel Cunningham's Regiment, October 5, 1776," *AA*, 5th ser., 2:873; "Return of the Field Officers Absent and Present of the Regiment Stationed at DeLancy's Mills," *AA*, 5th ser., 2:897; "General Return for the Army in the Service of the United States, November 3, 1776," *AA*, 5th ser., 3:500; Lord Stirling to General Washington, November 10, 1776, *AA*, 5th ser., 3:634.

20 John Harris to Lancaster Pennsylvania Committee, August 27, 1776, *AA*, 5th ser., 1:1181.

21 Committee Chamber, in Paxton, August 14, 1776, *AA*, 5th ser., 1:948.

22 John Harris to Lancaster Pennsylvania Committee, August 27, 1776, *AA*, 5th ser., 1:1181.

23 Andrew Berryhill to Chairman of Upper Paxton Township Committee, August 13, 1776, *AA*, 5th ser., 1:948.

24 George Washington to Colonel Joseph Reed, November 30, 1776, Founders Online, accessed June 25, 2019, https://founders.archives.gov/documents/ Washington/03-07-02-0171; David McCullough, *1776* (New York: Simon Schuster, 2005), 248–49.

25 *AA*, 5th ser., 3:500, shows that Edward Hand is listed as a general for the first time in a return of November 3, 1776. It appears that throughout the New York–New Jersey campaign, Lord Stirling, General Hand, and Colonels Cunningham and Haller were assigned together. See "Return of Militia at Trenton, December 1, 1776," *PA*, 2nd ser., 14:778–79. "Abstract of the Return of the troops now at or near Newark fit for duty, November, 1776," *AA*, 5th ser., 3:822, includes Hand's regiment, located in Newark, New Jersey. "Weekly Return of the First Regiment of Foot, in the Continental Service, Commanded by Colonel Edward Hand, November 30, 1776," *AA*, 5th ser., 3:921, shows Hand at Brunswick, New Jersey. "George Washington to the President of Congress, Brunswick, November 30, 1776," *AA*, 5th ser., 3:919, shows the Continental army in retreat. "Return of the Forces in the service of the States of America, Encamped and in Quarters on the Banks of Delaware, in the State of Pennsylvania…December 22, 1776," *AA*, 5th ser., 3:1401, shows Hand's regiment at 520 men, but Cunningham's and Holler's regiments are no longer listed separately. It could be that many of the enlistments had expired and the men went home.

26 Freeman, *George Washington*, 4:295n33.

27 George Ross to Lancaster Pennsylvania Committee, December 18, 1776, *AA*, 5th ser., 3:1272.

28 Circular, *AA*, 5th ser., 3:1273.

29 Colonel James Burd to General Thomas Mifflin, December 27, 1776, *AA*, 5th ser., 3:1448–49.

30 "Return of the Forces in the Service of the States of America," *AA*, 5th ser., 3:1401.

CHAPTER 4: BIG RUNAWAY

1 "Captain John Rutherford's Company," *PA*, 5th ser., 7:357–58.

2 "Captain Martin Weaver's Company," *PA*, 5th ser., 7:527.

3 Erick Trickey, "The Prussian Nobleman Who Helped Save the American Revolution," *Smithsonian*, April 26, 2017, https://www.smithsonianmag.com/history/baron-von-steuben-180963048/.

4 Barbara Graymont, *The Iroquois in the American Revolution* (Syracuse, NY: Syracuse University Press, 1972), 160.

5   Graymont, *The Iroquois in the American Revolution*, 160.

6   John F. Meginness, ed., *History of Lycoming County, Pennsylvania* (Chicago: Brown, Runk, 1892), chap. 6–10, https://archive.org/details/historyoflycomin00edit.

7   William Marion Schnure, comp., *Selinsgrove, Penna. Chronology: 1700–1850* (Middleburg, PA: Middleburg Post, 1918), 1:60, https://archive.org/details/selinsgrovepenn00schngoog. It is interesting and somewhat puzzling that a road, Isle of Que Road, winds its way through the old Woodside homestead in Lykens Valley.

8   Graymont, *The Iroquois in the American Revolution*, 168.

9   Meginness, *History of Lycoming County*, chap. 8.

10 Meginness, *History of Lycoming County*, chap. 7. Northumberland County in 1778 encompassed most of northern Pennsylvania.

11 "A Return of Capt. Martin Weavers Compy," *PA*, 5th ser., 7:386–87.

12 Rev. David Craft, "The Expedition of Col. Thomas Hartley against the Indians in 1778, to Avenge the Massacre of Wyoming," in *Proceedings and Collections of the Wyoming Historical and Geological Society*, ed. Rev. Horace Edwin Hayden (Wilkes-Barr, PA: E. B. Yordy, 1905), 9:191, https://catalog.hathitrust.org/Record/007854861.

13 Craft, "The Expedition of Col. Thomas Hartley against the Indians in 1778," 9:189–216.

14 Colin G. Calloway, *The American Revolution in Indian Country: Crisis and Diversity in Native American Communities* (Cambridge: Cambridge University Press, 1995), 124–25; Graymont, *The Iroquois in the American Revolution*, 181; Gary B. Nash, *The Unknown American Revolution: The Unruly Birth of Democracy and the Struggle to Create America* (New York: Viking, 2005), 256. William and Zebulon Butler fought on the American side during the war. John and Walter Butler fought with the British.

15 "Captain John Rutherford's Company," *PA*, 5th ser., 7:388–89.

16 Graymont, *The Iroquois in the American Revolution*, 202–3.

17 "Pay Role of Such a Part of Cap't Caldwell's Company," *PA*, 5th ser., 7:115.

18 George Washington to Major General John Sullivan, September 15, 1779, Founders Online, accessed June 26, 2019, https://founders.archives.gov/documents/Washington/03-22-02-0357.

19 Graymont, *The Iroquois in the American Revolution*, 213.

20 Frederick Cook, ed., *Journals of the Military Expedition of Major General John Sullivan against the Six Nations of Indians in 1779* (Auburn, NY: Knapp, Peck and Thomson, 1887), 296–305, https://catalog.hathitrust.org/Record/000362150.

CHAPTER 5: CHILLING OMENS

1 Gary B. Nash, *The Unknown American Revolution: The Unruly Birth of Democracy and the Struggle to Create America* (New York: Viking, 2005), 318.

2 C. Page Smith, "The Attack on Fort Wilson," *Pennsylvania Magazine of History and Biography* 78, no. 2 (April 1954): 177–88, https://www.jstor.org/stable/20088567.

3 "Pennsylvania Weather Records, 1644–1835," *Pennsylvania Magazine of History and Biography* 15, no. 1 (1891): 109–21, http://www.jstor.org/stable/20083411.

4 Robert C. Greiner, *Descendants of James Woodside of Dauphin County, PA* (Laurel, MD: Robert C. Greiner, 1994).

5 Frederick Houghton, "History of the Buffalo Creek Reservation," in *Publications of the Buffalo Historical Society*, ed. Frank H. Severance (Buffalo, NY: Buffalo Historical Society, 1920) 24:3–181, quotation at 62, https://catalog.hathitrust.org/Record/001636698.

6 Dean R. Snow, *The Iroquois* (Malden, MA: Blackwell, 1996), 88; Dean Snow, email message to author, September 12, 2011; William Ketchum, *An Authentic and Comprehensive History of Buffalo, with Some Account of Its Early Inhabitants Both Savage and Civilized, Comprising Historic Notices of the Six Nations or Iroquois Indians, Including a Sketch of the Life of Sir William Johnson*, vol. 1 (Buffalo, NY: Rockwell, Baker & Hill, 1864), https://catalog.hathitrust.org/Record/100299454.

7 Narrative of Colonel Thomas Procter, July 9, 1791, *American State Papers: Indian Affairs* 1:155, https://memory.loc.gov/ammem/amlaw/lwsp.html.

8 Ketchum, *An Authentic and Comprehensive History of Buffalo*, 358.

9 "Philadelphia, May 6," *The Pennsylvania Packet*, May 6, 1780, p. 3.

10 William Marion Schnure, comp., *Selinsgrove, Penna. Chronology: 1700–1850* (Middleburg, PA: Middleburg Post, 1918), 1:69–70, https://archive.org/details/selinsgrovepenn00schngoog. This is not to be confused with Buffalo Creek in western New York.

11 Ketchum, *An Authentic and Comprehensive History of Buffalo*, 357.

12 Barbara Graymont, *The Iroquois in the American Revolution* (Syracuse, NY: Syracuse University Press, 1972), 240, 245.

13 "A True and Exact List of the Names…,"*PA*, 5th ser., 7:1042–43; William Henry Egle, *History of the Counties of Dauphin and Lebanon in the Commonwealth of Pennsylvania: Biographical and Genealogical* (Philadelphia: Everts & Peck, 1883), 107, https://archive.org/details/historyofcountie01egle; *PA*, 5th ser., 7:995; J. I. Mombert, *An Authentic History of Lancaster*

County: In the State of Pennsylvania (Lancaster, PA: J. E. Barr, 1869), 314, https://archive.org/details/authentichistory00momb.

14 Rev. H. Harbaugh, *The Fathers of the German Reformed Church in Europe and America* (Lancaster, PA: J. M. Westhaeffer, 1872), 2:121–22, https://catalog.hathitrust.org/Record/012292426.

15 The Mingo were Iroquois who had migrated to the Ohio River Valley.

16 Graymont, *The Iroquois in the American Revolution*, 256. Graymont's footnote for the quotation lists several dates between October 28, 1782, and February 17, 1783.

17 *Minutes of the Supreme Executive Council of Pennsylvania from Its Organization to the Termination of the Revolution* (Harrisburg, PA: Theo. Fenn, 1853), 13:381, https://catalog.hathitrust.org/Record/009797062.

18 *Minutes of the Supreme Executive Council of Pennsylvania*, 13:368–71, 379–81.

CHAPTER 6: OUT OF THE CHAOS

1 Worthington C. Ford, ed., *Journals of the Continental Congress, 1774–1789* (Washington, DC: Government Printing Office, 1922), 25:681, http://memory.loc.gov/ammem/amlaw/lwjc.html.

2 Several types of coin of varying quality—Dutch, French, British, and Spanish—and paper money, including issues from each of the states, the Continental dollar issued by Congress, and commercial paper, were in circulation during and after the war. Converting one medium of exchange to another is an accounting nightmare, and any such conversions are approximations only. To arrive at the approximate US dollar amount, I used the following conversion calculators: the Bank of England inflation calculator, https://www.bankofengland.co.uk/monetary-policy/inflation; XE Currency Converter, https://www.xe.com/currencyconverter; and the CPI Inflation Calculator, http://www.in2013dollars.com/1860-dollars-in-2017?amount=1.

3 "List of Goods necessary towards effecting the purchase of unpurchased Territory within the State of Penna," *PA*, 1st ser., 10:318–20; "Commissioners for treating with the Indians, 1784," *PA*, 1st ser., 10:357; "Answer of the Six Nations to Commissioners, 1784," *PA*, 1st ser., 10:357–58; "Sam'l J. Atlee to Pres. Dickenson, 1784," *PA*, 1st ser., 10:360; "Commissioners for Treating with Indians, 1785," *PA*, 1st ser., 10:489; "Commissioners on Indian Treaty, 1785," *PA*, 1st ser., 10:496; "Pres. Dickinson to Wm. Maclay, 1785," *PA*, 1st ser., 10:510; "Obligation of Commissioners to Purchase from Indians, 1784," *PA*, 1st ser., 10:610.

4 Robert C. Greiner, *Descendants of James Woodside of Dauphin County, PA* (Laurel, MD: Robert C. Greiner, 1994).

5 For more on the craft of wheel making, including descriptions of tools

and techniques for building wheels for farm carts and carriages, see M. T. Richardson, comp., *Practical Carriage Building* (New York: M. T. Richardson, 1891), http://www.lostcrafts.com/Carriage-Building/Practical-Carriage-Building-Main.html.

6   Peter Lindert and Jeffrey Williamson, "America's Revolution: Economic Disaster, Development, and Equality," Vox, July 15, 2011, http://www.voxeu.org/article/america-s-revolution-economic-disaster-development-and-equality; Peter Lindert and Jeffrey Williamson, "American Incomes before and after the Revolution" (Working Paper 17211, National Bureau of Economic Research, 2011), https://ideas.repec.org/p/nbr/nberwo/17211.html.

7   James E. Ferguson, *The Power of the Purse: A History of American Public Finance, 1776–1790* (Chapel Hill: University of North Carolina Press, 1961), 333. This calculation is based on Ferguson's data and the 1790 census, which included 807,094 free white males sixteen years of age and older and 3,893,635 persons including all free white males, all free white females, and enslaved people.

8   Terry Bouton, *Taming Democracy: "The People," the Founders, and the Troubled Ending of the American Revolution* (Oxford: Oxford University Press, 2007), 83.

9   Bouton, *Taming Democracy*, 84.

10   Terry Bouton, "A Road Closed: Rural Insurgency in Post-Independence Pennsylvania," *Journal of American History* 87, no. 3 (December 2000): 855–87, specifically 864, https://www.jstor.org/stable/2675275.

11   Owen S. Ireland, *Religion, Ethnicity, and Politics: Ratifying the Constitution in Pennsylvania* (University Park: Pennsylvania State University Press, 1995), 184.

12   Bouton, *Taming Democracy*, 163.

13   John Ferling, *A Leap in the Dark: The Struggle to Create the American Republic* (Oxford: Oxford University Press, 2003), especially chap. 7 and 8; Woody Holton, *Unruly Americans and the Origins of the Constitution* (New York: Hill and Wang, 2007); Paul J. Selsam, *The Pennsylvania Constitution of 1776: A Study in Revolutionary Democracy* (Philadelphia: University of Pennsylvania Press, repr., New York: Octagon Books, 1971); Merrill Jensen, John P. Kaminski, and Gaspare J. Saladino, eds., *The Documentary History of the Ratification of the Constitution: Ratification of the Constitution by the States: Pennsylvania* (Madison: Wisconsin Historical Society Press, 1976); and especially Robert L. Brunhouse, *The Counter-revolution in Pennsylvania, 1776–1790* (Harrisburg: Pennsylvania Historical Commission, 1942; repr., New York: Octagon Books, 1971).

14   Peter Mancall, *Valley of Opportunity: Economic Culture along the Upper Susquehanna, 1700–1800* (Ithaca, NY: Cornell University Press, 1991), 180.

15   Mancall, *Valley of Opportunity*, 166.

16   George W. Franz, *Paxton, a Study of Community Structure and Mobility in the Colonial Pennsylvania Backcountry* (New York: Garland, 1989), especially chap. 8. Franz argues that high mobility contributed to a lack of community structure. By focusing on tax lists, however, Franz failed to take into account key residents who remained in the area for a long time and intermarried.

17   There is discrepancy between the tax lists, which show the Woodsides were taxed in 1782 on one hundred acres, and the data included in the warrantee township maps wherein the Woodsides' holdings by 1782 total 487 acres. An analysis of the tax data for 1782 places the Woodsides' wealth among the top third of Paxton residents, but because of the discrepancy between owned and taxed land, the analysis understates their wealth.

18   D. L. Elliott et al., *Wind Energy Resource Atlas of the United States* (Golden, CO: Solar Technical Information Program, Solar Energy Research Institute, 1991), especially http://rredc.nrel.gov/wind/pubs/atlas/maps/chap3/3-26m.html.

19   Greiner, *Descendants of James Woodside*. James Woodside's will was probated in 1805.

20   "A List of the Inhabitants of Turkey Foot Township Made Subject to the Militia Laws," *PA*, 6th ser., 3:44. Jonathan Sr. was listed in the militia roll at Bedford County in February 1789, so he probably moved sometime in 1788.

Chapter 7: The Rebel

1   Thomas P. Slaughter, *The Whiskey Rebellion: Frontier Epilogue to the American Revolution* (New York: Oxford University Press, 1986); William Hogeland, *The Whiskey Rebellion: George Washington, Alexander Hamilton, and the Frontier Rebels Who Challenged America's Newfound Sovereignty* (New York: Simon Schuster, 2006); Wythe Holt, "The Whiskey Rebellion of 1794: A Democratic Working-Class Insurrection" (paper presented at the Georgia Workshop in Early American History and Culture, Athens, GA, 2004), https://web.archive.org/web/20110925091324/http://www.uga.edu/colonialseminar/whiskeyrebellion-6.pdf.

2   Minutes of the meeting at Pittsburgh in 1791, *PA*, 2nd ser., 4:16–18.

3   *PA*, 2nd ser., 4:3–15.

4   David Bradford is not to be confused with US attorney general William Bradford.

5   The total population of Fayette, Westmoreland, Allegheny, and Wash-

ington Counties, according to the 1790 census, was 63,432. With about one-fourth being free white men older than sixteen, the voting population was in the neighborhood of 15,000.

6   Holt, "The Whiskey Rebellion of 1794," 61
7   The Old Northwest was the territory that would eventually include the states of Ohio, Michigan, Indiana, Illinois, Minnesota, and Wisconsin.
8   Simon P. Newman, *Parades and the Politics of the Street: Festive Culture in the Early American Republic* (Philadelphia: University of Pennsylvania Press, 1997), 145.
9   Richard H. Kohn, "The Washington Administration's Decision to Crush the Whiskey Rebellion," *Journal of American History* 59, no 3 (December 1972): 567–84, https://doi.org/10.2307/1900658.
10   The Militia Acts of 1792 provided for the organization of state militias and permitted the president to take command of state militias in times of imminent invasion or insurrection.
11   Mark H. Jones, "Herman Husband: Millenarian, Carolina Regulator, and Whiskey Rebel" (PhD diss., Northern Illinois University, 1982), 321.
12   Holt, "The Whiskey Rebellion of 1794," 62n129; Dorothy E. Fennell, "From Rebelliousness to Insurrection: A Social History of the Whiskey Rebellion, 1765–1802" (PhD diss., University of Pittsburgh, 1981).
13   Hugh Henry Brackenridge, *Incidents of the Insurrection in the Western Parts of Pennsylvania in the Year 1794* (Philadelphia: John M'Culloch, 1795), part 1:95–96, https://archive.org/details/incidentsofinsur00inbrac.
14   Brackenridge, *Incidents of the Insurrection*, part 1:111.
15   "Deposition of Judge Addison," *PA*, 2nd ser., 4:390–91.
16   "Report of the Commissioners, September 24," *PA*, 2nd ser., 4:359.
17   "Report of the Commissioners, September 24," *PA*, 2nd ser., 4:348–59.
18   "Return of the Officers of the Militia of the Several Regiments and Battalions of the County of Dauphin Composing John A. Hanna's Brigade," *PA*, 6th ser., 5:232–33, "Return of the 1st and 2nd Class of the Militia of the County of Dauphin Draughed [*sic*] and Ordered to March Against the Insurgents in the Western Parts of Pennsylvania," *PA*, 6th ser., 5:273–92; "Quota of the Several Brigades of Pennsylvania," *PA*, 2nd ser., 4:763–64.
19   "Pennsylvania Secretary Alexander Dallas Report to the Senate, September 10, 1794," *PA*, 2nd ser., 4:281–82.
20   Brackenridge, *Incidents of the Insurrection*, part 2:32.
21   Brackenridge, *Incidents of the Insurrection*, part 2:70–71.
22   Brackenridge, *Incidents of the Insurrection*, part 2:80.
23   William H. Welfley, E. Howard Blackburn, and William H. Koontz, *History of Bedford and Somerset Counties, Pennsylvania, with Genealogical and*

Personal History (New York: Lewis, 1906), 2:155.

24   *History of Bedford, Somerset, and Fulton Counties, Pennsylvania, with Illustrations and Biographical Sketches of Some of Its Pioneers and Prominent Men* (Chicago: Waterman, Watkins, 1884), 106n, https://catalog.hathitrust.org/Record/008726291.

25   Criminal Case Files of the US Circuit Court for the Eastern District of Pennsylvania, 1791–1840, National Archives Microfilm Publications M986, Roll 1, Case Files 1791–99, unpaginated.

26   Criminal Case Files of the US Circuit Court for the Eastern District of Pennsylvania.

27   Criminal Case Files of the US Circuit Court for the Eastern District of Pennsylvania.

28   Eugene Volokh, "Symbolic Expression and the Original Meaning of the First Amendment," *Georgetown Law Journal* 97, no. 4 (April 2009): 1057–84, http://www2.law.ucla.edu/volokh/symbolic.pdf; Johann N. Neem, "Freedom of Association in the Early Republic: The Republican Party, the Whiskey Rebellion, and the Philadelphia and New York Cordwainers' Cases," *Pennsylvania Magazine of History and Biography* 127, no. 3 (July 2003): 259–90, https://www.jstor.org/stable/20093635; Fennel, "From Rebelliousness to Insurrection," chap. 1; Thomas Slaughter, "Crowds in Eighteenth-Century America: Reflections and New Directions," *Pennsylvania Magazine of History and Biography* 115, no. 1 (January 1991): 3–34, http://www.jstor.org/stable/20092570.

29   Alexander Addison, *Reports of Cases in the County Courts of the Fifth Circuit, and in the High Court of Errors & Appeals, of the State of Pennsylvania* (Washington, DC: John Colerick, 1800), 126, https://archive.org/details/reportsofcasesin00penn.

30   Marco M. Sioli, "The Democratic Republican Societies at the End of the Eighteenth Century: The Western Pennsylvania Experience," *Pennsylvania History* 60, no. 3 (July 1993): 288–304, https://www.jstor.org/stable/27773649.

31   *Trial of Alexander Addison, Esq.* (Lancaster, PA: William Hamilton, 1803), https://archive.org/details/trialofalexander00addi.

32   John Caldwell, *William Findley from West of the Mountains: A Politician in Pennsylvania, 1783–1791* (Gig Harbor, WA: Red Apple, 2000).

33   Criminal Case Files of the US Circuit Court for the Eastern District of Pennsylvania.

34   Criminal Case Files of the US Circuit Court for the Eastern District of Pennsylvania.

35   William Findley, *History of the Insurrection in the Four Western Counties*

of Pennsylvania in the Year M.DCC.XCIV: With a Recital of the Circum-stances Specifically Connected Therewith, and an Historical Review of the Previous Situation of the Country (Philadelphia: Samuel Harrison Smith, 1796), 186–87, https://archive.org/details/historyinsurrec00findgoog.

36 Wikipedia, s.v. "Robert Philson," last modified February 19, 2020, 22:51, http://en.wikipedia.org/wiki/Robert_Philson; Somerset County was created out of part of Bedford County in 1795.

37 "History of Peter (Augenstein) Augustine," Somerset County Pennsylvania Genealogy, last modified March 2, 2007, http://www.pagenweb.org/~somerset/addison/augustine.htm.

38 Criminal Case Files of the US Circuit Court for the Eastern District of Pennsylvania; "Pennsylvania 1795, Commissioner, Somerset County," A New Nation Votes, last modified January 11, 2012, http://elections.lib.tufts.edu/catalog/tufts:pa.commissioner.somersetcounty.1795.

39 *History of Bedford, Somerset, and Fulton Counties, Pennsylvania*, 106.

40 Robert C. Greiner, *Descendants of James Woodside of Dauphin County, PA* (Laurel, MD: Robert C. Greiner, 1994).

41 My efforts, through the Somerset County Historical Society, Historical Society of Pennsylvania, and Pennsylvania Historical and Museum Commission, to figure out what the court summons was about have been unsuccessful. Here's a link to the document: http://www.pa-roots.org/data/read.php?723,779047.

CHAPTER 8: TWO ORATORS

1 Henry A. S. Dearborn, "Journals of Henry A. S. Dearborn," in *Publications of the Buffalo Historical Society*, ed. Frank H. Severance (Buffalo, NY: Buffalo Historical Society, 1904), 7:115, https://archive.org/details/publicationsbuf07socigoog.

2 The Second Bank of the United States was the second federally authorized bank in the United States and operated under a twenty-year federal charter from February 1816 to January 1836.

3 Thomas P. Govan, "Fundamental Issues of the Bank War," *Pennsylvania Magazine of History and Biography* 82, no. 3 (July 1958): 305–15, http://www.jstor.org/stable/20089097; Ralph C. H. Catterall, *The Second Bank of the United States* (1902; repr., Chicago: University of Chicago Press, 1968).

4 I have been unable to locate Woodside's anti-bank speech.

5 Jonathan F. Woodside, *An Oration Delivered in Chillicothe, July the 5th, 1830, by J. F. Woodside, Esq.* (Chillicothe, OH: J. C. Melcher, 1830), courtesy Ross County Historical Society.

6 J. Woodside, *An Oration Delivered in Chillicothe.*

7   J. Woodside, *An Oration Delivered in Chillicothe.*

8   J. Woodside, *An Oration Delivered in Chillicothe.*

9   J. Woodside, *An Oration Delivered in Chillicothe.*

10 J. Woodside, *An Oration Delivered in Chillicothe.*

11 Journal of the House of Representatives, 21st Cong., 1st Sess., May 26, 1830, pp. 726–27, https://memory.loc.gov/cgi-bin/query/r?ammem/hlaw:@field(DOCID+@lit(hj023135)); Wikipedia, s.v. "21st United States Congress," last modified March 27, 2018, 2:45, https://en.wikipedia.org/wiki/21st_United_States_Congress; Journal of the Senate, 21st Cong., 2nd Sess., February 2, 1831, p. 125, https://memory.loc.gov/cgi-bin/query/r?ammem/hlaw:@field(DOCID+@lit(sj02046)).

12 Jeffrey Ostler, *Surviving Genocide: Native Nations and the United States from the American Revolution to Bleeding Kansas* (New Haven, CT: Yale University Press, 2019).

13 James Monroe, "First Annual Message," December 2, 1817, American Presidency Project, accessed March 8, 2020, http://www.presidency.ucsb.edu/ws/index.php?pid=29459.

14 Francis Paul Prucha, *The Great Father: The United States Government and the American Indians* (Lincoln: University of Nebraska Press, 1984), 64.

15 Prucha, *The Great Father,* 69–70.

16 See Lewis Cass, "Removal of the Indians," *North American Review* 30, no. 66 (January 1830): 62–121, https://catalog.hathitrust.org/Record/100206040; Jeramiah Evarts, *Essays on the Present Crisis in the Condition of the American Indians: First Published in the National Intelligencer, under the Signature of William Penn* (Boston: Perkins & Marvin, 1829), https://archive.org/details/essaysonpresentc00evar.

17 Andrew Jackson, "First Annual Message," American Presidency Project, accessed March 8, 2020, https://www.presidency.ucsb.edu/documents/first-annual-message-3.

18 Many of the Iroquois resettled with Joseph Brant on the Grand River reservation in Ontario, Canada.

19 Charles J. Kappler, ed., "Treaty with the Six Nations, 1784," in *Indian Affairs: Laws and Treaties* (Washington, DC: Government Printing Office, 1904), 2:5, https://catalog.hathitrust.org/Record/000084638.

20 Supreme Court Chief Justice John Marshall enshrined the right of discovery in US law in Johnson and Graham's Lessee v. William M'Intosh, 21 U.S. 543 (1823), 8 Wheat. 543, 5 L.Ed. 681.

21 Preemptive right is like a first option to buy. The prerogatives that the preemptory right entailed would be the subject of legal battles for over a hundred years.

22 See William N. Fenton, *The Great Law and the Longhouse: A Political History of the Iroquois Confederacy* (Norman: University of Oklahoma Press, 1998), especially chap. 39–43, and p. 682.

23 The expression "came out of the ground" is an adaptation from Canasatego's speech (see chapter 2). The expression "spread their blankets" is an adaptation of a metaphor used by Red Jacket in a reply to Rev. John Alexander in Granville Ganter, ed., *The Collected Speeches of Sagoyewatha, or Red Jacket* (Syracuse, NY: Syracuse University Press, 2006), 164.

24 Ganter, *Collected Speeches of Sagoyewatha*, 88.

25 Ganter, *Collected Speeches of Sagoyewatha*, 79.

26 Barbara A. Chernow, "Robert Morris: Genesee Land Speculator," *New York History* 58, no. 2 (April 1977): 194–220, http://www.jstor.org/stable/23169915.

27 The First Bank of the United States, part of Alexander Hamilton's financial plan, was chartered for a term of twenty years, by the US Congress on February 25, 1791, and dissolved in 1811 when its charter expired.

28 Norman B. Wilkinson, "Robert Morris and the Treaty of Big Tree," *Mississippi Valley Historical Review* 40, no. 2 (September 1953): 257–78, specifically 270, https://doi.org/10.2307/1888927.

29 The Oil Spring and Tuscarora Reservations were added later, bringing the total to twelve reservations.

30 For the women's sellers' remorse, see Ganter, *Collected Speeches of Sagoyewatha*, 99.

31 Frederick Houghton, "History of the Buffalo Creek Reservation," in *Publications of the Buffalo Historical Society*, ed. Frank H. Severance (Buffalo, NY: Buffalo Historical Society, 1920), 24:3–181, https://catalog.hathitrust.org/Record/001636698. Houghton's classic work summarizes the history of the Buffalo Creek Reservation.

32 Charles J. Kappler, ed., "Agreement with the Seneca, 1797," in *Indian Affairs: Laws and Treaties* (Washington, DC: Government Printing Office, 1904), 2:1097, https://catalog.hathitrust.org/Record/000084638.

33 Theophile Cazenove to Joseph Ellicott, May 10, 1798, in Robert Warwick Bingham, ed., *Holland Land Company Papers: Reports of Joseph Ellicott as Chief of Survey (1797–1800) and as Agent (1800–1821) of the Holland Land Company's Purchase in Western New York* (Buffalo, NY: Buffalo Historical Society, 1937), 1:27.

34 Joseph Ellicott to Theophile Cazenove, September 25, 1798, in Bingham, *Holland Land Company Papers*, 1:42–43.

35 Alan Taylor, *The Divided Ground: Indians, Settlers, and the Northern Borderland of the American Revolution* (New York: Vintage Books, 2006), 316.

36 Laurence M. Hauptman, *Conspiracy of Interests: Iroquois Dispossession and the Rise of New York State* (Syracuse, NY: Syracuse University Press, 1999); For a chronological account of the treaties of 1826, 1838, and 1842, see Mary H. Conable, "A Steady Enemy: The Ogden Land Company and the Seneca Indians" (PhD diss., University of Rochester, 1994). Conable summarizes transactions regarding preemptive right on land west of the Genesee: Massachusetts to Phelps in 1888, Phelps back to Massachusetts in 1790, Massachusetts to Morris in 1791, Morris to the Holland Land Company in 1792/1793, and the preemptive right to the Indian reservations (only) to the Ogden Land Company in 1810.

37 Society of Friends Joint Committee on Indian Affairs, *The Case of the Seneca Indians in the State of New York* (Philadelphia: Merrihew and Thompson, 1840), 11, https://archive.org/details/caseofsenecaindi00join.

38 Ganter, *Collected Speeches of Sagoyewatha*, 198–219.

39 Henry S. Manley, "Red Jacket's Last Campaign: And an Extended Bibliographical and Biographical Note," *New York History* 31, no. 2 (April 1950): 155, http://www.jstor.org/stable/23149773.

40 At the time, the Office of Indian Affairs was under the jurisdiction of the war department.

41 Manley, "Red Jacket's Last Campaign," 156.

42 Hauptman, *Conspiracy of Interests*, 159–60; Manley, "Red Jacket's Last Campaign," 149–68; Christopher Densmore, *Red Jacket: Iroquois Diplomat and Orator* (Syracuse, NY: Syracuse University Press, 1999), chap. 9.

43 In Seneca Nation of Indians v. Christy, 162 U.S. 283 (1896), the Seneca Indians unsuccessfully challenged the sale.

44 Ganter, *Collected Speeches of Sagoyewatha*, 273–74.

45 A brief review of cases involving Georgia and the Cherokee, including Worcester v. Georgia, can be found at http://www.pbs.org/wnet/supreme-court/antebellum/landmark_cherokee.html.

46 For confirmation that the Seneca were aware of these events, see M. B. Pierce, *Address on the Present Condition and Prospects of the Aboriginal Inhabitants of North America, with Particular Reference to the Seneca Nation* (Buffalo, NY: Steele's Press, 1838), https://catalog.hathitrust.org/Record/009736457. Pierce was a Dartmouth-educated Seneca chief.

47 Nathaniel T. Strong, *Appeal to the Christian Community on the Condition and Prospects of the New York Indians: In Answer to a Book Entitled "The Case of the New-York Indians"* (Buffalo, NY: Thomas, 1841), 59, https://books.google.com/books?id=1JQLAAAAIAAJ. Strong was a Yale-educated Indian.

48 Conable, "A Steady Enemy," 119, 129.

49 Pierce, *Address on the Present Condition and Prospects*, 12.

50 Pierce, *Address on the Present Condition and Prospects*.

51 Conable, "A Steady Enemy," 110.

52 Conable, "A Steady Enemy," 129–31.

53 Charles J. Kappler, ed., "Treaty with the Cherokee, 1835," in *Indian Affairs: Laws and Treaties* (Washington, DC: Government Printing Office, 1904), 2:439, https://catalog.hathitrust.org/Record/000084638; Karim M. Tiro, *The People of the Standing Stone: The Oneida Nation from Revolution through the Era of Removal* (Amherst: University of Massachusetts Press, 2011), 157.

54 Conable, "A Steady Enemy," 129–30. The other original subcontractors were Orlando Allen and James Stryker. Stryker was the federal subagent to the New York Indians. Henry P. Willcox was added later.

55 See Senator Ambrose Sevier's speech, March 17, 1840, in Society of Friends Joint Committee on Indian Affairs, *The Case of the Seneca Indians*, 73–76; entire speech 65–93. Sevier was the chairman of the Indian Affairs committee, which recommended not to ratify the amended treaty.

56 Society of Friends Joint Committee on Indian Affairs, *A Further Illustration of the Case of the Seneca Indians in the State of New York, in a Review of a Pamphlet Entitled "An Appeal to the Christian Community" by Nathaniel T. Strong* (Philadelphia: Merrihew and Thompson, 1841), 48, https://archive.org/details/afurtherillustr00goog.

57 It was controversial at the time whether a majority or a two-thirds vote was required.

58 Society of Friends Joint Committee on Indian Affairs, *A Further Illustration*, 82.

59 Society of Friends Joint Committee on Indian Affairs, *A Further Illustration*, 80–82.

60 Harriet S. Caswell, *Our Life among the Iroquois Indians* (Boston: Congregational Sunday School and Publishing Society, 1892), 76, https://archive.org/details/ourlifeamongiroq00caswiala.

61 Laurence M. Hauptman, *The Tonawanda Senecas' Heroic Battle against Removal* (Albany: State University of New York Press, 2011).

62 Alexis de Tocqueville, *Democracy in America: Historical-Critical Edition of De la démocratie en Amérique*, edited by Eduardo Nolla, translated by James T. Schleifer (Indianapolis: Liberty Fund, 2010), vol. 4, appendix 2, https://oll.libertyfund.org/titles/2288.

63 Seneca Nation of Indians (website), accessed March 9, 2000, https://www.sni.org.

64 "Jonathan F. Woodside (1799–1845)," Office of the Historian, United

States Department of State, accessed March 9, 2020, http://history.state. gov/departmenthistory/people/woodside-jonathan-f.

65 Lyle S. Evans, ed., *A Standard History of Ross County, Ohio* (Chicago: Lewis, 1917), 2:550–53, https://archive.org/details/oh-ross-1917-evans-2.

66 Joseph P. Smith, ed., *History of the Republican Party in Ohio* (Chicago: Lewis, 1898), 1:116–17, https://archive.org/details/historyrepublic00smitgoog.

Chapter 9: Cattaraugus

1   Charles J. Kappler, ed., "Treaty with the Seneca, 1802," in *Indian Affairs: Laws and Treaties* (Washington, DC: Government Printing Office, 1904), 2:60–61, https://catalog.hathitrust.org/Record/000084638.

2   O. Turner, *Pioneer History of the Holland Purchase of Western New York: Embracing Some Account of the Ancient Remains* (Buffalo, NY: Jewett, Thomas, 1850), 417–18, https://archive.org/details/pioneerhistoryof00turn.

3   Granville Ganter, *The Collected Speeches of Sagoyewatha, or Red Jacket* (Syracuse, NY: Syracuse University Press, 2006), 95–99.

4   Vince Martonis, email message to author, October 12, 2014.

5   Vince Martonis, email message to author, October 12, 2014.

6   Vince Martonis, email message to author, October 12, 2014.

7   Vince Martonis, email message to author, October 12, 2014.

8   Vince Martonis, email message to author, October 12, 2014.

9   Vince Martonis, email message to author, October 12, 2014.

10 Vince Martonis, email message to author, October 12, 2014.

11 Vince Martonis, email message to author, October 12, 2014.

12 Matthew Dennis, email message to author, October 16, 2014.

13 Hercules [pseud.], "An Exposition of the Practicability of Constructing a Great Central Canal from Lake Erie to the Hudson through the Southern Tier of Counties in the State of New York," originally published as a series of articles in the *Western Star* newspaper, Westfield, NY, 1827. Facsimile courtesy of Special Collections, Grosvenor Room, Buffalo and Erie County Public Library.

14 Henry Willcox, "Irving on Lake Erie" (promotional brochure, printed by Charles Faxon, Buffalo, NY, 1837), courtesy of the Research Library at the Buffalo History Museum. Additional investors included Hiram Pratt of Buffalo; Pierre A. Barker of Buffalo; Henry P. Willcox, local physician; Thomas B. Stoddard, local lawyer; Hamlet Scrantom, leading Rochester merchant and civic leader; John V. L. Pruyn, Albany lawyer and businessman; Augustus C. Stevens of Buffalo; and William S. Johnson, New York attorney.

15 Thurlow Weed Barnes, "Memoir of Thurlow Weed," in *Life of Thurlow Weed Including His Autobiography and a Memoir* (Boston: Houghton Mifflin, 1884), 2:478, https://catalog.hathitrust.org/Record/000408044.

16 Mary H. Conable, "A Steady Enemy: The Ogden Land Company and the Seneca Indians" (PhD diss., University of Rochester, 1994), 131; Morgan Friedman's inflation calculator, accessed March 6, 2019, http://www.west-egg.com/inflation/.

17 Willcox, "Irving on Lake Erie."

18 Irene D. Neu, *Erastus Corning, Merchant and Financier, 1794–1872* (Ithaca, NY: Cornell University Press, 1960), 122.

19 Neu, *Erastus Corning*, 120–25.

20 Neu, *Erastus Corning*, 124.

21 Laurence M. Hauptmen, *Conspiracy of Interests: Iroquois Dispossession and the Rise of New York State* (Syracuse, NY: Syracuse University Press, 1999).

22 Theophile Cazenove to Joseph Ellicott, May 10, 1798, in Robert Warwick Bingham, ed., *Holland Land Company Papers: Reports of Joseph Ellicott as Chief of Survey (1797–1800) and as Agent (1800–1821) of the Holland Land Company's Purchase in Western New York* (Buffalo, NY: Buffalo Historical Society, 1937), 1:23.

23 Alan Taylor, *The Divided Ground: Indians, Settlers, and the Northern Borderland of the American Revolution* (New York: Vintage Books, 2006), 316.

24 Theophile Cazenove to Joseph Ellicott, May 10, 1798, in Bingham, *Holland Land Company Papers*, 1:23.

25 Joseph Ellicott to Theophile Cazenove, September 25, 1798, in Bingham, *Holland Land Company Papers*, 1:41–42.

26 Bingham, *Holland Land Company Papers*, 1:52; emphasis added.

27 Bingham, *Holland Land Company Papers*, 1:52.

28 Bingham, *Holland Land Company Papers*, 1:78.

29 "Rupport & Compte de L'arpentaye du Genesee par Mr. JH. Ellicott," in Bingham, *Holland Land Company Papers*, 1:91; emphasis in the original.

30 Vince Martonis, email message to author, October 12, 2014; emphasis added.

CHAPTER 10: SOLDIERS OF FORTUNE

1 Professor Eric Foner discusses the issue of slavery including the role played by the war with Mexico in ColumbiaLearn, "MOOC | The Mexican War & Expansion of Slavery | The Civil War and Reconstruction, 1850–1860 | 1.4.1," YouTube Video, 12:47, October 27, 2014, https://www.youtube.com/watch?v=KkgkZwQ9HgQ.

2   Timothy J. Henderson, *A Glorious Defeat: Mexico and Its War with the United States* (New York: Hill and Wang, 2007) focuses on the Mexican point of view. Sam W. Haynes, *James K. Polk and the Expansionist Impulse* (New York: Longman Publishing, 1997) is a short book that summarizes this president's impact on US history.

3   My main sources for information on Pennsylvania in the Mexican War are Robert Van Trombley, "Pennsylvania's Role in the Mexican American War" (master's thesis, Edinboro University of Pennsylvania, 2013); Randy W. Hackenburg, *Pennsylvania in the War with Mexico* (Shippensburg, PA: White Main, 1992); John S. D. Eisenhower, *So Far from God: The U.S. War with Mexico 1846–1848* (Norman: University of Oklahoma, 2000); and Justin H. Smith, *The War with Mexico*, vol. 2 (New York: Macmillan, 1919), https://archive.org/details/warwithmexicovol010848mbp.

4   Hackenburg, *Pennsylvania in the War with Mexico*, 262.

5   Van Trombley, "Pennsylvania's Role in the Mexican American War," 34.

6   Van Trombley, "Pennsylvania's Role in the Mexican American War," 37.

7   Van Trombley, "Pennsylvania's Role in the Mexican American War," 61.

8   Van Trombley, "Pennsylvania's Role in the Mexican American War," 61.

9   Van Trombley, "Pennsylvania's Role in the Mexican American War," 62.

10 Van Trombley, "Pennsylvania's Role in the Mexican American War," 68.

11 Smith, *The War with Mexico*, 2:157.

12 Hackenburg, *Pennsylvania in the War with Mexico*, 345–46.

13 Hackenburg, *Pennsylvania in the War with Mexico*, 347-350.

14 Hackenburg, *Pennsylvania in the War with Mexico*, 262.

15 Hackenburg, *Pennsylvania in the War with Mexico*, 258-265.

16 Alternative spellings for Colonel Richard are Ritcherd, Richards, and Ritscher.

17 "Muster Roll of a Company of Infantry," *PA*, 6th ser., 8:951–59.

18 A decent summary of Wyandot history can be found at http://touringohio.com/history/wyandot.html.

19 Colin G. Calloway, *The Shawnees and the War for America* (New York: Viking, 2007); John Sugden, *Tecumseh: A Life* (New York: Henry Holt, 1997).

20 Calloway, *The Shawnees and the War for America*, 139.

21 Calloway, *The Shawnees and the War for America*, 147.

22 Calloway, *The Shawnees and the War for America*, 155.

23 Randall L. Buchman, *A Sorrowful Journey* (Defiance, OH: Defiance College, 2007); *The History of Wyandot County Ohio* (Chicago: Leggett, Conaway, 1884), 299–301, https://archive.org/details/historyofwyandot00legg.

24 E. M. Violette, *History of Adair County Together with Reminiscences and*

Biographical Sketches (Kirksville, MO: Denslow History, 1911), 435, https://catalog.hathitrust.org/Record/008653285; George W. Cain, accessed May 4, 2018, http://maley.net/DAUPHIN/OnlineData/collections/isaac-novinger.htm.

25 George Korson, *Black Rock: Mining Folklore of the Pennsylvania Dutch* (New York: Arno Press, 1979), 147.

26 "Roll of Capt. Philip Fetterhoff's Company," *PA*, 2nd ser., 12:124–26.

27 Robert C. Greiner, *Descendants of James Woodside of Dauphin County, PA* (Laurel, MD: Robert C. Greiner, 1994); *PA*, 6th ser., 9:600.

28 Greiner, *Descendants of James Woodside.*

29 Robert E. Woodside, *My Life and Town* (Millersburg, PA: Robert E. Woodside, 1979), 67.

30 Greiner, *Descendants of James Woodside.*

31 Greiner, *Descendants of James Woodside.*

Chapter 11: A Man of His Time

1 Pocket Memorandum Book #1, Sallade-Bickel Family Papers, Manuscripts and Archives Division, The New York Public Library, Astor, Lenox, and Tilden Foundations.

2 "Jefferson Smith" is Jimmy Stewart's character in the movie *Mr. Smith Goes to Washington.*

3 William Henry Egle, ed., *Notes and Queries: Historical and Genealogical, Chiefly Relating to Interior Pennsylvania* (Harrisburg, PA: Harrisburg, 1896), 3:306–7, https://books.google.com/books?id=tNQUAAAAYAAJ.

4 William Henry Egle, ed., *Notes and Queries: Historical, Biographical, and Genealogical, Chiefly Relating to Interior Pennsylvania*, 3rd ser. (Harrisburg, PA: Daily Telegraph Print, 1887), 1:122, https://books.google.com/books?id=Z-gUAAAAYAAJ.

5 William Henry Egle, *Notes and Queries: Historical, Biographical, and Genealogical, Chiefly Relating to Interior Pennsylvania*, 3rd ser. (Harrisburg, PA: Harrisburg, 1891), 2:281, https://books.google.com/books?id=ru-gUAAAAYAAJ.

6 William Henry Egle, ed., *Commemorative Biographical Encyclopedia of Dauphin County, Pennsylvania* (Chambersburg, PA: J. M. Runk, 1896), 51–52, https://archive.org/details/commemorativebio00jmru.

7 The Indian captivity story appeared in histories written in the nineteenth century and continues to be circulated today. James D. Bowman wrote that some old family records say that Margaret was taken prisoner in 1753 and released to General John Forbes at Fort Duquesne in 1759. James D. Bowman is the great-grandson of Simon Sallade. See James D. Bowman,

"Early History of the 'Upper End' of Dauphin County, PA" (transcript of lecture, Historical Society of Dauphin County, Pennsylvania, 1940). The problem with this idea is that Forbes died in Philadelphia on March 11, 1759; see Alfred Procter James, ed., *Writings of General John Forbes Relating to His Service in North America* (Menasha, WI: Collegiate Press, 1938), xii, https://catalog.hathitrust.org/Record/000361863. Ian K. Steele, in *Setting All the Captives Free: Capture, Adjustment, and Recollection in Allegheny Country* (Canada: McGill-Queen's University Press, 2013), 470, wrote this about Margaret Eberhard: "Young daughter of George. Orphaned and captured on Shamokin Road, Oct 1755, Returned at Muskingum Nov 15, 1764." Steele cited "Lists of Pennsylvania Settlers Murdered, Scalped and Taken Prisoners by Indians, 1755–1756," *Pennsylvania Magazine of History and Biography* 32, no. 3 (1908): 309–19, Eberhard at 311; but that article, which used the Conrad Weiser papers as its primary source, states, "George Eberhard and his Wife and 5 Children Killed and scalp'd in the Month of Octr 1755, on the Shoemaker road over the Kittitiny hill." Further, Margaret Eberhard's name does not appear in the comprehensive list of Indian captives released to Colonel Henry Bouquet in 1764. However, not all the children in the lists are identified by name, and some are identified by their Indian name; see William S. Ewing, "Indian Captives Released by Colonel Bouquet," *Western Pennsylvania History Magazine* 39, no. 3 (Fall 1956): 187–203, https://journals.psu.edu/wph/article/view/2529.

8   Bowman, "Early History," 3.

9   Egle, *Commemorative Biographical Encyclopedia of Dauphin County*, 51–52; Bowman, "Early History," 3.

10 The *Aurora General Advertiser* (1790–1812) was a Republican paper edited between 1790 and 1798 by Benjamin Franklin Bache, the favorite grandson of his namesake, and, after Bache's death of yellow fever in 1798, by William Duane. *Porcupine's Gazette* (1798–1799) was a Federalist paper edited by William Cobbett.

11 Pennsylvania's political factions evolved. Generally speaking, those who identified as Republicans in 1776 became Federalists in 1787 and continued as such until about 1815. Those who identified as Constitutionalists (referring to the Pennsylvania constitution) in 1776 became Anti-Federalists in 1787 and Republicans (or Democratic Republicans) in 1800.

12 Paul Douglas Newman, *Fries's Rebellion: The Enduring Struggle for the American Revolution* (Philadelphia: University of Pennsylvania Press, 2004), 93. See also *Pennsylvania History* 67, no. 1 (Winter 2000), https://www.jstor.org/stable/i27774243; the entire issue is about Fries' Rebellion.

13 Alexander Graydon, *Memoirs of a Life, Chiefly Passed in Pennsylvania,*

within the Last Sixty Years (Edinburg: William Blackwood, 1822), 412, https://archive.org/details/memoirsalifechi00galtgoog. Graydon was prothonotary of Dauphin County at the time of Fries' Rebellion.

14 For an account of Cooper's activity, see James Morton Smith, *Freedom's Fetters: The Alien and Sedition Laws and American Civil Liberties* (Ithaca, NY: Cornell University Press, 1956), especially 308–9.

15 Thomas Cooper, *An Account of the Trial of Thomas Cooper, of Northumberland: On a Charge of Libel Against the President of the United States* (Philadelphia: J. Bioren, 1800), https://archive.org/details/DKC0017.

16 For the selection of presidential electors in Pennsylvania in 1800, in which there was no general election in Pennsylvania, see Harry Marlin Tinkcom, *The Republicans and Federalists in Pennsylvania, 1790–1801: A Study in National Stimulus and Local Response* (Harrisburg: Pennsylvania Historical and Museum Commission, 1950), chap. 13. For results of the 1796 and 1804 elections, see A New Nation Votes, Tufts Digital Collections and Archives, http://elections.lib.tufts.edu.

17 William Fairbairn, *Treatise on Mills and Millwork, Part I: On the Principles of Mechanism and on Prime Movers*, 3rd ed. (London: Longmans, Greens, 1871), x, https://catalog.hathitrust.org/Record/011613805.

18 Fairbairn, *Treatise on Mills and Millwork*, xiii.

19 Fairbairn, *Treatise on Mills and Millwork*, xiii.

20 "Colonial America's Pre-Industrial Age of Wood and Water," Building Community: Medieval Technology and American History, accessed June 24, 2020, http://www.engr.psu.edu/mtah/articles/colonial_wood_water. htm.

21 Patrick Gass, *A Journal of the Voyages and Travels of a Corps of Discovery* (Pittsburgh: David M'Keehan, 1808), https://archive.org/details/ cihm_57517.

22 Donald R. Hickey, *The War of 1812: A Forgotten Conflict*, bicentennial ed. (Urbana: University of Illinois Press, 2012), chap. 1.

23 Although Sallade is acknowledged as a colonel in his obituary and in some of the old stories about him, there is no extant record of his serving during the war in either the state militia or in the regular army.

24 Victor Sapio, "Expansion and Economic Depression as Factors in Pennsylvania's Support of the War of 1812: An Application of the Pratt and Taylor Theses to the Keystone State," *Pennsylvania History* 35, no. 4 (October 1968): 379–405, especially 395–405.

25 *Laws of the Commonwealth of Pennsylvania* (Philadelphia: J. Bioren, 1822), 6:154–71, https://books.google.com/books?id=ELUwAQAAMAAJ.

26 Philip Shriver Klein, *Pennsylvania Politics, 1817–1832: A Game without*

Rules (Philadelphia: Historical Society of Pennsylvania, 1940), 22.

27 Wikipedia, s.v. "Second Bank of the United States," last modified March 5, 2020, 2:10, https://en.wikipedia.org/wiki/Second_Bank_of_the_United_States.

28 Sean Wilentz, *The Rise of American Democracy: Jefferson to Lincoln* (New York: Norton, 2005), 207.

29 Klein, *Pennsylvania Politics*, 52–58.

CHAPTER 12: YOUNG POLITICIAN

1   For election returns, see A New Nation Votes, Tufts Digital Collections and Archives, http://elections.lib.tufts.edu/. Sallade is listed in Dauphin County under the name Solliday for this particular election.

2   Philip Shriver Klein, *Pennsylvania Politics, 1817–1832: A Game without Rules* (Philadelphia: Historical Society of Pennsylvania, 1940), 112.

3   *Annals of Congress*, 16th Cong., 1st sess., January 5, 1820, 70–72, https://memory.loc.gov/ammem/amlaw/lwaclink.html.

4   *Journal of the Thirtieth House of Representatives of the Commonwealth of Pennsylvania, Commenced at Harrisburg, Tuesday the Seventh of December, in the Year of Our Lord One Thousand Eight Hundred Nineteen and of the Commonwealth the Forty Fourth* (Harrisburg, PA: James Peacock, 1819–1820), 52–54, 98, 130, https://catalog.hathitrust.org/Record/100744482 (hereafter cited as *PA House Journal 1819–1820*).

5   *Annals of Congress*, 16th Cong., 1st sess., March 1, 1820, 1586–87, https://memory.loc.gov/ammem/amlaw/lwaclink.html.

6   *PA House Journal 1819–1820*, 990.

7   *PA House Journal 1819–1820*, 989, 1013, 1014.

8   *PA House Journal 1819–1820*, 338–41, 402, 1088. Text of the law is found in *Laws of the Commonwealth of Pennsylvania* (Philadelphia: John Bioren, 1922), 7:285–88, https://books.google.com/books/reader?id=sDhOAQAAIAAJ.

9   *Laws of the Commonwealth of Pennsylvania*, 7:285.

10 William R. Leslie, "The Pennsylvania Fugitive Slave Act of 1826," *Journal of Southern History* 18, no. 4 (November 1952): 429–445, https://doi.org/10.2307/2955218.

11 "Prigg v. Pennsylvania," Oyez, accessed January 12, 2020, https://www.oyez.org/cases/1789-1850/41us539.

12 *PA House Journal 1819–1820*, 73, 415–28, 459–66.

13 *PA House Journal 1819–1820*, 12.

14 *PA House Journal 1819–1820*, 428.

15 *PA House Journal 1819–1820*, 961–63.

16 Samuel Hazard, ed., "Report on the State of the Commonwealth," in *The*

Register of Pennsylvania (Philadelphia: Wm. F. Geddes, 1829), 4:136–42, 145–53, 166–69; questions are at 145–46, and Dauphin County answers are at 148, https://catalog.hathitrust.org/Record/008730775. The Dauphin County interviewee mentioned Millersburg. Since Millersburg was near Sallade's home and since Rutherford was from the south end of the county, it is logical that the Dauphin County representative to the committee was Sallade.

17 Hazard, "Report on the State of the Commonwealth," 4:136–42, 145–53, 166–69.
18 *PA House Journal 1819–1820*, 386.
19 *PA House Journal 1819–1820*, 389.
20 *PA House Journal 1819–1820*, 384–91.
21 *PA House Journal 1819–1820*, 883.
22 *PA House Journal 1819–1820*, 391, 534, 662, 788, 789, 792, 806–12, 816–31, 835–41, 849–64, 870–80, 883–84.
23 *PA House Journal 1819–1820*, 10, 100, 172, 220, 367, 586–612, 696–714, 715, 753–55.
24 For election returns, see A New Nation Votes, http://elections.lib.tufts.edu. Simon is listed in Dauphin County as Solliday in the 1819 election and as Sallade in the 1820 election.
25 "Pennsylvania Election Statistics: 1682–2006," accessed March 22, 2020, http://paelections.telcen.com/index.html. The compiler cites the *Oracle of Dauphin*, published November 18, 1820, in Harrisburg, as his source.
26 Klein, *Pennsylvania Politics*, 406–8.
27 *Journal of the Thirty-First House of Representatives of the Commonwealth of Pennsylvania, Commenced at Harrisburg, Tuesday the Fifth of December, in the Year of Our Lord, One Thousand Eight Hundred and Twenty* (Harrisburgh, PA: Hamilton & M'Ilwaine, 1820–1821), 43, https://catalog.hathitrust.org/Record/100744482 (hereafter cited as *PA House Journal 1820–1821*).
28 *PA House Journal 1820–1821*, 110–15.
29 Regarding the governor's salary, see *PA House Journal 1820–1821*, 91, 92, 97, 108, 110–15, 168. Regarding the gubernatorial election, see *PA House Journal 1820–1821*, 109, 110, 130, 133, 134, 137, 139.
30 *PA House Journal 1820–1821*, 51, 92, 93, 94, 341, 343, 864.
31 William Henry Egle, *Notes and Queries: Historical, Biographical, and Genealogical: Relating Chiefly to Interior Pennsylvania*, 4th ser. (Harrisburg, PA: Harrisburg, 1895), 2:170, https://books.google.com/books/reader?id=1dQUAAAAYAAJ.
32 "Pennsylvania 1822 House of Representatives, Dauphin County," A New Nation Votes, accessed March 22, 2020, http://elections.lib.tufts.edu/cata-

log/tufts:pa.assembly.dauphin.1822. By this time, the old political parties had disappeared, and the party assigned to a particular candidate was essentially meaningless.

CHAPTER 13: A PROJECT FROM HEAVEN

1   I calculated the acreage of the various individuals from the warrantee township maps of Dauphin County. Sallade's tracts are found in the following warrantee township maps: Jefferson, Washington, Jackson, Halifax, Wayne, and Upper Paxton; see http://www.phmc.state.pa.us/bah/dam/rg/di/r17-114CopiedSurveyBooks/r17-114MainInterfacePage.htm.

2   William Vincent Byars, ed., *B. and M. Gratz: Merchants in Philadelphia, 1754–1798* (Jefferson City, MO: Hugh Stephens, 1916), 7, 8, https://catalog.hathitrust.org/Record/100319910.

3   Byars, *B. and M. Gratz: Merchants in Philadelphia*, 32; Isaac Markens, *The Hebrews in America: A Series of Historical and Biographical Sketches* (New York: Isaac Markens, 1888), 78–81, https://archive.org/details/cu31924032763207; Sydney M. Fish, *Barnard and Michael Gratz: Their Lives and Times* (Lanham, MD: University Press of America, 1994); Toni Pitock, "Michael Gratz (1739–1811)," Immigrant Entrepreneurship: German-American Business Biographies, 1720 to the Present (website), German Historical Institute, last updated February 10, 2015, http://www.immigrantentrepreneurship.org/entry.php?rec=212.

4   Joseph R. Rosenbloom, *A Biographical Dictionary of Early American Jews: Colonial Times through 1800* (Lexington: University of Kentucky Press, 1960), 107; A. S. W. Rosenbach, *An Historical Sketch of the Congregation* (Philadelphia: Cahan, 1909), 6, https://archive.org/details/dedicationofnews00phil.

5   Henry Samuel Morais, *The Jews of Philadelphia: Their History from the Earliest Settlements to the Present Time* (Philadelphia: Levytype, 1894), 23, 50, https://archive.org/details/jewsofphiladelph00mora; Rosenbloom, *A Biographical Dictionary of Early American Jews*, 87; William Vincent Byars, "The Gratz Papers," *Publications of the American Jewish Historical Society* 23 (1915): 1–23, http://www.jstor.org/stable/43057967. For a transcription of Aaron Levy's will, see Isabella H. Rosenbach and Abraham S. Wolf Rosenbach, "Aaron Levy," *Publications of the American Jewish Historical Society* 2 (1894): 157–63, http://www.jstor.org/stable/43057420.

6   George Korson, *Black Rock: Mining Folklore of the Pennsylvania Dutch* (New York: Arno Press, 1979), 163–69.

7   J. Allen Barrett, ed., *Lykens-Williams Valley History: Directory and Pictorial Review Embracing the Entire Lykens and Williams Valley in the Effort to*

Preserve the Past and Perpetuate the Present (Lykens, PA: J. Allen Barrett, 1922), 52, https://archive.org/details/lykenswilliamsva00barr. The borough of Gratz was laid out in 1805. Barrett states the property was originally known as "Wild Cat Hill," which is also the name listed on the survey map of Aaron Levy's property; the survey map of the Gratz property indicates that its southern border was adjacent to the "top of short mountain."

8   Rosenbach, *An Historical Sketch of the Congregation*, 5–7, 11–12.

9   Congregation Mikveh Israel (website), accessed March 24, 2020, http://www.mikvehisrael.org.

10 Cope was not the original warrantee, and I have not been able to find details of this transaction. His ownership is documented in "Lykens Valley and the Coal Region," in *The Register of Pennsylvania*, edited by Samuel Hazard (Philadelphia: Wm. F. Geddes, 1833), 12:57–58, https://catalog.hathitrust.org/Record/008730775.

11 Ralph D. Gray, "Philadelphia and the Chesapeake and Delaware Canal, 1769–1823," *Pennsylvania Magazine of History and Biography* 84, no. 4 (October 1960): 401–23, https://www.jstor.org/stable/20089334; see also H. Niles and Son, eds., *Niles' Weekly Register from September 1826 to March 1827* (Baltimore: Franklin Press), 31:282, https://catalog.hathitrust.org/Record/006903835.

12 Joseph R. Chandler, "Pen and Pencil Sketches of Living Merchants.—No. 1.—Thomas P. Cope, Esq., of Philadelphia," *Merchants' Magazine and Commercial Review* 20 (January–June 1849): 355–63, https://catalog.hathitrust.org/Record/011570218.

13 Eliza Cope Harrison, ed., *Philadelphia Merchant: The Diary of Thomas P. Cope, 1800–1851* (South Bend, IN: Gateway Editions, 1978), 402.

14 George Rogers Taylor, *The Transportation Revolution, 1815–1860* (New York: Rinehart, 1951), 4:79, https://catalog.hathitrust.org/Record/000968070.

15 This James Buchanan is not the future president.

16 Charles L. Sheetz, "The Inception of the Rail-road to Lykens Valley" (master's thesis, Shippensburg University, 1968).

17 William Henry Egle, ed., *Notes and Queries: Historical and Genealogical, Chiefly Relating to Interior Pennsylvania* (Harrisburg, PA: Harrisburg, 1895), 1:147–48, https://books.google.com/books?id=mixBAQAAMAAJ.

18 Sheetz, "The Inception of the Rail-Road to Lykens Valley," 2–3.

19 Sheetz, "The Inception of the Rail-Road to Lykens Valley," 13. The minute books of the Lykens Valley Railroad and Coal Company can be found in the Pennsylvania State Archives, Manuscript Group 286, Penn Central Railroad Collection, roll MB20.

20 Sheetz, "The Inception of the Rail-road to Lykens Valley," 13.

21 Hugh Maxwell, "Dauphin County Coal Region," in *Register of Pennsylvania*, edited by Samuel Hazard (Philadelphia: Wm. F. Geddes, 1831), 7:312–13.

22 Walter R. Johnson, "Report of an Examination of the Bear Valley Coal District in Dauphin County, Pennsylvania," in *Report of a Survey and Exploration of the Coal and Ore Lands Belonging to the Allegheny Coal Company, in Somerset County, Pennsylvania* (Philadelphia: Joseph & William Kite, 1841), 16–17, https://books.google.com/books?id=OWE9AAAAYAAJ. The amounts do not add up, but are presented as reported in the original source.

23 "Lykens Valley Coal Mines," in *The Register of Pennsylvania*, edited by Samuel Hazard (Philadelphia: Wm. F. Geddes, 1834), 14:136.

24 Albert J. Churella, *The Pennsylvania Railroad* (Philadelphia: University of Pennsylvania Press, 2013); James L. Holton, *The Reading Railroad: History of a Coal Age Empire, Volume 1: The Nineteenth Century* (Laury's Station, PA: Garrigues House, 1989).

25 Charles Frederick Carter, *When Railroads Were New* (New York: Henry Holt, 1910), 1–2, https://catalog.hathitrust.org/Record/000458933.

Chapter 14: Bank Wars and Logrolling

1 Albert J. Churella, *The Pennsylvania Railroad* (Philadelphia: University of Pennsylvania Press, 2013), 65.

2 Charles McCool Snyder, *The Jacksonian Heritage: Pennsylvania Politics, 1833–1848* (Harrisburg: Pennsylvania Historical and Museum Commission, 1958), 80.

3 Churella, *The Pennsylvania Railroad*, 65.

4 Homer Tope Rosenberger, *The Philadelphia and Erie Railroad: Its Place in American Economic History* (Potomac, MD: Fox Hills Press, 1975), 74; *Proceedings of the Citizens of Philadelphia Relative to the Rail Road to Erie, and of the Convention at Williamsport, Lycoming County, PA* (Philadelphia: J. Thompson, 1836), https://books.google.com/books?id=1xg6AQAAMAAJ.

5 Snyder, *The Jacksonian Heritage*, 75–81.

6 "Northumberland and Erie Railroad Convention," *American Railroad Journal, and Advocate of Internal Improvements* 5, no. 49 (December 10, 1836): 776, https://catalog.hathitrust.org/Record/008717775.

7 "Northumberland and Erie Railroad Convention," 776–77.

8 Rosenberger, *The Philadelphia and Erie Railroad*, 90.

9 Snyder, *The Jacksonian Heritage*, chap. 5.

10 *Journal of the Forty-Seventh House of Representatives of the Commonwealth of Pennsylvania* (Harrisburg, PA: Samuel D. Patterson, 1836–1837), 445–49

(hereafter cited as *PA House Journal 1836–1837*), https://catalog.hathitrust. org/Record/100744482.

11 John Joseph Wallis, "What Caused the Crisis of 1839?" (NBER Working Paper Series on Historical Factors in Long Run Growth, Historical Paper 133, National Bureau of Economic Research, Cambridge, MA, April 2001), 20, 21, 42, http://econweb.umd.edu/~wallis/MyPapers/WhatCaused1839_ NBER.pdf.

12 "United States Bank," *Niles' Weekly Register* 51 (December 31, 1836): 273, https://catalog.hathitrust.org/Record/006903835.

13 Snyder, *The Jacksonian Heritage*, 92n42, 92.

14 Snyder, *The Jacksonian Heritage*, 92.

15 Snyder, *The Jacksonian Heritage*, 92.

16 Snyder, *The Jacksonian Heritage*, 95.

17 *PA House Journal 1836–1837*, 535; Snyder, *The Jacksonian Heritage*, 95.

18 "Coal-Susquehanna Canal," *American Railroad Journal, and Advocate of Internal Improvements* 6, no. 4 (January 28, 1837): 51, https://catalog. hathitrust.org/Record/008717775.

19 Paul G. Marr, "The Wiconisco Canal," *Canal History and Technology Proceedings* 24 (March 19, 2005): 5–21; Robert W. Keintz, "Wiconisco Canal Issue," *Canal Currents: Bulletin of the Pennsylvania Canal Society* (Spring 1988): 2; Historic American Engineering Record, *Wiconisco Canal Aqueduct No. 3, Spanning Powell Creek at State Route 147, Halifax, Dauphin County, PA*, documentation compiled after 1968, photograph, Library of Congress Prints and Photographs Division, Washington, DC, Call No. HAER PA,22-HAFX.V,1-, http://www.loc.gov/pictures/item/pa3667.

20 *PA House Journal 1836–1837*, 851.

21 *PA House Journal 1836–1837*, 852

22 Snyder, *The Jacksonian Heritage*, 94.

23 *PA House Journal 1836–1837*, 1056–57.

24 *PA House Journal 1836–1837*, 1065.

25 "Bank of the United States, Mr. Espy's Amendment," *Niles' Weekly Register* 52 (April 22, 1837): 119, https://catalog.hathitrust.org/Record/006903835.

CHAPTER 15: A PROJECT FROM HELL

1 Charles McCool Snyder, *The Jacksonian Heritage: Pennsylvania Politics, 1833–1848* (Harrisburg: Pennsylvania Historical and Museum Commission, 1958), 124.

2 "Report of the Committee to Investigate the Conduct of the Late Board of Canal Commissioners," in *Journal of the Forty-Ninth House of Representatives of the Commonwealth of Pennsylvania* (Harrisburg, PA: Boas &

Coplan, 1838–1839), vol. 2, part 2, p. 3 (hereafter cited as *PA House Journal 1838–1839*), https://catalog.hathitrust.org/Record/100744482.

3   John Rutherford was the son of William Rutherford. William Rutherford had served in the House alongside Sallade from 1819 to 1821.

4   *PA House Journal 1838–1839*, 5.

5   *PA House Journal 1838–1839*, 3–22.

6   "Report of the Minority of the Committee Appointed to Investigate the Conduct of the Late Board of Canal Commissioners," June 24, 1839, in *PA House Journal 1838–1839*, 400, 372–416.

7   *Report of the Committee Appointed to Enquire into the Causes of the Disturbances at the Seat of Government, in December, 1838* (Harrisburg, PA: Boas & Coplan, 1839), https://catalog.hathitrust.org/Record/008651716; William Henry Egle and Joseph Ritner, "The Buckshot War," *Pennsylvania Magazine of History and Biography* 23, no. 2 (1899): 137–56, https://www.jstor.org/stable/20085847; Sean Patrick Adams, "Hard Times, Loco-Focos, and the Buckshot Wars: The Panic of 1837 in Pennsylvania," *Pennsylvania Legacies* 11, no. 1 (May 2011): 12–17.

8   *Report of the Committee Appointed to Enquire into the Causes of the Disturbances at the Seat of Government*, 16.

9   *Report of the Committee Appointed to Enquire into the Causes of the Disturbances at the Seat of Government*, 21, 38, 46, 47, 87, 102, 129.

10 John Joseph Wallis, Richard E. Sylla, and Arthur Grinath III, "Land, Debt, and Taxes: Origins of the US State Default Crisis, 1839–1842," 19–21, September 15, 2020, https://www.frbatlanta.org/-/media/documents/news/conferences/2011/sovereign-debt/papers/Wallis.pdf, citing W. B. Smith, *Economic Aspects of the Second Bank of the United States* (Cambridge, MA: Harvard University Press, 1953), 179, for the $2 million cash bonus, which was only part of the total required cash bonus of $4.5 million. See also Avard Longley Bishop, "The State Works of Pennsylvania," *Transactions of the Connecticut Academy of Arts and Sciences* 13 (November 1907): 149–207, https://catalog.hathitrust.org/Record/006567007.

11 John Joseph Wallis, Richard E. Sylla, and Arthur Grinath III, "Sovereign Default and Repudiation: The Emerging-Market Debt Crisis in the US States, 1839–1843" (Working Paper 10753, National Bureau of Economic Research, Cambridge, MA, September 2004), 32, 34, https://www.nber.org/papers/w10753. The total in the table on p. 32 is given as $33,301,013 and in the table on p. 34 as $36,366,000.

12 John Joseph Wallis, "What Caused the Crisis of 1839?" (Working Paper H0133, National Bureau of Economic Research, Cambridge, MA, April 2001), 20.

13 Namsuk Kim and John Joseph Wallis, "The Market for American State Government Bonds in Britain and the United States, 1830–43," *Economic History Review* 58, no. 4 (February 2005): 736–64, specifically 753, https://www.nber.org/papers/w10108.

14 Kim and Wallis, "The Market for American State Government Bonds," 759.

15 Kim and Wallis, "The Market for American State Government Bonds," 759.

16 Kim and Wallis, "The Market for American State Government Bonds," 759.

17 Kim and Wallis, "The Market for American State Government Bonds," 754, 759.

18 Wallis, Sylla, and Grinath, "Sovereign Default and Repudiation," 33.

19 T. K. Worthington, "Historical Sketch of the Finances of Pennsylvania," *Publications of the American Economic Association* 2, no. 2 (May 1887): 171, http://www.jstor.org/stable/2696709.

20 Board of Canal Commissioners, *Annual Report of the Canal Commissioners, to the Governor of Pennsylvania, with the Accompanying Documents, for the Year Ending October 31, 1839, Read in the House of Representatives, January 23, 1840*, 40, 142–160, https://archive.org/details/messagefromgover03penn.

21 *Annual Report of the Board of Canal Commissioners, for the Year Ending 31st October, 1840, Read in the Senate, Jan. 15, 1841*, 40–41, https://archive.org/details/messagefromgover03penn.

22 *Journal of the Senate of the Commonwealth of Pennsylvania, Session 1842, Containing the Canal Commissioners Report and Accompanying Documents* (Harrisburg, PA: Boas & Patterson, 1842), 3:26–27, 38–40, 214–16, https://books.google.com/books?id=Rf1BAQAAMAAJ.

23 *Laws of the General Assembly of the Commonwealth of Pennsylvania, Passed at the Session of 1842, in the Sixty-Sixth Year of Independence* (Harrisburg, PA: M'Kinley & Lescurn, 1842), 351–60, https://books.google.com/books?id=61dNAQAAMAAJ. Letters patent were never issued in a timely manner under the authority of Act No. 113.

24 Walter R. Johnson, "Report of an Examination of the Bear Valley Coal District, in Dauphin County, Pennsylvania," in *Report of a Survey and Exploration of the Coal and Ore Lands Belonging to the Allegheny Coal Company, In Somerset County, Pennsylvania* (Philadelphia: Joseph & William Kite, 1841), 16–17, https://books.google.com/books?id=OWE9AAAAYAAJ.

25 Pocket Memorandum Book #4, Sallade-Bickel Family Papers, Manuscripts and Archives Division, New York Public Library, Astor, Lenox, and Tilden Foundations. Pocket Memorandum Book # 4.

26 Among the commissioners, George H. Thompson of Philadelphia was president of the Lykens Valley Coal Company and a director of the Lykens

Valley Railroad; Edward Gratz (Simon Gratz died in 1839) of Philadelphia was a director of the Lykens Valley Coal Company; Isaac Prince of Philadelphia was secretary and treasurer of the Lykens Valley Coal Company; Henry Sheaffer of Dauphin County was a director for the Lykens Valley Coal Company and the Lykens Valley Railroad; Simon Sallade was a director of the Lykens Valley Railroad; Simon Cameron was a Dauphin County resident and longtime supporter of transportation projects and would be elected to the US Senate on March 13, 1845; Thomas Elder and Jacob Haldeman owned extensive coal-producing land in Lykens Valley; and John Leebrick, John Rutherford, and James Martin (the same men who commandeered the state arsenal during the Buckshot War) had been contractors for the canal when it was owned by the state.

27   Pennsylvania State Archives, Harrisburg, RG 26, Records of the Department of State, Corporation Bureau, Letters Patent (series #26.111), June 17, 1845, Wiconisco Canal Company, courtesy Pennsylvania Historical and Museum Commission.

28   Johnson, "Report of an Examination of the Bear Valley Coal District"; *Laws of the General Assembly of the Commonwealth of Pennsylvania, Passed at the Session of 1845, in the Sixty-Ninth Year of Independence* (Harrisburg, PA: J. M. G. Lescure, 1845), 134–42, https://books.google.com/books?id=oSxOAQAAIAAJ.

29   Paul G. Marr, "The Wiconisco Canal," *Canal History and Technology Proceedings* 24 (March 2005), 13.

30   Marr, "The Wiconisco Canal," 13.

31   Marr, "The Wiconisco Canal," 3–21, quote at 13.

32   Wiconisco Canal Aqueduct No. 3 (Inglenook Aqueduct), HAER No. PA-496, Historic American Engineering Record, National Park Service, https://cdn.loc.gov/master/pnp/habshaer/pa/pa3600/pa3667/data/pa3667data.pdf.

Chapter 16: Seasoned Politician

1   Pocket Memorandum Book #4, Sallade-Bickel Family Papers, Manuscripts and Archives Division, New York Public Library, Astor, Lenox, and Tilden Foundations.

2   Pocket Memorandum Book #4, Sallade-Bickel Family Papers.

3   Pocket Memorandum Book #4, Sallade-Bickel Family Papers.

4   Pocket Memorandum Book #4, Sallade-Bickel Family Papers.

5   Pocket Memorandum Books #5, #6, and #7, Sallade-Bickel Family Papers.

6   "The Dauphin County Democratic Convention," *Sunbury American*, July 1, 1848, p. 2.

7   John F. Coleman, *The Disruption of the Pennsylvania Democracy, 1848–1860* (Harrisburg: Pennsylvania Historical and Museum Commission, 1975), 62.

8   *Laws of the General Assembly of the State of Pennsylvania Passed at the Session of 1854* (Harrisburg, PA: A. Boyd Hamilton, 1854), 54, 563–67, https://archive.org/details/lawsofgeneralas_1854penn.

9   Miles V. Miller, *Through the Years* (Valley View, PA: Valley Citizen, 1954), 10.

10 Miller, *Through the Years*, 10.

11 Donald H. Kent, "The Erie War of the Gauges," *Pennsylvania History* 15, no. 4 (October 1948): 254, https://www.jstor.org/stable/27766942

12 Kent, "The Erie War of the Gauges," 254; Homer Tope Rosenberger, *The Philadelphia and Erie Railroad: Its Place in American Economic History* (Potomac, MD: Fox Hills Press, 1975), 256–65; "To the Assembly Concerning the Franklin Canal Company," *PA*, 4th ser., 7:686–703.

13 Rosenberger, *The Philadelphia and Erie Railroad*, 262; L.S.B., "Important from Harrisburg, Erie and Pittsburgh Railroad, the Franklin Canal Railroad, Ohio and Pennsylvania Companies," *New York Times*, May 4, 1854, p. 2; L.S.B., "Charges of Bribery in the Pennsylvania Legislature," *New York Times*, May 4, 1854, p. 2; "Sunbury and Erie Railroad—The Deed Consummated," *New York Times*, May 8, 1854, p. 4.

14 Pocket Memorandum Books #2 and #3, Sallade-Bickel Family Papers.

15 *Journal of the Sixty-Fourth House of Representatives of the Commonwealth of Pennsylvania* (Harrisburg, PA: A. Boyd Hamilton, 1854), 528–34; Asa Earl Martin, "The Temperance Movement in Pennsylvania Prior to the Civil War," *Pennsylvania Magazine of History and Biography* 49, no. 3 (1925): 195–230.

16 Pocket Memorandum Book #1, Sallade-Bickel Family Papers.

CHAPTER 17: A KNOW-NOTHING EPISODE

1   "A large town meeting assembled at Harrisburg," *Jeffersonian* (Stroudsburg, PA), March 9, 1854, p. 2.

2   "The Pennsylvania Blacklist," *Morning Herald*, May 22, 1854, Secession Era Editorials Project, Furman University Department of History, http://history.furman.edu/editorials/see.py.

3   *The National Cyclopedia of American Biography* (New York: James T. White, 1900), 10:63, https://archive.org/details/nationalcyclopa03unkngoog.

4   For a timeline of the Pennsylvania temperance movement, see Asa Earl Martin, "The Temperance Movement in Pennsylvania Prior to the Civil War," *Pennsylvania Magazine of History and Biography* 49, no. 3 (1925): 195–230,

https://www.jstor.org/stable/20086574. For more about the Know-Nothings, see Michael F. Holt, "The Politics of Impatience: The Origins of Know Nothingism," *Journal of American History* 60, no. 2 (September 1973): 309–31, https://www.jstor.org/stable/2936778; William E. Gienapp, "Nebraska, Nativism, and Rum: The Failure of Fusion in Pennsylvania, 1854," *Pennsylvania Magazine of History and Biography* 109, no. 4 (October 1985): 425–71, https://www.jstor.org/stable/20091960; Tyler Anbinder, *Nativism and Slavery: The Northern Know Nothings and the Politics of the 1850s* (New York: Oxford University Press, 1992); and Mark Voss-Hubbard, *Beyond Party: Cultures of Antipartisanship in Northern Politics before the Civil War* (Baltimore: Johns Hopkins University Press, 2002).

5   Gerald G. Eggert, "'Seeing Sam': The Know Nothing Episode in Harrisburg," *Pennsylvania Magazine of History and Biography* 111, no. 3 (July 1987): 305–40, https://www.jstor.org/stable/20092119.

6   Voss-Hubbard, *Beyond Party*, 92–95.

7   Abraham Lincoln to Joshua Speed, August 24, 1855, in *The Collected Works of Abraham Lincoln*, edited by Roy P. Basler (New Brunswick, NJ: Rutgers University Press, 1953), 2:323.

8   Eggert, "'Seeing Sam,'" 308.

9   Eggert, "'Seeing Sam,'" 311.

10   Eggert, "'Seeing Sam,'" 311.

11   Simon Sallade to Richard M'Allister, September 8, 1854, printed in the *Democratic Union*, September 20, 1854, p. 1.

12   Richard M'Allister to Simon Sallade, September 14, 1854, printed in the *Democratic Union*, September 20, 1854, p. 1.

13   Simon Sallade to Richard M'Allister, September 16, 1854, printed in the *Democratic Union*, September 20, 1854, p. 1.

14   Sallade's sentiments toward Catholics and foreigners are unknown.

15   "Defining His Position," *Morning Herald*, September 21, 1854, p. 1.

16   Simon Sallada to Charles C. Rawn, September 16, 1854, printed in the *Morning Herald*, September 23, 1854.

17   "Prohibitory Liquor Law Meeting," *Morning Herald*, September 23, 1854.

18   "Local Department," *Morning Herald*, September 23, 1854.

19   "Sallade and Liberty," *Morning Herald*, September 24, 1854.

20   "Sallade and Liberty," *Morning Herald*, September 25, 1854. George M. Lauman was a distiller, farmer, and contractor, according to *Legislative Documents: Miscellaneous Documents Read in the Legislature of the Commonwealth of Pennsylvania, during the Session Which Commenced at Harrisburg, on the Second Day of January, 1855* (Harrisburg, PA: A. Boyd Hamilton, 1855), 642, https://books.google.com/books/reader?id=wz41AQAAMAAJ.

21 *Democratic Union*, October 4, 1854.

22 "Sallade and Liberty," *Morning Herald*, October 6, 1854.

23 Pocket Memorandum Book #1, Sallade-Bickel Family Papers, Manuscripts and Archives Division, New York Public Library, Astor, Lenox, and Tilden Foundations.

24 "Dauphin County Official for 1854," *Morning Herald*, October 14, 1854.

25 Advertisement in the *St. Cloud Visiter*, May 13, 1858, p. 3.

26 *St. Cloud Visiter*, May 13, 1858, pp. 1–4.

27 *St. Cloud Democrat*, August 5, 1858, p. 3.

28 *St. Cloud Democrat*, September 23, 1858, p. 2.

29 "The Indian Executions," *St. Cloud Democrat*, December 25, 1862, p. 2.

30 *The National Cyclopedia of American Biography*, 10:63; Duane Schultz, *Over the Earth I Come: The Great Sioux Uprising of 1862* (New York: St. Martin's Press, 1992), 255, 260; Wikipedia, s.v. "Dakota War of 1862," last modified May 1, 2020, https://en.wikipedia.org/wiki/Dakota_War_of_1862.

31 "Joseph H. Sallade," Find a Grave (website), accessed May 3, 2020, https://www.findagrave.com/memorial/16750125.

32 Find a Grave (website), accessed May 3, 2020, https://www.findagrave.com/memorial/69225123/simon-salada.

33 James D. Bowman, "Early History of the 'Upper End' of Dauphin County, PA" (transcript, address to the Historical Society of Dauphin County, 1940), 7.

Chapter 18: The Luck o' the Irish

1 Until 1772 the name Shamokin referred to present-day Sunbury. Today's city of Shamokin was incorporated in 1864.

2 "The Spelling Bee, First for Shamokin," *Shamokin Herald*, May 25, 1875. *Shamokin Herald* microfilm rolls were purchased by author from IMR Digital, West Hazleton, Pennsylvania. Citations will appear with the title of the article or with the first words of an article when there is no title. With few exceptions, the author of an article was not given.

3 *Book of Biographies: Biographical Sketches of Leading Citizens of the Seventeenth Congressional District, Pennsylvania* (Buffalo, NY: Biographical, 1899), 366–67.

4 See National Society of the Daughters of the American Revolution, *Lineage Book* (Washington, DC: Judd & Detweiler, 1930), 113:125, https://catalog.hathitrust.org/Record/007905197, which establishes the lineage of Stella Gallagher Hannon, including descent from John Woodside, Jonathan Woodside, Mary Ann Woodside (wife of George McEliece), and Mary McEliece (daughter of George and Mary Ann Woodside McEliece). Docu-

ments accepted with Hannon's application included an excerpt from an old letter in her posession that was signed by Benjamin Woodside (grandson of John Woodside and brother of Mary Ann Woodside) and affadavits from older acquaintances and members of the family who were told about John Woodside's Revolutionary War services by his sons and daughters. Among them was John E. Warfield, who resided with James Mardis and Jane Woodside Mardis in 1860 in Blacklick Township, Cambria, Pennsylvania. Jane Woodside (not to be confused with Jane Woodside Sallade) was the granddaughter of John Woodside and sister of Mary Ann Woodside. Also in the Mardis household at the time were James and Jane Mardis's children, including Joseph, age three. In Iowa, on the marriage certificate between Joseph Mardis and Louise Sophie Schmidt, dated May 23, 1886, Joseph's parents are listed as Jane Woodside and James Mardis. In the 1900 census, Joseph and Sophie Mardis are located in Cedar County, Iowa. Living with them was a daughter, Lucie Mardis, age ten. Lucie Mardis is listed as one of those who assisted Hannon with her Daughters of the American Revolution application. Also listed is Simon Sallade Bowman, grandson of Jane Woodside Sallade (John Woodside's daughter). John McEliece's descent from George and Mary Ann Woodside McEliece is established in several census records and a family bible. Thus the story is corroborated many times over.

5   Peter Way, *Common Labor: Workers and the Digging of North American Canals, 1780–1860* (Baltimore: Johns Hopkins University Press, 1997), 142.
6   Various spellings of McEliece appear throughout newspaper articles and census and other documents.
7   The Philadelphia and Sunbury Railroad is the same as the Philadelphia and Erie Railroad. Herbert C. Bell, ed., *History of Northumberland County, Pennsylvania* (Chicago: Brown, Runk, 1891), 942, https://archive.org/details/historyofnorthum00bell.
8   John's experience in the Civil War will be discussed later.
9   "Township Election," *Shamokin Herald*, February 26, 1863.
10 "Remarks Made at the School Gathering held in John's Hall on the Evening of April 1, 1874, by J. J. John," *Shamokin Herald*, April 9, 1874.
11 Bell, *History of Northumberland County*, 750–51.
12 Bell, *History of Northumberland County*, 378, 942.
13 Bell, *History of Northumberland County*, 896–98.
14 "Teacher's County Institute," *Sunbury American*, January 30, 1869. Citations for the *Sunbury American* will appear with the title of the article or with the first words of an article when there is no title. With few exceptions, the author of an article was not given.
15 Elizabeth McEliece turned up in the 1900 census, when she was listed as

head of household. She never married. In 1900 Belle's young children were living with Elizabeth; Belle was a widow. It is unknown where Belle lived in 1900. Perhaps she was employed outside of Shamokin.

16 John's first wife, Lydia Adams, died of smallpox and premature labor in 1864; John McEliece Pension File WC 593-714, National Archives and Records Administration, Washington, DC.

17 "Foundling," *Shamokin Herald,* October 21, 1869.

18 Diocese of Harrisburg archives, letter to author, May 17, 2011. Nothing more is known of George Alfred.

19 "The Washington Rifles of Locust Gap," *Shamokin Herald,* February 21, 1870; "Memorial Day," *Shamokin Herald,* June 3, 1870; "Monthly Report for Shamokin High School," *Shamokin Herald,* November 8, 1870; "The High School Literary Society," *Shamokin Herald,* February 2, 1871; "Military," *Shamokin Herald,* February 16, 1871; "Shamokin Progressive Literary Society," *Shamokin Herald,* April 6, 1871; "The Literary Society at the High School," *Shamokin Herald,* August 16, 1871; "A list of people appointed to solicit aid for the relief of the suffers of a hail storm," *Shamokin Herald,* August 31, 1871; "The following complementary notice of the military companies," *Shamokin Herald,* July 18, 1872; "Allotment of Schools in Coal township," *Shamokin Herald,* August 15, 1872; "Justices of the Peace," *Shamokin Herald,* July 24, 1873; "Following is a list of teachers chosen," *Shamokin Herald,* August 14, 1873; "The premium list of the Union Park and Agriculture Association Fair," *Shamokin Herald,* September 18, 1873; "Decoration Day," *Shamokin Herald,* May 28, 1874.

20 Margaret died on December 20, 1871, according to her grave marker in St. Edward's Cemetery, Shamokin.

CHAPTER 19: THE UNDOING OF GEORGE MCELIECE

1 Oyer and Terminer and Quarter Session Papers, 1877–1968, Pennsylvania State Archives, RG-47, microfilm rolls 16076 and 16077 (hereafter cited as trial transcript); films purchased by author.

2 *Shamokin Herald,* April 16, 1874, announces the opening of his liquor store; *Shamokin Herald,* May 5, 1877, lists him among those who were granted licenses to sell liquor.

3 "There appears to be trouble," *Sunbury American,* August 28, 1869, p. 2.

4 "The Two Platforms!" *Northumberland County Democrat,* August 13, 1869, p. 2.

5 "The Two Platforms!" *Northumberland County Democrat,* August 13, 1869, p. 2.

6 See, for example, Eric Foner and Joshua Brown, *Forever Free: The Story of*

Emancipation and Reconstruction (New York: Alfred A. Knopf, 2005), 29, 31.

7   Forrest G. Wood, *Black Scare: The Racist Response to Emancipation and Reconstruction* (Berkeley: University of California Press, 1968), 91.

8   Herbert C. Bell, ed., *History of Northumberland County, Pennsylvania* (Chicago: Brown, Runk, 1891), 282–83, https://archive.org/details/historyofnorthum00bell.

9   "Auditors' Report," *Sunbury American*, April 15, 1871.

10   Courthouse Ring, or Democratic Ring, was a pejorative used by the Republican editor of the *Sunbury American* to describe the local democrats.

11   "That $94,000," *Sunbury American*, April 22, 1871, p. 2; "That $94,000," *Sunbury American*, April 29, 1871, p. 2; "The County Finances," *Sunbury American*, May 6, 1871, p. 2; "County Finances," *Sunbury American*, May 20, 1871, p. 2; "Upheavings of the Ring," *Sunbury American*, May 27, 1871, p. 3.

12   "Teacher's County Institute," *Sunbury American*, January 30, 1869, p. 2.

13   Trial transcript, 838.

14   "Resigned," *Shamokin Herald*, August 18, 1870, p. 3.

15   Harold W. Aurand, *From the Molly Maguires to the United Mine Workers: The Social Ecology of an Industrial Union, 1869–1897* (Philadelphia: Temple University Press, 1971), 68.

16   "Meeting of the General Council of the M. and L. B. Associates," *Columbian and Bloomsberg Democrat*, July 15, 1870, p. 2.

17   "Resigned," *Shamokin Herald*, August 18, 1870, p. 3. By this time the WBA was known as the Miners' and Laborers' Benevolent Association.

18   Edward Pinkowski, *John Siney, the Miners' Martyr* (Philadelphia: Sunshine Press, 1963), 85. Pinkowski refers to a letter by Richard Trevellick in the *Workingman's Advocate*, June 25, 1870.

19   "The Democracy of this county," *Shamokin Herald*, June 8, 1871, p. 3.

20   "That $94,000" and "It is amusing to see the wire-pullers," *Sunbury American*, July 8, 1871, p. 2.

21   "The Democratic Convention," *Sunbury American*, June 10, 1871, p. 2.

22   "Primary Election Returns," *Sunbury American*, June 10, 1871, p. 2; June 17, 1871.

23   "Treverton, Sept. 19th, 1871," *Sunbury American*, September 23, 1871, p. 2.

24   "Primary Election Returns," *Sunbury American*, June 10, 1871, p. 2; June 17, 1871.

25   "Outstanding Taxes for 1865 and Previous Years," *Sunbury American*, April 21, 1866, p. 2; "Outstanding Taxes for 1866 and Previous Years," *Sunbury American*, April 6, 1867, p. 4.

26   "Awaiting Death," *New York Herald*, March 23, 1878, p. 6.

27   "Proceedings of Court," *Sunbury American*, January 9, 1864, p. 3.

28 Trial transcript, 1877.

29 "More Ring Villainy," *New York Times*, July 8, 1871, p. 4.

30 Kenneth D. Ackerman, *Boss Tweed: The Rise and Fall of the Corrupt Pol Who Conceived the Soul of Modern New York* (New York: Carroll & Graf, 2005), 52; "Ten Most Corrupt Politicians," Real Clear Politics, January 28, 2009, http://www.realclearpolitics.com/lists/most_corrupt_politicians.

31 "A Terrible Day," *New York Times*, July 13, 1871, p. 1.

32 Michael A. Gordon, *The Orange Riots: Irish Political Violence in New York City, 1870 and 1871* (Ithaca, NY: Cornell University Press, 1993).

33 "A Mask Removed," *Harper's Weekly* 15: 642, https://catalog.hathitrust.org/Record/000061498.

34 Father Isaac Thomas Hecker, "Infallibility," *Catholic World*, August 1871, 577–93, https://books.google.com/books/reader?id=yBU4AQAAIAAJ. For more on Father Hecker, see Boniface Hanley, OFM, "The Story of Servant of God Isaac Hecker," Paulist Fathers, accessed June 25, 2020, http://www.paulist.org/who-we-are/our-history/isaac-hecker.

35 "The Secular Not Supreme," 688.

36 "The Secular Not Supreme," 699, 701.

37 "A little hanging," *Sunbury American*, July 22, 1871, p. 2.

38 "A little hanging," *Sunbury American*, July 22, 1871, p. 2.

39 "The Flight of Tammany," *Sunbury American*, July 22, 1871, p. 2.

40 "The Masters of the Situation," *Sunbury American*, July 22, 1871, p. 2.

41 "The Masters of the Situation," *Sunbury American*, July 22, 1871, p. 2.

42 "The Real Murderers of New York," *Sunbury American*, August 12, 1871, p. 2.

43 "The Tammany Ring of New York," *Sunbury American*, August 5, 1871, p. 2.

44 "Orangemen vs Catholicism," *Sunbury American*, July 29, 1871, p. 2.

45 "Father Hecker asserts," *Sunbury American*, July 29, 1871, p. 2.

46 "The Great Danger," *Sunbury American*, September 2, 1871, p. 2.

47 *Yale University Obituary Record of Graduates Deceased during the Year Ending July 1, 1920* (New Haven, CT: Yale University, 1921), 1346, https://books.google.com/books?id=A55GAQAAMAAJ.

48 "Our neighbor of the Democrat," Sunbury *American*, July 29, 1871, p. 2.

49 "Come on with Your Affidavits," *Sunbury American*, September 23, 1871, p. 2; September 30, 1871, p. 2.

50 "The President Judgeship," *Sunbury American*, August 5, 1871, p. 2.

51 *Journal of the Proceedings of the Eighty-Seventh Convention of the Protestant Episcopal Church, in the Diocese of Pennsylvania, Held in St. Andrew's Church, Philadelphia, Commencing Tuesday, May 9, and Ending Thursday, May 11, 1871* (Philadelphia: M'Calla & Stavely, 1871), 14, https://books.google.com/books?id=k2PkAAAAMAAJ.

52 "Mr. Scott and the Catholics," *Sunbury American*, September 16, 1871, p. 2.

53 "Treverton, Sept. 19ᵗʰ, 1871, *Sunbury American*, September 23, 1871, p. 2.

54 "The Bible in the Schools," *New York Times*, January 17, 1870, p. 5.

55 "A Labor Union Meeting," *Sunbury American*, July 29, 1871, p. 3.

56 "Our Neighbors at the *Democratic Guard*," *Sunbury American*, August 12, 1871, p. 2.

57 "The Senior Editor of the *Democratic* Guard," *Sunbury American*, August 26, 1871, p. 2.

58 "A Labor Union Meeting," *Sunbury American*, July 29, 1871, p. 3; emphasis in original.

59 Bell, *History of Northumberland County*, 926–28.

60 "We are informed that speakers," *Sunbury American*, September 30, 1871, p. 2.

61 "We are informed that speakers," *Sunbury American*, September 30, 1871, p. 2.

62 "Our neighbors of the *Democratic Guard*," *Sunbury American*, August 12, 1871, p. 2.

63 "That $94,000," *Sunbury American*, August 5, 1871, p. 2.

64 "That $94,000," *Sunbury American*, August 12, 1871, p. 3.

65 "A Dream," *Sunbury American*, October 7, 1871, p. 1; *Shamokin Herald*, September 28, 1871. The author is anonymous, but the themes are consistent with Wilvert's opinions.

66 For more on Jim Fisk, see Willoughby Jones, *The Life of James Fisk, Jr.* (Philadelphia: Union Publishing, 1872), https://archive.org/details/lifejamesfiskjr00jonegoog. Fisk, the flamboyant robber baron, is notable for his legendary exploits. Among them was an attempt to corner the gold market on the New York Gold Exchange, a plot that also involved financier Jay Gould, assistant US Treasury secretary Daniel Butterfield, and Abel Corbin, the husband of President Grant's younger sister. Upon discovery of the plot, President Grant and Treasury secretary George S. Boutwell initiated countermeasures to break the Gold Ring, resulting in the crash of the price of gold on September 24, 1869, Black Friday. Fisk's greatest source of fame—or infamy—arose from his connection with the Erie Railroad and its no-holds-barred clash with Cornelius Vanderbilt, best known for building the New York Central Railway. The hijinks involved in the battle for control of the Erie Railway between the tycoons make for great reading and included the issuance of watered-down stock, bribery in the New York legislature, outrageous courtroom maneuvers, actual fisticuffs, and other shenanigans. Fisk, as spectacular in his death as he was in life, was caught on the losing end of an extortion scandal and love

triangle, resulting in his murder in 1872 by his business partner and rival in romance, Edward Stokes.

For more on Robert Bonners, see Wikipedia, s.v. "Robert E. Bonner," last modified March 24, 2020, https://en.wikipedia.org/wiki/Robert_E._ Bonner. Bonner was a publisher best known for the *New York Ledger*. He also had an interest in trotting horses.

For more on Horace Greeley, see Wikipedia, s.v. "Horace Greeley," last modified May 12, 2020, https://en.wikipedia.org/wiki/Horace_Greeley. Greeley was founder and editor the *New York Tribune*, among the great newspapers of its time. Long active in politics, he served briefly as a congressman from New York and was the unsuccessful candidate of the new Liberal Republican party in the 1872 presidential election against incumbent president Ulysses S. Grant.

67   "A Dream," *Sunbury American*, October 7, 1871, p. 1; *Shamokin Herald*, September 28, 1871.

68   "A Dream," *Sunbury American*, October 7, 1871, p. 1; *Shamokin Herald*, September 28, 1871.

69   A. N. Brice, "Court Proceedings," *Sunbury American*, August 17, 1872, p. 3; "Party Degradation and Shame," *Shamokin Herald*, August 15, 1872.

70   "Allotment of Schools in Coal Township," *Shamokin Herald*, August 15, 1872.

71   "A. J. Gallagher, intending to discontinue," *Shamokin Herald*, August 28, 1873.

72   "Election of County Superintendent," *Shamokin Herald*, May 6, 1875.

73   Trial transcript, 1877.

74   This is according to the 1880 US census, retrieved from https://www.familysearch.org.

75   Sarah Woodside Gallagher (Anthony J. Gallagher's great-granddaughter) email message to author, September 20, 2016.

76   John Frank Gallagher obituary, *Times Leader*, February 10, 2010, http://www.legacy.com/obituaries/timesleader/obituary.aspx?page=lifestory&pid=139271636.

77   S. John, "Report of the Grand Jury," *Shamokin Herald*, March 23, 1872, p. 3.

78   "The Ex-Treasurer," *Sunbury American*, March 23, 1872, p. 2.

79   "The Auditors' Report," *Sunbury American*, April 13, 1872, p. 2.

80   "Local Affairs," *Sunbury American*, March 15, 1873, p. 3.

81   "Expenditures and Receipts of Northumberland County," *Sunbury American*, March 27, 1874, p. 2.

82   "County Auditor's Report," *Sunbury Gazette*, March 15, 1878, p. 3; "Audi-

tors' Report," *Northumberland County Democrat*, March 7, 1884, p. 2.

83 "For County Commissioner, it was conceded," *Sunbury Gazette*, September 18, 1874, p. 2.

84 "The Democrats in Council," *Sunbury Gazette*, October 16, 1874, p. 2.

85 "A suit has been brought," *Northumberland County Democrat*, March 6, 1874, p. 3.

86 "Adding Insult to Injury," *Sunbury Gazette*, February 9, 1877, p. 3.

87 "Death of Geo. McEliece," *Sunbury American*, April 2, 1886, p. 3.

Chapter 20: Johnny's Gone for a Soldier

1 "Disunion," *Sunbury American*, April 6, 1861, p. 2.

2 "The Shamokin Volunteers," *Sunbury American*, April 27, 1861, p. 2.

3 Samuel P. Bates, *History of Pennsylvania Volunteers, 1861–1865* (Harrisburg, PA: B. Singerly, 1869–1871), 1:79, https://catalog.hathitrust.org/Record/000454271.

4 "The Sunbury Guards," *Sunbury American*, August 24, 1861, p. 2.

5 During the Civil War, the army was organized as follows: a regiment was eight hundred soldiers; a brigade was two to five regiments; a division was two to four brigades; a corps was two to three divisions; and an army was three corps.

6 George H. Gordon, *Brook Farm to Cedar Mountain in the War of the Great Rebellion, 1861–62* (Boston: Houghton Mifflin, 1885), https://catalog.hathitrust.org/Record/006578765.

7 Alpheus S. Williams, *From the Cannon's Mouth*, ed. Milo M. Quaife (Detroit: Wayne State University Press, 1959; repr., Lincoln: University of Nebraska Press, 1995).

8 United States War Department, *The War of the Rebellion: A Compilation of the Official Records of the Union and Confederate Armies* (Washington, DC: Government Printing Office, 1880–1901), https://catalog.hathitrust.org/Record/000625514 (hereafter cited as *Official Records*).

9 "Joseph Knipe, Hometown Hero," *The Bugle* 17, no. 2 (Summer 2007).

10 "Murder of Major Lewis," *New York Times*, September 24, 1861, p. 8.

11 Gordon, *Brook Farm*, 56; According to General S. Williams's Special Order No. 87, October 3, 1861, the Forty-Sixth had been temporarily assigned to Franklin's division when it arrived in DC but was reassigned to Brigadier General Samuel P. Heintzelman's division on October 3. This conflicts with the accounts of General George H. Gordon and General Alpheus S. Williams, and perhaps because of the confusion at the time, it appears Special Order No. 87 was never implemented; "Special Orders, No. 87," *Official Records*, ser. 1, vol. 51, part 1, chap. 63, p. 491.

12 "Our Baltimore Correspondence, Another Female Soldier," *New York Times*, October 9, 1861, p. 2.

13 Williams, *From the Cannon's Mouth*, 18; Gordon, *Brook Farm*, 59.

14 Williams, *From the Cannon's Mouth*, 29.

15 Williams, *From the Cannon's Mouth*, 35.

16 For an account and interpretation of this battle, see William Marvel, "Battle of Ball's Bluff," accessed May 14, 2020, http://www.historynet.com/battle-of-balls-bluff-2.htm. A good map of the area, which shows several of the places mentioned in John's story, is the map of the Chesapeake and Ohio Canal by the National Park Service: https://www.nps.gov/choh/planyourvisit/upload/CHOHmap-full-140922-v7-accessible.pdf.

17 "Report of Maj. Gen. Nathaniel P. Banks, U.S. Army, of march to re-enforce General Stone, Headquarters, Edwards Ferry, October 22, 1861," *Official Records*, ser. 1, vol. 5, chap. 14, pp. 338–39.

18 Gordon, *Brook Farm*, 63.

19 Gordon, *Brook Farm*, 63–64.

20 Gordon, *Brook Farm*, 64.

21 Williams, *From the Cannon's Mouth*, 24–25.

22 "Important from the Upper Potomac," *New York Times*, October 27, 1861, p. 1.

23 Williams, *From the Cannon's Mouth*, 38.

24 Williams, *From the Cannon's Mouth*, 44.

25 "Affairs on the Upper Potomac," *New York Times*, December 22, 1861, p. 8; December 23, 1861, p. 8.

26 "From Gen. Banks' Command," *New York Times*, January 9, 1862, p. 1; "Fighting on the Upper Potomac," *New York Times*, January 6, 1862, p. 1.

27 "Special Orders, No. 3, Hdqrs. General Banks' Division, Frederick City, Md., January 5, 1862," *Official Records*, ser. 1, vol. 5, chap. 14, p. 694; "Important from the Upper Potomac," *New York Times*, January 8, 1862, p. 8; Williams, *From the Cannon's Mouth*, 53, 54.

28 Williams, *From the Cannon's Mouth*, 52, 53, 54.

29 Williams, *From the Cannon's Mouth*, 60.

30 "Headquarters Department of the Shenandoah, Strasburg, May 22, 1862," *Official Records*, ser. 1, vol. 12, chap. 24, part 3, pp. 524–25.

31 "Winchester, March 22, 1862," *Official Records*, ser. 1, vol. 12, chap. 24, part 3, pp. 12–13; "Headquarters, Army of the Potomac, March 23, 1862," ser. 1, vol. 12, chap. 24, part 3, pp. 15; Williams, *From the Cannon's Mouth*, 65–66.

32 "Abstract from 'Record of Events' in Cavalry Brigade, Department of the Shenandoah," *Official Records*, ser. 1, vol. 12, chap. 24, part 1, p. 427.

33 "New Market, April 24, 1862," *Official Records*, ser. 1, vol. 12, chap. 24, part 1, pp. 446–47.

34 Williams, *From the Cannon's Mouth*, 73–75.

35 "Headquarters Department of the Shenandoah, May 18, 1862, 10:30 p. m.," *Official Records*, ser. 1, vol. 12, chap. 24, part 1, p. 523.

36 "Strasburg, Va., May 21, 1862, 5:00 p. m.," *Official Records*, ser. 1, vol. 12, chap. 24, part 1, p. 523.

37 "Headquarters Department of the Shenandoah, Strasburg, Va., May 22, 1862," *Official Records*, ser. 1, vol. 12, chap. 24, part 1, p. 524.

38 "From Gen. Banks' Army," *New York Times*, June 5, 1862, p. 8.

39 "Gen. Banks' Department," *New York Times*, June 8, 1862, p. 8.

40 "June 29–30, 1862, Reconnaissance from Front Royal to Luray, Va., and skirmish," *Official Records*, ser. 1, vol. 12, chap. 24, part 2, pp. 94–95.

41 Gordon, *Brook Farm*, 263.

42 "Return of Casualties in the Union Forces, Maj. Gen. John Pope Commanding, at the Battle of Cedar Mountain, Va., August 9, 1862," *Official Records*, ser. 1, vol. 12, chap. 24, part 2, pp. 136–37.

43 Banks' Second Division was commanded by General Christopher Augur.

44 Gordon, *Brook Farm*, 275.

45 Gordon, *Brook Farm*, 276.

46 "General Orders, No. 18, Headquarters Army of Virginia, near Sperryville, Va., August 6, 1862," *Official Records*, ser. 1, vol. 12, chap. 24, part 2, p. 52.

47 Robert K. Krick, *Stonewall Jackson at Cedar Mountain* (Chapel Hill: University of North Carolina Press, 1990), 17. Krick's book is the most comprehensive account of the battle that I have found.

48 The statement in the county histories that John was imprisoned at Libby Prison and Belle Isle after being released from the hospital in Staunton, Virginia, is contradicted by the report in John's pension file, which states that he was located at Fort McHenry in September and November. The official pension file is the more credible source.

49 "The Shamokin Company," *Sunbury American*, July 4, 1863, p. 3.

50 The information about the Thirty-Sixth Regiment is primarily from (1) a document compiled by Robert E. Nale, a descendant of one of the soldiers, and Jean A. Suloff of the Mifflin County Historical Society titled *The 36th Regiment, Pennsylvania Volunteer Militia, July and August, 1863*, accessed June 25, 2020, http://www.nale.org/36thpvm.pdf, and (2) Gregory A. Coco, *A Strange and Blighted Land: Gettysburg: The Aftermath of a Battle* (Gettysburg, PA: Thomas Publications, 1995).

51 Coco, *A Strange and Blighted Land*, 6.

52 Daniel Pearl, "In Gujarat, Stench Provides a Constant Reminder of Death,"

Wall Street Journal, February 5, 2001, https://www.wsj.com/articles/
SB981323645338299940.
53 "Some half a dozen of our citizens," *Sunbury American*, July 18, 1863, p. 3.
54 Nale and Suloff, *The 36th Regiment*.
55 "Return of Northumberland County Volunteers," *Sunbury American*,
August 15, 1863, p. 3.

Chapter 21: A Case against the Molly Maguires

1 The lifelong friend's name is illegible in John's pension file.
2 The dates of death of Michael's parents are from David Lukens. David
(now deceased) is the great-grandson of Frederick Walter Lukens, Ann
Ellen's brother.
3 Jill J. Hurd, *The Ancestors and Descendants of Jan Lucken* (Baltimore:
Gateway Press, 1989), 26, 123, 183.
4 Katherine Jaeger, "The Molly Maguires of Northumberland County, Pennsylvania," April 2001, accessed May 18, 2020, http://files.usgwarchives.net/
pa/northumberland/areahistory/mollymag.txt.
5 The population of Northumberland County was 28,922 in 1860, 41,444 in
1870, and 53,123 in 1880.
6 "2018 Crime in the United States," Criminal Justice Information Services
Division, table 1, https://ucr.fbi.gov/crime-in-the-u.s/2018/crime-in-the-
u.s.-2018/tables/table-1.
7 "Murder—During the afternoon of Saturday last," *Shamokin Herald*,
October 22, 1868.
8 Andruss Library Special Collections, Bloomsburg University, accessed
May 16, 2020, https://library.bloomu.edu/Archives/SC/MollieMaguires/
mollieindex.htm.
9 "Outrage at Locust Gap," *Shamokin Herald*, August 5, 1869.
10 "Three Mollies Gobbled," *Shamokin Herald*, August 26, 1876; emphasis
added.
11 "Com. vs John Mahan," *Shamokin Herald*, August 11, 1870.
12 A. N. Brice, "Court Proceedings," *Shamokin Herald*, January 16, 1873.
13 "The Washington Rifles of Locust Gap," *Shamokin Herald*, February 24, 1870
(includes reference to Weaver's Hotel); "Memorial Day," *Shamokin Herald*,
June 3, 1870; "Mr. Editor: On the morning of the 4th," *Shamokin Herald*,
July 11, 1872; "The following complimentary notice," *Shamokin Herald*,
July 18, 1872 (includes "the Washington boys behaved admirably); "On
Thursday last the 8th Division N. G. of Pa.," *Shamokin Herald*, November
6, 1873; "Decoration Day," *Shamokin Herald*, May 28, 1874; "The following
communication received," *Shamokin Herald*, October 1, 1874.

14   "Military," *Shamokin Herald*, February 16, 1871; "On Thursday last the
      8th Division N. G. of Pa.," *Shamokin Herald*, November 6, 1873; "Military,"
      Shamokin Herald, August 6, 1874.
15   John Binns, *Binn's Justice, or Magistrate's Daily Companion: A Treatise on
      the Office and Duties of Aldermen and Justices of the Peace, in the Com-
      monwealth of Pennsylvania*, 8th ed. (Philadelphia: Kay & Brother, 1870),
      490–523, https://books.google.cg/books?id=gLc4AAAAIAAJ.
16   Anthony F. C. Wallace, *St. Clair: A Nineteenth-Century Coal Town's Expe-
      rience with a Disaster-Prone Industry* (Ithaca, NY: Cornell University Press,
      1981), 350–58.
17   "Mr. Beers' Surprise Party," *Pacific Commercial Advertiser*, June 5, 1875, p. 4.
18   "The Molly Maguires of Pennsylvania," *Pulaski Citizen*, May 20, 1875, p. 2.
19   "Chicago's coal heavers have struck," *Yankton Daily Press and Dakotan*,
      June 7, 1875, p. 2.
20   "A Quarrel among the Doctors," *New Orleans Bulletin*, July 17, 1875, p. 2.
21   "The Coal Conspiracy," *Chicago Tribune*, April 17, 1875, p. 8. The National
      Industrial Congress, also referred to as the Industrial Brotherhood, was
      a short-lived labor union that succeeded the National Labor Union and
      preceded the Knights of Labor. It met in Ohio in 1873; in Rochester, New
      York, in 1874; and probably in Indianapolis in 1875. For the history of the
      National Industrial Congress, see T. V. Powderly, *Thirty Years of Labor:
      1859–1889* (Columbus, OH: Excelsior, 1890), 106–30, https://archive.org/
      details/thirtyyearsoflab00powduoft.
22   Oyer and Terminer and Quarter Session Papers, 1877–1968, Pennsylvania
      State Archives, RG-47, microfilm rolls 16076 and 16077.
23   Rea murder documents accessed through Andruss Library Special Col-
      lections at Bloomsburg University of Pennsylvania, https://library.bloomu.
      edu/Archives/SC/MollieMaguires/mollieindex.htm.
24   Kevin Kenny, *Making Sense of the Molly Maguires* (New York: Oxford
      University Press, 1998), 286.
25   Wallace, *St. Clair*, 358.
26   Wallace, *St. Clair*, 359.
27   Wallace, *St. Clair*, 360.
28   Wallace, *St. Clair*, 361.
29   Kevin Kenny, "The 'Molly Maguires,' the Ancient Order of Hibernians, and
      the Bloody Summer of 1875," *Pennsylvania Legacies* 14, no. 2 (Fall 2014): 18–25.

CHAPTER 22: DOWN IN THE COAL MINE

1   Abandoned in 1990 due to structural problems and safety concerns, the
     cathedral has since been rebuilt two hundred feet below the original

structure. See "Colombia's Salt Cathedral Is a Marvel of Architecture and a Popular House of Worship," National Public Radio, April 20, 2019, https://www.npr.org/2019/04/20/714609074/colombias-salt-cathedral-is-a-marvel-of-architecture-and-a-popular-house-of-wors.

2 Wikipedia, s.v. "Salt Cathedral of Zipaquirá," last modified May 16, 2020, https://en.wikipedia.org/wiki/Salt_Cathedral_of_Zipaquir%C3%A1#Old_cathedral.

3 Ninth Census of the United States, 1870, National Archives and Records Administration, RG-29, Pub. No. M593, Roll No. 1385.

4 Herbert C. Bell, ed., *History of Northumberland County, Pennsylvania* (Chicago: Brown, Runk, 1891), 943, https://archive.org/details/historyof-northum00bell.

5 *The Charter and By-Laws of the Locust Gap Improvement Company, with Reports on Their Coal Land* (Philadelphia: McLaughlin Brothers, 1854), https://books.google.com/books/reader?id=pxkxAQAAMAAJ.

6 Henry Samuel Morais, *The Jews of Philadelphia: Their History from the Earliest Settlements to the Present Time* (Philadelphia: Levytype, 1894), 309–10.

7 *Reports of the Inspectors of Coal Mines of the Anthracite Coal Regions of Pennsylvania for the Year 1870* (Harrisburg, PA: B. Singerly, 1871), 221. Hereafter, reports are cited as *Inspectors' Reports* followed by the year and page number. The reports are available online through the Pennsylvania State University Libraries system: https://libraries.psu.edu/about/collections/pennsylvania-geology-resources/pennsylvania-annual-report-mines-year-1870-1979.

8 *Inspectors' Reports 1873*, 164.

9 *Inspectors' Reports 1874*, 69, 149.

10 *Inspectors' Reports 1878*, 56–57.

11 Grace Palladino, *Another Civil War: Labor, Capital, and the State in the Anthracite Regions of Pennsylvania, 1840–68* (Urbana: University of Illinois Press, 1990), 9.

12 Palladino, *Another Civil War*, 9.

13 Harold W. Aurand, *From the Molly Maguires to the United Mine Workers: The Social Ecology of an Industrial Union, 1869–1897* (Philadelphia: Temple University Press, 1971), 67.

14 Marvin W. Schlegel, "America's First Cartel," *Pennsylvania History* 13, no. 1 (January 1946): 1–16, https://journals.psu.edu/phj/article/view/21564. The Reading was the primary shipper of coal mined in the western middle coal field, which included mines near Mahanoy City, Shenandoah, and Ashland in Schuylkill County; Centralia in Columbia County; and Mount

Carmel and Shamokin in Northumberland County.

15 J. J. John, "Coal Department, the New Compromise," *Shamokin Herald,* October 6, 1870.

16 *Inspectors' Reports 1870,* 6, 16, 17, 25, 26.

17 It is unknown at which colliery Henry Hoffman's death occurred.

18 *Inspectors' Reports 1878,* 35–46. For the Henry Clay fatalities in 1873, see *Inspectors' Reports 1873,* 145.

19 For details about casualties on John's watch, see the appendix.

Chapter 23: The Bitter Cry of Children

1 *Inspectors' Reports 1878,* 42.

2 *Inspectors' Reports 1883,* 81.

3 Since the age of those injured was not consistently reported, this list probably understates the number of injured boys. For example, although an injury to Daniel Kehler (more on him later) is listed in the coal inspectors' report for 1882, his age (fourteen) is not given in the report.

4 *Inspectors' Reports 1871,* 219; *Inspectors' Reports 1874,* 24; *Inspectors' Reports 1882,* 90, 93; *Inspectors' Reports 1883,* 87.

5 Ninth Census of the United States, 1870, National Archives and Records Administration, RG 29, Pub. No. M-593, Roll-1385 (hereafter cited as 1870 census). Household numbers: 132, 198, 246, 295, 365, 369, 400, 413, 51, 200, 225. I tabulated census data three times and each time came up with different numbers. The difference can be attributed to problems of legibility and human error (mine). That said, the difference was minimal.

6 Owen R. Lovejoy, "Child Labor in the Coal Mines," *Annals of the American Academy of Political and Social Science* 27 (1906): 35–41, https://www.jstor.org/stable/pdf/1010788.pdf; Owen R. Lovejoy, "The Extent of Child Labor in the Anthracite Coal Industry," *Annals of the American Academy of Political and Social Science* 29 (January 1907): 35–49, http://www.jstor.org/stable/1010416.

7 Walter I. Trattner, *Crusade for the Children: A History of the National Child Labor Committee and Child Labor Reform in America* (Chicago: Quadrangle Books, 1970), 70–74.

8 Hugh D. Hindman, *Child Labor: An American History* (Armonk, NY: M. E. Sharpe, 2002), 35–36.

9 Herbert C. Bell, ed., *History of Northumberland County, Pennsylvania* (Chicago: Brown, Runk, 1891), 668–69, https://archive.org/details/historyofnorthum00bell; "Education: Mount Carmel High School Graduates, 1887–1892, Mt Carmel, Northumberland Co, PA," file contributed for use in USGenWeb Archives by Sandy Jensen, http://files.usgwarchives.net/pa/northumberland/education/mchs0001.txt.

10 Tenth Census of the United States, 1980, National Archives and Records
    Administration, 1880, RG-29, Pub. No. T-9, Roll 1164 Part 1 and Roll 1164
    Part 2 (hereafter cited as 1880 census). Household numbers: 75, 87, 93, 143,
    156, 164, 245, 278, 280, 183, 425.
11 *Inspectors' Reports 1878*, 94.
12 1880 census. Household numbers: 56, 70, 97, 191, 235, 265, 301, 326.
13 Alan Dickerson, *Black Lung: Anatomy of a Public Health Disaster* (Ithaca,
    NY: Cornell University Press, 1998), 46.
14 *Inspectors' Reports 1871*, 215–16. The pump rod is the rod to which the
    bucket of a pump is fastened and which is attached to the brake or handle.
15 Florence Kelley, *Our Toiling Children* (Chicago: Women's Temperance Pub-
    lication Association, 1889), http://nrs.harvard.edu/urn-3:FHCL:409534.
16 Edith Abbott, "A Study of the Early History of Child Labor in America,"
    American Journal of Sociology 14, no. 1 (July 1908): 15, http://www.jstor.
    org/stable/2762758.
17 Abbott, "A Study of the Early History of Child Labor in America," 15–37.

CHAPTER 24: SEEDS OF REFORM

1   A hopper is a container for a bulk material such as grain, rock, or trash,
    typically one that tapers downward and is able to discharge its contents
    at the bottom.
2   *Inspectors' Reports 1878*, 163.
3   *Inspectors' Reports 1878*, 166.
4   *Inspectors' Reports 1878*, 166.
5   *Inspectors' Reports 1879*, 87.
6   "Dr. John's Education Bill," *Sunbury American*, March 3, 1876, p. 3.
7   *Inspectors' Reports 1881*, 10–11.
8   *Inspectors' Reports 1881*, 11.
9   The act (PL 218) of June 30, 1885, was titled "An Act to Provide for the
    Health and Safety of Persons Employed in and about the Anthracite Coal
    Mines of Pennsylvania, and for the Protection and Preservation of Prop-
    erty Connected Therewith."
10 Spragging involved inserting a stout stick or bar between the spokes of a
    wheel to check its motion.
11 Alexander Trachtenberg, *The History of Legislation for the Protection of
    Coal Miners in Pennsylvania, 1824–1915* (New York: International, 1942),
    116–21.
12 *Inspectors' Reports 1882*, 293.
13 *Inspectors' Reports 1882*, 293.
14 *Inspectors' Reports 1882*, 256.

15   *Inspectors' Reports 1882*, 257.

16   *Inspectors' Reports 1882*, 256–57.

17   *Inspectors' Reports 1882*, 261.

18   *Inspectors' Reports 1882*, 261.

19   *Inspectors' Reports 1882*, 261.

20   Jonathan L. Schaffer, "The History of Pennsylvania's Workmen's Compensation: 1900–1916," *Pennsylvania History* 53, no. 1 (January 1986): 26–55, https://journals.psu.edu/phj/article/view/24554.

21   *Report of the Bureau of Mines of the Department of Internal Affairs of Pennsylvania, 1899*, Official Document No. 10 (Harrisburg, PA: W. M. Stanley Ray, 1900), ix.

22   John Fabian Witt, *The Accidental Republic: Crippled Workingmen, Destitute Widows, and the Remaking of American Law* (Cambridge, MA: Harvard University Press, 2004), 235n79; see also G. Edward White, *Law in American History, Volume II, From Reconstruction through the 1920s* (New York: Oxford University Press, 2016), 241–42.

23   Witt, *The Accidental Republic*, 55–56.

24   Witt, *The Accidental Republic*, 56.

25   *Inspectors' Reports 1882*, 92.

26   Sequence of events: 1882, injury; 1883, lawsuit commenced in the Court of Common Pleas of Northumberland County; 1886, trial took place in that court before president judge William E. Rockefeller with judgment for plaintiff; 1888, Schwenk v. Kehler, 122 Pa. 67, 15 A. 694 judgment reversed and order for new trial; 18??, new trial in Northumberland county with judgment in favor of defendant; 1891, Kehler v. Schwenk, 144 Pa. 348, 22 A. 910, judgment reversed and new trial (again); 18??, another trial in Northumberland County (Judge Sittser), judgment for plaintiff; 1892, Kehler v. Schwenk, 151 Pa. 505, 25 A. 130, judgment for plaintiff affirmed.

27   The Kehler v. Schwenk case did not show up in Witt's search, perhaps because it was listed as a "loss of service of a minor" case instead of a "personal injury" case. The six cases in Witt's search are McClafferty v. Fisher, 1 Sadler 161 (1885); Massey v. Snowden, 149 Pa. 410 (1892); Welsh v. Lehigh & Wilkesbarre Coal Co., 2 Sadler 319 (1886); Union Pacific Railway Company v. McDonald, 152 U.S. 262 (1894); Ebright v. Mineral Railroad & Mining Co., 2 Monag. 126 (1888); and Lineoski v. Susquehanna Coal Co., 157 Pa. St. 153 (1893).

28   United States census, 1870, Eldred Township, Schuylkill County, Pennsylvania, https://www.familysearch.org; *Genealogical and Biographical Annals of Northumberland County, Pennsylvania* (Chicago: J. L. Floyd, 1911), 263–64, https://archive.org/details/genealogicalbiog00floy.

29 Samuel T. Wiley, *Biographical and Portrait Cyclopedia of Schuylkill County Pennsylvania Comprising a Historical Sketch of the County* (Philadelphia: Rush, West, 1893), 619–20, https://archive.org/details/cu31924028854598.

30 Jim Robertson, "How Umbrella Policies Started, Part 1: Early Liability Coverage," International Risk Management Institute, March 2000, https://www.irmi.com/articles/expert-commentary/how-umbrella-policies-started-part-1-early-liability-coverage.

31 The judicial system concerning claims against an employer for personal injury was based in common law. Common law is law developed in the course of time from the rulings of judges, as compared to law embodied in statutes passed by legislatures (statutory law) or law embodied in a written constitution (constitutional law).

32 *Genealogical and Biographical Annals of Northumberland County*, 694–97.

33 S. Higginbotham, email message to author, July 6, 2017.

34 *Pennsylvania Suggested Standard Civil Jury Instructions*, 4th ed., 2016 Supplement, Chapter 13, Negligence Actions, Date of Last Revision, December 2012 (PA-JICIV 13.80, Pa SSJI (Civ), 13.80 (2013).

35 White, *Law in American History*, 257–58.

36 White, *Law in American History*, 258.

37 *Genealogical and Biographical Annals of Northumberland County Pennsylvania*, 263.

38 Wiley, *Biographical and Portrait Cyclopedia of Schuylkill County Pennsylvania*, 619.

39 "Five Popular Candidates for Governor," *Pittsburg Dispatch*, February 16, 1890, p. 9.

40 *Genealogical and Biographical Annals of Northumberland County Pennsylvania*, 695–97.

41 "Coal Operators Heard: Lawyers Outline Their Case Before the Strike Commission," *New York Times*, December 18, 1902, p. 3.

42 Anthracite Coal Strike Commission, *Report to the President on the Anthracite Coal Strike of May–October, 1902* (Washington, DC: Government Printing Office, 1903), 125, https://catalog.hathitrust.org/Record/001432256.

43 Anthracite Coal Strike Commission, *Report to the President*, 126.

44 Anthracite Coal Strike Commission, *Report to the President*, 84.

45 Anthracite Coal Strike Commission, *Report to the President*, 84.

46 Hugh D. Hindman, *Child Labor: An American History* (Armonk, NY: M. E. Sharpe, 2002), 90.

47 Owen R. Lovejoy, "The Extent of Child Labor in the Anthracite Coal Industry," *Annals of the American Academy of Political and Social Science*

29 (January 1907): 35–49, http://www.jstor.org/stable/1010416.

48   Hindman, *Child Labor*, 293–319, 320; "Human Trafficking of Children in the United States," US Department of Education, accessed May 23, 2020, https://www2.ed.gov/about/offices/list/oese/oshs/factsheet.html.

Chapter 25: Lights

1   "First Electric Light Historical Marker," ExplorePAhistory.com, accessed May 25, 2020, http://explorepahistory.com/hmarker.php?marker-Id=1-A-399.

2   "The Electric Light," *Shamokin Herald*, September 13, 1883.

3   "The Electric Light," *Shamokin Herald*, September 13, 1883.

4   Herbert C. Bell, ed., *History of Northumberland County, Pennsylvania* (Chicago: Brown, Runk, 1891), 647, https://archive.org/details/historyof-northum00bell.

5   "Former Selectman Dead," *Philadelphia Inquirer*, April 17, 1904, p. 7.

6   "Tuesday evening fire destroyed," *Northumberland County Democrat*, September 6, 1889, p. 4.

7   Richard White, *The Republic for Which It Stands: The United States during Reconstruction and the Gilded Age, 1865–1896* (New York: Oxford University Press, 2017), 477–82.

8   "Shamokin's Sensation," *Sunbury Gazette*, April 17, 1891, p. 1.

9   "The Case Settled," *Sunbury Weekly News*, April 23, 1891, p. 1.

10   *Book of Biographies: Biographical Sketches of Leading Citizens of the Seventeenth Congressional District, Pennsylvania* (Buffalo, NY: Biographical, 1899), 368; Herbert C. Bell, ed., *History of Northumberland County, Pennsylvania* (Chicago: Brown, Runk, 1891), 942–43.

11   S. Rep. No. 1411, 58th Cong., 2nd Sess., "John McEliece." See John McEliece Pension File WC 593-714, National Archives and Records Administration, Washington, DC; see also *Catalogue of United States Public Documents Issued Monthly by the Superintendent of Documents* (Washington DC: Government Printing Office, January, 1904), 124, 209, 713, https://archive.org/details/monthlycatalogof190410unit.

Chapter 26: Healing Hands

1   Allison Lantero, "The War of the Currents: AC vs. DC Power," US Department of Energy, November 18, 2014, https://www.energy.gov/articles/war-currents-ac-vs-dc-power.

2   "The Largest Steel Plant in the World," *Iron Age* 73 (January 7, 1904): 49–73, https://catalog.hathitrust.org/Record/009798831.

3   "United States Census, 1910," database with images, FamilySearch, https://
     familysearch.org, citing NARA microfilm publication T624 (Washington,
     DC: National Archives and Records Administration, n.d.).

4   "Hospital Notes," *Buffalo Medical Journal* 60, no. 3 (October 1904): 198,
     https://archive.org/details/buffalomedicalj32unkngoog.

5   Mary Gerald Pierce, *Unto All—His Mercy: The First Hundred Years of the
     Sisters of Mercy in the Diocese of Buffalo, 1858-1958* (Buffalo, NY: Savage
     Litho, 1979), 152–59, 169–78.

6   Father Mario Brown to author, January 4, 2002.

7   Pierce, *Unto All*, 97–98. In its early years the parish was called Sacred Heart.

8   Pierce, *Unto All*, 142.

9   Father Mario Brown to author, January 4, 2002.

10   "Buffalo University," *Buffalo Medical Journal* 57, no. 11 (June 1902): 840–41.

11   "Hospital Notes," *Buffalo Medical Journal* 60, no. 4 (November 1904): 260.
     I suspect the designation as an alternate was a reflection of Dr. Brown's
     lack of experience at that time.

12   US Department of Health, Education, and Welfare, "200 Years of Amer-
     ican Medicine (1776–1976)," Pub. No. (NIH) 76-1069, https://www.nlm.
     nih.gov/hmd/pdf/200years.pdf.

13   Harry Burns, "Germ Theory: Invisible Killers Revealed," *British Medical Journal*
     334, no. S1 (January 2007): S11, https://doi.org/10.1136/bmj.39044.597292.94.

14   United States Department of Commerce, Bureau of the Census, *Mortal-
     ity Statistics, 1910*, 11th annual report (Washington, DC: Government
     Printing Office, 1913), 16, https://www.cdc.gov/nchs/data/vsushistorical/
     mortstatsh_1910.pdf.

15   M. Stephen Pendleton, "Ernest Wende and Buffalo's Transition to Modern
     Public Health Policy, 1892–1910," *New York History* 90, no. 4 (Fall 2009):
     294, http://www.jstor.org/stable/23185130. Dr. Robert Koch was the
     founder of modern bacteriology. He discovered the specific causative
     agents of tuberculosis, anthrax, and cholera.

16   Pendleton, "Ernest Wende and Buffalo's Transition," 289.

17   Pendleton, "Ernest Wende and Buffalo's Transition," 296.

18   Pendleton, "Ernest Wende and Buffalo's Transition," 310.

19   United States Department of Commerce, Bureau of the Census, *Mortal-
     ity Statistics, 1934*, 35th annual report (Washington, DC: Government
     Printing Office, 1936), 30, https://www.cdc.gov/nchs/data/vsushistorical/
     mortstatsh_1934.pdf.

20   Thomas P. Duffy, "The Flexner Report—100 Years Later," *Yale Journal of
     Biology and Medicine* 84, no. 3 (September 2011): 274, https://www.ncbi.
     nlm.nih.gov/pmc/articles/PMC3178858,

21   Duffy, "The Flexner Report," 274,

22   Duffy, "The Flexner Report," 276,

23   Abraham Flexner, *Medical Education in the United States and Canada: A Report to the Carnegie Foundation for the Advancement of Teaching* (Boston: D. B. Updike, Merrymount Press, 1910), 267.

24   Flexner, *Medical Education*, 267.

25   Flexner, *Medical Education*, 267

26   Flexner, *Medical Education*, 267

27   Flexner, *Medical Education*, 147.

28   As a child, I lived next door and was familiar with the setup.

29   Lillian Brown Diggins to author, March 3, 2010.

30   Lillian Brown Diggins to author, May 10, 2008.

31   Pierce, *Unto All*, 317.

32   Sister Mary Innocentia Fitzgerald, *A Historical Sketch of the Sisters of Mercy in the Diocese of Buffalo, 1857–1942* (Buffalo, NY: Mount Mercy Academy, 1942), 99–103; Pierce, *Unto All*, 317, 320–21.

33   Pierce, *Unto All*, 324.

34   Lillian Brown Diggins to author, March 3, 2010.

35   "Mission and Values," Society of St. Vincent de Paul, accessed May 25, 2020, http://www.svdpusa.org/About-Us/Mission-and-Values.

36   "Funeral Rites on Monday for Dr. J. J. Brown," *Buffalo Times*, February 24, 1934.

37   "Our Story," Baker Victory Services, accessed May 25, 2020, https://www.bakervictoryservices.org/our-story.

38   Excerpt from "Annals of Mercy," included in materials from Sister Helen Parot, RSM, to author, November 25, 2008.

APPENDIX C: CASUALTIES AT LOCUST GAP MINE

1   Herbert C. Bell, ed., *History of Northumberland County, Pennsylvania* (Chicago: Brown, Runk, 1891), 383, https://archive.org/details/historyof-northum00bell; *Reports of the Inspectors of Coal Mines of the Anthracite Coal Regions of Pennsylvania for the Year 1870* (Harrisburg, PA: B. Singerly, 1871), 17, 25. Hereafter, reports are cited as *Inspectors' Reports* followed by the year to which the report applies and page number. The reports are available online through the Pennsylvania State University Libraries system: https://libraries.psu.edu/about/collections/pennsylvania-geolo-gy-resources/pennsylvania-annual-report-mines-year-1870-1979.

2   *Inspectors' Reports* for 1871, 19, 20, 24, 25, 27.

3   *Inspectors' Reports* for 1873, 18, 22, 146, 164.

4   *Inspectors' Reports* for 1874, 14, 20, 22–24, 26, 149.

5   *Shamokin Herald*, October 7, 1875; June 3, 1875; *Inspectors' Reports* for 1875, 113.
6   *Shamokin Herald*, March 16, 1876; *Inspectors' Reports* for 1876, 9, 10.
7   *Inspectors' Reports* for 1877, 36, 37, 42.
8   *Inspectors' Reports* for 1878, 38, 43, 45.
9   *Inspectors' Reports* for 1879, 55-62.
10 *Inspectors' Reports* for 1880, 79.
11 *Inspectors' Reports* for 1881, 110, 122.
12 *Inspectors' Reports* for 1882, 81, 90–93.
13 *Inspectors' Reports* for 1883, 77, 87–90.
14 *Inspectors' Reports* for 1884, 61, 74, 77.

BIBLIOGRAPHY

Abbott, Edith. "A Study of the Early History of Child Labor in America." *American Journal of Sociology* 14, no. 1 (July 1908): 15–37. http://www.jstor.org/stable/2762758.

Ackerman, Kenneth D. *Boss Tweed: The Rise and Fall of the Corrupt Pol Who Conceived the Soul of Modern New York.* New York: Carroll & Graf, 2005.

Adams, Richard C. *A Brief History of the Delaware Indians.* 59th Cong., 1st sess., Senate Doc. 501. Washington, DC: US Government Printing Office, 1906.

Adams, Sean Patrick. "Hard Times, Loco-Focos, and the Buckshot Wars: The Panic of 1837 in Pennsylvania." *Pennsylvania Legacies* 11, no. 1 (May 2011): 12–17.

Addison, Alexander. *Reports of Cases in the County Courts of the Fifth Circuit, and in the High Court of Errors & Appeals, of the State of Pennsylvania.* Washington, DC: John Colerick, 1800. https://archive.org/details/reportsofcasesin00penn.

Adler, Jeanne Winston, ed. *Chainbreaker's War: A Seneca Chief Remembers the American Revolution.* Hensonville, NY: Black Dome Press, 2002.

Aldrich, Mark. "The Perils of Mining Anthracite: Regulation, Technology and Safety, 1870–1945." *Pennsylvania History* 64 (Summer 1997): 361–83. https://www.jstor.org/stable/27773999.

Ambrose, Stephen E. *Nothing Like It in the World: The Men Who Built the Transcontinental Railroad, 1863–1869.* New York: Simon Schuster, 2000.

———. *Undaunted Courage: Meriwether Lewis, Thomas Jefferson, and the Opening of the American West.* New York: Simon Schuster, 1996.

American State Papers: Indian Affairs, vol. 1. http://memory.loc.gov/ammem/amlaw/lwsp.html.

Anbinder, Tyler. *Nativism and Slavery: The Northern Know Nothings and the Politics of the 1850s.* New York: Oxford University Press, 1992.

"Andrew Jackson Document Signed." Inkwell Autograph Gallery. http://www.inkwellgallery.com/Products/historical/presidential/jacksona-9.htm.

Anthracite Coal Commission. *Report to the President on the Anthracite Coal Strike of May–October, 1902.* Washington, DC: Government Printing Office, 1903. https://catalog.hathitrust.org/Record/001432256.

Appleby, Joyce. *Inheriting the Revolution: The First Generation of Americans.* Cambridge, MA: Belknap Press, 2000.

Armstrong County Pennsylvania: Her People, Past and Present, Embracing a History of the County. Vol. 2. Chicago: J. H. Beers, 1914. https://archive. org/details/armstrongcounty00cogoog.

Arnold, Andrew B. *Fueling the Gilded Age: Railroads, Miners, and Disorder in Pennsylvania Coal Country.* New York: New York University Press, 2014.

Aurand, Harold W. *Coalcracker Culture: Work and Values in Pennsylvania Anthracite, 1835–1935.* Selinsgrove, PA: Susquehanna University Press, 2013.

———. "Early Mine Workers' Organizations in the Anthracite Region." *Pennsylvania History* 58, no. 4 (October 1991): 298–310. https://www.jstor.org/ stable/27773483.

———. *From the Molly Maguires to the United Mine Workers: The Social Ecology of an Industrial Union, 1869–1897.* Philadelphia: Temple University Press, 1971.

———. "Mine Safety and Social Control in the Anthracite Industry." *Pennsylvania History* 52, no. 4 (October 1985): 227–41. https://www.jstor.org/ stable/27773071.

Aurand, Harold, and William Gudelunas. "The Mythical Qualities of Molly Maguire." *Pennsylvania History* 49, no. 2 (April 1982): 91–105. https://www. jstor.org/stable/27772818.

Axtell, James, and William C. Sturtevant. "The Unkindest Cut, or Who Invented Scalping." *William and Mary Quarterly* 37, no. 3 (July 1980): 451–72. https:// www.jstor.org/stable/1923812.

Baker, Richard Lee. *"Villainy and Madness": Washington's Flying Camp.* Baltimore: Published for Clearfield by Genealogical, 2011.

Barendse, Michael A. *Social Expectations and Perception: The Case of the Slavic Anthracite Workers.* University Park: Pennsylvania State University Press, 1981.

Barrett, J. Allen, ed. *Lykens-Williams Valley History: Directory and Pictorial Review Embracing the Entire Lykens and Williams Valley in the Effort to Preserve the Past and Perpetuate the Present.* Lykens, PA: J. Allen Barrett, 1922. https://archive.org/details/lykenswilliamsva00barr.

Bartram, John. *Observations on the Inhabitants, Climate, Soil, Rivers, Productions, Animals, and Other Matters Worthy of Notice Made by Mr. John Bartram in His Travels from Pensilvania to Onondago, Oswego, and the Lake Ontario in Canada.* London: J. Whiston and B. Write, 1751. https:// archive.org/details/cihm_11915.

Basler, Roy P., ed. *The Collected Works of Abraham Lincoln.* New Brunswick, NJ: Rutgers University Press, 1953.

Bates, Samuel P. *History of Pennsylvania Volunteers, 1861–1865.* Harrisburg, PA: B. Singerly, 1869–1871. https://catalog.hathitrust.org/Record/000454271.

"Battle of Long Island." BritishBattles.com. Accessed June 24, 2020. http://www. britishbattles.com/long-island.htm.

Bauman, Richard. *For the Reputation of Truth: Politics, Religion, and Conflict among the Pennsylvania Quakers, 1750–1800.* Baltimore: Johns Hopkins Press, 1971.

Beckert, Sven. *Empire of Cotton: A Global History.* New York: Alfred A. Knopf, 2014.

Bell, Herbert C., ed. *History of Northumberland County, Pennsylvania.* Chicago: Brown, Runk, 1891. https://archive.org/details/historyofnorthum00bell.

Benn, Carl. *The Iroquois in the War of 1812.* Toronto: University of Toronto Press, 1998.

Berthoff, Rowland. "The Social Order of the Anthracite Region, 1825–1902." *Pennsylvania Magazine of History and Biography* 89, no. 3 (July 1965): 261–91. http://www.jstor.org/stable/20089815.

Bezanson, Anne. *Prices and Inflation during the American Revolution: Pennsylvania, 1770–1790.* Philadelphia: University of Pennsylvania Press, 1951.

Bimba, Anthony. *The Molly Maguires: The True Story of Labor's Martyred Pioneers in the Coalfields.* New York: International Publishers, 1975.

Bingham, Robert Warwick, ed. *Holland Land Company Papers: Reports of Joseph Ellicott as Chief of Survey (1797–1800) and as Agent (1800–1821) of the Holland Land Company's Purchase in Western New York.* Vol. 1. Buffalo, NY: Buffalo Historical Society, 1937.

Binns, John. *Binn's Justice, or Magistrate's Daily Companion: A Treatise on the Office and Duties of Aldermen and Justices of the Peace, in the Commonwealth of Pennsylvania,* 8th ed. Philadelphia: Kay & Brother, 1870. https:// books.google.cg/books?id=gLc4AAAAIAAJ.

Bishop, Avard Longley. "The State Works of Pennsylvania." *Transactions of the Connecticut Academy of Arts and Sciences* 13 (November 1907): 149–207. https://catalog.hathitrust.org/Record/006567007.

Blackhawk, Ned. *Violence over the Land: Indians and Empires in the Early American West.* Cambridge, MA: Harvard University Press, 2006.

Bloom, Robert L. "'We Never Expected a Battle': The Civilians at Gettysburg, 1863." *Pennsylvania History* 55, no. 4 (October 1988): 161–200. https:// journals.psu.edu/phj/article/view/24708.

Bockelman, Wayne L. "Local Politics in Pre-Revolutionary Lancaster County." *Pennsylvania Magazine of History and Biography* 97 (January 1973): 45–74. https://journals.psu.edu/pmhb/article/view/42918.

Bogart, Ernest L. "Taxation of the Second Bank of the United States by Ohio."

American Historical Review 17, no. 2 (January 1912): 312–31. https://doi. org/10.2307/1833001.

Bonnicksen, Thomas M. *America's Ancient Forests: From the Ice Age to the Age of Discovery.* New York: Wiley, 2000.

Book of Biographies: Biographical Sketches of Leading Citizens of the Seventeenth Congressional District, Pennsylvania. Buffalo, NY: Biographical Publishing Company, 1899.

Bouton, Terry. "'No Wonder the Times Were Troublesome': The Origins of Fries Rebellion, 1783–1799." *Pennsylvania History* 67, no. 1 (Winter 2000): 21–42. https://www.jstor.org/stable/27774246.

———. "A Road Closed: Rural Insurgency in Post-Independence Pennsylvania." *Journal of American History* 87, no. 3 (December 2000): 855–87. https:// www.jstor.org/stable/2675275.

———. *Taming Democracy: "The People," the Founders, and the Troubled Ending of the American Revolution.* Oxford: Oxford University Press, 2007.

Bowen, Eli. "Coal, and the Coal-Mines of Pennsylvania." *Harper's New Monthly Magazine* 15 (June–November 1857): 451–69. https://catalog.hathitrust. org/Record/008919716.

Bowman, James D. "Early History of the 'Upper End' of Dauphin County, PA." Transcript of lecture, Historical Society of Dauphin County, Pennsylvania, 1940.

Boyd, Steven R., ed. *The Whiskey Rebellion: Past and Present Perspectives.* Westport, CT: Greenwood Press, 1985.

Boylston, James R., and Allen J. Wiener. *David Crockett in Congress: The Rise and Fall of the Poor Man's Friend.* Houston, TX: Bright Sky Press, 2009.

Brackenridge, Hugh Henry. *Incidents of the Insurrection in the Western Parts of Pennsylvania in the Year 1794.* Philadelphia: John M'Culloch, 1795. https:// archive.org/details/incidentsofinsur00inbrac.

Bray, George A. III. "Scalping during the French and Indian War." *Early America Review* 3 (Spring–Summer 1998). https://www.varsitytutors.com/ earlyamerica/early-america-review/volume-3/scalping-during-the-french- and-indian-war.

Breer, T. H. *The Marketplace of Revolution: How Consumer Politics Shaped American Independence.* New York: Oxford University Press, 2004.

Broehl, Wayne G. *The Molly Maguires.* New York: Chelsea House, 1983.

Brooks, David. "Ben Franklin's Nation." *New York Times*, December 14, 2010. https://www.nytimes.com/2010/12/14/opinion/14brooks.html.

Brooks, N. C. *A Complete History of the Mexican War: Its Causes, Conduct, and Consequences.* Philadelphia: Grigg, Elliot, 1849. https://archive.org/details/ completehistoryo01broo.

Brubaker, Jack. *Down the Susquehanna to the Chesapeake*. University Park: Pennsylvania State University Press, 2002.

Brunhouse, Robert L. *The Counter-revolution in Pennsylvania: 1776–1790*. Harrisburg: Pennsylvania Historical Commission, 1942. Reprint, New York: Octagon Books, 1971.

Buchman, Randall. *A Sorrowful Journey*. Defiance, OH: Defiance College Press, 2007.

Buck, Solon J., and Elizabeth Hawthorn Buck. *The Planting of Civilization in Western Pennsylvania*. Pittsburgh: University of Pittsburgh Press, 1939.

Burns, Harry. "Germ Theory: Invisible Killers Revealed." *British Medical Journal* 334, no. S1 (January 2007): S11. https://doi.org/10.1136/bmj.39044.597292.94.

Bushman, Richard L. "The Genteel Republic." *Wilson Quarterly* (Winter 2014). https://wilsonquarterly.com/quarterly/winter-2014-four-decades-of-classic-essays/the-genteel-republic/.

Butterfield, L. H. "The Jubilee of Independence July 4, 1826." *Virginia Magazine of History and Biography* 61, no. 2 (April 1953): 119–40. http://www.jstor.org/stable/4245917.

Byars, William Vincent, ed. *B. and M. Gratz: Merchants in Philadelphia, 1754–1798*. Jefferson City, MO: Hugh Stephens, 1916. https://catalog.hathitrust.org/Record/100319910.

———. "The Gratz Papers." *Publications of the American Jewish Historical Society* 23 (1915): 1–23. http://www.jstor.org/stable/43057967.

Cain, George W., transcriber. "A Biographical Sketch of Isaac Novinger and His Family." 1889. Dauphin County Geneology Resource Center. Accessed May 21, 2010. http://maley.net/DAUPHIN/OnlineData/collections/isaac-novinger.htm.

Caldwell, John. *William Findley from West of the Mountains: A Politician in Pennsylvania, 1783–1791*. Gig Harbor, WA: Red Apple, 2000.

Calkin, Homer L. "Pamphlets and Public Opinion during the American Revolution." *Pennsylvania Magazine of History and Biography* 64, no. 1 (January 1940): 22–42. https://www.jstor.org/stable/20087256.

Calloway, Colin G. *The American Revolution in Indian Country: Crisis and Diversity in Native American Communities*. Cambridge: Cambridge University Press, 1995.

———. *The Shawnees and the War for America*. New York: Viking, 2007.

Cammerhoff, John Christopher Frederick, and John W. Jordan. "Bishop J. C. F. Cammerhoff's Narrative of a Journey to Shamokin, Penna., in the Winter of 1748." *Pennsylvania Magazine of History and Biography* 29, no. 2 (1905): 160–79. http://www.jstor.org/stable/20085277.

Carlson, Robert E. "The Pennsylvania Improvement Society and Its Promotion of Canals and Railroads, 1824–1826." *Pennsylvania History* 31, no. 3 (July 1964): 295–310. https://www.jstor.org/stable/27770269.

Carter, Charles Frederick. *When Railroads Were New.* New York: Henry Holt, 1910. https://catalog.hathitrust.org/Record/000458933.

Carter, Edward C., II. "A 'Wild Irishman' under Every Federalist's Bed: Naturalization in Philadelphia, 1789–1806." *Pennsylvania Magazine of History and Biography* 94, no. 3 (July 1970): 331–46. http://jstor.org/stable/20090446.

Cashman, Sean Dennis. *America in the Gilded Age: From the Death of Lincoln to the Rise of Theodore Roosevelt.* 3rd ed. New York: New York University Press, 1984.

Cass, Lewis. "Removal of the Indians." *North American Review* 30, no. 66 (January 1830): 62–121. https://catalog.hathitrust.org/Record/100206040.

Caswell, Harriet S. *Our Life among the Iroquois.* Boston: Congregational Sunday School and Publishing Society, 1892. https://archive.org/details/ourlifeamongiroq00caswiala.

Catterall, Ralph C. H. *The Second Bank of the United States.* Chicago: University of Chicago Press, 1968. First published in 1902.

Champagne, Raymond W., Jr., and Thomas J. Rueter. "Jonathan Roberts and the 'War Hawk' Congress of 1811–1812." *Pennsylvania Magazine of History and Biography* 104, no. 4 (October 1980): 434–49. https://www.jstor.org/stable/20091512.

Chandler, Alfred D. "Anthracite Coal and the Beginnings of the Industrial Revolution in the United States." *Business History Review* 46, no. 2 (Summer 1972): 141–81. https://doi.org/10.2307/3113503.

Chandler, Joseph R. "Pen and Pencil Sketches of Living Merchants.—No. 1.—Thomas P. Cope, Esq., of Philadelphia." *Merchants' Magazine and Commercial Review* 20 (January–June 1849): 355–63. https://catalog.hathitrust.org/Record/011570218.

Chernow, Barbara A. "Robert Morris: Genesee Land Speculator." *New York History* 58, no. 2 (April 1977): 194–220. http://www.jstor.org/stable/23169915.

Chernow, Ron. *Grant.* New York: Penguin Press, 2017.

Churchill, Robert H. "Popular Nullification, Fries' Rebellion, and the Waning of Radical Republicanism, 1798–1801." *Pennsylvania History* 67, no. 1 (Winter 2000): 105–40. https://www.jstor.org/stable/27774249.

Churella, Albert J. *The Pennsylvania Railroad.* Philadelphia: University of Pennsylvania Press, 2013.

Clark, Martha Bladen. "Lazarus Stewart." *Journal of the Lancaster County Historical Society* 14, no. 10 (1910): 301–9. https://www.lancasterhistory.org/images/stories/JournalArticles/vol14no10pp301_309_235447.pdf.

Clinton Brown Company Architecture. *Historic Resources: Intensive Level Survey, Triangle Neighborhood.* Prepared for the City of Buffalo Urban Renewal Agency in conjunction with the Buffalo Preservation Board and New York State Office of Parks, Recreation, and Historic Preservation, May 2004.

Cobbett, William. *Porcupine's Works.* Vol. 9. London: Cobbett and Morgan, 1801. https://archive.org/details/porcupinesworks08cobbgoog.

Cockley, Marguerite, comp. "1796 Assessment Tax Somerset Co., Pa." Accessed June 24, 2020. http://www.ourfamilyhistories.com/hsdurbin/tax-lists/1796-pasomer-tax.html.

Coco, Gregory A. *A Strange and Blighted Land: Gettysburg: The Aftermath of a Battle.* Gettysburg, PA: Thomas, 1995.

Coleman, John F. *The Disruption of the Pennsylvania Democracy, 1848–1860.* Harrisburg: Pennsylvania Historical and Museum Commission, 1975.

"Colonial America's Pre-Industrial Age of Wood and Water." Building Community: Medieval Technology and American History. Accessed June 24, 2020. http://www.engr.psu.edu/mtah/articles/colonial_wood_water.htm.

Commons, John R., David J. Saposs, Helen L. Sumner, E. B. Mittelman, H. E. Hoagland, John B. Andrews, and Selig Perlman. *History of Labour in the United States.* Vol. 2. New York: Macmillan, 1918.

Conable, Mary H. "A Steady Enemy: The Ogden Land Company and the Seneca Indians." PhD diss., University of Rochester, 1994.

Conover, George S. *Sayenqueraghta, King of the Senecas.* Waterloo, NY: Observer Steam Job Printing House, 1885. https://catalog.hathitrust.org/Record/100381950.

Cook, Frederick, ed. *Journals of the Military Expedition of Major John Sullivan against the Six Nations of Indians in 1779.* Auburn, NY: Knapp, Peck and Thomson, 1887. https://catalog.hathitrust.org/Record/000362150.

Cooke, Jacob E. "The Whiskey Insurrection: A Re-evaluation." *Pennsylvania History* 30, no. 3 (July 1963): 316–46. http://www.jstor.org/stable/27770195.

Cooper, Thomas. *An Account of the Trial of Thomas Cooper, of Northumberland: On a Charge of Libel against the President of the United States.* Philadelphia: J. Bioren, 1800. https://archive.org/details/DKC0017.

Copeland, David A. "How Newspapers Covered the French and Indian War." Accessed September 12, 2020. https://www.varsitytutors.com/earlyamerica/early-america-review/volume-2/how-newspapers-covered-the-french-and-indian-war.

Cornell, Saul. "Mobs, Militias, and Magistrates: Popular Constitutionalism and the Whiskey Rebellion." *Chicago-Kent Law Review* 81, no. 3 (2006): 883–903. https://scholarship.kentlaw.iit.edu/cklawreview/vol81/iss3/6/.

Craft, Rev. David. "The Expedition of Col. Thomas Hartley against the Indians in 1778, to Avenge the Massacre of Wyoming." In Vol. 9, *Proceedings and Collections of the Wyoming Historical and Geological Society*, edited by Rev. Horace Edwin Hayden, 189–216. Wilkes-Barr, PA: E. B. Yordy, 1905. https://books.google.com/books?id=vbmEVD8Eb1MC.

Criminal Case Files of the US Circuit Court for the Eastern District of Pennsylvania, 1791–1840. National Archives Microfilm Publication M986. https://www.archives.gov/digitization/digitized-by-partners.

Crist, Robert Grant. "Highwater 1863: The Confederate Approach to Harrisburg." *Pennsylvania History* 30, no. 2 (April 1963): 158–83. https://www.jstor.org/stable/27770174.

"Currency Converter: 1270–2017." National Archives. March 2, 2020. http://www.nationalarchives.gov.uk/currency/results.asp#mid.

Current, Richard N. "Love, Hate, and Thaddeus Stevens." *Pennsylvania History* 14, no. 4 (October 1947): 259–72. https://www.jstor.org/stable/27766829.

Davis, Jeffrey A. "Guarding the Republican Interest: The Western Pennsylvania Democratic Societies and the Excise Tax." *Pennsylvania History* 67, no. 1 (Winter 2000): 43–62. https://www.jstor.org/stable/27774247.

Deane, Ruthven. "Abundance of the Passenger Pigeon in Pennsylvania in 1850." *The Auk* 48, no. 2 (April 1931): 264–265. https://sora.unm.edu/sites/default/files/journals/auk/v048n02/p0264-p0265.pdf.

Dearborn, Henry A. S. "Journals of Henry A. S. Dearborn." In Vol. 7, *Publications of the Buffalo Historical Society*, edited by Frank H. Severance, 35–228. Buffalo, NY: Buffalo Historical Society, 1904. https://archive.org/details/publicationsbuf07socigoog.

DeLancey, Edward F. "Mount Washington and Its Capture on the 16th of November, 1776." *Magazine of American History* 1, no. 2 (February 1877): 65–90, https://catalog.hathitrust.org/Record/000550040.

Dennis, Matthew. *Cultivating a Landscape of Peace: Iroquois-European Encounters in Seventeenth-Century America*. Ithaca, NY: Cornell University Press, 1993.

———. *Seneca Possessed: Indians, Witchcraft, and Power in the Early American Republic*. Philadelphia: University of Pennsylvania Press, 2010.

Densmore, Christopher. *Red Jacket: Iroquois Diplomat and Orator*. Syracuse, NY: Syracuse University Press, 1999.

Derickson, Alan. *Black Lung: Anatomy of a Public Health Disaster*. Ithaca, NY: Cornell University Press, 1998.

Devine, Francis E. "The Pennsylvania Flying Camp, July–November, 1776." *Pennsylvania History* 46, no. 1 (January 1979): 59–78. https://www.jstor.org/stable/27772569.

Dixon, David. *Never Come to Peace Again: Pontiac's Uprising and the Fate of the British Empire in North America.* Norman: University of Oklahoma Press, 2005.

Doddridge, Joseph. *Notes on the Settlement and Indian Wars.* Pittsburgh, PA: John S. Ritenour and Wm. T. Lindsey, 1912. https://archive.org/details/notesonsettlemen00doddrich.

Downes, Randolph C. *Council Fires on the Upper Ohio: A Narrative of Indian Affairs in the Upper Ohio Valley until 1795.* London: Baker & Taylor, 1989.

Drury, Bob, and Tom Clavin. *The Heart of Everything That Is: The Untold Story of Red Cloud, An American Legend.* New York: Simon Schuster, 2013.

Duane, William J. *Letters Addressed to the People of Pennsylvania Respecting the Internal Improvement of the Commonwealth by Means of Roads and Canals.* Philadelphia: Jane Aitken, 1811. https://catalog.hathitrust.org/Record/000964349.

Duffy, Thomas P. "The Flexner Report—100 Years Later." *Yale Journal of Biology and Medicine* 84, no. 3 (September 2011): 269–76. https://www.ncbi.nlm.nih.gov/pmc/articles/PMC3178858.

Dunaway, Wayland F. *The Scotch-Irish of Colonial Pennsylvania.* Chapel Hill: University of North Carolina Press, 1944.

Earle, Alice Morse. *Home Life in Colonial Days.* New York: Macmillan, 1917. https://archive.org/details/homelifeincoloni00earl.

Egge, Marion F. *Pennsylvania German Roots across the Ocean.* Philadelphia: Genealogical Society of Pennsylvania, 2000.

Eggert, Gerald G. "'Seeing Sam': The Know Nothing Episode in Harrisburg." *Pennsylvania Magazine of History and Biography* 111, no. 3 (July 1987): 305–40. https://www.jstor.org/stable/20092119.

Egle, William Henry. *Col. Timothy Green, of the Army of the Revolution.* Harrisburg, PA: George Bergner, 1874. https://archive.org/details/timothy_green.

———, ed. *Commemorative Biographical Encyclopedia of Dauphin County Pennsylvania Containing Sketches of Prominent and Representative Citizens and Many of the Early Scotch-Irish and German Settlers.* Chambersburg, PA: J. M. Runk, 1896. https://archive.org/details/commemorativebio00jmru.

———. *History of the Counties of Dauphin and Lebanon in the Commonwealth of Pennsylvania: Biographical and Genealogical.* Philadelphia: Everts & Peck, 1883. https://archive.org/details/historyofcountie01egle.

———. *An Illustrated History of the Commonwealth of Pennsylvania: Civil, Political, and Military.* Harrisburg, PA: De Witt C. Goodrich, 1876. https://archive.org/details/illustratedhisto02egle.

———. *Notes and Queries: Historical, Biographical, and Geneological, Chiefly Relating to Interior Pennsylvania.* 3rd ser. Vol. 1. Harrisburg, PA: Daily Telegraph Print, 1887. https://books.google.com/books?id=Z-gUAAAAYAAJ.

———. *Notes and Queries: Historical, Biographical, and Geneological, Chiefly Relating to Interior Pennsylvania.* 3rd ser. Vol. 2. Harrisburg, PA: Harrisburg, 1891. https://books.google.com/books?id=rugUAAAAYAAJ.

———. *Notes and Queries: Historical, Biographical, and Genealogical: Relating Chiefly to Interior Pennsylvania.* 4th ser. Vol. 2. Harrisburg, PA: Harrisburg, 1895. https://books.google.com/books/?id=1dQUAAAAYAAJ.

———. *Notes and Queries: Historical and Genealogical, Chiefly Relating to Interior Pennsylvania.* Vol 1. Harrisburg, PA: Harrisburg, 1895. https://books.google.com/books?id=mixBAQAAMAAJ.

———. *Notes and Queries: Historical and Genealogical, Chiefly Relating to Interior Pennsylvania.* Vol. 3. Harrisburg, PA: Harrisburg, 1896. https://books.google.com/books?id=tNQUAAAAYAAJ.

———. *Pennsylvania Genealogies: Scotch-Irish and German.* Harrisburg, PA: Lane S. Hart, 1886. https://books.google.com/books/?id=d7_akH9VO_cC.

Egle, William Henry, and Joseph Ritner. "The Buckshot War." *Pennsylvania Magazine of History and Biography* 23, no. 2 (1899): 137–56. https://www.jstor.org/stable/20085847.

Eisenhower, John S. D. *So Far From God: The U.S. War with Mexico, 1846–1848.* Norman: University of Oklahoma Press, 2000.

Elliott, D. L., C. G. Holladay, W. R. Barchet, H. P. Foote, and W. F. Sandusky. *Wind Energy Resource Atlas of the United States.* Golden, CO: Solar Technical Information Program, Solar Energy Research Institute, 1986. http://rredc.nrel.gov/wind/pubs/atlas/atlas_index.html.

Ellis, Joseph J. *American Creation: Triumphs and Tragedies at the Founding of the Republic.* New York: Alfred A. Knopf, 2007.

Elting, John R. *Amateurs, to Arms!: A Military History of the War of 1812.* Chapel Hill, NC: Algonquin Books of Chapel Hill, 1991.

Empire State Society of the Sons of the American Revolution, with Reginald Pelham Bolton. *Fort Washington: An Account of the Identification of the Site of Fort Washington, New York City, and the Erection and Dedication of a Monument thereon Nov. 16, 1901.* New York: Empire State Society of the Sons of the American Revolution, 1902. https://catalog.hathitrust.org/Record/000362425.

Eshleman, H. Frank. "Items of Local Interest from the Pennsylvania Gazette, from 1761 to 1770." *Historical Papers and Addresses of the Lancaster County Historical Society* 24 (1920): 5–23. https://catalog.hathitrust.org/Record/000051657.

———. *Lancaster County Indians: Annals of the Susquehannocks and Other Indian Tribes of the Susquehanna Territory from About the Year 1500 to*

1763, the Date of Their Extinction. Lancaster, PA: Express Printing, 1908.
https://catalog.hathitrust.org/Record/008981995.

Evans, Lyle S., ed. *A Standard History of Ross County, Ohio.* Vol. 2. Chicago:
Lewis, 1917. https://archive.org/details/oh-ross-1917-evans-2.

Evans, Griffith, and Hallock F. Raup. "Notes and Documents: Journal of Griffith
Evans, 1784–1785." *Pennsylvania Magazine of History and Biography* 65, no.
2 (April 1941): 202–33. https://www.jstor.org/stable/20087373.

Evarts, Jeremiah. *Essays on the Present Crisis in the Condition of the American
Indians: First Published in the National Intelligencer, under the Signature of
William Penn.* Boston: Perkins & Marvin, 1829. https://archive.org/details/
essaysonpresentc00evar.

Everett, Edward. "John Smilie, Forgotten Champion of Early Western Pennsylvania." *Western Pennsylvania Historical Magazine* 33, nos. 3–4 (September–December 1950): 77–89. https://journals.psu.edu/wph/article/
view/2356/2189.

Ewing, William S. "Indian Captives Released by Colonel Bouquet." *Western
Pennsylvania History Magazine* 39, no. 3 (Fall 1956): 187–203. https://
journals.psu.edu/wph/article/view/2529.

Fairbairn, William. *Treatise on Mills and Millwork, Part I: On the Principles
of Mechanism and on Prime Movers.* 3rd ed. London: Longmans, Green,
1871. https://catalog.hathitrust.org/Record/011613805.

Fenn, Elizabeth. *Encounters at the Heart of the World: A History of the Mandan
People.* New York: Hill and Wang, 2014.

Fennell, Dorothy E. "From Rebelliousness to Insurrection: A Social History of
the Whiskey Rebellion, 1765–1802." PhD diss., University of Pittsburgh,
1981.

Fenton, William N. *The Great Law and the Longhouse: A Political History of
the Iroquois Confederacy.* Norman: University of Oklahoma Press, 1998.

Ferguson, E. James. *The Power of the Purse: A History of American Public
Finance, 1776–1790.* Chapel Hill: University of North Carolina Press, 1961.

Ferling, John. *A Leap in the Dark: The Struggle to Create the American Republic.*
Oxford: Oxford University Press, 2003.

Fike, Jean. *Terrestrial & Palustrine Plant Communities of Pennsylvania.* Harrisburg: Pennsylvania Department of Conservation and Natural Resources,
1999. http://www.naturalheritage.state.pa.us/fikebook.aspx.

Findley, William. *History of the Insurrection in the Four Western Counties of
Pennsylvania in the Year M.DCC.XCIV: With a Recital of the Circumstances
Specifically Connected Therewith, and an Historical Review of the Previous
Situation of the Country.* Philadelphia: Samuel Harrison Smith, 1796.
https://archive.org/details/historyinsurrec00findgoog.

Fischer, David Hackett. *Albion's Seed: Four British Folkways in America.* New York: Oxford University Press, 1989.

———. *Washington's Crossing.* New York: Oxford University Press, 2004.

Fish, Sydney M. *Barnard and Michael Gratz: Their Lives and Times.* Lanham, MD: University Press of America, 1994.

Fisher, H. L. *Olden Times: or, Pennsylvania Rural Life, Some Fifty Years Ago, and Other Poems.* York, PA: Fisher Bros., 1888. https://archive.org/details/oldentimesorpenn00fish.

Fiske, John. *The American Revolution.* Vols. 1–2 Boston: Houghton Mifflin, 1891. https://archive.org/details/americanrevoluti010168mbp.

Fitch, John A. "Labor in the Steel Industry: The Human Side of Large Outputs." *Annals of the American Academy of Political and Social Science* 33, no. 2 (March 1909): 83–91. https://www.jstor.org/stable/1011566.

Fleming, James, Jr. "Contributory Negligence." *Yale Law Journal* 62 (April 1953): 691–735. https://digitalcommons.law.yale.edu/fss_papers/3077/.

Flexner, Abraham. *Medical Education in the United States and Canada: A Report to the Carnegie Foundation for the Advancement of Teaching.* Boston: D. B. Updike, Merrymount Press, 1910. http://archive.carnegiefoundation.org/pdfs/elibrary/Carnegie_Flexner_Report.pdf.

Foner, Eric. *Forever Free: The Story of Emancipation and Reconstruction.* New York: Knopf, 2005.

Foner, Philip S. *History of the Labor Movement in the United States.* Vol. 1. New York: International, 1947.

Force, Peter. *American Archives.* 6 series. Washington, DC: M. St. Claire Clarke and Peter Force, 1837–1853. https://catalog.hathitrust.org/Record/000346548.

Ford, Worthington C., ed. *Journals of the Continental Congress, 1774–1875.* Washington, DC: Government Printing Office, 1904–1937. http://memory.loc.gov/ammem/amlaw/lwjc.html.

Frantz, John B., and William Pencak, eds. *Beyond Philadelphia: The American Revolution in the Pennsylvania Hinterland.* University Park: Pennsylvania State University Press, 1998.

Franz, George W. *Paxton, a Study of Community Structure and Mobility in the Colonial Pennsylvania Backcountry.* New York: Garland, 1989.

Frear, Ned. *The Whiskey Rebellion.* Bedford, PA: Frear, 1999.

Freeman, Douglas S. *George Washington.* Vol. 4. New York: Scribner 1951. Reprint, Fairfield, NJ: Augustus M. Kelley, 1981.

Freese, Barbara. *Coal: A Human History.* Cambridge, MA: Perseus, 2003.

Gallagher, John J. *The Battle of Brooklyn, 1776.* Edison, NJ: Castle Books, 2002.

Gallatin, Albert. *The Speech of Albert Gallatin, a Representative from the*

County of Fayette, in the House of Representatives of the General Assembly of Pennsylvania on the Important Question Touching the Validity of the Elections in the Four Western Counties of the State. Philadelphia: William W. Woodward, 1795. https://digital.library.pitt.edu/islandora/object/pitt:31735056287380.

Ganter, Granville, ed. *The Collected Speeches of Sagoyewatha, or Red Jacket.* Syracuse, NY: Syracuse University Press, 2006.

———. "Red Jacket and the Decolonization of Republican Virtue." *American Indian Quiarterly* 31, no. 4 (Fall 2007): 559–81. http://www.jstor.org/stable/30113977.

Gass, Patrick. *A Journal of the Voyages and Travels of a Corps of Discovery.* Pittsburgh, PA: David M'Keehan, 1808. https://archive.org/details/cihm_57517.

Geiser, Karl Frederick. "Redemptioners and Indentured Servants in the Colony and Commonwealth of Pennsylvania." Supplement, *Yale Review* 10, no. 2 (August 1901). https://archive.org/details/redemptionersind01geis.

Genealogical and Biographical Annals of Northumberland County, Pennsylvania. Chicago: J. L. Floyd, 1911. https://archive.org/details/genealogicalbiog-00floy.

Genetin-Pilawa, C. Joseph. *Crooked Paths to Allotment: The Fight over Federal Indian Policy after the Civil War.* Chapel Hill: University of North Carolina Press, 2012.

Gerrity, Frank. "The Masons, the Antimasons, and the Pennsylvania Legislature, 1834–1836." *Pennsylvania Magazine of History and Biography* 99, no. 2 (April 1975): 180–206. https://www.jstor.org/stable/20090944.

Gibson, James E., John Morton, John Hancock, Dan'l Roberdeau, Henry Haller, Charles Shoemaker, Joseph Heister, Mark Bird, and Thos. McKean. "The Pennsylvania Provincial Conference of 1776." *Pennsylvania Magazine of History and Biography* 58, no. 4 (1934): 312–41. http://www.jstor.org/stable/20086878.

Gienapp, William E. "Nebraska, Nativism, and Rum: The Failure of Fusion in Pennsylvania, 1854." *Pennsylvania Magazine of History and Biography* 109, no. 4 (October 1985): 425–71. https://www.jstor.org/stable/20091960.

Glatfelter, Charles H. "The Eighteenth Century German Lutheran and Reformed Clergymen in the Susquehanna Valley." *Pennsylvania History* 20, no. 1 (January 1953): 57–68. https://www.jstor.org/stable/27769384.

Goldman, Mark. *City on the Edge: Buffalo, New York.* Amherst, NY: Prometheus Books, 2007.

———. *High Hopes: The Rise and Decline of Buffalo, New York.* Albany: State University of New York Press, 1983.

Goloboy, Jennifer L. "The Early American Middle Class." *Journal of the*

Early Republic 25, no. 4 (Winter 2005): 537–45. https://www.jstor.org/stable/30043362.

Good, James I. "The German Reformed Church in Colonial America." Reformed Church in the United Staes, April 4, 2009. http://www.rcus.org/reformed-colonial.

Gordon, George H. *Brook Farm to Cedar Mountain in the War of the Great Rebellion, 1861–62*. Boston: Houghton Mifflin, 1885. https://catalog.hathitrust.org/Record/006578765.

Gordon, Michael A. *The Orange Riots: Irish Political Violence in New York City, 1870 and 1871*. Ithaca, NY: Cornell University Press, 1993.

Gould, William. "Journal of Major William Gould, of the New Jersey Infantry, during an Expedition into Pennsylvania in 1794." *Proceedings of the New Jersey Historical Society* 3 (1848–1849): 175–91. https://catalog.hathitrust.org/Record/000053736.

Govan, Thomas P. "Fundamental Issues of the Bank War." *Pennsylvani Magazine of History and Biography* 82, no. 3 (July 1958): 305–15. http://www.jstor.org/stable/20089097.

Grann, David. *Killers of the Flower Moon: The Osage Murders and the Birth of the FBI*. New York: Doubleday, 2017.

Gray, Ralph D. "Philadelphia and the Chesapeake and Delaware Canal, 1769–1823." *Pennsylvania Magazine of History and Biography* 84, no. 4 (October 1960): 401–23. https://www.jstor.org/stable/20089334.

Graydon, Alexander. *Memoirs of a Life, Chiefly Passed in Pennsylvania, within the Last Sixty Years*. Edinburgh: William Blackwood, 1822. https://archive.org/details/memoirsalifechi00galtgoog.

Graymont, Barbara. *The Iroquois in the American Revolution*. Syracuse, NY: Syracuse University Press, 1972.

Greene, Homer. *Coal and the Coal Mines*. Boston: Houghton Mifflin, 1889. https://archive.org/details/coalandcoalmine00greegoog.

Greiner, Robert C. *Descendants of James Woodside of Dauphin County, PA*. Laurel, MD: Robert C. Greiner, 1994.

Griffin, Patrick. *American Leviathan: Empire, Nation, and Revolutionary Frontier*. New York: Hill and Wang, 2007.

Guyton, Gregory P. "A Brief History of Workers' Compensation." *Iowa Orthopaedic Journal* 19 (1999): 106–10. https://www.ncbi.nlm.nih.gov/pmc/articles/PMC1888620.

Hackenburg, Randy W. *Pennsylvania in the War with Mexico*. Shippensburg, PA: White Main, 1992.

Hain, H. H. *History of Perry County, Pennsylvania, Including Descriptions of Indian and Pioneer Life from the Time of Earliest Settlement*. Harrisburg,

PA: Hain-Moore, 1922. https://archive.org/details/historyofperryco00hain.

Hanley, Boniface, OFM. "The Story of Servant of God Isaac Hecker." Paulist Fathers. Accessed June 25, 2020. http://www.paulist.org/who-we-are/our-history/isaac-hecker.

Hansel, William Usher. "The Scotch-Irish." *Historical Papers and Addresses of the Lancaster County Historical Society* 9 (1904–1905): 246–66. https://books.google.com/books?id=5A08AAAAIAAJ.

Harbaugh, Rev. H. *The Fathers of the German Reformed Church in Europe and America.* Vol. 2. Lancaster, PA: J. M. Westhaeffer, 1872. https://archive.org/details/fathersofgermanr02harb.

Harper, R. Eugene. *The Transformation of Western Pennsylvania, 1770–1800.* Pittsburgh: University of Pittsburgh Press, 1991.

Harris, George H. "The Life of Horatio Jones." In Vol. 6, *Publications of the Buffalo Historical Society,* edited by Frank H. Severance, 383–514. Buffalo, NY: Buffalo Historical Society, 1904. https://books.google.com/books?id=6k1D7OfDd04C.

Harrison, Eliza Cope, ed. *Philadelphia Merchant: The Diary of Thomas P. Cope, 1800–1851.* South Bend, IN: Gateway Editions, 1978.

Hauptman, Laurence M. *Conspiracy of Interests: Iroquois Dispossession and the Rise of New York State.* Syracuse, NY: Syracuse University Press, 1999.

———. *Seven Generations of Iroquois Leadership: The Six Nations since 1800.* Syracuse, NY: Syracuse University Press, 2008.

———. *The Tonawanda Senecas' Heroic Battle against Removal.* Albany: State University of New York Press, 2011.

Hawke, David. *In the Midst of a Revolution: The Politics of Confrontation in Colonial America.* Philadelphia: University of Pennsylvania Press, 1961.

Haynes, Sam W. *James K. Polk and the Expansionist Impulse.* New York: Longman, 1997.

Haywood, William D. *Bill Haywood's Book: The Autobiography of William D. Haywood.* New York: International, 1929.

Hazard, Samuel, ed. *The Register of Pennsylvania.* 16 vols. Philadelphia: Wm. F. Geddes, 1828–1835. https://catalog.hathitrust.org/Record/008730775.

Hecker, Father Isaac. "Infallibility." *Catholic World,* August 1871, 577–93. https://books.google.com/books/reader?id=yBU4AQAAIAAJ.

Heckewelder, John Gottlieb Ernestus. *A Narrative of the Mission of the United Brethren among the Delaware and Mohegan Indians.* Philadelphia: McCarty & Davis, 1820. https://archive.org/details/narrativeofmissi00heck.

Henderson, Dwight F. "Treason, Sedition, and Fries' Rebellion." *American Journal of Legal History* 14, no. 4 (October 1970): 308–18. https://www.jstor.org/stable/844332.

Henderson, Elizabeth K. "The Attack on the Judiciary in Pennsylvania, 1800–1810." *Pennsylvania Magazine of History and Biography* 61, no. 2 (April 1937): 113–36. http://www.jstor.org/stable/20087035.

Henderson, Rodger C. "Demographic Patterns and Family Structure in Eighteenth-Century Lancaster County, Pennsylvania." *Pennsylvania Magazine of History and Biography* 114, no. 3 (July 1990): 349–83. http://www.jstor.org/stable/20092502.

Hennessy, John J. *Return to Bull Run: The Campaign and Battle of Second Manassas.* Norman: University of Oklahoma Press, 1999.

Henning, D. C. *Tales of the Blue Mountains: Indian Paths.* Vol. 3, *Publications of the Historical Society of Schuylkill County.* Pottsville, PA: Daily Republican Book Rooms, 1911. https://archive.org/details/publicationsofhi03hist.

Hibbert, Christopher. *Redcoats and Rebels: The American Revolution through British Eyes.* New York: Norton, 1990.

Hickey, Donald R. *The War of 1812: A Forgotten Conflict.* Bicentennial ed. Urbana: University of Illinois Press, 2012.

Higginbotham, Sanford W. *The Keystone in the Democratic Arch: Pennsylvania Politics, 1800–1816.* Harrisburg: Pennsylvania Historical and Museum Commission, 1952.

Hill, Henry Wayland. *Municipality of Buffalo, New York: A History, 1720–1923.* Vol. 1. New York: Lewis Historical, 1923.

Hindman, Hugh D. *Child Labor: An American History.* Armonk, NY: M. E. Sharpe, 2002.

History of Bedford, Somerset, and Fulton Counties, Pennsylvania, with Illustrations and Biographical Sketches of Some of Its Pioneers and Prominent Men. Chicago: Waterman, Watkins, 1884. https://catalog.hathitrust.org/Record/008726291.

History of Crawford County and Ohio. Chicago: Baskin & Battey, 1881. https://archive.org/details/historyofcrawfor00bask.

The History of Wyandot County, Ohio. Chicago: Leggett, Conaway, 1884. https://archive.org/details/historyofwyandot00legg.

Hoffer, Peter Charles. *The Free Press Crisis of 1800: Thomas Cooper's Trial for Seditious Libel.* Lawrence: University Press of Kansas, 2011.

Hogeland, William. *The Whiskey Rebellion: George Washington, Alexander Hamilton, and the Frontier Rebels Who Challenged America's Newfound Sovereignty.* New York: Simon Schuster, 2006.

Holt, Michael F. "The Politics of Impatience: The Origins of Know Nothingism." *Journal of American History* 60, no. 2 (September 1973): 309–31. https://www.jstor.org/stable/2936778.

Holt, Wythe. "The Whiskey Rebellion of 1794: A Democratic Working-Class

Insurrection." Paper presented at the Georgia Workshop in Early American History and Culture, Athens, GA, 2004. https://web.archive.org/web/20110925091324/http://www.uga.edu/colonialseminar/whiskeyrebellion-6.pdf.

Holton, James L. *The Reading Railroad: History of a Coal Age Empire, Volume 1: The Nineteenth Century.* Laury's Station, PA: Garrigues House, 1989.

Holton, Woody. *Unruly Americans and the Origins of the Constitution.* New York: Hill and Wang, 2007.

Homrighaus, Barbara Knox. *Dangerous Work Must Be Done: Oral Histories of Child Labor.* Pottsville, PA: Schuylkill County Council for the Arts, 1987.

Houghton, Frederick. "History of the Buffalo Creek Reservation." In Vol. 24, *Publications of the Buffalo Historical Society,* edited by Frank H. Severance, 3–181. Buffalo, NY: Buffalo Historical Society, 1920. https://catalog.hathitrust.org/Record/001636698.

Howe, Daniel Walker. *What God Hath Wrought: The Transformation of America, 1815–1848.* New York: Oxford University Press, 2007.

Humphries, Jane. "Childhood and Child Labour in the British Industrial Revolution." *Economic History Review* 66, no. 2 (May 2013): 395–418. https://www.jstor.org/stable/i40112158.

Hurd, Jill J. *The Ancestors and Descendants of Jan Lucken.* Baltimore: Gateway Press, 1989.

Husband, David. *Recollections of Somerset County's Earliest Years.* Compiled by Ronald G. Bruner. Rockwood, PA: Somerset County Historical and Genealogical Society, 2005. First published in the *Somerset Standard,* 1870.

Huston, James L. "The Demise of the Pennsylvania American Party, 1854–1858." *Pennsylvania Magazine of History and Biography* 109, no. 4 (October 1985): 473–97. https://www.jstor.org/stable/20091961.

Ireland, Owen S. "The Invention of American Democracy: The Pennsylvania Federalists and the New Republic." *Pennsylvania History* 67, no. 1 (Winter 2000): 161–71. https://www.jstor.org/stable/27774251.

———. "The People's Triumph: The Federalist Majority in Pennsylvania, 1787–1788." *Pennsylvania History* 56, no. 2 (April 1989): 93–113. https://www.jstor.org/stable/27773296.

———. *Religion, Ethnicity, and Politics: Ratifying the Constitution in Pennsylvania.* University Park: Pennsylvania State University Press, 1995.

Jaeger, Katherine. "The Molly Maguires of Northumberland County." April 2001. http://files.usgwarchives.net/pa/northumberland/areahistory/Mollymag.txt.

James, Alfred Procter, ed. *Writings of General John Forbes Relating to His Service in North America.* Menasha, WI: Collegiate Press, 1938. https://catalog.hathitrust.org/Record/000361863.

Jamieson, Patrick C. "Foreign Criticisms of the 1871 Paris Commune: The Role of British and American Newspapers and Periodicals." *Intersections* 11, no. 1 (Summer 2010): 100–115. https://depts.washington.edu/chid/intersections_Summer_2010/Patrick_Jamieson_Foreign_Criticisms_of_the_1871_Paris_Commune.pdf.

Jensen, Merrill. *The Articles of Confederation: An Interpretation of the Social-Constitutional History of the American Revolution, 1774–1781.* Madison: University of Wisconsin Press, 1940.

Jensen, Merrill, John P. Kaminski, and Gaspare Saladino, eds. *The Documentary History of the Ratification of the Constitution: Ratification of the Constitution by the States: Pennsylvania.* Vol. 2. Madison: Wisconsin Historical Society Press, 1976.

Jensen, Richard. "No Irish Need Apply: A Myth of Victimization." *Journal of Social History* 36, no. 2 (Winter 2002): 405–29. https://www.jstor.org/stable/3790116.

John, Andrew. "Response by John Andrew." In *A History of the Treaty of Big Tree,* edited by the Livingston County Historical Society, 57–60. Dansville, NY: Livingston County Historical Society, 1904. https://archive.org/stream/historyoftreatyo00livi#page/n3/mode/2up.

Johnson, Walter R. "Report of an Examination of the Bear Valley Coal District in Dauphin County, Pennsylvania." In *Report of a Survey and Exploration of the Coal and Ore Lands Belonging to the Allegheny Coal Company, in Somerset County, Pennsylvania,* 16–17. Philadelphia: Joseph & William Kite, 1841. https://books.google.com/books?id=OWE9AAAAYAAJ.

Johnston, Henry P. *Memoirs of the Long Island Historical Society, Vol. 3: The Campaign of 1776 around New York and Brooklyn.* Brooklyn: Long Island Historical Society, 1878. https://archive.org/details/campaignaroundn-00johngoog.

Jones, Mark H. "Herman Husband: Millenarian, Carolina Regulator, and Whiskey Rebel." PhD diss., Northern Illinois University, 1982.

Jordan, Brian Matthew. *Marching Home: Union Veterans and Their Unending Civil War.* New York: Liveright, 2014.

Jordan, Donald E. *Land and Popular Politics in Ireland: County Mayo from the Plantation to the Land Wars.* Cambridge: Cambridge University Press, 1994.

Jordan, John W., ed. *Colonial and Revolutionary Families of Pennsylvania.* Vol. 1. New York: Lewis, 1911. https://archive.org/details/colonialrevoluti01jord.

Journal of the Forty-Ninth House of Representatives of the Commonwealth of Pennsylvania. Harrisburg, PA: Boas & Coplan, 1838–1839. https://catalog.hathitrust.org/Record/100744482.

Journal of the Forty-Seventh House of Representatives of the Commonwealth of

Pennsylvania. Harrisburg, PA: Samuel D. Patterson, 1836–1837. https://
catalog.hathitrust.org/Record/100744482.

Journal of the House of Representatives of the United States. Washington, DC:
Government Printing Office, 1789–1875. https://memory.loc.gov/ammem/
amlaw/lwhj.html.

*Journal of the Senate of the Commonwealth of Pennsylvania, Session 1842, Con-
taining the Canal Commissioners Report and Accompanying Documents.*
Vol. 3. Harrisburg, PA: Boas & Patterson, 1842. https://books.google.com/
books?id=Rf1BAQAAMAAJ.

*Journal of the Sixty-Fourth House of Representatives of the Commonwealth of
Pennsylvania.* Harrisburg, PA: A. Boyd Hamilton, 1854.

*Journal of the Thirtieth House of Representatives of the Commonwealth of
Pennsylvania, Commenced at Harrisburg, Tuesday the Seventh of December, in the Year of Our Lord One Thousand Eight Hundred Nineteen.* Harrisburg, PA: James Peacock, 1819–1820. https://catalog.hathitrust.org/
Record/100744482.

*Journal of the Thirty-First House of Representatives of the Commonwealth of
Pennsylvania, Commenced at Harrisburg, Tuesday the Fifth of December, in
the Year of Our Lord, One Thousand Eight Hundred Twenty.* Harrisburgh,
PA: Hamilton & M'Ilwaine, 1820–1821. https://catalog.hathitrust.org/
Record/100744482.

Joy, Mark S. *American Expansionism, 1783–1860: A Manifest Destiny?* London:
Pearson/Longman, 2003.

Kalm, Peter. *Travels into North America; Containing Its Natural History, and a
Circumstantial Account of Its Plantations and Agriculture in General, with
the Civil, Ecclesiastical, and Commercial State of the Country, the Manners
of Its Inhabitants, and Several Curiou.* Warrington, England: William Eyres,
1770. https://archive.org/details/travelsintonorth01inkalm.

Kapp, Freidrich. *The Life of Frederick William von Steuben, Major General in
the Revolutionary Army.* New York: Mason Brothers, 1859. https://archive.
org/details/lifeoffrederickw00kappuoft.

Kappler, Charles Joseph, ed. *Indian Affairs: Laws and Treaties.* Vol. 2. Washington, DC: Government Printing Office, 1904. https://catalog.hathitrust.
org/Record/000084638.

Karsten, Peter. "Enabling the Poor to Have Their Day in Court: The Sanctioning
of Contingency Fee Contracts, a History to 1940." *DePaul Law Review*
47 (1998): 231–60. https://via.library.depaul.edu/law-review/vol47/iss2/3/.

Keet, James H., Jr. "Contributory Negligence of Children." *Cleveland-Marshall
Law Review* 12 (1963): 395–411. https://engagedscholarship.csuohio.edu/
clevstlrev/vol12/iss3/2/.

Keil, Thomas J., and Wayne M. Usui. "The Family Wage System in Pennsylvania's Anthracite Region: 1850–1900." *Social Forces* 67, no. 1 (September 1988): 185–205. https://doi.org/10.2307/2579106.

Keintz, Robert W. "Wiconisco Canal Issue." *Canal Currents: Bulletin of the Pennsylvania Canal Society* (Spring 1988): 2.

Kelker, Luther Reily. *History of Dauphin County: With Genealogical Memoirs.* Vol. 3. New York: Lewis, 1907. https://catalog.hathitrust.org/Record/011262520.

Keller, Kenneth W. "Cultural Conflict in Early Nineteenth-Century Pennsylvania Politics." *Pennsylvania Magazine of History and Biography* 110, no. 4 (October 1986): 509–30. http://www.jstor.org/stable/20092043.

Kelley, Florence. *Our Toiling Children.* Chicago: Women's Temperance Publication Association, 1889. http://nrs.harvard.edu/urn-3:FHCL:409534.

Kenny, Kevin. *The American Irish.* Essex, UK: Longman, 2000.

———. *Making Sense of the Molly Maguires.* New York: Oxford University Press, 1998.

———. "The 'Molly Maguires,' the Ancient Order of Hibernians, and the Bloody Summer of 1875." *Pennsylvania Legacies* 14, no. 2 (Fall 2014): 18–25.

———, ed. *New Directions in Irish-American History.* Madison: University of Wisconsin Press, 2003.

———. *Peaceable Kingdom Lost: The Paxton Boys and the Destruction of William Penn's Holy Experiment.* Oxford: Oxford University Press, 2009.

Kent, Donald H. "The Erie War of the Gauges." *Pennsylvania History* 15, no. 4 (October 1948): 253–75. https://www.jstor.org/stable/27766942.

Kenyon, Cecelia M. "Republicanism and Radicalism in the American Revolution: An Old-Fashioned Interpretation." *William and Mary Quarterly* 19, no. 2 (April 1962): 153–82. https://doi.org/10.2307/1921921.

Ketcham, Ralph, ed. *The Anti-Federalist Papers; and, the Constitutional Convention Debates.* New York: New American Library, 1986.

Ketchum, William. *An Authentic and Comprehensive History of Buffalo, with Some Account of Its Early Inhabitants Both Savage and Civilized, Comprising Historic Notices of the Six Nations or Iroquois Indians, Including a Sketch of the Life of Sir William Johnson.* Vol. 1. Buffalo, NY: Rockwell, Baker & Hill, 1964. https://catalog.hathitrust.org/Record/100299454.

Kim, Namsuk, and John Joseph Wallis. "The Market for American State Government Bonds in Britain and the United States, 1830–43." *Economic History Review* 58, no. 4 (February 2005): 736–64. https://www.nber.org/papers/w10108.

King, Byron. "The Whiskey Rebellion: Whiskey Taxes: The Real Thing." *Daily Reckoning*, December 17, 2004. https://dailyreckoning.com/the-whiskey-rebellion-whiskey-taxes-the-real-thing.

Klein, Philip Shriver. *Pennsylvania Politics, 1817–1832: A Game without Rules.*
    Philadelphia: Historical Society of Pennsylvania, 1940.

Knouff, Gregory T. *The Soldiers' Revolution: Pennsylvania in Arms and the
    Forging of Early American Identity.* University Park: Pennsylvania State
    University Press, 2004.

Kohn, Richard H. "The Washington Administration's Decision to Crush the
    Whiskey Rebellion." *Journal of American History* 59, no. 3 (December
    1972): 567–84. https://www.jstor.org/stable/1900658.

Korson, George. *Black Rock: Mining Folklore of the Pennsylvania Dutch.* New
    York: Arno Press, 1979.

———. *Minstrels of the Mine Patch: Songs and Stories of the Anthracite Industry.*
    Hatboro, PA: Folklore Associates, 1964.

———, ed. *Pennsylvania Songs and Legends.* Philadelphia: University of Penn-
    sylvania Press, 1949.

Kozuskanich, Nathan R. "'For the Security and Protection of the Community':
    The Frontier and the Makings of Pennsylvanian Constitutionalism." PhD
    diss., Ohio State University, 2005.

———. "Pennsylvania, the Militia, and the Second Amendment." *Pennsylvania
    Magazine of History and Biography* 133, no. 2 (April 2009): 119–47. http://
    www.jstor.org/stable/40543453.

Krause, Eleanor, and Isabel V. Sawhill. "Seven Reasons to Worry about the
    American Middle Class." *Social Mobility Memos*, June 5, 2018. https://www.
    brookings.edu/blog/social-mobility-memos/2018/06/05/seven-reasons-to-
    worry-about-the-american-middle-class/.

Krick, Robert K. *Stonewall Jackson at Cedar Mountain.* Chapel Hill: University
    of North Carolina Press, 1990.

Kukla, Jon. *A Wilderness So Immense: The Louisiana Purchase and the Destiny
    of America.* New York: Anchor Books, 2003.

Landsman, Stephan. "The History of Contingency and the Contingency of
    History." *DePaul Law Review* 47, no. 2 (1998): 261–65. https://papers.ssrn.
    com/sol3/papers.cfm?abstract_id=110536.

"The Largest Steel Plant in the World." *Iron Age* 73 (January 7, 1904): 49–73.
    https://catalog.hathitrust.org/Record/009798831.

*Laws of the Commonwealth of Pennsylvania, Republished under the Authority
    of the Legislature, with Notes and References.* 10 vols. Philadelphia: John
    Bioren, 1810–1844. https://catalog.hathitrust.org/Record/008596137.

*Laws of the General Assembly of the Commonwealth of Pennsylvania, Passed at
    the Session of 1845, in the Sixty-Ninth Year of Independence.* Harrisburg,
    PA: J. M. G. Lescure, 1845. https://books.google.com/books?id=oSxOA-
    QAAIAAJ.

Laws of the General Assembly of the Commonwealth of Pennsylvania, Passed at the Session of 1842, in the Sixty-Sixth Year of Independence. Harrisburg, PA: M'Kinley & Lescurn, 1842. https://books.google.com/books?id=61d-NAQAAMAAJ.

Laws of the General Assembly of the State of Pennsylvania Passed at the Session of 1854. Harrisburg, PA: A. Boyd Hamilton, 1854. https://catalog.hathitrust. org/Record/008892032.

Lee, J. J., and Marion R. Casey, eds. *Making the Irish American: History and Heritage of the Irish in the United States.* New York: New York University Press, 2006.

Legislative Documents: Miscellaneous Documents Read in the Legislature of the Commonwealth of Pennsylvania, during the Session Which Commenced at Harrisburg, on the Second Day of January, 1855. Harrisburg, PA: A. Boyd Hamilton, 1855. https://books.google.com/books/reader?id=wz41AQAAMAAJ.

Lehman, Forrest K. "'Seditious Libel' on Trial, Political Dissent on the Record: 'An Account of the Trial of Thomas Cooper' as Campaign Literature." *Pennsylvania Magazine of History and Biography* 132, no. 2 (April 2008): 117–39. http://www.jstor.org/stable/20093994.

Lehmann, Hartmut, Hermann Wellenreuther, and Renate Wilson, eds. *In Search of Peace and Prosperity: New German Settlements in Eighteenth-Century Europe and America.* University Park: Pennsylvania State University Press, 2000.

Lemon, James T. *The Best Poor Man's Country: A Geographical Study of Southeastern Pennsylvania.* New York: Norton, 1972.

Lens, Sidney. *The Labor Wars: From the Molly Maguires to the Sitdowns.* Garden City, NY: Doubleday, 1973.

Lepler, Jessica M. *The Many Panics of 1837: People, Politics, and the Creation of a Transatlantic Financial Crisis.* New York: Cambridge University Press, 2013.

Levinson, Sanford. *Our Undemocratic Constitution: Where the Constitution Goes Wrong (And How We the People Can Correct It).* Oxford: Oxford University Press, 2008.

Leyburn, James Graham. *The Scotch-Irish: A Social History.* Chapel Hill: University of North Carolina Press, 1962.

Lincoln, Charles Henry. *The Revolutionary Movement in Pennsylvania 1760–1776.* Philadelphia: University of Pennsylvania, 1901. https://archive.org/ details/revolutionarymov00linc.

Lindert, Peter, and Jeffrey Williamson. "American Incomes before and after the Revolution." Working Paper 17211, National Bureau of Economic Research, 2011. https://ideas.repec.org/p/nbr/nberwo/17211.html.

———. "America's Revolution: Economic Disaster, Development, and Equality."

Vox, July 15, 2011. http://www.voxeu.org/article/america-s-revolution-eco-
    nomic-disaster-development-and-equality.
"Lists of Pennsylvania Settlers Murdered, Scalped and Taken Prisoners by Indi-
    ans, 1755–1756." *Pennsylvania Magazine of History and Biography* 32, no.
    3 (1908): 309–19. http://www.jstor.org/stable/20085436.
Lord, Arthur C. "The Pre-Revolutionary Agriculture of Lancaster County,
    Pennsylvania." *Journal of the Lancaster County Historical Society* 79, no.
    1 (1975): 23–42.
Loudon, Archibald. *A Selection of the Most Interesting Narratives, of Outrages,
    Committed by the Indians, in Their Wars with the White People.* 2 vols.
    Carlisle, PA: A. Loudon (Whitehall), 1808. https://catalog.hathitrust.org/
    Record/100330943.
Lovejoy, Owen R. "Child Labor in the Coal Mines." *Annals of the American
    Academy of Political and Social Science* 27 (1906): 35–41. https://www.jstor.
    org/stable/pdf/1010788.pdf.
———. "The Extent of Child Labor in the Anthracite Coal Industry." *Annals of
    the American Acedemy of Political and Social Science* 29 (January 1907):
    35–49. http://www.jstor.org/stable/1010416.
Lu, Chunlong. "Middle Class and Democracy: Structural Linkage." *Interna-
    tional Review of Modern Sociology* 31, no. 2 (Autumn 2005): 157–78. https://
    www.jstor.org/stable/i40069196.
Maier, Pauline. *Ratification: The People Debate the Constitution, 1787–1788.*
    New York: Simon Schuster, 2010.
Majewski, John. "Toward a Social History of the Corporation: Shareholding in
    Pennsylvania, 1800–1840." In *The Economy of Early America: Historical
    Perspectives and New Directions,* edited by Cathy Matson, 294–316. Uni-
    versity Park: Pennsylvania State University Press, 2006.
Malone, Dumas. *The Public Life of Thomas Cooper, 1783–1839.* New
    Haven, CT: Yale University Press, 1926. https://catalog.hathitrust.org/
    Record/000365470.
Mancall, Peter. *Valley of Opportunity: Economic Culture along the Upper Susque-
    hanna, 1700–1800.* Ithaca, NY: Cornell University Press, 1991.
Mancini, Alexandra. "The Paxton Boys and the Pamphlet Frenzy: Politics, Reli-
    gion, and Social Structure in Eighteenth-Century Pennsylvania." *Concept*
    30 (2006). https://concept.journals.villanova.edu/article/view/278.
Manley, Henry S. "Buying Buffalo from the Indians." *New York History* 28, no.
    3 (July 1947): 313–29. http://www.jstor.org/stable/23149888.
———. "Red Jacket's Last Campaign: And an Extended Bibliographical and
    Biographical Note." *New York History* 31, no. 2 (April 1950): 149–68. http://
    www.jstor.org/stable/23149773.

Markens, Isaac. *The Hebrews in America: A Series of Historical and Biographical Sketches.* New York: Isaac Markens, 1888. https://archive.org/details/cu31924032763207.

Marker, Linda. "Cemeteries: Younkin Cemetery, Upper Turkeyfoot Twp., Somerset Co., PA." 1998. http://www.pagenweb.org/~somerset/cemetery/tf/TUZZYJ.htm.

Marr, Paul G. "The Wiconisco Canal." *Canal History and Technology Proceedings* 24 (March 2005): 3–21.

Marr, Paul, and Michael Ross. "Socioeconomic Conditions on the Pennsylvania Frontier: The Germans and Scots-Irish of Cumberland County, 1765–1775." *Middle States Geographer* 41 (2008): 1–8. https://msaag.aag.org/middle-states-geographer/past-journals/middle-states-geographer-volume-41-2008/.

Marsh, George P. *The Earth as Modified by Human Action.* New York: Scribner, Armstrong, 1874. https://catalog.hathitrust.org/Record/100437878.

Martin, Asa Earl. "The Temperance Movement in Pennsylvania Prior to the Civil War." *Pennsylvania Magazine of History and Biography* 49, no. 3 (1925): 195–230. https://www.jstor.org/stable/20086574.

Marvel, William. "Battle of Ball's Bluff." August 8, 2011. http://www.historynet.com/battle-of-balls-bluff-2.htm.

McAfee, Ward. "A Reconsideration of the Origins of the Mexican-American War." *Southern California Quarterly* 62, no. 1 (Spring 1980): 49–65. https://doi.org/10.2307/41170855.

McCullough, David. *1776.* New York: Simon Schuster, 2005.

McMahon, Seán. *A Short History of Ireland.* Dublin: Mercier Press, 1996.

McPherson, James M. *Battle Cry of Freedom: The Civil War Era.* New York: Oxford University Press, 1988.

Meacham, Jon. *American Lion: Andrew Jackson in the White House.* New York: Random House, 2008.

Meginness, John F., ed. *History of Lycoming County, Pennsylvania.* Chicago: Brown, Runk, 1892. https://archive.org/details/historyoflycomin00edit.

Merritt, Jane T. *At the Crossroads: Indians and Empires on a Mid-Atlantic Frontier, 1700–1763.* Chapel Hill: University of North Carolina Press, 2003.

Miller, Kerby A. *Emigrants and Exiles: Ireland and the Irish Exodus to North America.* New York: Oxford University Press, 1985.

Miller, Miles V. *Through the Years.* Valley View, PA: Valley Citizen, 1954.

Miller, Randall M., and William Pencak. *Pennsylvania: A History of the Commonwealth.* Harrisburg: Pennsylvania Historical and Museum Commission, 2002.

Miller, William. "The Democratic Societies and the Whiskey Insurrection."

Pennsylvania Magazine of History and Biography 62, no. 3 (July 1938): 324–49. https://www.jstor.org/stable/20087127.

Miner, H. Craig, and William E. Unrau. *The End of Kansas: A Study of Cultural Revolution, 1854–1871.* Lawrence: University Press of Kansas, 1990. First published 1978 by Regents Press of Kansas.

Minutes of the Provincial Council of Pennsylvania, from the Organization to the Termination of the Proprietary Government. Vols. 4 and 6. Harrisburg, PA: Theo. Fenn, 1851. https://catalog.hathitrust.org/Record/011262481.

Minutes of the Supreme Executive Council of Pennsylvania, from Its Organization to the Termination of the Revolution. Vol. 13. Harrisburg, PA: Theo. Fenn, 1853. https://archive.org/details/minutessupremee03coungoog.

Mombert, J. I. *An Authentic History of Lancaster County: In the State of Pennsylvania.* Lancaster, PA: J. E. Barr, 1869. https://archive.org/details/authentichistory00momb.

Montgomery, Thomas Lynch, ed. *Report of the Commission to Locate the Site of the Frontier Forts of Pennsylvania.* 2nd ed. Harrisburg, PA: W. M. Stanley Ray, 1916. https://catalog.hathitrust.org/Record/008651785.

Moody, John. *The Railroad Builders: A Chronicle of the Welding of the States.* New Haven, CT: Yale University Press, 1919. https://catalog.hathitrust.org/Record/000439021.

Moody, T. W., F. X. Martin, and Dermot Keogh, eds. *The Course of Irish History.* Lanham, MD: Roberts Rinehart, 1995.

Morais, Henry Samuel. *The Jews of Philadelphia: Their History from the Earliest Settlements to the Present Time.* Philadelphia: Levytype, 1894. https://archive.org/details/jewsofphiladelph00mora.

Morris, Richard B. "Class Struggle and the American Revolution." *William and Mary Quarterly* 19, no. 1 (January 1962): 3–29. https://doi.org/10.2307/1919955.

Mt. Pleasant, Alyssa. "After the Whirlwind: Maintaining a Haudenosaunee Place at Buffalo Creek, 1780–1825." PhD diss., Cornell University, 2007.

Nagy, John A. *Rebellion in the Ranks: Mutinies of the American Revolution.* Yardley, PA: Westholme, 2008.

Nale, Robert E., and Jean A. Suloff. *The 36th Regiment, Pennsylvania Volunteer Militia, July and August, 1863.* Accessed June 25, 2020. http://www.nale.org/36thpvm.pdf.

Nash, Gary B. "The American Clergy and the French Revolution." *William and Mary Quarterly* 22, no. 3 (July 1965): 392–412. http://www.jstor.org/stable/1920453.

———. *Quakers and Politics: Pennsylvania, 1681–1726.* Princeton, NJ: Princeton University Press, 1968.

———. *The Unknown American Revolution: The Unruly Birth of Democracy and the Struggle to Create America*. New York: Viking, 2005.

National Cyclopedia of American Biography. Vol. 10. New York: James T. White, 1900. https://archive.org/details/nationalcyclopa03unkngoog.

National Park Service. "Whiskey Rebellion." Last updated February 26, 2015. http://www.nps.gov/frhi/historyculture/whiskeyrebellion.htm.

Neem, Johann N. "Freedom of Association in the Early Republic: The Republican Party, the Whiskey Rebellion, and the Philadelphia and New York Cordwainers' Cases." *Pennsylvania Magazine of History and Biography* 127, no. 3 (July 2003): 259–90. https://www.jstor.org/stable/20093635.

Neible, George W. "Accounts of Servants Bound and Assigned before James Hamilton, Mayor of Philadelphia." *Pennsylvania Magazine of History and Biography* 32, no. 3 (July 1908): 358. https://archive.org/details/pennsylvaniamaga32hist.

Neu, Irene D. *Erastus Corning, Merchant and Financier, 1794–1872*. Ithaca, NY: Cornell University Press, 1960.

Newman, Paul Douglas. "The Federalists' Cold War: The Fries Rebellion, National Security, and the State, 1787–1800." *Pennsylvania History* 67, no. 1 (Winter 2000): 63–104. https://www.jstor.org/stable/27774248.

———. *Fries's Rebellion: The Enduring Struggle for the American Revolution*. Philadelphia: University of Pennsylvania Press, 2004.

———. "Fries' Rebellion and American Political Culture, 1798–1800." *Pennsylvania Magazine of History and Biography* 119, no. 1/2 (January–April 1995): 37–73. http://www.jstor.org/stable/20092925.

Newman, Simon P. *Parades and the Politics of the Street: Festive Culture in the Early American Republic*. Philadelphia: University of Pennsylvania Press, 1997.

———. "The World Turned Upside Down: Revolutionary Politics, Fries' and Gabriel's Rebellions, and the Fears of the Federalists." *Pennsylvania History* 67, no. 1 (Winter 2000): 5–20. https://www.jstor.org/stable/27774245.

Nolt, Steven M. *Foreigners in Their Own Land: Pennsylvania Germans in the Early Republic*. University Park: Pennsylvania State University Press, 2002.

"Northumberland and Erie Railroad Convention." *American Railroad Journal, and Advocate of Internal Improvements* 5, no. 49 (December 10, 1836): 776–77. https://catalog.hathitrust.org/Record/008717775.

Ostler, Jeffrey. *Surviving Genocide: Native Nations and the United States from the American Revolution to Bleeding Kansas*. New Haven, CT: Yale University Press, 2019.

Painter, Nell Irvin. *Standing at Armageddon: A Grassroots History of the Progressive Era*. New York: Norton, 2008.

Palladino, Grace. *Another Civil War: Labor, Capital, and the State in the Anthracite Regions of Pennsylvania, 1840–68*. Urbana: University of Illinois Press, 1990.

Parker, Arthur Caswell. *Red Jacket, Seneca Chief*. Lincoln: University of Nebraska Press, 1998.

Parkman, Francis. *The Conspiracy of Pontiac, and the Indian War after the Conquest of Canada*. Vol. 2. Boston: Little, Brown, 1902. https://catalog. hathitrust.org/Record/100730923.

Pasley, Jeffrey L. *The First Presidential Contest: 1796 and the Founding of American Democracy*. Lawrence: University Press of Kansas, 2013.

———. "Popular Constitutionalism in Philadelphia: How Freedom of Expression Was Secured by Two Fearless Newspaper Editors." *Pennsylvania Legacies* 8, no. 1 (May 2008): 6–11. https://www.jstor.org/stable/i27765122.

———. *"The Tyranny of Printers": Newspaper Politics in the Early American Republic*. Charlottesville: University Press of Virginia, 2001.

Pearl, Daniel. "In Gujarat, Stench Provides a Constant Reminder of Death." *Wall Street Journal*, February 5, 2001. https://www.wsj.com/articles/ SB981323645338299940.

Peattie, Donald Culross. *A Natural History of Trees of Eastern and Central North America*. 2nd ed. Boston: Houghton Mifflin, 1966.

Peeling, James Hedley. "Governor McKean and the Pennsylvania Jacobins (1799–1808)." *Pennsylvania Magazine of History and Biography* 54, no. 4 (1930): 320–54. http://www.jstor.org/stable/20086750.

Pendleton, M. Stephen. "Ernest Wende and Buffalo's Transition to Modern Public Health Policy, 1892–1910." *New York History* 90, no. 4 (Fall 2009): 287–311. http://www.jstor.org/stable/23185130.

Pennsylvania Annual Report of Mines by Year: 1870–1890. PennState University Libraries. https://libraries.psu.edu/about/collections/pennsylvania-geology-resources/pennsylvania-annual-report-mines-year-1870-1979.

Pennsylvania Archives. HathiTrust Digital Library. https://catalog.hathitrust. org/Record/003912969.

Pennsylvania Colonial Records. Hathitrust Digital Library. https://catalog. hathitrust.org/Record/000540855.

Pennsylvania State Archives. Pennsylvania Historical Museum Commission. https://www.phmc.pa.gov/Archives/Pages/default.aspx.

"Pennsylvania Weather Records, 1644–1835." *Pennsylvania Magazine of History and Biography* 15, no. 1 (1891): 109–21. http://www.jstor.org/stable/20083411.

Pessen, Edward. "The Ideology of Stephen Simpson, Upperclass Champion of the Early Philadelphia Workingmen's Movement." *Pennsylvania History* 22, no. 4 (October 1955): 328–40. https://www.jstor.org/stable/27769623.

Phillips, Kim T. "Democrats of the Old School in the Era of Good Feelings."

Pennsylvania Magazine of History and Biography 95, no. 3 (July 1971): 363–82. http://www.jstor.org/stable/20090571.

———. "The Pennsylvania Origins of the Jackson Movement." *Political Science Quarterly* 91, no. 3 (Autumn 1976): 489–508. http://www.jstor.org/stable/2148938.

———. "William Duane, Philadelphia's Democratic Republicans, and the Origin of Modern Politics." *Pennsylvania Magazine of History and Biography* 101, no. 3 (July 1977): 365–87. https://www.jstor.org/stable/20091178.

———. "William Duane, Revolutionary Editor." PhD diss., University of California, Berkeley, 1968.

Pierce, M. B. *Address on the Present Condition and Prospects of the Aboriginal Inhabitants of North America, with Particular Reference to the Seneca Nation.* Buffalo, NY: Steele's Press, 1838. https://catalog.hathitrust.org/Record/009736457.

Pierce, Mary Gerald. *Unto All—His Mercy: The First Hundred Years of the Sisters of Mercy in the Diocese of Buffalo, 1858–1958.* Buffalo, NY: Savage Litho, 1979.

Pinkowski, Edward. *John Siney, The Miners' Martyr.* Philadelphia: Sunshine Press, 1963.

———. "Joseph Battin: Father of the Coal Breaker." *Pennsylvania Magazine of History and Biography* 73, no. 3 (July 1849): 337–48. https://www.jstor.org/stable/20079508.

Pitock, Toni. "Michael Gratz (1739–1811)." Immigrant Entrepreneurship: German-American Business Biographies, 1720 to the Present (website), German Historical Institute. Last updated February 10, 2015. https://www.immigrantentrepreneurship.org/entry.php?rec=212%20.

Pletcher, David M. "James K. Polk and the US Mexican War: A Policy Appraisal." PBS.org. Accessed July 3, 2019. http://www.pbs.org/kera/usmexicanwar/prelude/jp_jp_and_the_mexican_war.html.

Poor, Henry V. *History of Railroads and Canals in the United States of America.* New York: John H. Schultz, 1860. https://catalog.hathitrust.org/Record/000969922.

Potts, William John. "British Views of American Trade and Manufactures during the Revolution." *Pennsylvania Magazine of History and Biography* 7, no. 2 (1883): 194–99. https://www.jstor.org/stable/20084601.

Powderly, T. V. *Thirty Years of Labor: 1859–1889.* Columbus, OH: Excelsior, 1890. https://archive.org/details/thirtyyearsoflab00powduoft.

Powell, H. Benjamin. "Coal and Pennsylvania's Transportation Policy, 1825–1828." *Pennsylvania History* 38, no. 2 (April 1971): 134–51. https://www.jstor.org/stable/27771927.

———. "The Pennsylvania Anthracite Industry, 1769–1976." *Pennsylvania History* 47, no. 1 (January 1980): 3–27. https://journals.psu.edu/phj/article/view/24141.

Pownall, Thomas. *A Topographical Description of the Dominions of the United States of America.* 2nd ed. Edited by Lois Mulkearn. Pittsburgh: University of Pittsburgh Press, 1949. https://catalog.hathitrust.org/Record/000600774.

Priestley, Joseph. *Letters to the Inhabitants of Northumberland and Its Neighbuorhood.* Northumberland, PA: Andrew Kennedy, 1799. https://archive.org/details/letterstoinhabit00prierich.

———. *Memoirs of Dr. Joseph Priestley, to the Year 1795, Written by Himself.* Northumberland, PA: John Binns, 1806. https://catalog.hathitrust.org/Record/009706579.

Proceedings of the Citizens of Philadelphia Relative to the Rail Road to Erie, and of the Convention at Williamsport, Lycoming County, PA. Philadelphia: J. Thompson, 1836. https://catalog.hathitrust.org/Record/001353380.

Proceedings of the Commissioners of Indian Affairs, Appointed by Law for the Extinguishment of Indian Titles in the State of New York. Vol. 1. Albany, NY: Joel Munsell, 1861. https://archive.org/stream/proceedingsofcom01newy#mode/2up.

The Proceedings Relative to the Calling the Conventions of 1776 and 1790. Harrisburg, PA: John S. Wiestling, 1825. https://archive.org/details/proceedingsrela01convgoog.

Proud, Robert, and R. P. Theophilus. "Autobiography of Robert Proud, the Historian." *Pennsylvania Magazine of History and Biography* 13, no. 4 (January 1890): 430–40. https://www.jstor.org/stable/20083339.

Provincial Conference of Committees, of the Province of Pennsylvania; Held at the Carpenter's Hall at Philadelphia. Philadelphia: W. & T. Bradford, 1776. http://www.ushistory.org/pennsylvania/birth3.html.

Prucha, Francis Paul. *The Great Father: The United States Governmant and the American Indians.* Lincoln: University of Nebraska Press, 1984.

Reeves, Richard V. "How to Build a Stronger Middle Class: With Respect." May 21, 2018. https://www.brookings.edu/blog/up-front/2018/05/21/how-to-build-a-stronger-middle-class-with-respect/.

———. *A Little Respect: Can We Restore Relational Equality?* Washington, DC: Brookings Institution, 2018. https://www.brookings.edu/wp-content/uploads/2018/07/ES_20180702_Reeves-Respect.pdf.

———. "The Respect Deficit." August 9, 2018. https://www.brookings.edu/blog/up-front/2018/08/09/the-respect-deficit/.

Reeves, Richard V., Katherine Guyot, and Eleanor Krause. "Defining the Middle Class: Cash, Credentials, or Culture?" May 7, 2018. https://www.brookings.

edu/research/defining-the-middle-class-cash-credentials-or-culture/.

Reichel, William C., ed. "Zinzendorf's Narrative of a Journey from Bethlehem to Shamokin in September of 1742." In Vol. 1, *Memorials of the Moravian Church*, 62–99. Philadelphia: J. B. Lippincott, 1870. https://archive.org/details/moravianchurch00reicrich.

Report of the Committee Appointed to Enquire into the Causes of the Disturbances at the Seat of Government, in December, 1838. Harrisburg, PA: Boas & Coplan, 1839. https://catalog.hathitrust.org/Record/008651716.

Richards, Henry M. M. *The Pennsylvania-German in the French and Indian War: A Historical Sketch*. Lancaster, PA: New Era Printing, 1905. https://archive.org/details/pennsylvaniage00rich.

Richardson, M. T., comp. *Practical Carriage Building*. New York: M. T. Richardson, 1891. http://www.lostcrafts.com/Carriage-Building/Practical-Carriage-Building-Main.html.

Richter, Conrad. *The Trees*. New York: Alfred A. Knopf, 1940.

Richter, Daniel K. *Facing East from Indian Country: A Native History of Early America*. Cambridge, MA: Harvard University Press, 2001.

———. *The Ordeal of the Longhouse: The Peoples of the Iroquois League in the Era of European Colonization*. Chapel Hill: University of North Carolina Press, 1992.

Ridgway, Whitman H. "Fries in the Federalist Imagination: A Crisis of Republican Society." *Pennsylvania History* 67, no. 1 (Winter 2000): 141–60. https://www.jstor.org/stable/27774250.

Roberts, Alasdair. *America's First Great Depression: Economic Crisis and Political Disorder after the Panic of 1837*. Ithaca, NY: Cornell University Press, 2012.

Roberts, Peter. *Anthracite Coal Communities: A Study of the Demography, the Social, Educational and Moral Life of the Anthracite Regions*. New York: Macmillan, 1904. https://archive.org/details/anthracitecoalco00roberich.

Robertson, Jim. "How Umbrella Policies Started, Part 1: Early Liability Coverage." International Risk Management Institute, March 2000. https://www.irmi.com/articles/expert-commentary/how-umbrella-policies-started-part-1-early-liability-coverage.

Robson, David W. "Anticipating the Brethren: The Reverend Charles Nisbet Critiques the French Revolution." *Pennsylvania Magazine of History and Biography* 121, no. 4 (October 1997): 303–28. http://www.jstor.org/stable/20093156.

Rosenbach, A. S. W. *An Historical Sketch of the Congregation*. Philadelphia: Cahan, 1909. https://archive.org/details/dedicationofnews00phil.

Rosenbach, Isabella H., and Abraham S. Wolf Rosenbach. "Aaron Levy." *Pub-*

lications of the American Jewish Historical Society 2 (1894): 157–63. http:// www.jstor.org/stable/43057420.

Rosenberg, Norman L. "Alexander Addison and the Pennsylvania Origins of Federalist First-Amendment Thought." *Pennsylvania Magazine of History and Biography* 108, no. 4 (October 1984): 399–417. http://www.jstor.org/ stable/20091884.

Rosenberger, Homer Tope. *The Philadelphia and Erie Railroad: Its Place in American Economic History*. Potomac, MD: Fox Hills Press, 1975.

Rosenbloom, Joseph R. *A Biographical Dictionary of Early American Jews: Colonial Times through 1800*. Lexington: University of Kentucky Press, 1960.

Rosier, Paul C. "Dam Building and Treaty Breaking: The Kinzua Dam Controversy, 1936–1958." *Pennsylvania Magazine of History and Biography* 119, no. 4 (October 1995): 345–68. https://www.jstor.org/stable/20092990.

Rosswurm, Steven. *Arms, Country, and Class: The Philadelphia Militia and the "Lower Sort" during the American Revolution, 1775–1783*. New Brunswick: Rutgers University Press, 1987.

Rothbard, Murray. *The Panic of 1819: Reactions and Policies*. Auburn, AL: Ludwig von Mises Institute, 2007.

Runkle, Stephen A. *Native American Waterbody and Place Names within the Susquehanna River Basin and Surrounding Subbasins*. Publication 229. Harrisburg, PA: Susquehannah River Basin Commission, 2003. https://www.srbc.net/our-work/reports-library/technical-reports/229-native-american-names/.

Rupp, I. Daniel. *History of Lancaster County: To which Is Prefixed a Brief Sketch of the Early History of Pennsylvania*. Lancaster, PA: Gilbert Hills, 1844. https://archive.org/details/historylancas00rupp.

Ryerson, Richard Alan. *The Revolution Is Now Begun: The Radical Committees of Philadelphia, 1765–1776*. Philadelphia: University of Pennsylvania Press, 1978.

Sallade-Bickel Family Papers. Manuscripts and Archives Division. New York Public Library. Astor, Lenox and Tilden Foundation.

Sandoz, Mari. *Crazy Horse: The Strange Man of the Oglalas*. Lincoln: University of Nebraska Press, 1992.

Sapio, Victor A. "Expansion and Economic Depression as Factors in Pennsylvania's Support of the War of 1812: An Application of the Pratt and Taylor Theses to the Keystone State." *Pennsylvania History* 35, no. 4 (October 1968): 379–405. https://journals.psu.edu/phj/issue/view/1482.

———. *Pennsylvania & the War of 1812*. Lexington: University Press of Kentucky, 1970.

Schaffer, Jonathan L. "The History of Pennsylvania's Workmen's Compensation:

1900–1916." *Pennsylvania History* 53, no. 1 (January 1986): 26–55. https://journals.psu.edu/phj/article/view/24554.

Scharf, J. Thomas, and Thompson Westcott. *History of Philadelphia, 1609–1884.* 3 vols. Philadelphia: L. H. Everts, 1884. https://catalog.hathitrust.org/Record/100899626.

Schlegel, Marvin W. "America's First Cartel." *Pennsylvania History* 13, no. 1 (January 1946): 1–16. https://journals.psu.edu/phj/article/view/21564.

———. *Ruler of the Reading: The Life of Frank B. Gowen, 1836–1889.* Harrisburg, PA: Archives Publishing Company of Pennsylvania, 1947.

———. "The Workingmen's Benevolent Association: First Union of Anthracite Miners." *Pennsylvania History* 10, no. 4 (October 1943): 243–67. https://www.jstor.org/stable/27766575.

Schmidt, James D. *Industrial Violence and the Legal Origins of Child Labor.* New York: Cambridge University Press, 2010.

Schnure, William Marion, comp. *Selinsgrove, Penna. Chronology: 1700–1850.* Vol. 1. Middleburg, PA: Middleburg Post, 1918. https://archive.org/details/selinsgrovepenn00schngoog.

Schuman, Michael. "History of Child Labor in the United States—Part 1: Little Children Working." *Monthly Labor Review,* January 2017. https://www.bls.gov/opub/mlr/2017/article/history-of-child-labor-in-the-united-states-part-1.htm.

———. "History of Child Labor in the United States—Part 2: The Reform Movement." *Monthly Labor Review,* January 2017. https://www.bls.gov/opub/mlr/2017/article/history-of-child-labor-in-the-united-states-part-2-the-reform-movement.htm.

Seaver, James Everett. *A Narrative of the Life of Mary Jemison: The White Woman of Genesee.* 20th edition. New York: American Scenic & Historic Preservation Society, 1918. https://catalog.hathitrust.org/Record/000249945.

"The Secular Not Supreme." *Catholic World,* August 1871, 685–701. https://books.google.com/books/reader?id=yBU4AQAAIAAJ.

Sellers, Charles. *The Market Revolution: Jacksonian America, 1815–1846.* New York: Oxford University Press, 1991.

Selsam, Paul J. *The Pennsylvania Constitution of 1776: A Study in Revolutionary Democracy.* New York: Octogan Books, 1971.

Shankman, Andrew. *Crucible of American Democracy: The Struggle to Fuse Egalitarianism & Capitalism in Jeffersonian Pennsylvania.* Lawrence: University Press of Kansas, 2004.

Sharp, James Roger. *American Politics in the Early Republic: The New Nation in Crisis.* New Haven, CT: Yale University Press, 1993.

Sheetz, Charles L. "The Inception of the Rail-road to Lykens Valley." Master's thesis, Shippensburg University, 1968.

Shelling, Richard. "Philadelphia and the Agitation in 1825 for the Pennsylvania Canal." *Pennsylvania Magazine of History and Biography* 62, no. 2 (April 1938): 175–204. https://www.jstor.org/stable/20087108.

Shimmell, Lewis S. *Border Warfare in Pennsylvania during the Revolution.* Harrisburg, PA: R. L. Myers, 1901. https://catalog.hathitrust.org/Record/100555469.

Shoemaker, Henry W. *Extinct Pennsylvania Animals: Part I, The Panther and the Wolf.* Altoona, PA: Altoona Tribune, 1917. https://catalog.hathitrust.org/Record/008595561.

———. *Extinct Pennsylvania Animals, Part II: Black Moose, Elk, Bison, Beaver, Pine Marten, Fisher, Glutton, Canada Lynx.* Altoona, PA: Altoona Tribune, 1919. https://catalog.hathitrust.org/Record/008595561.

Shrager, David S., and Carol Nelson Shepherd. "History, Development, and Analysis of the Pennsylvania Comparative Negligence Act: An Overview." *Villanova Law Review* 24 (1979): 422–52. https://digitalcommons.law.villanova.edu/vlr/vol24/iss3/2/.

Shy, John. *A People Numerous and Armed: Reflections on the Military Struggle for American Independence.* Ann Arbor: University of Michigan Press, 1990.

Silver, Peter. *Our Savage Neighbors: How the Indian War Transformed Early America.* New York: Norton, 2008.

Simpson, Stephen. *The Working Man's Manual: A New Theory of Political Economy, on the Principle of Production the Source of Wealth.* Philadelphia: Thomas L. Bonsal, 1831. https://catalog.hathitrust.org/Record/006593672.

Sioli, Marco. "The Democratic Republican Societies at the End of the Eighteenth Century: The Western Pennsylvania Experience." *Pennsylvania History* 60, no. 3 (July 1993): 288–99. https://www.jstor.org/stable/27773649.

———. "Where Did the Whiskey Rebels Go?" Accessed September 15, 2020. https://ir.vanderbilt.edu/handle/1803/7202.

———. "The Whiskey Rebellion as Republican Citizenship." Accessed September 15, 2020. https://ir.vanderbilt.edu/handle/1803/7183. http://www.library.vanderbilt.edu/Quaderno/Quaderno3/Q3.C4.Soli.pdf.

Sipe, C. Hale. *The Indian Wars of Pennsylvania.* Harrisburg, PA: Telegraph Press, 1929.

Sisters of Mercy. *Annals Mercy Hospital.* Buffalo, NY: Sisters of Mercy, Buffalo Archives, 1934.

Skaggs, David Curtis, and Larry L. Nelson. *The Sixty Years' War for the Great Lakes, 1754-1814.* East Lansing: Michigan State University Press, 2001.

Slaughter, Thomas P. "Crowds in Eighteenth-Century America: Reflections and New Directions." *Pennsylvania Magazine of History and Biography* 115, no.

1 (January 1991): 3–34. http://www.jstor.org/stable/20092570.

———. *The Whiskey Rebellion: Frontier Epilogue to the American Revolution.* New York: Oxford University Press, 1986.

Smith, C. Page. "The Attack on Fort Wilson." *Pennsylvania Magazine of History and Biography* 78, no. 2 (April 1954): 177–88. https://www.jstor.org/stable/20088567.

Smith, James Morton. "The 'Aurora' and the Alien and Sedition Laws: Part II: The Editorship of William Duane." *Pennsylvania Magazine of History and Biography* 77, no. 2 (April 1953): 123–55. http://www.jstor.org/stable/20088454.

———. *Freedom's Fetters: The Alien and Sedition Laws and American Civil Liberties.* Ithaca, NY: Cornell University Press, 1956.

Smith, Joseph P., ed. *History of the Republican Party in Ohio.* Vol. 1. Chicago: Lewis, 1898. https://archive.org/details/historyrepublic00smitgoog.

Smith, Justin H. *The War with Mexico.* Vol. 2. New York: Macmillan, 1919. https://archive.org/details/warwithmexicovol010848mbp.

Smith, Page. *The Rise of Industrial America: A People's History of the Post-Reconstruction Era.* Vol. 6. New York: McGraw-Hill, 1984.

Smith, R. Scudder, ed. "Berner's Auction Gallery advertisement for auction of Jonathan F. Woodside collection." Advertisement. *Antiques and the Arts Weekly*, March 26, 2010, 91.

Smith, Matthew, and James Gibbon. *A Declaration and Remonstrance of the Distressed and Bleeding Frontier Inhabitants of the Province of Pennsylvania, Presented by Them to the Honourable the Governor and the Assembly of the Province, Showing the Causes of Their Late Discontent and Uneasiness under Which They Have Laboured, and Which They Humbly Pray to Have Redress'd.* Philadelphia: W. Bradford, 1764. http://archive.org/details/declarationremon00smit.

Smyth, Albert Henry, ed. *The Writings of Benjamin Franklin.* Vol. 4. New York: Macmillan, 1906. https://catalog.hathitrust.org/Record/000365746.

Snow, Dean R. *The Iroquois.* Malden, MA: Blackwell, 1996.

Snyder, Charles McCool. *The Jacksonian Heritage: Pennsylvania Politics, 1833–1848.* Harrisburg, PA: Pennsylvania Historical and Museum commission, 1958.

Society of Friends Joint Committee on Indian Affairs. *The Case of the Seneca Indians in the State of New York.* Philadelphia: Merrihew and Thompson, 1840. https://archive.org/details/caseofsenecaindi00join.

———. *A Further Illustration of the Case of the Seneca Indians in the State of New York, in a Review of a Pamphlet Entitled "An Appeal to the Christian Community" by Nathaniel T. Strong.* Philadelphia: Merrihew and Thompson, 1841. https://archive.org/details/afurtherillustr00goog.

Soltow, Lee, and Kenneth W. Keller. "Rural Pennsylvania in 1800: A Portrait from the Septennial Census." *Pennsylvania History* 49, no. 1 (January 1982): 25–47. https://www.jstor.org/stable/27772791.

Sowers, Gladys Bucher. *Lebanon County, Pennsylvania: United States Direct Tax of 1798 for Bethel Township, East Hanover Township, Heidelberg Township, Lebanon Township, Londonderry Township.* Westminster, MD: Heritage Books, 2006.

Spangenberg, A. G. "Spangenberg's Notes of Travel to Onondaga in 1745." *Pennsylvania Magazine of History and Biography* 2, no. 4 (1878): 424–32. http://www.jstor.org/stable/20084365.

Speakman, Joseph M. "The Inspector and His Critics: Child Labor Reform in Pennsylvania." *Pennsylvania History* 69, no. 2 (Spring 2002): 266–86. https://www.jstor.org/stable/27774412.

Speeches on the Passage of the Bill for the Removal of the Indians, Delivered in the Congress of the United States, April and May, 1830. Edited by Jeremiah Evarts. Boston: Perkins and Marvin, 1830. https://catalog.hathitrust.org/ Record/008586608.

Splitter, Wolfgang. "The Gremans in Pennsylvania Politics, 1758–1790: A Quantitative Analysis." *Pennsylvania Magazine of History and Biography* 122, no. 1/2 (January–April 1998): 39–76. http://www.jstor.org/stable/20093187.

Stannard, David E. *American Holocaust: Columbus and the Conquest of the New World.* New York: Oxford University Press, 1992.

Steele, Ian K. *Setting All the Captives Free: Capture, Adjustment, and Recollection in Allegheny Country.* Canada: McGill-Queen's University Press, 2013.

Stoever, Johann Casper. *Early Lutheran Baptisms and Marriages in Southeastern Pennsylvania.* Baltimore: Genealogical, 1998.

———. *Records of Rev. John Casper Stoever, Baptismal and Marriage, 1730–1779.* Harrisburg, PA: Harrisburg, 1896. https://archive.org/details/recordsof-revjohn01stoe.

Stone, William L. *The Life and Times of Sa-Go-Ye-Wat-Ha, or Red Jacket.* Albany, NY: J. Munsell, 1866. https://catalog.hathitrust.org/Record/000287499.

———. *Life of Joseph Brant (Thayendanegea).* 2 vols. New York: A. V. Blake, 1838. https://catalog.hathitrust.org/Record/008376067.

Stoudt, John Joseph. "Count Zinzendorf and the Pennsylvania Congregation of God in the Spirit: The First American Oecumenical Movement." *Church History* 9 (December 1940): 366–80. https://doi.org/10.2307/3160914.

Strong, Nathaniel T. *Appeal to the Christian Community on the Condition and Prospects of the New York Indians: In Answer to a Book Entitled* The Case of the New York Indians. Buffalo, NY: Thomas, 1841. https://books.google. com/books?id=1JQLAAAAIAAJ.

Stryker, William S. *The Battles of Trenton and Princeton*. Boston: Houghton Mifflin, 1898.

Suddath, Claire. "A Brief History of the Middle Class." *Time*, February 27, 2009. http://content.time.com/time/nation/article/0,8599,1882147,00.html.

Sugarman, Stephen D. "A Century of Change in Personal Injury Law." *California Law Review* 88, no. 6 (December 2000): 2405–35. https://doi.org/10.2307/3481219.

Sugden, John. *Tecumseh: A Life*. New York: Henry Holt, 1997.

Sullivan, William A. "The Industrial Revolution and the Factory Operative in Pennsylvania." *Pennsylvania Magazine of History and Biography* 78, no. 4 (October 1954): 476–94. http://www.jstor.org/stable/20088638.

Sylvis, James C. *The Life, Speeches, Labors and Essays of William H. Sylvis*. Philadelphia: Claxton, Remsen, Haffelfinger, 1872. https://archive.org/details/lifespeecheslab00sylvgoog.

Taft, Philip. *Organized Labor in American History*. New York: Harper & Row, 1964.

Taylor, Alan. *The Civil War of 1812: American Citizens, British Subjects, Irish Rebels, and Indian Allies*. New York: Alfred A. Knopf, 2010.

———. *The Divided Ground: Indians, Settlers, and the Northern Borderland of the American Revolution*. New York: Vintage Books, 2006.

———. "The Divided Ground: Upper Canada, New York, and the Iroquois Six Nations, 1783–1815." *Journal of the Early Republic* 22, no. 1 (Spring 2002): 55–75. https://doi.org/10.2307/3124858.

Taylor, George Rogers. *The Transportation Revolution, 1815–1860*. Vol. 4, *The Economic History of the United States*. New York: Rinehart, 1951. https://catalog.hathitrust.org/Record/000968070.

Tepper, Michael, ed. *Emigrants to Pennsylvania, 1641–1819: A Consolidation of Ship Passenger Lists from the* Pennsylvania Magazine of History and Biography. Baltimore: Genealogical, 1975.

Thayer, Theodore. *Pennsylvania Politics and the Growth of Democracy: 1740–1776*. Harrisburg: Pennsylvania Historical and Museum Commission, 1953.

Thomson, Charles, and Christian Frederick Post. *Causes of the Alienation of the Delaware and Shawanese Indians from the British Interest*. Philadelphia: John Campbell, 1867. https://catalog.hathitrust.org/Record/100279164.

Thrap, G. Cary. "The Land between the Rivers." In *Prose and Poetry of the Susquehanna and Juniata Rivers*, edited by Zenas J. Gray, 56–57. Harrisburg, PA: Harrisburg, 1893. https://catalog.hathitrust.org/Record/009594588.

Tinkcom, Harry Marlin. *The Republicans and Federalists in Pennsylvania, 1790–1801: A Study in National Stimulus and Local Response*. Harrisburg: Pennsylvania Historical and Museum Commission, 1950.

Tiro, Karim M. "A 'Civil War'? Rethinking Iroquois Participation in the American Revolution." *Explorations in Early American Culture* 4 (2000): 148–65. https://www.jstor.org/stable/23549298.

———. *The People of Standing Stone: The Oneida Nation from Revolution through the Era of Removal.* Amherst: University of Massachusetts Press, 2011.

Tocqueville, Alexis de. *Democracy in America.* Vol. 1. New York: Vintage Classics, 1990.

———. *Democracy in America: Historical-Critical Edition of De la démocratie en Amérique.* Edited by Eduardo Nolla. Translated by James T. Schleifer. Vol. 4. Indianapolis: Liberty Fund, 2010. https://oll.libertyfund.org/titles/2288.

Tomes, Nancy J. "American Attitudes toward the Germ Theory of Disease: Phyllis Allen Richmond Revisited." *Journal of the History of Medicine and Allied Sciences* 52, no. 1 (January 1997): 17–50. https://doi.org/10.1093/jhmas/52.1.17.

Trachtenberg, Alexander. *The History of Legislation for the Protection of Coal Miners in Pennsylvania, 1824–1915.* New York: International, 1942.

Trattner, Walter I. *Crusade for the Children: A History of the National Child Labor Committee and Child Labor Reform in America.* Chicago: Quadrangle Books, 1970.

A Treaty, Held at the Town of Lancaster, in Pennsylvania, by the Honourable the Lieutenant-Governor of the Province and the Honourable the Commissioners for the Provinces of Virginia and Maryland, with the Indians of the Six Nations, in June, 1744. Philadelphia: B. Franklin, 1744. http://treatiesportal.unl.edu/earlytreaties/treaty.00003.html?q=lancaster,%201744.

Treuer, David. *The Heartbeat of Wounded Knee: Native America from 1890 to the Present.* New York: Riverhead Books, 2019.

Trial of Alexander Addison, Esq. Lancaster, PA: William Hamilton, 1803. https://archive.org/details/trialofalexander00addi.

Trombley, Robert Van. "Pennsylvania's Role in the Mexican American War." Master's thesis, Edinboro University of Pennsylvania, 2013.

Turner, O. *Pioneer History of the Holland Land Purchase of Western New York.* Buffalo, NY: Jewett, Thomas, 1850. https://archive.org/details/pioneerhistoryof00turne.

United States Department of Labor, Children's Bureau. *Child Labor and the Welfare of Children in the Anthracite Coal-Mining District.* Bureau Publication No. 106, Washington, DC: Government Printing Office, 1922. https://catalog.hathitrust.org/Record/012480479.

United States War Department. *The War of the Rebellion: A Compilation of the Official Records of the Union and Confederate Armies.* Washington, DC: Government Printing Office, 1880–1901. https://catalog.hathitrust.org/Record/000625514.

Violette, E. M. *History of Adair County Together with Reminincenses and Biographical Sketches.* Kirksville, MO: Denslow History, 1911. https:// catalog.hathitrust.org/Record/008653285.

Virtue, G. O. "The Anthracite Combinations." *Quarterly Journal of Economics* 10, no. 3 (April 1896): 296–323. http://www.jstor.org/stable/1882587.

Volokh, Eugene. "Symbolic Expression and the Original Meaning of the First Amendment." *Georgetown Law Journal* 97, no. 4 (April 2009): 1057–84. http://www2.law.ucla.edu/volokh/symbolic.pdf.

Voss-Hubbard, Mark. *Beyond Party: Cultures of Antipartisanship in Northern Politics before the Civil War.* Baltimore: Johns Hopkins University Press, 2002.

Wallace, Anthony F. C. *The Death and Rebirth of the Seneca.* New York: Alfred A. Knopf, 1970.

———. *The Long, Bitter Trail: Andrew Jackson and the Indians.* New York: Hill and Wang. 1993.

———. *St. Clair: A Nineteenth-Century Coal Town's Experience with a Disaster-Prone Industry.* Ithaca, NY: Cornell University Press, 1981.

Wallace, Paul A. W. *Conrad Weiser: Friend of Colonist and Mohawk.* Philadelphia: University of Pennsylvania Press, 1945. Reprint, Lewisburg, PA: Wennawoods, 1996.

Wallis, John Joseph. "What Caused the Crisis of 1839?" NBER Working Paper Series on Historical Factors in Long Run Growth, Historical Paper 133, National Bureau of Economic Research, Cambridge, MA, April 2001. http://econweb.umd.edu/~wallis/MyPapers/WhatCaused1839_NBER.pdf.

Wallis, John Joseph, Richard E. Sylla, and Arthur Grinath III. "Land, Debt, and Taxes: Origins of the US State Default Crisis, 1839–1842." Accessed September 15, 2020. https://www.frbatlanta.org/-/media/documents/news/ conferences/2011/sovereign-debt/papers/Wallis.pdf.

———. "Sovereign Debt and Repudiation: The Emerging-Market Debt Crisis in the U. S. States, 1839–1843." NBER Working Paper 10753, September 2004. https://www.nber.org/papers/w10753.

Ward, Christopher. *The War of the Revolution.* 2 vols. Edited by John Richard Alden. New York: Macmillan, 1952.

Way, Peter. *Common Labor: Workers and the Digging of North American Canals, 1780–1860.* Baltimore: Johns Hopkins University Pressm, 1997.

Weaver, Abraham E., ed. *A Standard History of Elkhart County, Indiana.* Vol. 2. Chicago: American Historical Society, 1916. https://catalog.hathitrust. org/Record/008652933.

Weed Barnes, Thurlow. "Memoir of Thurlow Weed." In *Life of Thurlow Weed Including His Autobiography and a Memoir.* Boston: Houghton Mifflin,

1884. https://catalog.hathitrust.org/Record/000408044.

Weigley, Russell F. "Emergency Troops in the Gettysburg Campaign." *Pennsylvania History* 25, no. 1 (January 1858): 39–57. https://www.jstor.org/stable/27769781.

Welfley, William H, E. Howard Blackburm, and William H. Koontz. *History of Bedford and Somerset Counties, Pennsylvania, with Genealogical and Personal History.* Vol. 2. New York: Lewis, 1906.

Wellenreuther, Hermann, ed. "The Political Dilemma of the Quakers in Pennsylvania, 1681–1748." *Pennsylvania Magazine of History and Biography* 94, no. 2 (April 1970): 135–72. https://www.jstor.org/stable/20090418.

———. *The Revolution of the People: Thoughts and Documents on the Revolutionary Process in North America, 1774–1776.* Göttingen: Universitätsverlag, 2006.

Wenning, Ronald, and Kristen Wenning, eds. *Chief Logan: An Anthology.* Lewisburg, PA: Wennawoods, 2006.

Wert, Jonathan. "History of Wirth's Evangelical Lutheran Church and Cemetery." Wert Family History Association, revised 1995. http://jncass.tripod.com/wert.htm.

Weslager, C. A. *The Delaware Indians: A History.* New Brunswick, NJ: Rutgers University Press, 1972.

Wharton, Francis. *State Trials of the United States during the Administrations of Washington and Adams.* Philadelphia: Carey and Hart, 1849. https://archive.org/details/statetrialsunit00whargoog.

White, G. Edward. "The Emergence and Doctrinal Development of Tort Law, 1870–1930." *University of St. Thomas Law Journal* 11 (2014): 463–527. https://ir.stthomas.edu/ustlj/vol11/iss3/6.

———. *Law in American History, Volume II, From Reconstruction through the 1920s.* New York: Oxford University Press, 2016.

White, Richard. *The Middle Ground: Indians, Empires, and Republics in the Great Lakes Region, 1650–1815.* New York: Cambridge University Press, 2011.

———. *The Republic for Which It Stands: The United States during Reconstruction and the Gilded Age, 1865–1896.* New York: Oxford University Press, 2017.

Wilcox, General Cadmus M. *History of the Mexican War.* Edited by Mary Rachel Wilcox. Washington DC: Church News, 1892. https://archive.org/details/historyofmexican00wilc.

Wilentz, Sean. *The Rise of American Democracy: Jefferson to Lincoln.* New York: Norton, 2005.

Wiley, Samuel T. *Biographical and Portrait Cyclopedia of Schuylkill County Pennsylvania Comprising a Historical Sketch of the County.* Philadelphia:

Rush, West, 1893. https://archive.org/details/cu31924028854598.

Wilkinson, Norman B. "Robert Morris and the Treaty of Big Tree." *Mississippi Valley Historical Review* 40, no. 2 (September 1953): 257–78. https://doi.org./10.2307/1888927.

Willcox, Henry. "Irving on Lake Erie." Buffalo, NY: Charles Faxon, 1837.

Williams, Alpheus S. *From the Cannon's Mouth.* Edited by Milo M. Quaife. Lincoln: University of Nebraska Press, 1995.

Wilson, Janet. "The Bank of North America and Pennsylvania Politics: 1781–1787." *Pennsylvania Magazine of History and Biography* 66 (January 1942): 3–28. https://journals.psu.edu/pmhb/article/view/29750.

Wingert, Cooper H. *The Confederate Approach on Harrisburg: The Gettysbug Campaign's Northernmost Reaches.* Charleston, SC: History Press, 2012.

Winik, Jay. *April 1865: The Month That Saved America.* New York: Harper-Collins, 2001.

Witt, John Fabian. *The Accidental Republic: Crippled Workingmen, Destitute Widows, and the Remaking of American Law.* Cambridge, MA: Harvard University Press, 2004.

———. "From Loss of Services to Loss of Support: The Wrongful Death Statutes, the Origins of Modern Tort Law, and the Making of the Nineteenth-Century Family." *Law and Social Inquiry,* (Faculty Scholarship Series 397, 25 (2000): 717–55. http://digitalcommons.law.yale.edu/fss_papers/397/.

Wokeck, Marianne S. *Trade in Strangers: The Beginnings of Mass Migration to North America.* University Park: Pennsylvania State University Press, 1999.

Wolensky, Robert, and Joseph M. Keating. *Tragedy at Avondale.* Easton, PA: Canal History and Technology Press, 2008.

Wolfe, Theresa L., and the Tifft Farm History Committee, comps. *Tifft Farm: A History of Man and Nature.* Buffalo, NY: The Committee, 1983.

Wood, Forrest G. *Black Scare: The Racist Response to Emancipation and Reconstruction.* Berkeley: University of California Press, 1968.

Wood, Gordon S. *The American Revolution: A History.* New York: Modern Library, 2003.

———. *The Creation of the American Republic, 1776–1787.* Chapel Hill: University of North Carolina Press, 1969.

———. *Empire of Liberty: A History of the Early Republic, 1789–1815.* Oxford: Oxford University Press, 2009.

———. *The Radicalism of the American Revolution.* New York: Vintage Books, 1993.

———. "Rhetoric and Reality in the American Revolution." *William and Mary Quarterly* 23, no. 1 (January 1966): 3–32. https://doi.org/10.2307/2936154.

Woodside, Jonathan F. *An Oration Delivered in Chillicothe, July the 5th, 1830, by J. F. Woodside, Esq.* Chillicothe, OH: J. C. Melcher, 1830. Courtesy Ross County Historical Society.

Woodside, Robert E. *My Life and Town.* Millersburg, PA: Robert E. Woodside, 1979.

Worthington, T. K. "Historical Sketch of the Finances of Pennsylvania." *Publications of the American Economic Association* 2, no. 2 (May 1887): 7–206. https://www.jstor.org/stable/i346049.

Wright, Robert K., Jr. *The Continental Army.* Washington, DC: Center of Military History United States Army, 1983.

Yale University Obituary Record of Graduates Deceased during the Year Ending July 1, 1920. New Haven: Yale University, 1921. https://google.com/books/reader?id=A55GAQAAMAAJ.

Young, Alfred F., ed. *Beyond the American Revolution: Explorations in the History of American Radicalism.* DeKalb: Northern Illinois University Press, 1993.

Young, Alfred F., Gary B. Nash, and Ray Raphael, eds. *Revolutionary Founders: Rebels, Radicals, and Reformers in the Making of the Nation.* New York: Alfred A. Knopf, 2011.

INDEX

Pages in *italic* mark photos or figures, while
pages in **bold** indicate tables.

Made in the USA
Middletown, DE
05 October 2021